The 4th XoveTIC Conference

The 4th XoveTIC Conference

Editors

Joaquim de Moura
Marco A. González
Javier Pereira Loureiro
Manuel G. Penedo

MDPI • Basel • Beijing • Wuhan • Barcelona • Belgrade • Manchester • Tokyo • Cluj • Tianjin

Editors
Joaquim de Moura
Universidade da Coruña
Spain

Marco A. González
Universidade da Coruña
Spain

Javier Pereira Loureiro
Universidade da Coruña
Spain

Manuel G. Penedo
Universidade da Coruña
Spain

Editorial Office
MDPI
St. Alban-Anlage 66
4052 Basel, Switzerland

This is a reprint of articles from the Conference Proceedings published online in the open access journal *Engineering Proceedings* (ISSN 2673-4591) (available at: https://www.mdpi.com/2673-4591/7/1).

For citation purposes, cite each article independently as indicated on the article page online and as indicated below:

LastName, A.A.; LastName, B.B.; LastName, C.C. Article Title. *Journal Name* **Year**, *Volume Number*, Page Range.

ISBN 978-3-0365-2496-2 (Hbk)
ISBN 978-3-0365-2497-9 (PDF)

Cover image courtesy of Pixebay license

© 2021 by the authors. Articles in this book are Open Access and distributed under the Creative Commons Attribution (CC BY) license, which allows users to download, copy and build upon published articles, as long as the author and publisher are properly credited, which ensures maximum dissemination and a wider impact of our publications.

The book as a whole is distributed by MDPI under the terms and conditions of the Creative Commons license CC BY-NC-ND.

Contents

About the Editors xi

Preface to "The 4th XoveTIC Conference" xiii

Joaquim de Moura, Lucía Ramos, Plácido L. Vidal, Milena Cruz, Laura Abelairas, Eva Castro, Jorge Novo and Marcos Ortega
Computational Radiological Screening of Patients with COVID-19 Using Chest X-ray Images from Portable Devices [†]
Reprinted from: *Eng. Proc.* **2021**, 7, 1, doi:10.3390/engproc2021007001 1

Mateo Gende, Joaquim de Moura, Jorge Novo, Pablo Charlón and Marcos Ortega
Automatic Segmentation and Visualisation of the Epirretinal Membrane in OCT Scans Using Densely Connected Convolutional Networks [†]
Reprinted from: *Eng. Proc.* **2021**, 7, 2, doi:10.3390/engproc2021007002 5

Manuel Merino-Monge, Alberto Jesús Molina-Cantero, Juan Antonio Castro-García, Clara Lebrato-Vázquez, and Isabel María Gómez-González
Promoting Physical Activity in People with Functional Diversity through a Multiplayer Musical Game [†]
Reprinted from: *Eng. Proc.* **2021**, 7, 3, doi:10.3390/engproc2021007003 9

Clara Lebrato-Vázquez, Alberto J. Molina-Cantero, Juan A. Castro-García, Manuel Merino-Monge, and Isabel M. Gómez-González
Development and Testing of Motion-Detection Techniques for People with Cerebral Palsy [†]
Reprinted from: *Eng. Proc.* **2021**, 7, 4, doi:10.3390/engproc2021007004 13

Plácido L. Vidal, Joaquim de Moura, Jorge Novo and Marcos Ortega
COVID-19 Lung Radiography Segmentation by Means of Multiphase Transfer Learning [†]
Reprinted from: *Eng. Proc.* **2021**, 7, 5, doi:10.3390/engproc2021007005 17

Daniel I. Morís, Joaquim de Moura, Jorge Novo and Marcos Ortega
Portable Chest X-ray Synthetic Image Generation for the COVID-19 Screening [†]
Reprinted from: *Eng. Proc.* **2021**, 7, 6, doi:10.3390/engproc2021007006 21

Alba Ortolan-Soto, Juan A. Castro-García, Alberto J. Molina-Cantero, Manuel Merino-Monge and Isabel M. Gómez-González
Smart Bracelet for Emotional Enhancement in Children with Autism Spectrum Disorder [†]
Reprinted from: *Eng. Proc.* **2021**, 7, 7, doi:10.3390/engproc202100707 25

Mariña González-Pena, Juan A. Castro-García, Alberto J. Molina-Cantero, Manuel Merino-Monge and Isabel M. Gómez-González
Study of Blood-Pressure Measurement Using Noninvasive Methods [†]
Reprinted from: *Eng. Proc.* **2021**, 7, 8, doi:10.3390/engproc2021007008 29

David Rivas-Villar, José Rouco, Rafael Carballeira, Manuel G. Penedo and Jorge Novo
Automatic Pipeline for Detection and Classification of Phytoplankton Specimens in Digital Microscopy Images of Freshwater Samples [†]
Reprinted from: *Eng. Proc.* **2021**, 7, 9, doi:10.3390/engproc2021007009 33

Aida Vidal-Balea, Oscar Blanco-Novoa, Paula Fraga-Lamas, Miguel Vilar-Montesinos and Tiago M. Fernández-Caramés
Collaborative Augmented Digital Twin: A Novel Open-Source Augmented Reality Solution for Training and Maintenance Processes in the Shipyard of the Future [†]
Reprinted from: *Eng. Proc.* **2021**, 7, 10, doi:10.3390/engproc2021007010 37

Javier Díaz-Santiso and Paula Fraga-Lamas
E-Voting System Using Hyperledger Fabric Blockchain and Smart Contracts [†]
Reprinted from: *Eng. Proc.* **2021**, 7, 11, doi:10.3390/engproc2021007011 41

Jaime Mas-Santillán, Francisco Javier Acevedo-Rodríguez and Roberto Javier López-Sastre
Embedding ROS and AI-Based Perception Capabilities in a Novel Low-Cost Assistive Robotic Platform [†]
Reprinted from: *Eng. Proc.* **2021**, 7, 12, doi:10.3390/engproc2021007012 45

Rubén Pérez-Jove, Roberto R. Expósito and Juan Touriño
RGen: Data Generator for Benchmarking Big Data Workloads [†]
Reprinted from: *Eng. Proc.* **2021**, 7, 13, doi:10.3390/engproc2021007013 49

Ignacio D. Lopez-Miguel
Survey on Preprocessing Techniques for Big Data Projects [†]
Reprinted from: *Eng. Proc.* **2021**, 7, 14, doi:10.3390/engproc2021007014 53

Rita Costa, Paulo Veloso Gomes, António Correia, António Marques and Javier Pereira
The Influence of Brain Activity on the Interactive Process through Biofeedback Mechanisms in Virtual Reality Environments [†]
Reprinted from: *Eng. Proc.* **2021**, 7, 15, doi:10.3390/engproc2021007015 57

Alvaro Michelena, Francisco Zayas-Gato, Esteban Jove, and José Luis Calvo-Rolle
Detection of DoS Attacks in an IoT Environment with MQTT Protocol Based on Intelligent Binary Classifiers [†]
Reprinted from: *Eng. Proc.* **2021**, 7, 16, doi:10.3390/engproc2021007016 61

Wende Clarence Safari, Ignacio López-de-Ullibarri and María Amalia Jácome
Nonparametric Inference for Mixture Cure Model When Cure Information Is Partially Available [†]
Reprinted from: *Eng. Proc.* **2021**, 7, 17, doi:10.3390/engproc2021007017 65

Iván Froiz-Míguez, Paula Fraga-Lamas and Tiago M. Fernández-Caramés
Design, Implementation and Validation of a Bluetooth 5 Real-Time Monitoring System for Large Indoor Environments [†]
Reprinted from: *Eng. Proc.* **2021**, 7, 18, doi:10.3390/engproc2021007018 69

Joana Cunha, Paulo Veloso Gomes, António Marques and Javier Pereira
The Effect of Music on Brain Activity an Emotional State [†]
Reprinted from: *Eng. Proc.* **2021**, 7, 19, doi:10.3390/engproc2021007019 73

Ainhoa Molinero Rodríguez, Carla Guerra Tort, Victoria Suárez Ulloa, José M. López Gestal, Javier Pereira, Vanessa Aguiar Pulido
Training of Machine Learning Models for Recurrence Prediction in Patients with Respiratory Pathologies [†]
Reprinted from: *Eng. Proc.* **2021**, 7, 20, doi:10.3390/engproc2021007020 77

Ainhoa Molinero-Rodríguez, Rubén Carneiro-Medín, Carmen Miranda-Duro, Laura Nieto-Riveiro, Paula M. Castro and Adriana Dapena
Development of Dual Activities with Micro:Bit for Interventions in People with Cerebral Palsy [†]
Reprinted from: *Eng. Proc.* **2021**, *7*, 21, doi:10.3390/engproc2021007021 81

José Morano, Álvaro S. Hervella, Jorge Novo and José Rouco
Deep Multi-Segmentation Approach for the Joint Classification and Segmentation of the Retinal Arterial and Venous Trees in Color Fundus Images [†]
Reprinted from: *Eng. Proc.* **2021**, *7*, 22, doi:10.3390/engproc2021007022 85

Jorge Gabín, Anxo Pérez and Javier Parapar
Multiple-Choice Question Answering Models for Automatic Depression Severity Estimation [†]
Reprinted from: *Eng. Proc.* **2021**, *7*, 23, doi:10.3390/engproc2021007023 89

Patricia Concheiro-Moscoso, Miguel Pereira, Francisco José Martínez-Martínez, Thais Pousada and Javier Pereira
Applicability of Clinical Decision Support in Management among Patients Undergoing Cardiac Surgery in Intensive Care Unit: A Systematic Review [†]
Reprinted from: *Eng. Proc.* **2021**, *7*, 24, doi:10.3390/engproc2021007024 93

Patricia Concheiro-Moscoso, Betania Groba, Sílvia Monteiro-Fonseca, Nereida Canosa and Cristina Queirós
SQoF-WEAR Project. The Use of Wearable Devices to Identify the Impact of Stress on Workers' Quality of Life [†]
Reprinted from: *Eng. Proc.* **2021**, *7*, 25, doi:10.3390/engproc2021007025 97

Raquel Vázquez Díaz, Martiño Rivera-Dourado, Rubén Pérez-Jove, Pilar Vila Avendaño, José M. Vázquez-Naya
Address Space Layout Randomization Comparative Analysis on Windows 10 and Ubuntu 18.04 LTS [†]
Reprinted from: *Eng. Proc.* **2021**, *7*, 26, doi:10.3390/engproc2021007026 101

María Isabel Limaylla, Nelly Condori-Fernandez and Miguel R. Luaces
Towards a Semi-Automated Data-Driven Requirements Prioritization Approach for Reducing Stakeholder Participation in SPL Development [†]
Reprinted from: *Eng. Proc.* **2021**, *7*, 27, doi:10.3390/engproc2021007027 105

Rebeca Peláez Suárez, Ricardo Cao Abad, Juan M. Vilar Fernández
Bootstrap Selector for the Smoothing Parameter of Beran's Estimator [†]
Reprinted from: *Eng. Proc.* **2021**, *7*, 28, doi:10.3390/engproc2021007028 109

Nieves R. Brisaboa, Pablo Gutiérrez-Asorey, Miguel R. Luaces and Tirso V. Rodeiro
Succinct Data Structures in the Realm of GIS [†]
Reprinted from: *Eng. Proc.* **2021**, *7*, 29, doi:10.3390/engproc2021007029 113

David Barreiro-Villaverde, Marcos Lema and Anne Gosset
Numerical Simulations and Modal Analysis to Investigate the Defects in a Coating Process [†]
Reprinted from: *Eng. Proc.* **2021**, *7*, 30, doi:10.3390/engproc2021007030 117

Sergio Roget, Marcos Lema and Anne Gosset
Simulation of the Fluid–Structure Interaction in Fishing Nets [†]
Reprinted from: *Eng. Proc.* **2021**, *7*, 31, doi:10.3390/engproc2021007031 121

Alejandro Puente-Castro, Daniel Rivero, Alejandro Pazos and Enrique Fernandez-Blanco
Using Reinforcement Learning in the Path Planning of Swarms of UAVs for the Photographic Capture of Terrains [†]
Reprinted from: *Eng. Proc.* **2021**, *7*, 32, doi:10.3390/engproc2021007032 . . . . **125**

Delfina Ramos-Vidal and Guillermo de Bernardo
Tool for SPARQL Querying over Compact RDF Representations [†]
Reprinted from: *Eng. Proc.* **2021**, *7*, 33, doi:10.3390/engproc2021007033 . . . . **129**

Marco Martínez-Sánchez, Roberto R. Expósito and Juan Touriño
Performance Optimization of a Parallel Error Correction Tool [†]
Reprinted from: *Eng. Proc.* **2021**, *7*, 34, doi:10.3390/engproc2021007034 . . . . **133**

Mauro Alberto de los Santos Nodar, Tiago Manuel Fernández Caramés
COVID-19 Digital Vaccination Passport Based on Blockchain with Its Own Cryptocurrency as a Reward and Mobile App for Its Use [†]
Reprinted from: *Eng. Proc.* **2021**, *7*, 35, doi:10.3390/engproc2021007035 . . . . **137**

María González Taboada and Hiram Varela Rodríguez
On the Adaptive Numerical Solution to the Darcy–Forchheimer Model [†]
Reprinted from: *Eng. Proc.* **2021**, *7*, 36, doi:10.3390/engproc2021007036 . . . . **141**

Brais Galdo, Enrique Fernandez-Blanco and Daniel Rivero
Detection of Chocolate Properties Using Near-Infrared Spectrophotometry [†]
Reprinted from: *Eng. Proc.* **2021**, *7*, 37, doi:10.3390/engproc2021007037 . . . . **147**

Brais Galdo, Daniel Rivero and Enrique Fernandez-Blanco
Development of a Server for the Implementation of Data Processing Pipelines and ANN Training [†]
Reprinted from: *Eng. Proc.* **2021**, *7*, 38, doi:10.3390/engproc2021007038 . . . . **151**

José Bobes-Bascarán, Eduardo Mosqueira-Rey and David Alonso-Ríos
Improving Medical Data Annotation Including Humans in the Machine Learning Loop [†]
Reprinted from: *Eng. Proc.* **2021**, *7*, 39, doi:10.3390/engproc2021007039 . . . . **155**

Iker González-Santamaría, Minia Manteiga and Carlos Dafonte
Close Binary Stars in Planetary Nebulae through Gaia EDR3 [†]
Reprinted from: *Eng. Proc.* **2021**, *7*, 40, doi:10.3390/engproc2021007040 . . . . **159**

Joel Pérez Villarino and Álvaro Leitao Rodríguez
Deep Learning-Based Method for Computing Initial Margin [†]
Reprinted from: *Eng. Proc.* **2021**, *7*, 41, doi:10.3390/engproc2021007041 . . . . **163**

Isabel Méndez-Fernández, Silvia Lorenzo-Freire and Ángel Manuel González-Rueda
A Bi-Objective Scheduling Problem in a Home Care Business [†]
Reprinted from: *Eng. Proc.* **2021**, *7*, 42, doi:10.3390/engproc2021007042 . . . . **167**

Manuel Lagos, Jessica Martín, Ángel Gómez and Thais Pousada
Virtual Reality at the Service of People with Functional Diversity: Personalized Intervention Spaces [†]
Reprinted from: *Eng. Proc.* **2021**, *7*, 43, doi:10.3390/engproc2021007043 . . . . **171**

Alejandro Fernández-Fraga, Jorge González-Domínguez and Juan Touriño
A Parallel Tool for the Identification of Differentially Methylated Regions in Genomic Analyses [†]
Reprinted from: *Eng. Proc.* **2021**, *7*, 44, doi:10.3390/engproc2021007044 175

Alberto Manzano, Daniele Musso, Álvaro Leitao, Andrés Gómez, Carlos Vázquez, Gustavo Ordóñez and María Rodríguez-Nogueiras
Quantum Arithmetic for Directly Embedded Arrays [†]
Reprinted from: *Eng. Proc.* **2021**, *7*, 45, doi:10.3390/engproc2021007045 179

Pedro Nogueiras, Paula M. Castro and Adriana Dapena
PreLectO: An App for Cognitive Stimulation through Games in Early Childhood [†]
Reprinted from: *Eng. Proc.* **2021**, *7*, 46, doi:10.3390/engproc2021007046 183

Victoria Noci-Luna, Sergio Lafuente-Arroyo, Saturnino Maldonado-Bascón and Pilar Martin-Martin
Proposal and Integration of Functionalities for an Assistive Platform in Complex Indoor Environments [†]
Reprinted from: *Eng. Proc.* **2021**, *7*, 47, doi:10.3390/engproc2021007047 187

Alejandro Puente-Castro, Brais Galdo, Ismael Said Criado, David Baltar Boileve, Juan R. Rabuñal, Alejandro Pazos and Modesto Martínez-Pillado
PRACTICUM DIRECT Simulator for Decision Making during Pandemics [†]
Reprinted from: *Eng. Proc.* **2021**, *7*, 48, doi:10.3390/engproc2021007048 191

Daniel Juanatey, Martin Naya, Tamara Baamonde and Francisco Bellas
Developing a Simulation Model for Autonomous Driving Education in the Robobo SmartCity Framework [†]
Reprinted from: *Eng. Proc.* **2021**, *7*, 49, doi:10.3390/engproc2021007049 195

María del Carmen Miranda-Duro, Laura Nieto-Riveiro, Betania Groba and Nereida Canosa
Monitoring of Older Adults' Daily Activity and Sleep with Xiaomi Mi Band 2 [†]
Reprinted from: *Eng. Proc.* **2021**, *7*, 50, doi:10.3390/engproc2021007050 199

Rubén Pérez-Jove, Cristian R. Munteanu, Alejandro Pazos Sierra, José M. Vázquez-Naya
Applying Artificial Intelligence for Operating System Fingerprinting [†]
Reprinted from: *Eng. Proc.* **2021**, *7*, 51, doi:10.3390/engproc2021007051 203

Noé Vila-Muñoz, Paula M. Castro and Óscar Fresnedo
PICTOTEMPO: An App for Personal Organization in Autism Spectrum Disorders [†]
Reprinted from: *Eng. Proc.* **2021**, *7*, 52, doi:10.3390/engproc2021007052 207

Ángel Carro-Lagoa, Valentín Barral, Miguel González-López, Carlos J. Escudero and Luis Castedo
Alternatives for Locating People Using Cameras and Embedded AI Accelerators: A Practical Approach [†]
Reprinted from: *Eng. Proc.* **2021**, *7*, 53, doi:10.3390/engproc2021007053 211

Rita Veloso, Renato Magalhães, António Marques, Paulo Veloso Gomes and Javier Pereira
Mixed Reality in an Operating Room Using Hololens 2—The Use of the Remote Assistance from Manufacturers Techinicians during the Surgeries [†]
Reprinted from: *Eng. Proc.* **2021**, *7*, 54, doi:10.3390/engproc2021007054 215

Erick Gonzalez-Martin, Alberto Alvarellos, Virginia Mato-Abad, Juan Manuel Pias-Peleteiro, Isabel Jimenez-Martin and Francisco Cedron
Application for Decision-Making on MildCognitive Impairments [†]
Reprinted from: *Eng. Proc.* **2021**, 7, 55, doi:10.3390/engproc2021007055 219

Martiño Rivera-Dourado, Marcos Gestal and José M. Vázquez-Naya
An Analysis of the Current Implementations Based on the WebAuthn and FIDO Authentication Standards [†]
Reprinted from: *Eng. Proc.* **2021**, 7, 56, doi:10.3390/engproc2021007056 223

Dariel Pereira-Ruisánchez, Darian Pérez-Adán and Luis Castedo
A Deep Learning-Based Strategy to Predict Self-Interference in SFN DTT [†]
Reprinted from: *Eng. Proc.* **2021**, 7, 57, doi:10.3390/engproc2021007057 227

Pedro Fernández-Arruti, Julio J. Estévez-Pereira, Francisco J. Nóvoa, Jose C. Dafonte and Diego Fernández
Low Cost Automated Security Audit System [†]
Reprinted from: *Eng. Proc.* **2021**, 7, 58, doi:10.3390/engproc2021007058 231

Sara Alvarez-Gonzalez and Ivan Erill
Design of Machine Learning Models for the Prediction of Transcription Factor Binding Regions in Bacterial DNA [†]
Reprinted from: *Eng. Proc.* **2021**, 7, 59, doi:10.3390/engproc2021007059 235

Ángel López-Oriona, Pierpaolo D'Urso, José A. Vilar and Borja Lafuente-Rego
Robust Methods for Soft Clustering of Multidimensional Time Series [†]
Reprinted from: *Eng. Proc.* **2021**, 7, 60, doi:10.3390/engproc2021007060 239

About the Editors

Joaquim de Moura (Ph.D.) received his degree in Computer Engineering in 2014 from the University of A Coruña (Spain). In 2016, he received his M.Sc. degree in Computer Engineering from the same university and his Ph.D. degree (cum Laude) in Computer Science and Artificial Intelligence in 2019. He has also worked as a visiting researcher at the INESC-TEC (Portugal), in the development of different methodologies for DME diagnosis with OCT images. He is currently a postdoctoral researcher in the Center for Research in Information and Communication Technologies (CITIC) at the University of A Coruña. His main research interests include computer vision, biomedical imaging and video processing.

Marco A. González (Ph.D.) is a postdoctoral researcher in the Center for Research in Information and Communication Technologies (CITIC) at the University of A Coruña. He received his degrees in Computer Engineering, M.Sc. in Computer Engineering and Ph.D. (cum Laude) in Information and Communication Technologies from the University of A Coruña (Spain) in 2014, 2015 and 2019, respectively. He is also a member of the Data Processing and Analysis Consortium (DPAC) of the Gaia Mission of the European Space Agency (ESA) and member of the Astronomy Spanish Society (SEA). His main research interests include data mining, data visualisation and the application of Artificial Intelligence techniques in Astronomy and security in communication networks.

Javier Pereira Loureiro (Ph.D.) is an associate professor at the Faculty of Health Science from the Universidade da Coruña (UDC), Spain. He received his B.Sc., Master's degree and Ph.D. in Computer Science from the UDC in 1995, 1997 and 2004, respectively. Currently, he is deputy director of the Centre for Information and Communications Technology Research (CITIC) and Head of Master of Bioinformatics. His research interests include medical informatics and assistive technologies for people with disabilities.

Manuel G. Penedo (Ph.D.) received his B.S. and Ph.D. degrees in Physics from the University of Santiago de Compostela, Spain, in 1990 and 1997, respectively. He is currently Professor at the Department of Computer Science in the University of A Coruña, Spain, and the director of the Center for Research in Information and Communication Technologies (CITIC). His main research interests include computer vision, biomedical image processing and video processing.

Preface to "The 4th XoveTIC Conference"

The 4th XoveTIC Conference (A Coruña, Spain, 7–8 October 2021), organized by the Research Center of Information and Communication Technologies (CITIC) of the University of A Coruña (UDC), is a platform for young pre- and postdoctoral researchers to present short communications in different research areas, such as big data, artificial intelligence, the Internet of Things, HPC (High-performance computing), cybersecurity, bioinformatics or natural language processing. The aim of the conference is to complement and improve the training of young researchers by providing them with a space for debate and scientific exchange. This fourth edition is intended to serve as a basis for this event to consolidate over time and acquire international.

Financial support from Vice-rectorate for Science Policy, Research and Transfer of Universidade da Coruña and Consellería de Cultura, Educación e Universidade of the Xunta de Galicia (Convenio I+D+i Centro de investigación de Galicia 2019–2022) and the European Union (European Regional Development Fund- ERDF) is gratefully acknowledged.

Joaquim de Moura, Marco A. González, Javier Pereira Loureiro, Manuel G. Penedo
Editors

Proceeding Paper

Computational Radiological Screening of Patients with COVID-19 Using Chest X-ray Images from Portable Devices [†]

Joaquim de Moura [1,2,*], Lucía Ramos [1,2], Plácido L. Vidal [1,2], Milena Cruz [3], Laura Abelairas [3], Eva Castro [3], Jorge Novo [1,2] and Marcos Ortega [1,2]

1. Centro de Investigación CITIC, Universidade da Coruña, 15071 A Coruña, Spain; l.ramos@udc.es (L.R.); placido.francisco.lizancos.vidal@udc.es (P.L.V.); jnovo@udc.es (J.N.); mortega@udc.es (M.O.)
2. Grupo VARPA, Instituto de Investigación Biomédica de A Coruña (INIBIC), Universidade da Coruña, 15006 A Coruña, Spain
3. Servicio de Radiodiagnóstico, Complexo Hospitalario Universitario de A Coruña (CHUAC), 15006 A Coruña, Spain; nmilena19@hotmail.com (M.C.); Laura.Abelairas.Lopez@sergas.es (L.A.); casloeva@gmail.com (E.C.)
* Correspondence: joaquim.demoura@udc.es; Tel.: +34-981-167-000 (ext. 1330)
† Presented at the 4th XoveTIC Conference, A Coruña, Spain, 7–8 October 2021.

Abstract: This work presents a fully automatic system for the screening of chest X-ray images from portable devices under the analysis of three different clinical categories: normal, pathological cases of pulmonary diseases with findings similar to those of COVID-19, and COVID-19 cases. Our methodology was validated using a dataset retrieved specifically for this study, which was provided by the Radiology Service of the Complexo Hospitalario Universitario A Coruña (CHUAC). Despite the poor quality conditions of chest X-ray images acquired by portable devices, satisfactory results were obtained, demonstrating the robustness and great potential of the proposed system to help front-line clinicians in the diagnosis and treatment of patients with COVID-19.

Keywords: computer-aided diagnosis; portable chest X-ray imaging; COVID-19; pneumonia; deep learning

1. Introduction

COVID-19 is a disease caused by a new severe acute respiratory syndrome coronavirus 2 (SARS-CoV-2), which was initially identified in Wuhan (capital of the Hubei province, China) in early December 2019. The World Health Organization (WHO) declared the COVID-19 outbreak a global pandemic on 11 March 2020. According to the WHO, more than 187 million cases have been confirmed, including more than 4 million deaths, making it one of the deadliest pandemics in history. Moreover, this highly infectious disease has the potential to mutate and infect non-immune populations [1].

According to the American College of Radiology (ACR), portable chest X-ray devices should be used instead of conventional fixed machinery in order to prevent the spread of the COVID-19 pathogen, which is considered critical in this pandemic scenario [2]. A portable X-ray device is a compact equipment that allows the clinician to perform radiological examinations of the patient in a hospital bed or the emergency room. In this type of device, the X-ray tube is connected to a flexible arm that extends over the patient, while a radiographic image recording plate is placed under the patient to facilitate the imaging process. In this context, chest X-ray images acquired with portable devices are widely used by clinicians to assess confirmed, suspected, and probable cases of COVID-19 disease from data collected directly on site, without the necessity of transferring potentially COVID-19-infected patients to another location, and thus preventing cross-contamination [3]. Despite its great importance and usefulness in the pandemic, the use of portable equipment implies a greater challenge for the automatic diagnosis of COVID-19, since the acquired images are of a lower quality and a lower level of detail in comparison with the conventional fixed machinery.

2. Methodology

In this work, we present a fully automatic system for the screening of chest X-ray images from portable devices under the analysis of 3 different categories [4]: (I) normal, (II) pathological cases of pulmonary diseases with findings similar to those of COVID-19, and (III) COVID-19 cases. To analyze the differentiation between these 3 categories and explore the full potential of the available dataset, the proposed methodology integrates 3 complementary approaches: (I) normal vs. pathological/COVID-19, (II) normal/pathological vs. COVID-19, and (III) normal vs. pathological vs. COVID-19. Figure 1 shows representative examples of portable chest X-ray images related to the presented 3 clinical categories. To perform the classification process, we used a Densely Connected Convolutional Network (DenseNet-161) [5] architecture, which was adapted to our issue due to its flexibility and simplicity and its preceding promising results in other classification tasks [6,7].

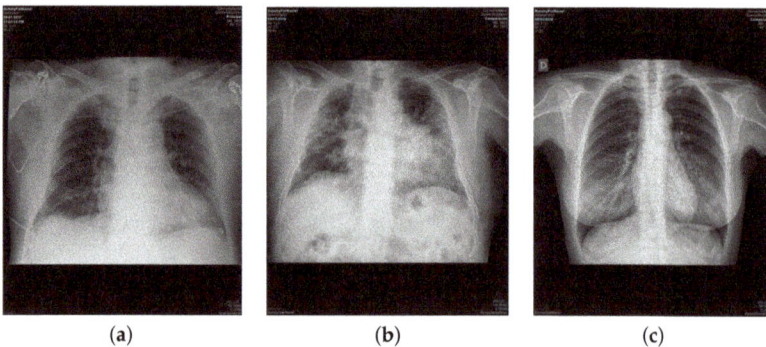

Figure 1. Representative examples of portable chest X-ray images. (**a**) Portable chest X-ray images from normal patients. (**b**) Portable chest X-ray images from pathological patients without COVID-19 but diagnosed with other pleural or pulmonary diseases. (**c**) Portable chest X-ray images from patients with COVID-19.

3. Results and Conclusions

The dataset that was used for this research study has been provided by the Radiology Service of the Complexo Hospitalario Universitario A Coruña (CHUAC). Specifically, this dataset consists of 1616 portable chest X-ray images divided into 728 normal, 648 pathological, and 240 COVID-19 cases. All the images were inspected by specialist graders in order to find relevant features representative of pulmonary affectation and, in the case of the COVID-19 samples, this was corroborated by external RT-PCR tests. Despite the poor quality of the chest X-ray images that is inherent to the nature of the portable equipment, the presented approaches provided global accuracy values of 79.62%, 90.27%, and 79.86%, respectively. Complementarily, Figure 2 presents the confusion matrices with the experimental results of all the presented approaches. As we can see, all the results that were obtained show the robustness of the presented system in the classification of the three categories of chest X-ray images considered in this work.

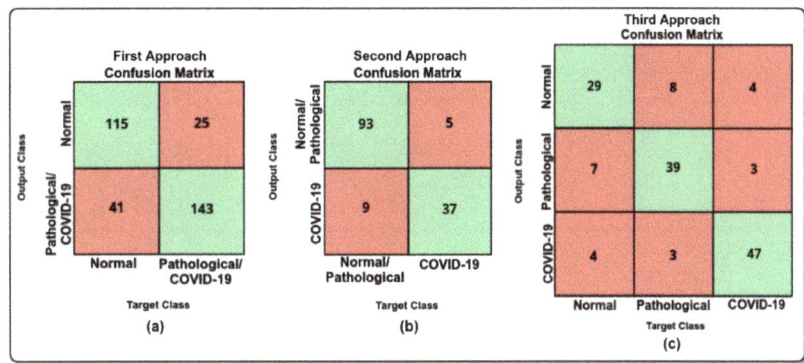

Figure 2. Experimental results of the proposed approaches for the classification of COVID-19 in portable chest X-ray images. (**a**) first experiment: analyzing the normal vs. pathological/COVID-19 approach. (**b**) second experiment: analyzing the normal/pathological vs. COVID-19 approach. (**c**) third experiment: analyzing the normal vs. pathological vs. COVID-19 approach.

Author Contributions: J.d.M., L.R. and P.L.V. contributed to the analysis and design of the computer methods and the experimental evaluation methods. M.C., L.A. and E.C. contributed with clinical knowledge and data collection. J.N. and M.O. contributed with domain-specific knowledge, supervision and project administration. J.d.M. was responsible for drafting the manuscript, and all the authors participated in its critical revision and final approval. All authors have read and agreed to the published version of the manuscript.

Funding: This research was funded by Instituto de Salud Carlos III, Government of Spain, DTS18/00136 research project; Ministerio de Ciencia e Innovación y Universidades, Government of Spain, RTI2018-095894-B-I00 research project, as well as through Ayudas para la formación de profesorado universitario (FPU), Ref. FPU18/02271; Ministerio de Ciencia e Innovación, Government of Spain through the research project with reference PID2019-108435RB-I00; Consellería de Cultura, Educación e Universidade, Xunta de Galicia through the postdoctoral grant contract ref. ED481B 2021/059; and Grupos de Referencia Competitiva, grant ref. ED431C 2020/24; Axencia Galega de Innovación (GAIN), Xunta de Galicia, grant ref. IN845D 2020/38; CITIC, Centro de Investigación de Galicia ref. ED431G 2019/01, received financial support from Consellería de Educación, Universidade e Formación Profesional, Xunta de Galicia, through the ERDF (80%) and Secretaría Xeral de Universidades (20%).

Institutional Review Board Statement: The study was approved by the Ethics Review Board y Data Management Technical Commission of Galician Health Ministry for High Impact studies with protocol code 2020-007.

Conflicts of Interest: The authors declare no conflict of interest.

References

1. Pollard, C.A.; Morran, M.P.; Nestor-Kalinoski, A.L. The COVID-19 pandemic: A global health crisis. *Physiol. Genom.* **2020**, *52*, 549–557. [CrossRef] [PubMed]
2. Kooraki, S.; Hosseiny, M.; Myers, L.; Gholamrezanezhad, A. Coronavirus (COVID-19) outbreak: What the department of radiology should know. *J. Am. Coll. Radiol.* **2020**, *17*, 447–451. [CrossRef] [PubMed]
3. Vidal, P.L.; de Moura, J.; Novo, J.; Ortega, M. Multi-stage transfer learning for lung segmentation using portable X-ray devices for patients with COVID-19. *Expert Syst. Appl.* **2021**, *173*, 114677. [CrossRef] [PubMed]
4. de Moura, J.; Ramos, L.; Vidal, P.L.; Cruz, M.; Abelairas, L.; Castro, E.; Novo, J.; Ortega, M. Deep Convolutional Approaches for the Analysis of COVID-19 Using Chest X-ray Images from Portable Devices. *IEEE Access* **2020**, *8*, 195594–195607. [CrossRef]
5. Huang, G.; Liu, S.; Van der Maaten, L.; Weinberger, K.Q. Condensenet: An efficient densenet using learned group convolutions. In Proceedings of the IEEE Conference on Computer Vision and Pattern Recognition, Salt Lake City, UT, USA, 18–22 June 2018; pp. 2752–2761. [CrossRef]

6. Morís, D.I.; de Moura, J.; Novo, J.; Ortega, M. Cycle Generative Adversarial Network Approaches to Produce Novel Portable Chest X-rays Images for COVID-19 Diagnosis. In Proceedings of the ICASSP 2021—2021 IEEE International Conference on Acoustics, Speech and Signal Processing (ICASSP), Toronto, ON, Canada, 6–11 June 2021; pp. 1060–1064. [CrossRef]
7. de Moura, J.; Novo, J.; Ortega, M. Fully automatic deep convolutional approaches for the analysis of COVID-19 using chest X-ray images. *medRxiv* **2020**. [CrossRef]

Proceeding Paper

Automatic Segmentation and Visualisation of the Epirretinal Membrane in OCT Scans Using Densely Connected Convolutional Networks [†]

Mateo Gende [1,2,*], Joaquim de Moura [1,2], Jorge Novo [1,2], Pablo Charlón [3,4] and Marcos Ortega [1,2]

1. Centro de Investigación CITIC, Universidade da Coruña, 15071 A Coruña, Spain; joaquim.demoura@udc.es (J.d.M.); jnovo@udc.es (J.N.); mortega@udc.es (M.O.)
2. Grupo VARPA, Instituto de Investigación Biomédica de A Coruña (INIBIC), Universidade da Coruña, 15006 A Coruña, Spain
3. Instituto Oftalmológico Victoria de Rojas, 15009 A Coruña, Spain; pcharlon@gmail.com
4. Hospital HM Rosaleda, 150701 Santiago de Compostela, Spain
* Correspondence: m.gende@udc.es; Tel.: +34-981-167-000 (ext. 5522)
† Presented at the 4th XoveTIC Conference, A Coruña, Spain, 7–8 October 2021.

Citation: Gende, M.; de Moura, J.; Novo, J.; Charlón, P.; Ortega, M. Automatic Segmentation and Visualisation of the Epirretinal Membrane in OCT Scans Using Densely Connected Convolutional Networks. *Eng. Proc.* **2021**, *7*, 2. https://doi.org/10.3390/engproc2021007002

Academic Editors: Joaquim de Moura, Marco A. González, Javier Pereira and Manuel G. Penedo

Published: 28 September 2021

Publisher's Note: MDPI stays neutral with regard to jurisdictional claims in published maps and institutional affiliations.

Copyright: © 2021 by the authors. Licensee MDPI, Basel, Switzerland. This article is an open access article distributed under the terms and conditions of the Creative Commons Attribution (CC BY) license (https://creativecommons.org/licenses/by/4.0/).

Abstract: The Epiretinal Membrane (ERM) is an ocular disease that appears as a fibro-cellular layer of tissue over the retina, specifically, over the Inner Limiting Membrane (ILM). It causes vision blurring and distortion, and its presence can be indicative of other ocular pathologies, such as diabetic macular edema. The ERM diagnosis is usually performed by visually inspecting Optical Coherence Tomography (OCT) images, a manual process which is tiresome and prone to subjectivity. In this work, we present a methodology for the automatic segmentation and visualisation of the ERM in OCT volumes using deep learning. By employing a Densely Connected Convolutional Network, every pixel in the ILM can be classified into either healthy or pathological. Thus, a segmentation of the region susceptible to ERM appearance can be produced. This methodology also produces an intuitive colour map representation of the ERM presence over a visualisation of the eye fundus created from the OCT volume. In a series of representative experiments conducted to evaluate this methodology, it achieved a Dice score of 0.826 ± 0.112 and a Jaccard index of 0.714 ± 0.155. The results that were obtained demonstrate the competitive performance of the proposed methodology when compared to other works in the state of the art.

Keywords: epiretinal membrane; machine learning; medical diagnostic imaging; optical coherence tomography

1. Introduction

The Epiretinal Membrane (ERM) is an ocular disease that consists of scar tissue that is formed over the boundary between the retina and the vitreous body of the eye, an area known as the Inner Limiting Membrane (ILM). As the ERM appears over the retina, it may start to contract, exerting a traction and producing puckers or wrinkles over the underlying tissue. This may cause vision blurring, distortion, and metamorphopsia.

Several authors have approached the automatic detection of the ERM using Optical Coherence Tomography (OCT) images. In References [1,2], the authors identify the ILM layer using classical machine learning algorithms and local luminosity patterns; Lo et al. [3] proposes the use of a Residual Neural Network for the screening of ERM in cross-sectional OCT images, while, in Sonobe et al. [4], the authors compare the use of classical machine learning algorithms and deep learning for the detection of ERM, with deep learning outperforming the classical methods. These works, however, deal only with the screening of ERM, a simpler problem than its precise segmentation. In this regard, only Baamonde et al. [5,6] has approached the problem of segmenting the ERM in OCT images, using classical machine learning methods in this case.

In this work, we present an automatic methodology for the segmentation of the ERM in OCT volumes by using deep learning. This methodology consists of three phases, corresponding to the detection of the region of interest, the segmentation of the ERM via the classification of window samples of the ILM, and the visualisation and post-processing of the segmentation map [7]. This process produces a representation of the ERM presence and absence over the eye fundus in the form of a 2D colour map. This map can be used to aid clinicians in the detection and posterior removal of the ERM via pars plana vitrectomy.

2. Methodology

The ERM segmentation methodology consists of three steps. In the first one, the ILM is segmented using active contours [8]. The position of the ILM is modeled as a height value for every image column, since the retina appears as an irregular horizontal line in OCT images. The active contour models are allowed to contract downwards until they converge over the ILM. With the region of interest segmented, the ILM can be sampled via sliding window. The next step consists of sample classification. A Densely Connected Convolutional Neural Network [9] is then used to classify each of the 112 × 112 pixel sliding window samples into either healthy or pathological. These classes are then assigned to the central pixel around which each sliding window was extracted, effectively producing a segmentation of each OCT scan. This process is illustrated in Figure 1. In the final step, all the slice segmentations are combined to produce a 2D preliminary segmentation map of the whole eye fundus. A post-processing step is then applied to this map in order to soften the boundary of the ERM and eliminate some misclassifications caused by image artifacts. This post-processed map is then overlaid on a reconstruction of the eye fundus to produce an intuitive visualisation of the ERM presence over the eye tissue, as illustrated in Figure 2.

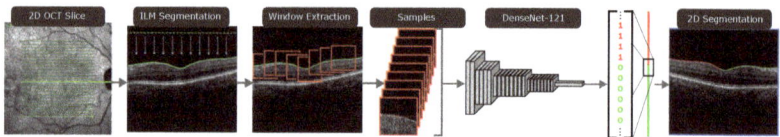

Figure 1. The first two steps of the proposed methodology, producing a 2D segmentation of the ERM in a single OCT slice.

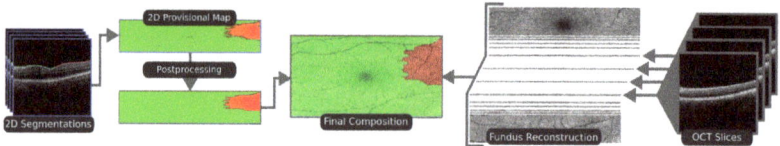

Figure 2. The final steps of the proposed methodology. Slice segmentations are stacked to form a map. This map is post-processed and overlaid on a reconstruction of the eye fundus.

3. Results and Conclusions

The proposed methodology was evaluated in terms of its ability to correctly segment the ERM, with preliminary maps achieving a Dice score of 0.800 ± 0.100 and a Jaccard index of 0.676 ± 0.141. When applying the post-processing stage, these results were improved up to 0.826 ± 0.112 and 0.714 ± 0.155. A comparison between the proposed methodology and the state-of-the-art proposal [6], which only takes into account ERM-positive eyes, can be found in Table 1. These results show that the proposed system is able to accurately segment the ERM, even surpassing the current state of the art before the application of the post-processing stage.

Table 1. Comparison of Dice and Jaccard indexes of the previous work and the deep learning method proposed in this work for the segmentation and post-processing stages.

		ERM-Positive Eyes Only			
		Baamonde et al. [6]		Our Proposal	
		Segmentation	Post-Processing	Segmentation	Post-Processing
Dice	Mean	0.670	0.780	0.810	0.833
	SD	±0.110	±0.092	±0.099	±0.091
Jaccard	Mean	0.515	0.649	0.689	0.725
	SD	±0.140	±0.128	±0.139	±0.129

Author Contributions: Author Contributions: Conceptualization, J.N., J.d.M., and M.O.; methodology, M.G.; software, M.G.; validation, M.G.; formal analysis, M.G.; investigation, M.G.; resources, J.N., J.d.M., P.C., and M.O.; data curation, P.C. and M.G-; writing—original draft preparation, M.G.; writing—review and editing, J.N., J.d.M., and M.O.; visualization, M.G.; supervision, J.N., J.d.M. and M.O.; project administration, J.N., J.d.M., and M.O.; funding acquisition, J.N., J.d.M., and M.O. All authors have read and agreed to the published version of the manuscript.

Funding: This research was funded by Instituto de Salud Carlos III, Government of Spain, DTS18/00136 research project; Ministerio de Ciencia e Innovación y Universidades, Government of Spain, RTI2018-095894-B-I00 research project; Ministerio de Ciencia e Innovación, Government of Spain through the research project with reference PID2019-108435RB-I00; Consellería de Cultura, Educación e Universidade, Xunta de Galicia through the predoctoral and postdoctoral grant contracts ref. ED481A 2021/161 and ED481B 2021/059, respectively; and Grupos de Referencia Competitiva, grant ref. ED431C 2020/24; Axencia Galega de Innovación (GAIN), Xunta de Galicia, grant ref. IN845D 2020/38; CITIC, Centro de Investigación de Galicia ref. ED431G 2019/01, receives financial support from Consellería de Educación, Universidade e Formación Profesional, Xunta de Galicia, through the ERDF (80%) and Secretaría Xeral de Universidades (20%).

Institutional Review Board Statement: The study was conducted according to the guidelines of the Declaration of Helsinki, and approved by the local Ethics Committee of Investigation from A Coruña/Ferrol (2014/437) the 24 November 2014.

Informed Consent Statement: Informed consent was obtained from all subjects involved in the study.

Conflicts of Interest: The authors declare no conflict of interest.

References

1. Baamonde, S.; de Moura, J.; Novo, J.; Rouco, J.; Ortega, M. Feature Definition and Selection for Epiretinal Membrane Characterization in Optical Coherence Tomography Images. In *Image Analysis and Processing—ICIAP 2017*; Springer International Publishing: Basel, Switzerland, 2017; pp. 456–466. [CrossRef]
2. Baamonde, S.; de Moura, J.; Novo, J.; Ortega, M. Automatic Detection of Epiretinal Membrane in OCT Images by Means of Local Luminosity Patterns. In *Advances in Computational Intelligence*; Springer International Publishing: Basel, Switzerland, 2017; pp. 222–235. [CrossRef]
3. Lo, Y.C.; Lin, K.H.; Bair, H.; Sheu, W.H.H.; Chang, C.S.; Shen, Y.C.; Hung, C.L. Epiretinal Membrane Detection at the Ophthalmologist Level using Deep Learning of Optical Coherence Tomography. *Sci. Rep.* **2020**, *10*, 8424. [CrossRef] [PubMed]
4. Sonobe, T.; Tabuchi, H.; Ohsugi, H.; Masumoto, H.; Ishitobi, N.; Morita, S.; Enno, H.; Nagasato, D. Comparison between support vector machine and deep learning, machine-learning technologies for detecting epiretinal membrane using 3D-OCT. *Int. Ophthalmol.* **2018**, *39*, 1871–1877. [CrossRef] [PubMed]
5. Baamonde, S.; de Moura, J.; Novo, J.; Charlón, P.; Ortega, M. Automatic identification and characterization of the epiretinal membrane in OCT images. *Biomed. Opt. Express* **2019**, *10*, 4018. [CrossRef] [PubMed]
6. Baamonde, S.; de Moura, J.; Novo, J.; Charlón, P.; Ortega, M. Automatic Identification and Intuitive Map Representation of the Epiretinal Membrane Presence in 3D OCT Volumes. *Sensors* **2019**, *19*, 5269. [CrossRef] [PubMed]
7. Gende, M.; De Moura, J.; Novo, J.; Charlón, P.; Ortega, M. Automatic Segmentation and Intuitive Visualisation of the Epiretinal Membrane in 3D OCT Images Using Deep Convolutional Approaches. *IEEE Access* **2021**, *9*, 75993–76004. [CrossRef]

8. Gawlik, K.; Hausser, F.; Paul, F.; Brandt, A.U.; Kadas, E.M. Active contour method for ILM segmentation in ONH volume scans in retinal OCT. *Biomed. Opt. Express* **2018**, *9*, 6497–6518. [CrossRef] [PubMed]
9. Huang, G.; Liu, Z.; Maaten, L.V.D.; Weinberger, K.Q. Densely Connected Convolutional Networks. In Proceedings of the 2017 IEEE Conference on Computer Vision and Pattern Recognition (CVPR), Honolulu, HI, USA, 21–26 July 2017; pp. 2261–2269. [CrossRef]

Proceeding Paper

Promoting Physical Activity in People with Functional Diversity through a Multiplayer Musical Game [†]

Manuel Merino-Monge *, Alberto J. Molina-Cantero, Juan A. Castro-García, Clara Lebrato-Vázquez and Isabel M. Gómez-González

Departamento de Tecnología Electrónica, E.T.S. Ingeniería Informática, Universidad de Sevilla, 41012 Sevilla, Spain; almolina@us.es (A.J.M.-C.); jacastro@us.es (J.A.C.-G.); clebrato@us.es (C.L.-V.); igomez@us.es (I.M.G.-G.)
* Correspondence: manmermon@dte.us.es; Tel.: +34-954-552787
† Presented at the 4rd XoveTIC Conference, A Coruña, Spain, 7–8 October 2021.

Abstract: Physical activity (PA) performed in group can slow down the decline in motor functions in people with disabilities. With this objective, Interactive Rehab Orchestra (IRO) was developed. IRO is an interactive multiplayer musical game that looks for reducing sedentary lifestyles by promoting PA. The individuals are responsible for playing the melody correctly. To do that, they must perform a movement when the on-screen avatar reaches a certain area. If the action is not performed, the melody will stop playing for a certain time interval. IRO is highly configurable, allowing the controller to be adapted to player skills. The customization of melodies and images is also possible according to the players' preferences, which helps to enhance player engagement. In addition, a configurable color code allows identifying when to perform an action. IRO incorporates a statistical summary to assess the evolution of the user. In this way, IRO aims at encouraging PA through music to maintain/improve muscle tone and the subjects' mobility, quantifying PA intensity, in relation to motor skills, and promoting PA so that participants can adhere to a specific program with long-term follow-up.

Keywords: physical activity; functional diversity; multiplayer musical game

1. Introduction

Many people with disabilities and limited motor functions, such as cerebral palsy, exhibit sedentary behavior (SB), which contributes to reducing motor functions, increasing body fat, muscle stiffness, and health issues [1]. The World Health Organization guidelines [2] recommend the practice of regular PA to reduce health risks. Three factors are important in PA: duration, frequency, and intensity. By increasing all of them, better health benefits can be achieved. Exercising in groups endows people with a higher level of engagement in the activity, allows increasing the PA, and results in an improvement in physical capabilities [3]. Additionally, the use of music to evoke emotions [4] and obtain higher levels of engagement and attention to the PA is also important [5].

This paper describes the multiplayer musical game denominated Interactive Rehab Orchestra (IRO), which aims at reducing SB lifestyles by promoting individual or group PA. The application is highly configurable and can be adapted to the user's needs, providing statistical summaries to therapists for the assessment of the players.

2. Software

IRO (https://github.com/manmermon/IRO, accessed on 22 July 2021) is a cross-platform software, developed using Java technology (version 1.8) under development but in a sufficient state so that it can be used by potential users. In this multiplayer musical game, based on midi files, the player must perform a movement when the avatar reaches a certain area. Missing actions mute the melody for a while. Therefore, the players are

responsible for the correct sounding of the melody. IRO contains three parts: the video game itself, the controller or the user interface, and the therapist interface. As players' motor skills can be very different, IRO does not set any default controller.

2.1. Videogame

During the game, the user must perform a movement when the avatar reaches a certain area, such that any missing action would mute the melody for a time equal to the player's reaction time. In this way, motor capabilities, concentration, and reaction are worked on.

The game's screen (Figure 1b) shows a bar with the reached level of action (BRAL) with 3 areas (recovery level (RL) in green, action level (AL) in red, and intermediate zone in yellow) plotting the player's movement, which allows a feedback; therefore, external instructions are unnecessary. Another element is the action area. When the avatars enter this area, the player must perform the action for a limited time defined by the configurable parameter time to reach the action level (TAL). In addition, the action is split in two parts: AL and time at action target (TAT). If AL is not reached and maintained for TAT time, then music is muted. The local multiplayer session is implemented to increase fun and player involvement. The number of players is limited to 4 people, where each player will be assigned a specific controller, a BRAL, and a different avatar color.

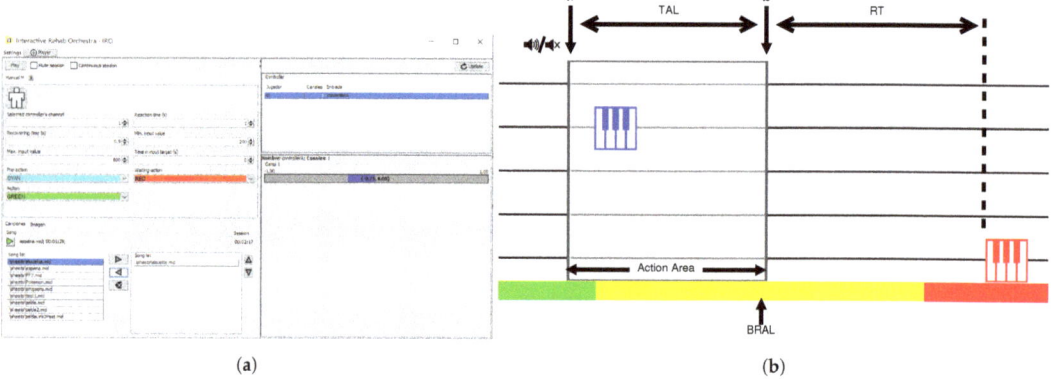

Figure 1. IRO interfaces: (**a**) therapist interface; (**b**) video-game scheme.

2.2. Game Controller

IRO allows using a wide range of controllers that can be adapted to players' motor skills. To achieve this, we included the Lab-Streaming Layer (LSL) library (https://github.com/sccn/labstreaminglayer, accessed on 22 July 2021). This is a cross-platform library (Windows/Linux/MacOS and 32/64-bit computer architecture) that provides a unified interface for centralized data collection, synchronization in (near) real-time, and the ability to register multiple devices at the same time. Thus, LSL is responsible for the communication between IRO and the controller.

The therapist sets six parameters per player to interact with IRO: stream channel (SC), AL, TAT, TAL, RL, and recovery time (RT). As any controller can send several data streams at the same time, you need to select a specific data stream. For example, a gyroscope sends the angle velocity of the X, Y, Z axes associated with a movement. If you are interested in torsional motions, the stream to be used would be the one associated with the X axis. Thus, the SC parameter selects exactly the control source. The AL, TAT, and TAL parameters set the range of motion to perform, which includes the time TAT to reach the preset AL level when the avatar enters the action zone, and the time TAL to remain above the level for IRO to determine that an action has been correctly performed. Finally, RL and RT determine the starting value to which the player must return before performing the next action (which compels subjects to perform complete movements), and the time the therapist considers enough for the player to recover, before performing the next movement (which only determines when the next note is displayed on the screen). In this way, the parameters TAL and RT determine the temporal distance between the musical notes in the game (Figure 1b).

2.3. Therapist Interface

The therapist interface is oriented to configure the sessions (Figure 1a). Firstly, the default music session is not set, and therapists can add new midi files. The songs must be selected so that the players' preferences can be taken into account, which will improve their engagement. The background and avatar images can be customized. Similarly, the color of the active zone can be changed to make it easier for players to identify when to perform an action. Moreover, the therapist is responsible for selecting and configuring the control interface.

In addition to these above elements, the therapist can access the statistics of each player, so that they can analyze the evolution. This is still under development. However, data logging is already implemented. Fourteen different events associated with each player are stored in a SQLite database (when an avatar is displayed/disappears on the screen, when the avatar enters/exits the action zone, when the action starts, and so on), as well as the score achieved by each player and the data of all the controller channels. With this information, the therapist can assess the evolution of the users (score, reaction time, number of errors, average time taken to reach the recovery zone in the controller, and so on).

3. Conclusions

IRO is a highly configurable game that is independent of any controller hardware, and that takes into consideration the preferences of the players. This application aims at encouraging PA by using music to maintain/improve muscle tone and mobility. It also allows quantifying PA levels in relation to motor skills and promoting PA so that participants can adhere to a specific program with long-term follow-up.

Author Contributions: M.M.-M. developed IRO following the advice of the other authors. All authors have contributed equally in conducting the research and writing the paper. All authors have read and agreed to the published version of the manuscript.

Funding: This research was funded by the Spanish Ministry of Science and Innovation, State Plan 2017-2020: Challenges-R&D&I Projects with grant code PID2019-104323RB-C32.

Conflicts of Interest: The authors declare no conflict of interest.

References

1. WHO. *A Guide for Population-Based Approaches to Increasing Levels of Physical Activity: Implementation of the WHO Global Strategy on Diet, Physical Activity and Health*; World Health Organization: Geneva, Switzerland, 2007; p. 20.
2. WHO. *Global Priority Research Agenda for Improving Access to High-Quality Affordable Assistive Technology*; World Health Organization: Genève, Switzerland, 2017; p. 24.
3. Raghavan, P.; Geller, D.; Guerrero, N.; Aluru, V.; Eimicke, J.P.; Teresi, J.A.; Ogedegbe, G.; Palumbo, A.; Turry, A. Music Upper Limb Therapy—Integrated: An enriched collaborative approach for stroke rehabilitation. *Front. Hum. Neurosci.* **2016**, *10*, 498. [CrossRef] [PubMed]
4. Yip, H.; Moore, K.S. Music Therapy for Multisensory and Body Awareness in Children and Adults with Severe to Profound Multiple Disabilities: The MuSense Manual. *J. Music. Ther.* **2017**, *54*, 479–483. [CrossRef]
5. Davies, C.; Shurdington, J.; Murray, K.; Slater, L.; Pearson, D. Music for Wellness in rehabilitation patients: Programme description and evaluation results. *Public Health* **2021**, *194*, 109–115. [CrossRef] [PubMed]

Proceeding Paper

Development and Testing of Motion-Detection Techniques for People with Cerebral Palsy †

Clara Lebrato-Vázquez *, Alberto J. Molina-Cantero, Juan A. Castro-García and Manuel Merino-Monge and Isabel M. Gómez-González

Departamento de Tecnología Electrónica. E.T.S. Ingeniería Informática, Universidad de Sevilla, 41004 Sevilla, Spain; almolina@us.es (A.J.M.-C.); jacastro@us.es (J.A.C.-G.); manmermon@dte.us.es (M.M.-M.); igomez@us.es (I.M.G.-G.)

* Correspondence: clebrato@us.es
† Presented at the 4th XoveTIC Conference, A Coruña, Spain, 7–8 October 2021.

Abstract: This paper describes several computer access methods tested by Eva, a woman with choreoathetosic cerebral palsy. This disease prevents her from controlling the peripherals and configurations that normally give access to information and communication technologies, further limiting her independence. To make Eva access a computer, we focused our efforts on the methodologies that Eva could control by just moving her neck and head. These sensors were: Kinect, inertial measurement units (IMU), and video. Kinect, composed of a system of cameras and sensors, gives the option to interact and control the devices contactlessly. The IMU is a device consisting of an accelerometer and a gyroscope that measure velocity, orientation, and gravitational forces. For live image processing, a common webcam was used. During the development of the experiment, Eva must follow a sequence shown on the computer screen that alternates movement of the head with rest. These movements involved moving the head up, down, right, or left. Our results showed that the Kinect system could not be used effectively, while the image-processing algorithm obtained the best performance.

Keywords: cerebral palsy; choreoathetosis; accessibility; IMU; Kinect; image processing

1. Introduction

Cerebral palsy is a non-degenerative and permanent neurodevelopmental disorder that affects one in 500 people [1] (https://www.overleaf.com/project/6150b68910a2214a792fc158 (accessed on 23 September 2021)). It is caused by a neurological injury that occurs during the development of the fetus, childbirth, or in early childhood [1], which can be due to varied causes [2]. In boys and girls, it is the most frequent cause of disability [3], and the degree differs widely in each person [4], depending on the intensity, location, and duration of the injury [5]. Among the different types of cerebral palsy, we focused on the choreoathetosic, which happens when chorea and athetosis occur simultaneously. Chorea is characterized by involuntary, irregular, brief, repetitive, and somewhat rapid movements, while athetosis is a continuous flow of slow, twisting, and sinuous involuntary movements that alternate with parts of the body that remain rigid. When given together, the person has a mixture of twisting movements at a variable speed. Normally, subjects have slow movements in the head, neck, and extremities due to athetosis combined with large shaking in the arms and hands by the chorea. They together alter all the activity, capacity, and posture of the person with these uncontrolled movements.

In the literature, we found several research articles devoted to the design of devices for pointer control [5,6] using techniques based on movement detection sensors or software interfaces for a traditional mouse that are capable of filtering or isolating voluntary movements from the involuntary ones [7].

This work aims to help Eva access the computer autonomously. Eva has little control over her limbs, due to the spastic movements. These characteristics make it difficult for her to use adapted peripherals. With great effort, she has some control over her neck and head. Therefore, we exploited this to detect her instructions via head movements using three different sensors: Kinect, IMU, and video.

2. Materials and Methods

Due to the limited length of this communication, we have only focused here on describing the methods and results associated with the image-processing technique. Those based on Kinect and IMU will be presented at the conference.

The image-processing method is based on detecting the head position in the image captured by the webcam using the Viola–Jones algorithm [8]. This algorithm is based on dividing the image in small patches to which a set of cascade classifiers determines if they contain facial features, and, eventually, a face. This allows for fast face-tracking with high detection rates that provides us with face coordinates.

We have developed a user graphic interface (GUI) which allows us to test each of the devices under study and to guide the user throughout the experiment, providing them with stimuli or hints for the actions that they need to complete, in the form of arrows.

The experiment consists of a series of movements that the subject must reproduce from the initial position. The directions are right, left, up and down. They complete 10 repetitions per movement, in a random order. The time duration of each arrow is 6 s with another 6 s allocated for the user to move back to the origin. The idle time can seem relatively long, but it was found to be needed by Eva during the initial tests.

Two women have taken part in the experiment: S1 without any disability and Eva (whose characteristics have been aforementioned). All of them are adults (27 and 48 years of age) and with higher-education degrees. Before the experiment, they were thoroughly informed of the details and provided their consent.

3. Results and Discussion

The position (x, y) of the center of the frame returned by the Viola–Jones algorithm for each movement was stored for both subjects. Then, their distinguish ability was studied by extracting the average and standard error in both x and y directions. Figure 1 shows the results obtained by this method, in which each ellipse corresponds to the area containing 98% of the positions associated with the four movements plus the resting period. The figure contains the data of one session with both subjects.

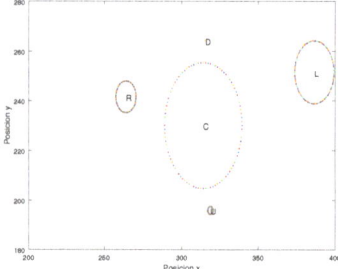
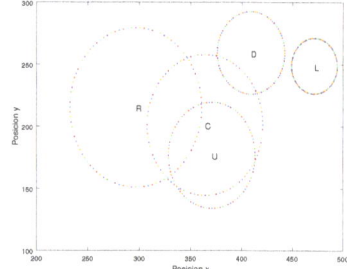

Figure 1. Representation of the results obtained by image processing of the x and y axes of the facial center. On the (**left**), results from S1, while on the (**right**) the data that corresponds to Eva.

As can be observed, for S1, the four movements plus the resting state are perfectly identifiable and separable. For Eva, those states overlap more, which implies greater difficulty in their identification. Nevertheless, there are some states that, without any further processing, could be identified (e.g., the movement to the left).

Looking at the results, the use of four movements seems not to be appropriate for Eva. A better option should only include a subset of movements. For example, movement to the left was easier for Eva, but at least three states (left, down, and rest) could be differentiated. With these detection possibilities, Eva could access most adapted software applications that use the scanning of their elements. Two gestures in the proposed technique (rest and left), will be enough to send a selection command to accept highlighted element during the scanning.

The Kinect detection system did not achieve the expected results. We believe that the main problem lies in the software driver that links the Kinect to the library used to synchronize the data.

The results obtained with the accelerometer for Eva were unclear. The movement she performed was not unequivocally identified and could not be improved after applying the Kalman filter. Despite other studies having obtained good results with this filter [9], we believe that the strong involuntary movements that Eva has makes this approach not work properly.

The processing of images obtained by the webcam seems to be the most feasible method, since some head gestures could be identified without any additional processing.

4. Conclusions

Among the systems used, we found that the system based on image processing gave better results since it had a higher probability in identifying some head movements. In addition, this system has several advantages with respect to the use of sensor type IMU or any that requires the placement of a device on the user [10]. Another clear advantage is that most people are familiar with webcams, which makes it easier for the caregiver to connect the system properly and easily.

Author Contributions: All authors have equally contributed to this paper. All authors have read and agreed to the published version of the manuscript.

Funding: This research was funded by Spanish Ministry of Science and Innovation, State Plan 2017–2020: Challenges—R&D&I Projects with grant codes PID2019-104323RB-C32.

Institutional Review Board Statement: The study was conducted according to the guidelines of the Declaration of Helsinki, and approved by the Ethics Committee of Junta de Andalucía (protocol code C.P. TAIS-C.I. 1130-N-17, 2018).

Informed Consent Statement: All participants agreed to take part in the experiments.

Conflicts of Interest: The authors declare no conflict of interest.

References

1. Nelson, K.B.; Ellenberg, J.H. Antecedents of cerebral palsy. *N. Engl. J. Med.* **1986**, *315*, 81–86. [CrossRef] [PubMed]
2. MacLennan, A.H.; Thompson, S.C.; Gecz, J. Cerebral palsy: Causes, pathways, and the role of genetic variants. *Am. J. Obstet. Gynecol.* **2015**, *213*, 779–788. [CrossRef] [PubMed]
3. Reddihough, D.S.; Collins, K.J. The epidemiology and causes of cerebral palsy. *Aust. J. Physiother.* **2003**, *49*, 7–12. [CrossRef]
4. Krigger, K.W. Cerebral palsy: An overview. *Am. Fam. Physician* **2006**, *73*, 91–100. [PubMed]
5. Almanji, A.; Davies, T.C.; Stott, N.S. Using cursor measures to investigate the effects of impairment severity on cursor control for youths with cerebral palsy. *Int. J. Hum. Comput. Stud.* **2014**, *72*, 349–357. [CrossRef]
6. Betke, M.; Gips, J.; Fleming, P. The Camera Mouse: Visual tracking of body features to provide computer access for people with severe disabilities. *IEEE Trans. Neural Syst. Rehabil. Eng.* **2002**, *10*, 1–10. [CrossRef] [PubMed]
7. Almanji, A.; Davies, C.; Amor, R. A Dynamic Adjustment of Control-Display Gain Based on Curvature Index. In Proceedings of the 2nd International Conference on Human-Computer Interaction, Prague, Czech Republic, 14–15 August 2014; pp. 1–9.
8. Hjelmås, E.; Low, B.K. Face detection: A survey. *Comput. Vis. Image Underst.* **2001**, *83*, 236–274. [CrossRef]
9. Raya, R.; Rocon, E.; Gallego, J.A.; Ceres, R.; Pons, J.L. A robust kalman algorithm to facilitate human-computer interaction for people with cerebral palsy, using a new interface based on inertial sensors. *Sensors* **2012**, *12*, 3049–3067. [CrossRef] [PubMed]
10. Molina-Cantero, A.J.; Lebrato-Vázquez, C.; Merino-Monge, M.; Quesada-Tabares, R.; Castro-García, J.A.; Gómez-González, I.M. Communication Technologies Based on Voluntary Blinks: Assessment and Design. *IEEE Access* **2019**, *7*, 70770–70798. [CrossRef]

Proceeding Paper

COVID-19 Lung Radiography Segmentation by Means of Multiphase Transfer Learning †

Plácido L. Vidal [1,2,*], Joaquim de Moura [1,2], Jorge Novo [1,2] and Marcos Ortega [1,2]

1. Centro de investigación CITIC, Universidade da Coruña, Campus de Elviña, s/n, 15071 A Coruña, Spain; joaquim.demoura@udc.es (J.d.M.); jnovo@udc.es (J.N.); mortega@udc.es (M.O.)
2. Grupo VARPA, Instituto de Investigación Biomédica de A Coruña (INIBIC), Universidade da Coruña, Xubias de Arriba, 84, 15006 A Coruña, Spain
* Correspondence: placido.francisco.lizancos.vidal@udc.es
† Presented at the 4th XoveTIC Conference, A Coruña, Spain, 7–8 October 2021.

Abstract: COVID-19 is characterized by its impact on the respiratory system and, during the global outbreak of 2020, specific protocols had to be designed to contain its spread within hospitals. This required the use of portable X-ray devices that allow for a greater flexibility in terms of their arrangement in rooms not specifically designed for such purpose. However, their poor image quality, together with the subjectivity of the expert, can hinder the diagnosis process. Therefore, the use of automatic methodologies is advised. Even so, their development is challenging due to the scarcity of available samples. For this reason, we present a COVID-19-specific methodology able to segment these portable chest radiographs with a reduced number of samples via multiple transfer learning phases. This allows us to extract knowledge from two related fields and obtain a robust methodology with limited data from the target domain. Our proposal aims to help both experts and other computer-aided diagnosis systems to focus their attention on the region of interest, ignoring unrelated information.

Keywords: CAD system; radiography; X-ray; lung segmentation; COVID-19; transfer learning

1. Introduction

In 2020, a new variant of coronavirus spread around the world, known as SARS-CoV-2. This variant, which causes the COVID-19 pathology, is known to cause a viral pneumonia and severe acute respiratory syndrome as its main symptoms. Due to the aerosol transmission capabilities of the virus and the possibility of contagion through surfaces, specific protocols and independent circuits were designed in the health services in order to avoid cross-contamination between hospital personnel and patients. Chest X-rays and computerized tomography scans are mainly used to diagnose this pathology in order to determine the degree of the affliction of the patients, which allows us to see the state of the lungs in a non-invasive way. However, this medical imaging equipment is usually set up in rooms specifically designed for them, with certain safety measures. For this reason, to prevent said cross-contamination, the use of portable X-ray devices that can be used in these alternative circuits is recommended. On the other hand, these devices only allow a limited range of planes from which images of the patient can be extracted. Moreover, due to their nature, the images tend to be of lesser quality. These two factors, together with the emergency situation and the inherent subjectivity of a human expert, can result in challenges in making a quick, correct and repeatable diagnosis for further monitoring of the afflicted. It is precisely for this reason that the use of computer-based diagnostic support systems to assist in the task is necessary.

The main problem that emerged in the development of these methodologies derives from the scarcity of available samples due to the exceptionality of the scenario as well as the target domain. For this reason, methodologies were developed based on the prominent classical lung radiographs from fixed devices [1,2]. Even so, the results from these automatic methodologies were not as accurate as would be desired, as they were unprepared to work with these portable devices. This way, there were attempts to develop both methodologies trained with a reduced dataset with networks robust to this data scarcity [3], methodologies that proposed generating synthetic samples from zero to train more powerful networks weak to this data scarcity [4] and, like in the work proposed here, methodologies that aim to assist both clinicians and other computer-aided diagnosis systems by reducing the presence of extraneous elements [5]: a robust lung segmentation strategy for chest radiographs from portable devices.

2. Materials and Methods

For the development of our proposal we employed three different domains represented in Figure 1. Using as baseline brain magnetic resonance images for glioma segmentation, we took advantage of a pretrained U-Net model from the work of *Buda* [6]. These pathological bodies (and also natural structures present in the image) show similar gradient and texture patterns as lung regions afflicted by different respiratory tract diseases. The second domain consists in chest radiographs that were obtained with classical X-ray devices [7,8] to further approximate the deep features of the network to the target images from portable devices (introducing it to the patterns of the target organ and pathology). Finally, the third (and target) domain is composed of images that were captured during live clinical practice from a local hospital during the COVID-19 pandemic (the Universitary Hospital Complex of A Coruña or CHUAC, by its acronym in Spanish) with portable chest X-ray devices. To ensure that the system would be able to properly perform in a real clinical scenario in even the most borderline cases, both chest radiography datasets include both COVID-19 and healthy patients, but also a third class of pathological lung radiographs with a similar profile as patients with COVID-19 (but not being actually afflicted by it). These scenarios mainly include similar cases of viral and bacterial pneumonia that leave a very similar trace in the chest radiographs.

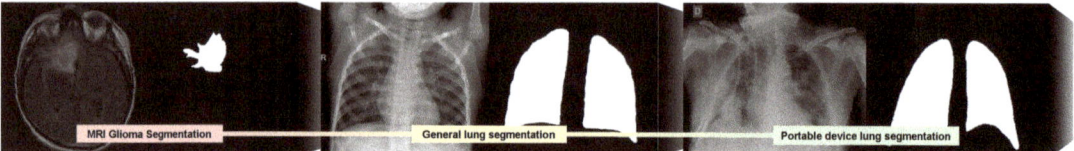

Figure 1. Representation in order of the three domains from which we will perform the knowledge transfer.

This way, we first adapt the classification layer of the U-Net pretrained with glioma images dataset and resume the training with the general lung radiographs. This allows the network to learn to segment these radiographs in a reduced number of epochs. Afterwards, we further refine the classification of this model by resuming the training, but now with images from our dataset composed by chest radiographs from portable devices.

3. Results and Discussion

The results attained in both transfer learning stages can be seen in Table 1. In both cases, the results are shown with the same independent dataset with images that were extracted by means of portable X-ray devices. As we can see, the results that were obtained by the system are satisfactory with all the studied metrics. However, we see two metrics that clearly stand out from the rest after the second phase of transfer learning: the Dice and the sensitivity that improve by 0.0688 and 0.0804 on average in the three classes, respectively. These metrics indicate that, while in both cases the system was able to obtain an approximate segmentation to the lung region, after the second phase of knowledge transfer these segmentations are more adjusted to the regions of interest established by the experts (even despite the aforementioned deterioration in image quality and limitations).

For this reason, we can see that, in fact, we have obtained a more robust system compared to those trained only with classical lung radiographs thanks to the progressive adaptation of the latent features of the network, and only needing a reduced number of samples.

Table 1. Test results from the inter domain (a) and inter device type (b) knowledge transfer phases.

(a)			
	COVID-19	Normal	Pathological
Accuracy	0.9570 ± 0.0293	0.9555 ± 0.0439	0.9476 ± 0.0294
Sensitivity	0.8729 ± 0.0745	0.8576 ± 0.0973	0.8536 ± 0.0608
Specificity	0.9844 ± 0.0230	0.9864 ± 0.0197	0.9754 ± 0.0286
Dice	0.8936 ± 0.0698	0.8854 ± 0.0731	0.8536 ± 0.0928
(b)			
	COVID-19	Normal	Pathological
Accuracy	0.9761 ± 0.0100	0.9801 ± 0.0104	0.9769 ± 0.0111
Sensitivity	0.9444 ± 0.0443	0.9470 ± 0.0373	0.9340 ± 0.0525
Specificity	0.9867 ± 0.0108	0.9906 ± 0.0059	0.9891 ± 0.0077
Dice	0.9447 ± 0.0241	0.9528 ± 0.0161	0.9414 ± 0.0322

Author Contributions: P.L.V.: Conceptualization, methodology, software, formal analysis, investigation, data curation, writing—original draft, writing—review and editing, visualization. J.d.M.: conceptualization, validation, investigation, data curation, writing—review and editing, supervision, project administration. J.N.: validation, investigation, data curation, writing—review and editing, supervision, project administration, funding acquisition. M.O.: validation, investigation, data curation, writing—review and editing, supervision, project administration, funding acquisition. All authors have read and agreed to the published version of the manuscript.

Funding: Instituto de Salud Carlos III, Government of Spain, DTS18/00136 research project; Ministerio de Ciencia e Innovación y Universidades, Government of Spain, RTI2018-095894-B-I00 research project, Ayudas para la formación de profesorado universitario (FPU), grant ref. FPU18/02271; Ministerio de Ciencia e Innovación, Government of Spain through the research project with reference PID2019-108435RB-I00; Consellería de Cultura, Educación e Universidade, Xunta de Galicia, Grupos de Referencia Competitiva, grant ref. ED431C 2020/24 and through the postdoctoral grant contract ref. ED481B 2021/059; Axencia Galega de Innovación (GAIN), Xunta de Galicia, grant ref. IN845D 2020/38; CITIC, Centro de Investigación de Galicia ref. ED431G 2019/01, receives financial support from Consellería de Educación, Universidade e Formación Profesional, Xunta de Galicia, through the ERDF (80%) and Secretaría Xeral de Universidades (20%).

Institutional Review Board Statement: The study was approved by the Ethics Review Board y Data Management Technical Commission of Galician Health Ministry for High Impact studies with protocol code 2020-007.

Conflicts of Interest: The authors declare no conflict of interest. The funders had no role in the design of the study; in the collection, analyses, or interpretation of data; in the writing of the manuscript, or in the decision to publish the results.

References

1. Ozturk, T.; Talo, M.; Yildirim, E.A.; Baloglu, U.B.; Yildirim, O.; Acharya, U.R. Automated detection of COVID-19 cases using deep neural networks with X-ray images. *Comput. Biol. Med.* **2020**, *121*, 103792. [CrossRef] [PubMed]
2. de Moura, J.; Novo, J.; Ortega, M. Fully automatic deep convolutional approaches for the analysis of Covid-19 using chest X-ray images. *IEEE Access* **2020**, *8*, 195594–195607. [CrossRef]
3. de Moura, J.; Garcia, L.R.; Vidal, P.L.; Cruz, M.; Lopez, L.A.; Lopez, E.C.; Novo, J.; Ortega, M. Deep Convolutional Approaches for the Analysis of COVID-19 Using Chest X-Ray Images From Portable Devices. *IEEE Access* **2020**, *8*, 195594–195607. [CrossRef]
4. Moris, D.I.; de Moura, J.; Novo, J.; Ortega, M. Cycle Generative Adversarial Network Approaches to Produce Novel Portable Chest X-Rays Images for Covid-19 Diagnosis. In Proceedings of the ICASSP 2021—2021 IEEE International Conference on Acoustics, Speech and Signal Processing (ICASSP), Toronto, ON, Canada, 6–11 June 2021. [CrossRef]
5. Vidal, P.L.; de Moura, J.; Novo, J.; Ortega, M. Multi-stage transfer learning for lung segmentation using portable X-ray devices for patients with COVID-19. *Expert Syst. Appl.* **2021**, *173*, 114677. [CrossRef] [PubMed]

6. Buda, M. U-Net for Brain MRI, Pytorch Hub. 2020. Available online: https://pytorch.org/hub/mateuszbuda_brain-segmentation-pytorch_unet/ (accessed on 20 October 2020).
7. Kermany, D. Labeled Optical Coherence Tomography (OCT) and Chest X-Ray Images for Classification. Mendeley Data. 2018. Available online: https://data.mendeley.com/datasets/rscbjbr9sj/2 (accessed on 1 September 2020). [CrossRef]
8. Cohen, J.P.; Morrison, P.; Dao, L.; Roth, K.; Duong, T.Q.; Ghassemi, M. COVID-19 Image Data Collection: Prospective Predictions Are the Future. *arXiv* **2020**, arXiv:2006.11988.

Proceeding Paper

Portable Chest X-ray Synthetic Image Generation for the COVID-19 Screening †

Daniel I. Morís [1,2,*], Joaquim de Moura [1,2], Jorge Novo [1,2] and Marcos Ortega [1,2]

1. Centro de Investigación CITIC, Universidade da Coruña, 15071 A Coruña, Spain; joaquim.demoura@udc.es (J.d.M.); jnovo@udc.es (J.N.); mortega@udc.es (M.O.)
2. Grupo Varpa, Instituto de Investigación Biomédica de A Coruña (INIBIC), Universidade da Coruña, 15006 A Coruña, Spain
* Correspondence: daniel.iglesias.moris@udc.es; Tel.: +34-981-167-000 (ext. 1330)
† Presented at the 4th XoveTIC Conference, A Coruña, Spain, 7–8 October 2021.

Abstract: The global pandemic of COVID-19 raises the importance of having fast and reliable methods to perform an early detection and to visualize the evolution of the disease in every patient, which can be assessed with chest X-ray imaging. Moreover, in order to reduce the risk of cross contamination, radiologists are asked to prioritize the use of portable chest X-ray devices that provide a lower quality and lower level of detail in comparison with the fixed machinery. In this context, computer-aided diagnosis systems are very useful. During the last years, for the case of medical imaging, they are widely developed using deep learning strategies. However, there is a lack of sufficient representative datasets of the COVID-19 affectation, which are critical for supervised learning when training deep models. In this work, we propose a fully automatic method to artificially increase the size of an original portable chest X-ray imaging dataset that was specifically designed for the COVID-19 diagnosis, which can be developed in a non-supervised manner and without requiring paired data. The results demonstrate that the method is able to perform a reliable screening despite all the problems associated with images provided by portable devices, providing an overall accuracy of 92.50%.

Keywords: COVID-19; portable chest X-ray images; oversampling; CycleGAN; deep learning

1. Introduction

COVID-19, declared as a global pandemic by the World Health Organization (WHO) in March 2020, mainly affects the respiratory tissues [1]. Chest X-ray imaging plays an important role in supporting the screening and early detection of the disease. In this context, radiologists are asked to prioritize the use of portable chest X-ray devices that are important to reduce the risk of cross contamination [2]. However, these devices provide a lower quality and a lower level of detail in comparison with fixed machinery [3]. In this critical scenario, computer-aided diagnosis (CAD) systems can be very useful for clinical practice. During recent years, in the scope of biomedical imaging, these diagnostic systems were usually developed using computer vision techniques as well as machine learning techniques and, specifically, deep learning strategies, which have increased their importance. However, in the context of supervised learning, deep learning models require a great amount of labeled data to be trained.

Regarding medical imaging, data scarcity is an aspect to take into account as, in many occasions, it critically affects the amount of labeled data. One of the ways to overcome data scarcity is to generate synthetic images with several network architectures, as is the case of many variants of Generative Adversarial Networks (GANs) [4]. One example of this kind of GAN model is the CycleGAN, a model that is able to translate images from a certain scenario to another different scenario.

In this work, due to the low availability of samples that show COVID-19 affectation, we present novel approaches to artificially increase the size of a portable chest X-ray image dataset to diagnose COVID-19, combining three different and complementary CycleGAN architectures to perform an oversampling using a non-supervised strategy that can be performed without paired data.

2. Methodology

Thus, the presented methodology is divided in 2 different parts. The first part performs the synthetic image generation. The second part uses the novel set of generated images in order to augment the dimensionality of the original dataset, which is proven in a COVID-19 screening scenario.

2.1. Approaches for Data Augmentation

In order to increase the size of the original chest X-ray dataset, we considered 3 different complementary scenarios, which correspond to all the possible combinations given the classes of the dataset. For the first scenario, normal vs. pathological, normal samples are translated to their pathological representation and vice versa. For the second scenario, normal vs. COVID-19, normal samples are converted to their hypothetical representation showing COVID-19 affectation and vice versa, and for the third scenario, pathological vs. COVID-19, we perform the same task as in the previous cases but to convert pathological samples to COVID-19 and vice versa. It is important to remark that all the images from the original dataset are used to train the CycleGAN model [5].

2.2. Approaches for Screening Tasks

For this second stage, we assess the degree of separability among the generated images and the suitability of the novel set of generated synthetic images, with the oversampled dataset. We used a Dense Convolutional Network Architecture (DenseNet) [6] model, pretrained on the ImageNet dataset, with the same training details as stated in [7,8] due to their suitability to this particular problem.

3. Results and Conclusions

The chest X-ray image dataset was provided by the Radiology Service of the Complexo Hospitalario Universitario de A Coruña (CHUAC) and is composed of 600 patients that were divided into 3 different classes [9], having 200 normal cases (i.e., from patients without evidence of pulmonary pathologies), 200 pathological cases (i.e., from patients with pulmonary pathologies other than COVID-19) and 200 COVID-19 genuine cases.

In order to demonstrate the separability and the suitability of the generated synthetic images, we conducted 4 different experiments, where the first 3 correspond to the separability among the generated images and the fourth experiment corresponds to the suitability of the novel set of generated images, evaluating the screening using the oversampled dataset. The first 3 experiments demonstrate that there is a proper separability among generated images for the 3 possible scenarios. For the fourth experiment, the model obtained a global accuracy of 0.9250 for the test. Additionally, Figure 1 shows the performance of the model for the test set for all the 4 experiments, obtaining remarkable correct classification ratios in every case.

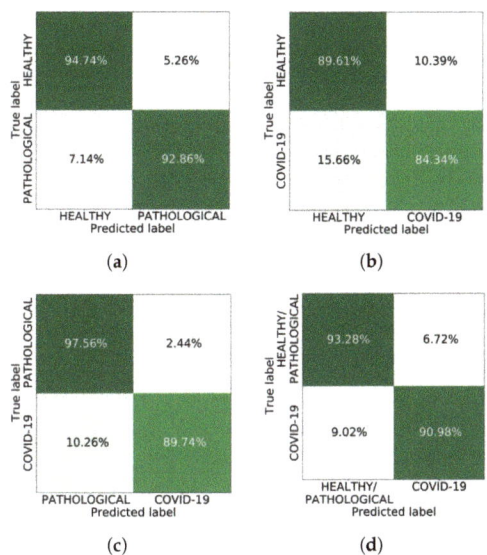

Figure 1. Confusion matrices for the four conducted experiments. (**a**) 1st experiment (Healthy vs. Pathological); (**b**) 2nd experiment (Healthy vs. COVID-19); (**c**) 3rd experiment (Pathological vs. COVID-19); (**d**) 4th experiment (Healthy and Pathological vs. COVID-19).

Author Contributions: Conceptualization, D.I.M., J.d.M., J.N. and M.O.; methodology, D.I.M., J.d.M., J.N. and M.O.; software, D.I.M. and J.d.M.; validation, J.d.M., J.N. and M.O.; investigation, J.N. and M.O.; data curation, J.N. and M.O.; writing—original draft preparation, D.I.M.; writing—review and editing, D.I.M., J.d.M., J.N. and M.O.; visualization, D.I.M.; supervision, J.d.M., J.N. and M.O.; project administration, J.N. and M.O.; funding acquisition, M.O. All authors have read and agreed to the published version of the manuscript.

Funding: This research was funded by Instituto de Salud Carlos III, Government of Spain, DTS18/00136 research project; Ministerio de Ciencia e Innovación y Universidades, Government of Spain, RTI2018-095894-B-I00 research project; Ministerio de Ciencia e Innovación, Government of Spain through the research project with reference PID2019-108435RB-I00; Consellería de Cultura, Educación e Universidade, Xunta de Galicia through the predoctoral and postdoctoral grant contracts ref. ED481A 2021/196 and ED481B 2021/059, respectively; and Grupos de Referencia Competitiva, grant ref. ED431C 2020/24; Axencia Galega de Innovación (GAIN), Xunta de Galicia, grant ref. IN845D 2020/38; CITIC, Centro de Investigación de Galicia ref. ED431G 2019/01, receives financial support from Consellería de Educación, Universidade e Formación Profesional, Xunta de Galicia, through the ERDF (80%) and Secretaría Xeral de Universidades (20%).

Institutional Review Board Statement: The study was approved by the Ethics Review Board y Data Management Technical Commission of Galician Health Ministry for High Impact studies with protocol code 2020-007.

Conflicts of Interest: The authors declare no conflict of interest.

References

1. Pollard, C.A.; Morran, M.P.; Nestor-Kalinoski, A.L. The COVID-19 pandemic: A global health crisis. *Physiol. Genom.* **2020**, *52*, 549–557. [CrossRef] [PubMed]
2. Kooraki, S.; Hosseiny, M.; Myers, L.; Gholamrezanezhad, A. Coronavirus (COVID-19) outbreak: What the department of radiology should know. *J. Am. Coll. Radiol.* **2020**, *17*, 447–451. [CrossRef] [PubMed]
3. Vidal, P.L.; de Moura, J.; Novo, J.; Ortega, M. Multi-stage transfer learning for lung segmentation using portable X-ray devices for patients with COVID-19. *Expert Syst. Appl.* **2021**, *173*, 114677. [CrossRef] [PubMed]
4. Creswell, A.; White, T.; Dumoulin, V.; Arulkumaran, K.; Sengupta, B.; Bharath, A.A. Generative adversarial networks: An overview. *IEEE Signal Process. Mag.* **2018**, *35*, 53–65. [CrossRef]

5. Zhu, J.Y.; Park, T.; Isola, P.; Efros, A.A. Unpaired Image-to-Image Translation using Cycle-Consistent Adversarial Networks. In Proceedings of the 2017 IEEE International Conference on Computer Vision (ICCV), Venice, Italy, 22–29 October 2017. [CrossRef]
6. Huang, G.; Liu, Z.; van der Maaten, L.; Weinberger, K.Q. Densely Connected Convolutional Networks. In Proceedings of the 2017 IEEE Conference on Computer Vision and Pattern Recognition (CVPR), Honolulu, HI, USA, 21–26 July 2017. [CrossRef]
7. de Moura, J.; Novo, J.; Ortega, M. Fully automatic deep convolutional approaches for the analysis of Covid-19 using chest X-ray images. *medRxiv* **2020**. [CrossRef]
8. Morís, D.I.; de Moura, J.; Novo, J.; Ortega, M. Cycle Generative Adversarial Network Approaches to Produce Novel Portable Chest X-Rays Images for Covid-19 Diagnosis. In Proceedings of the ICASSP 2021—2021 IEEE International Conference on Acoustics, Speech and Signal Processing (ICASSP), Toronto, ON, Canada, 6–11 June 2021; pp. 1060–1064. [CrossRef]
9. De Moura, J.; García, L.R.; Vidal, P.F.L.; Cruz, M.; López, L.A.; Lopez, E.C.; Novo, J.; Ortega, M. Deep convolutional approaches for the analysis of covid-19 using chest x-ray images from portable devices. *IEEE Access* **2020**, *8*, 195594–195607. [CrossRef]

Proceeding Paper

Smart Bracelet for Emotional Enhancement in Children with Autism Spectrum Disorder [†]

Alba Ortolan-Soto *, Juan A. Castro-García *, Alberto J. Molina-Cantero, Manuel Merino-Monge and Isabel M. Gómez-González

Departamento de Tecnología Electrónica, E.T.S. Ingeniería Informática, Universidad de Sevilla, 41012 Sevilla, Spain; almolina@us.es (A.J.M.-C.); manmermon@dte.us.es (M.M.-M.); igomez@us.es (I.M.G.-G.)
* Correspondence: alba.ortolan@gmail.com (A.O.-S.); jacastro@us.es (J.A.C.-G.)
† Presented at the 4rd XoveTIC Conference, A Coruña, Spain, 7–8 October 2021.

Abstract: People with autism spectrum disorder (ASD) have great difficulties in social interaction and in the management of personal and other people's emotions. This work aimed at developing an intelligent bracelet, capable of inferring the children's emotional state, transmitting it to others, and, above all, informing the patients themselves so that they can learn to recognise, control, and work with, as well as to improve their self-knowledge and their relationship with their environment. Electrodermal activity (EDA) and photoplethysmography (PPG) are useful in combined psychophysiological and medical studies to determine the mood of patients. Due to COVID-19, no experiments with subjects could be carried out, although the modules were validated, and a public database was used to test the system's application. The results concluded that, in general, when an individual is altered or becomes nervous, either positively or negatively (also known as valence) to a stimulus, their heart rate and sweating increase. This is the kind of relationship between physiological signals and external stimuli that the design of these circuits was intended to confirm. Finally, with the indicators of nervous system activity and knowing the behaviour of skin conductance in response to each basic emotion, it can be determined whether the subject is in a situation of pleasure or frustration in response to each reaction.

Keywords: autism; ASD; PPG; EDA; IoT; wearable; low cost

1. Introduction

Nowadays, there are some devices available in the market focused on the processing of biomedical signals in relation to the emotions of individuals, but they are neither numerous nor affordable to all. Focusing on those applied to autism, again, we find that those that exist are not accessible. The cost ranges from EUR 300 to EUR 2000. The aim of this project was to develop a bracelet able to measure electrodermal activity (EDA) and photoplethysmography (PPG) signals in autistic children but developing an accessible and affordable device for the public. This type of technology is very useful in helping the emotional control and development of children on the autistic spectrum. The processing of their heart rate (HR) and electrodermal activity helps to classify the individual into one of the basic emotions. This information allows both the subject and their tutors or relatives to assess this emotional state and to act, respond, and evolve accordingly. In other words, this device is a tool for the growth, education, and personal development of these individuals.

2. Materials and Methods

The hardware design had an EDA and a PPG module. An Arduino Nano-programmed using the library BSP [1] at 256 Hz of sampling frequency was used for data acquisition and sent them via Bluetooth (HC05). The EDA circuit was presented in [2]. The PPG circuit had a first-order [0.7–28] Hz bandpass filter and a total gain of 100.

The PCB board developed for the prototype is shown in Figure 1. It was made with surface-mounting device (SMD) components, with the intention of reducing the size of the board as much as possible.

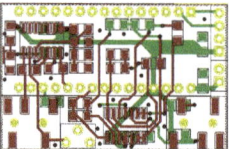

Figure 1. The resulting dimensions of the prototype are 2.95 cm wide and 4.73 cm high.

Due to the COVID-19 pandemic, it was not possible to test the prototype on volunteers. However, the circuits used during this project (EDA and PPG) had previously been tested in [2,3]; then, we used a database [4] that collected some biological signals— EDA, PPG, EEG, EMG, BVP, breath rate, etc.—when participants were playing the Pacman game, to test the algorithms to apply. This version of the game was designed to introduce the loss of control (LOC) states and measure physiological reactions in volunteers. The controls were reduced to two buttons for the index fingers of both hands. The left one rotated the game avatar clockwise by 90 degrees, and the right one rotated it dual clockwise. The experimental design consisted of introducing the LOC into the game in two-minute blocks, interspersed with unmodified blocks of the same duration. In total, each session lasted 30 min. The blocks with LOC were distributed evenly throughout the experiment, building a series from sequences of three blocks; one LOC and two normal blocks. Modifications to induce LOC consisted of randomly ignoring 15% of the actions typed by the subject and occasionally freezing the screen to produce a delay in the image. After each block, the subjects rated their mental state in terms of valence (pleasure), arousal, and dominance (subjective feelings of control) on a scale presented with the Software Asset Management (SAM) assessment test [5].

Data Processing

The PPG signal was processed in 3 steps: firstly, we calculated the derivative of the signal, then a bandpass filter was applied, and finally, the Wavelet transform. This algorithm calculates the time difference between two consecutive RR segments and determines the individual's cardiac variability (HRV) [6]. PPG and electrocardiography (ECG) are signals that could be considered redundant, as we were interested in analysing the heart rate and its variability. The derivative was performed to resemble the PPG signal to the ECG and process it with one of the algorithms commonly used to analyse these types of signals, such as the Wavelet. The bandpass filter has a cutoff frequency of 1 Hz and 40 Hz. It does not allow frequencies lower than 1 Hz or higher than 40 Hz.

For the processing of the EDA signal, the variables extracted with Ledalab [7], an open source EDA signal processing package for MATLAB, were used. For the Ledalab processing, software-understandable events were manually added every 10 s to evaluate the EDA signal in 10 s windows within each block. The continuous decomposition analysis (CDA) method was applied, which aimed to recover the underlying signal characteristics of the sudomotor nerve.

3. Results and Discussions

As an example of the results of the statistical processing of the PPG, some of the data obtained for the individual s4 is shown below. The discrete analysis recording of the EDA signal for subject s0 shows that during the course of the entire video game, he underwent four steps of increase in skin conductance. This was consistent over time with the blocks of frustration and with the peak values of phasic activity, as can be seen in Figure 2.

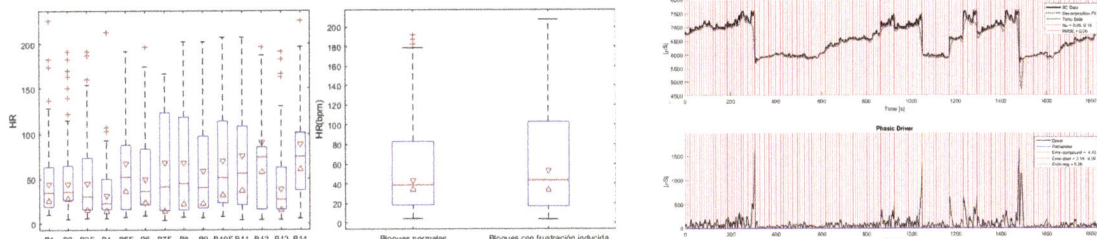

Figure 2. Left graph: HR of s4 during the whole experiment divided by blocks. The blocks where frustration was introduced had an F added at the end of the name. **Middle graph**: HR of s4 grouped by blocks with and without induced frustration. **Right graph**: EDA signal for S0 (upper graph), and the phasic activity (bottom graph).

4. Conclusions

The developed device allows the PPG and EDA of individuals to be measured correctly. It has been determined that, when an individual becomes upset or nervous, either positively or negatively to a stimulus, their heart rate and sweating increase. This is the relationship between these signals and external stimuli that this project was intended to confirm. In addition, with the indicators of autonomic nervous system (ANS) activity (acquired from the analysis of cardiac variability obtained through the PPG recording) and knowing the behaviour of skin conductivity in response to each stimulus, it is possible to determine whether the subject is in a situation of pleasure or frustration in response to each observed reaction.

Funding: This research was funded by the Spanish Ministry of Science and Innovation, State Plan 2017–2020: Challenges—R&D&I Projects with grant codes PID2019-104323RB-C32.

Institutional Review Board Statement: The study was conducted according to the guidelines of the Declaration of Helsinki, and approved by the Ethics Committee of *Junta de Andalucía* (protocol code C.P. TAIS-C.I. 1130-N-17, 2018).

Informed Consent Statement: Informed consent was obtained from all subjects involved in the study.

Conflicts of Interest: The authors declare no conflict of interest.

References

1. Molina-Cantero, A.J.; Castro-García, J.A.; Lebrato-Vázquez, C.; Gómez-González, I.M.; Merino-Monge, M. Real-time processing library for open-source hardware biomedical sensors. *Sensors* **2018**, *18*, 1033. [CrossRef] [PubMed]
2. Castro-García, J.A.; Molina-Cantero, A.J.; Merino-Monge, M.; Gómez-González, I.M. An Open-Source Hardware Acquisition Platform for Physiological Measurements. *IEEE Sens. J.* **2019**, *19*, 11526–11534. [CrossRef]
3. Molina, A.J.; Gómez, I.M.; Guerrero, J.; Merino, M.; Castro, J.A.; Quesada, R.; Berrazueta, S.; Hermoso-de-Mendoza, M. A HW/SW Platform to Acquire Bioelectrical Signals. A Case Study: Characterizing Computer Access through Attention. In *Proceedings of the 4th International Conference on Physiological Computing Systems*; SciTePress: Setúbal, Portugal, 2017; pp. 76–83.
4. Reuderink, B.; Nijholt, A.; Poel, M. Affective Pacman: A Frustrating Game for Brain-Computer Interface Experiments. In *Intelligent Technologies for Interactive Entertainment*; Nijholt, A., Reidsma, D., Hondorp, H., Eds.; Springer: Berlin/Heidelberg, Germany, 2009; pp. 221–227.
5. Bradley, M.M.; Lang, P.J. Measuring emotion: The self-assessment manikin and the semantic differential. *J. Behav. Ther. Exp. Psychiatry* **1994**, *25*, 49–59. [CrossRef]
6. Shaffer, F.; Ginsberg, J.P. An Overview of Heart Rate Variability Metrics and Norms. *Front. Public Health* **2017**, *5*, 258. [CrossRef] [PubMed]
7. Benedek, M.; Kaernbach, C. A continuous measure of phasic electrodermal activity. *J. Neurosci. Methods* **2010**, *190*, 80–91. [CrossRef] [PubMed]

Proceeding Paper

Study of Blood-Pressure Measurement Using Noninvasive Methods [†]

Mariña González-Pena *, Juan A. Castro-García *, Alberto J. Molina-Cantero, Manuel Merino-Monge and Isabel M. Gómez-González

Departamento de Tecnología Electrónica, ETS, Ingeniería Informática, Universidad de Sevilla, 41012 Sevilla, Spain; almolina@us.es (A.J.M.-C.); manmermon@dte.us.es (M.M.-M.); igomez@us.es (I.M.G.-G.)
* Correspondence: marinagonzalezpena10@gmail.com (M.G.-P.); jacastro@us.es (J.A.C.-G.)
† Presented at the 4th XoveTIC Conference, A Coruña, Spain, 7–8 October 2021.

Abstract: The correct diagnosis of high blood pressure is important to avoid cardiovascular diseases. In this work, we propose a low-cost noninvasive blood-pressure measurement unit composed of a photoplethysmograph and an electrocardiograph. It is based on pulse transit time measurement, thus performing nonocclusive measurement. To test the effectiveness of this parameter, a total of five subjects were measured, verifying their effectiveness at all times.

Keywords: blood pressure; PTT; pulse transit time; PPG; ECG

1. Introduction

Cardiovascular diseases are a group of disorders related to the circulatory system that may affect the heart. According to the World Health Organisation World Health Organisation (WHO), 17.9 million people die from cardiopathy, with high blood pressure (BP) being one of the major risk factors for cardiovascular disease [1]. The periodic measurement of the BP is recommended. Some methods for it have the disadvantage of being occlusive, which may cause discomfort to patients, apart from requiring health personnel. In recent years, a method of BP measurement based on the pulse wave velocity (PWV) concept has been investigated, which has the great advantage of being nonocclusive.

PWV is defined as the velocity of pressure pulses as they propagate along the arterial tree. Any variation in the biomechanical properties of the aorta induces changes in pulse propagation velocity; see [2] for further details. In general, different proposals are based on the following simplification: given an arterial segment of length D, the PWV is defined as quotient of D divided by pulse transit time (PTT) $PWV = D/PTT$, where PTT is the time of flight of the pressure wave. More exactly, PTT corresponds to the difference between the arrival times of the pressure pulse at the distal end and the proximity of the heart $PTT = PAT_d - PAT_p$ (see Figure 1). The wave peak R of the electrocardiography (ECG) offers information about when heart contraction starts. Thus, it represents to some extent PAT_p time, while the systolic peak of the photoplethysmography (PPG) indicates the distal PAT_d.

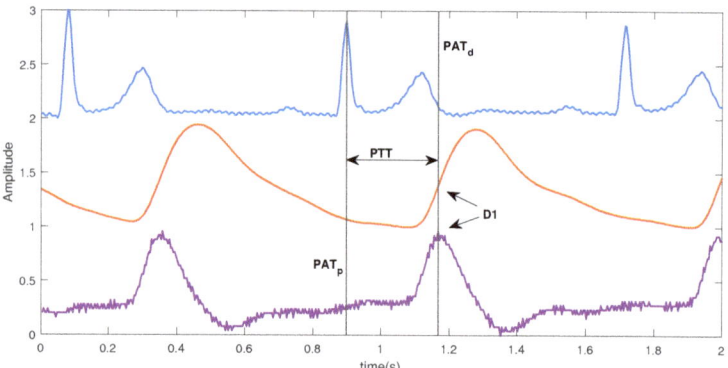

Figure 1. ECG (blue), PPG (orangle), and VPG (purple). Signal amplitudes were normalized.

2. Materials and Methods

With the aim of quantifying the PTT, an Arduino shield called Galicia was developed. It contains an ECG and a PPG. An Arduino Uno, programmed using library BSP [3] at 256 Hz of sampling frequency, has only been used for data acquisition. The ECG circuit was presented in [4], with electrodes placed following the Einthoven lead II schema. The PPG is formed by an TCRT100, a high-pass filter with a cut-off frequency of 0.7 Hz, a low pass filter of 28.2 Hz, and a total gain of 100. In order to make the design portable, an external battery was added along with an expansion port for a Bluetooth connection through the HC05 module. Between the R peak of the ECG signal and the systolic peak of the PPG signal, there is a delay of the order of hundreds of milliseconds that remains constant throughout the measurement. This delay obeys the response time between the electrical activation of the myocardium and the mechanical ejection of the ventricular blood towards the aorta. In the ECG signal, the R peak is the most commonly used critical point, whereas for the PPG, there is no defined convention for this point. In this case, the maximum of the first derivative of the PPG signal, the so-called velocity of PPG (VPG), was chosen; this point is also known as $D1$. The Pan–Tompkins algorithm [5] is used for the detection of the R and $D1$ points in offline processing.

The principal aim of the development of this study was to use the concept of PTT to estimate arterial BP, finding out the relationship among systolic pressure (SP), arm length, and PTT. In addition, the effect of physical exercise on BP reduction was analyzed to process ECG and PPG data taken from a total of five people (3 men and 2 women) with an age range of 22 to 34 years. Only one participant, S2, had been subjected to a 2.5 min of soft exercise before the corresponding measurements were taken, to verify that there was a decrease in BP [6].

The method is similar for both situations and comprises the following steps: (1) measurement of diastolic and SP before of the experiment using a sphygmomanometer; (2) arm-length measurement; (3) ECG and PPG data recorded for 2.5 min, and (4) measurement of diastolic and SP. During Step (3), all volunteers were at rest except in the physical condition, in which one volunteer was pedalling.

3. Results and Discussions

The following relationships were analysed: SP, arm length, and PTT. First, a higher PTT value is related to a higher BP, as Table 1 shows, where the participant with less arterial pressure was the one who had less PTT. The relationship between PTT and the ratio of SP to arm length (SPAL) was then analyzed. The definition of PTT shows that the lower the value of such a ratio is, the lower the PTT (SPAL in Table 1), with the exception of participant S2, who did not fulfil this condition. Therefore, the existence of a relationship between PTT and systolic pressure was demonstrated. According to the consulted bibliography, this relationship can be very useful in the detection of patients in a sleep unit since it provides relevant information about refractory hypertension [7].

Lastly, for participant S2 who was performing physical exercise for 2 min 30 s, blood pressure obtained prior and after working out was compared. PTT decreased when the subject underwent physical activity, which agreed with some published studies [8]. Although obtained results were conclusive with the consulted bibliography, they were not statistically significant since the tests were performed only on five people.

Table 1. BP, heart rate (HR), arm length, PTT and SPAL per participant.

ID	BP-Pre (mmHg)	HR-Pre (bpm)	BP-Post (mmHg)	HR-Post (bpm)	Arm Length (m)	PTT (ms)	SPAL (mmHg/m)
1	100/67	91	101/70	83	0.700	251	143
2	123/74	67	110/65	61	0.855	301	144
3	125/81	83	120/82	83	0.830	262	151
4	145/72	86	119/73	61	0.835	305	174
5	121/77	58	113/76	58	0.730	298	165
2_e	112/75	75	103/65	64	0.855	266	131

Two devices based on this technology are currently on the market: the ASUS VivoWatch BP and the RT1025 Cardioid PAD. Both integrate ECG and PPG sensors with a cost of EUR 139 and EUR 75.75, respectively. The price of these devices is far from the one designed for this work, which costs EUR 25.

4. Conclusions

In this work, we used the concept of PTT for the measurement of BP using electrocardiographic and photoplethysmographic signals. The relationship among concepts such as PTT, SP or PTT, and physical exercise were tested. In summary, the designed hardware device, PCB GALICIA, fulfilled the initial objective, being useful for analyzing PPG and ECG signals.

Funding: This research was funded by Spanish Ministry of Science and Innovation, State Plan 2017–2020: Challenges—R&D&I Projects with grant codes PID2019-104323RB-C32.

Institutional Review Board Statement: The study was conducted according to the guidelines of the Declaration of Helsinki, and approved by the Ethics Committee of *Junta de Andalucía* (protocol code C.P. TAIS-C.I. 1130-N-17, 2018).

Informed Consent Statement: Informed consent was obtained from all subjects involved in the study.

Conflicts of Interest: The authors declare no conflict of interest.

References

1. World Health Organization. Cardiovascular Diseases (CVDs). 2021. Available online: https://www.who.int/en/news-room/fact-sheets/detail/cardiovascular-diseases-(cvds) (accessed on 8 September 2021).
2. Solà i Carós, J.M. Continuous Non-Invasive Blood Pressure Estimation. Ph.D. Thesis, ETH Zurich, Zurich, Switzerland, 2011.
3. Molina-Cantero, A.J.; Castro-García, J.A.; Lebrato-Vázquez, C.; Gómez-González, I.M.; Merino-Monge, M. Real-Time Processing Library for Open-Source Hardware Biomedical Sensors. *Sensors* **2018**, *18*, 1033. [CrossRef] [PubMed]
4. Castro-García, J.A.; Molina-Cantero, A.J.; Merino-Monge, M.; Gómez-González, I.M. An Open-Source Hardware Acquisition Platform for Physiological Measurements. *IEEE Sens. J.* **2019**, *19*, 11526–11534. [CrossRef]
5. Pan, J.; Tompkins, W.J. A Real-Time QRS Detection Algorithm. *IEEE Trans. Biomed. Eng.* **1985**, *BME-32*, 230–236. [CrossRef] [PubMed]
6. Ferrer Mileo, V. Estudio de la Viabilidad de la Estimación del Grado de Adherencia a Estilos de Vida Saludables a Partir de Medidas Cardíacas Oportunistas. Ph.D. Thesis, Universitat Politècnica de Catalunya, Barcelona, Spain, 2019.

7. Gómez García, M.T.; Troncoso Acevedo, M.F.; Rodriguez Guzmán, M.; Alegre de Montaner, R.; Fernández Fernández, B.; del Río Camacho, G.; González-Mangado, N. Can Pulse Transit Time Be Useful for Detecting Hypertension in Patients in a Sleep Unit? *Arch. Bronconeumol.* **2014**, *50*, 278–284. [CrossRef] [PubMed]
8. Mateu-Mateus, M.; Guede-Fernández, F.; García-González, M.A.; Ramos-Castro, J.J.; Fernández-Chimeno, M. Camera-Based Method for Respiratory Rhythm Extraction From a Lateral Perspective. *IEEE Access* **2020**, *8*, 154924–154939. [CrossRef]

Proceeding Paper

Automatic Pipeline for Detection and Classification of Phytoplankton Specimens in Digital Microscopy Images of Freshwater Samples †

David Rivas-Villar [1,2,*], **José Rouco** [1,2], **Rafael Carballeira** [3], **Manuel G. Penedo** [1,2] **and Jorge Novo** [1,2]

1. Centro de Investigación CITIC, Universidade da Coruña, 15071 A Coruña, Spain; jrouco@udc.es (J.R.); mgpenedo@udc.es (M.G.P.); jnovo@udc.es (J.N.)
2. Grupo VARPA, Instituto de Investigación Biomédica de A Coruña (INIBIC), Universidade da Coruna, 15006 A Coruña, Spain
3. Centro de Investigacions Científicas Avanzadas (CICA), Facultade de Ciencias, Universidade da Coruna, 15071 A Coruña, Spain; r.carballeira@udc.es
* Correspondence: david.rivas.villar@udc.es
† Presented at the 4th XoveTIC Conference, A Coruña, Spain, 7–8 October 2021.

Abstract: Phytoplankton blooming can compromise the quality of the water and its safety due to the negative effects of the toxins that some species produce. Therefore, the continuous monitoring of water sources is typically required. This task is commonly and routinely performed by specialists manually, which represents a major limitation in the quality and quantity of these studies. We present an accurate methodology to automate this task using multi-specimen images of phytoplankton which are acquired by regular microscopes. The presented fully automatic pipeline is capable of detecting and segmenting individual specimens using classic computer vision algorithms. Furthermore, the method can fuse sparse specimens and colonies when needed. Moreover, the system can differentiate genuine phytoplankton from other similar non-phytoplanktonic objects like zooplankton and detritus. These genuine phytoplankton specimens can also be classified in a target set of species, with special focus on the toxin-producing ones. The experiments demonstrate satisfactory and accurate results in each one of the different steps that compose this pipeline. Thus, this fully automatic system can aid the specialists in the routine analysis of water sources.

Keywords: microscope images; phytoplankton detection; colony merging; gabor filters; deep features; bag of visual words

1. Introduction

Phytoplankton has retained scientific attention over the years for various reasons. It is the basis of the food chain in all aquatic environments, producing oxygen through photosynthesis and being able to fix carbon. Furthermore, several species produce toxins which can contaminate drinking water sources [1]. Thus, continuous monitoring of phytoplankton populations is not only a purely scientific activity, it is also a matter of public health. The monitoring of water sources is done manually by experts, therefore, automating part of the process is highly desirable. In this work, we present an accurate method that uses a systematic microscopic imaging approach which can liberate experts from operating the microscope [2]. The presented system can segment, identify and classify phytoplankton species, with special focus on the toxin-producing ones [3].

2. Materials and Methods

The presented method is divided into several steps. Firstly, the foreground-background stage uses an adaptive Gaussian threshold [4] over each of the input image channels to binarize the image. The results are merged with an OR operator to preserve the highest amount of information. Next, to detect every specimen, we employ Suzuki and Abe's Algorithm [5]. In this step, we discard any detection smaller than 5 µm^2, since, due to their size, they can not be phytoplankton. Moreover, incomplete specimens cut by the image borders are discarded. Following this step, we present an algorithm to fuse sparse specimens and colonies, which do not have evident visual links among their parts. We employ a Delaunay Triangulation [6] linking neighbouring detections. We prune the graph according to a colour similarity metric, keeping only the similar neighbours. Finally, the neighbouring detections are fused if they are still connected after the pruning step. The output of these first steps are a set of bounding boxes enclosing each specimen.

Once the specimens are segmented we must classify them. Firstly, a step to separate genuine phytoplankton from non-phytoplanktonic elements is devised. This is due to the tuning towards recall of the previous steps, as they capture most of the phytoplankton but they also mistakenly let through some similar specimens. Therefore, the first classification step separates phytoplankton from other similar objects like zooplankton, mineral particles or organic detritus. After this, another classification is needed, separating the genuine phytoplankton specimens into a set of relevant species. In this case the focus is set on two toxin-producing ones *Woronichinia naegeliana* and *Anabaena spiroides* and a harmless but complex one, *Dinobryon sociale*. Lastly, this classification will also have an "Others" tag which includes all the other phytoplankton species.

For these classification steps we test several features. To capture texture information we use Gabor Filter banks with a Bag of Visual Words (BoVW). Furthermore, colour information is also gathered using a BoVW, capturing the information of each of the RGB channels. Finally, we also use Deep Features, extracted from a ResNet50 [7] pretrained using ImageNet [8]. The different features are tested, masked and unmasked. This means that, either the features are obtained from the whole bounding box or just from the area of the specimen, using the segmentation mask. These features are used in combination with Random Forest (RF) and Support Vector Machines (SVM) as classifiers.

All the experiments were carried out in the same microscopic image dataset. Contrary to the state of the art, this dataset was captured using fixed focal points and magnification. This greatly complicates the automated task but frees the specialists from operating the microscope, as any technician can follow the systematic approach. The first steps, the segmentation of specimens, are trained on a random subset of 50 images. The rest of the images are the test set to evaluate the algorithms. The classification steps employ an 80-20% split on a 10-fold crossvalidation with grid search to determine the best parameters for the features and classifiers.

The ground truth of the dataset are bounding boxes containing the phytoplankton specimens, with an associated label identifying the species as marked by an expert.

3. Results and Conclusions

For the specimen detection and merging steps, we obtain a False Negative Rate (FNR) of 0.4%. We count as positives the cases where bounding boxes enclose at least 50% of the specimens' area. Overall this step is satisfactory, missing very few specimens.

In terms of phytoplankton identification, separating it from other spurious elements, we evaluate it using precision at high levels of recall, like 90% or 95%. In particular, the best result at 90% of recall is a 84.07%, obtained using an SVM that only uses unmasked Deep Features, as adding any other feature reported no benefit. In terms of precision at 95% of recall, the best result is RF with the combination of all unmasked features. Overall, masking the features showed no improvement in this step, on the contrary. Despite the complexities due to the heterogeneity of the classes, the first classification step shows accurate results.

Regarding the species classification, the best performance is obtained with masked features and mixing Deep Features with colour features. In this case, RF performs better than SVM, obtaining a top result of 87.50% global classification accuracy and a 87.99% of F1-Score. In terms of particular results for each species, *W. naegeliana* obtains an accuracy of 94.53%, *A. spiroides* 97.66%, *D. sociale* 94.53% and the others class results in a 88.28% of accuracy. This step demonstrates a satisfactory performance despite the complexities of classifying among species has, like morphological similarities among different species.

Image examples of the results of the classification steps can be seen in Figure 1, which also represent the bounding boxes that the system detects.

Overall, the performance in each of the different steps has been satisfactory, despite the particular complexities that each one of them shows, like similarities among different phytoplankton species or the variations among a single species. Therefore, we can say that the methodology presented in this work can be of notable help to the trained taxonomists that usually carry out potability analysis in water sources.

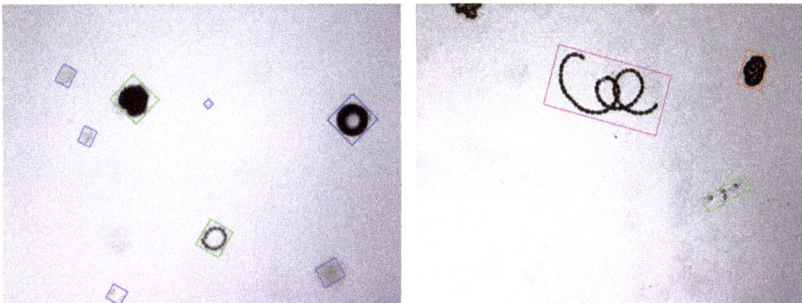

Figure 1. Examples of phytoplankton detection (**left**) and species classification (**right**). In the left image, true positives are represented in green and true negatives in blue. In the right image *W. naegeliana* in red, *A. spiroides* in magenta and *D. sociale* in green.

Author Contributions: Conceptualization, J.R. and J.N.; methodology, D.R.-V.; software, D.R.-V.; validation, D.R.-V.; formal analysis, D.R.-V.; investigation, D.R.-V.; resources, M.G.P., R.C., J.R. and J.N.; data curation, R.C. and D.R.-V.; writing—original draft preparation, D.R.-V.; writing—review and editing, J.R. and J.N.; visualization, D.R.-V.; supervision, J.R. and J.N.; project administration, J.R. and J.N.; funding acquisition, J.R. and J.N. All authors have read and agreed to the published version of the manuscript.

Funding: This research was funded by Consellería de Cultura, Educación e Universidade, Xunta de Galicia through the predoctoral grant contract ref. ED481A 2021/147 and Grupos de Referencia Competitiva, grant ref. ED431C 2020/24; CITIC, Centro de Investigación de Galicia ref. ED431G 2019/01, receives financial support from Consellería de Educación, Universidade e Formación Profesional, Xunta de Galicia, through the ERDF (80%) and Secretaría Xeral de Universidades (20%).

Conflicts of Interest: The authors declare no conflict of interest.

References

1. Zamyadi, A.; Choo, F.; Newcombe, G.; Stuetz, R.; Henderson, R.K. A review of monitoring technologies for real-time management of cyanobacteria: Recent advances and future direction. *Trends Analyt. Chem.* **2016**, *85*, 83–96. [CrossRef]
2. Rivas-Villar, D.; Rouco, J.; Penedo, M.G.; Carballeira, R.; Novo, J. Automatic Detection of Freshwater Phytoplankton Specimens in Conventional Microscopy Images. *Sensors* **2020**, *20*, 6704. [CrossRef] [PubMed]
3. Rivas-Villar, D.; Rouco, J.; Carballeira, R.; Penedo, M.G.; Novo, J. Fully automatic detection and classification of phytoplankton specimens in digital microscopy images. *Comput. Methods Programs Biomed.* **2021**, *200*, 105923. [CrossRef] [PubMed]
4. Parker, J.R. *Algorithms for Image Processing and Computer Vision*, 2nd ed.; Wiley Publishing: Indianapolis, IN, USA, 2010.
5. Suzuki, S.; Abe, K. Topological structural analysis of digitized binary images by border following. *Comput. Vis. Image Underst.* **1985**, *30*, 32–46. [CrossRef]
6. Delaunay, B. Sur la sphère vide. *Bulletin de l'Académie des Sciences de l'URSS, Classe des Sciences Mathématiques et Naturelles* **1934**, *6*, 793–800.
7. He, K.; Zhang, X.; Ren, S.; Sun, J. Deep Residual Learning for Image Recognition. In Proceedings of the 2016 IEEE Conference on Computer Vision and Pattern Recognition (CVPR), Las Vegas, NV, USA, 27–30 June 2016; pp. 770–778.
8. Deng, J.; Dong, W.; Socher, R.; Li, L.-J.; Li, K.; Li, F.-F. ImageNet: A large-scale hierarchical image database. In Proceedings of the 2009 IEEE Conference on Computer Vision and Pattern Recognition (CVPR), Miami, FL, USA, 20–25 June 2009; pp. 248–255. [CrossRef]

Proceeding Paper

Collaborative Augmented Digital Twin: A Novel Open-Source Augmented Reality Solution for Training and Maintenance Processes in the Shipyard of the Future [†]

Aida Vidal-Balea [1,2,*], Oscar Blanco-Novoa [1,2], Paula Fraga-Lamas [1,2,*], Miguel Vilar-Montesinos [3] and Tiago M. Fernández-Caramés [1,2]

1. Department of Computer Engineering, Faculty of Computer Science, Universidade da Coruña, 15071 A Coruña, Spain; o.blanco@udc.es (O.B.-N.); tiago.fernandez@udc.es (T.M.F.-C.)
2. Centro de Investigación CITIC, Universidade da Coruña, 15071 A Coruña, Spain
3. Navantia S. A., Astillero de Ferrol, 15403 Ferrol, Spain; mvilar@navantia.es
* Correspondence: aida.vidal@udc.es (A.V.-B.); paula.fraga@udc.es (P.F.-L.); Tel.: +34-981167000 (P.F.-L.)
† Presented at the 4th XoveTIC Conference, A Coruña, Spain, 7–8 October 2021.

Abstract: Large companies use a lot of resources on workshop operator training and industrial machinery maintenance since the lack of this practice or its poor implementation increases the cost and risks of operating and handling sensitive and/or hazardous machinery. Industrial Augmented Reality (IAR), a major technology in the Industry 4.0 paradigm that may enhance worker performance, minimize hazards and improve manufacturing processes, could be beneficial in this situation. This paper presents an IAR solution that allows for visualizing and interacting with the digital twin of a critical system. Specifically, the augmented digital twin of an industrial cooler was developed. The proposed IAR system provides a dynamic way to perform operator training with a full-size model of the actual equipment and to provide step-by-step guidance so that maintenance processes can be performed more safely and efficiently. The proposed system also allows several users to use devices at the same time, creating a new type of collaborative interaction by viewing the model in the same place and state. Performance tests with many simultaneous users have been conducted, with response latency being measured as the number of connected users grows. Furthermore, the suggested IAR system has been thoroughly tested in a real-world industrial environment.

Keywords: industrial augmented reality; collaborative augmented reality; mixed reality; Industry 4.0; maintenance; training

1. Introduction

The introduction of new technologies that optimize production processes has increased growth to the point of being considered a fourth industrial revolution. Thus, the term Industry 4.0 was established to name this new stage in which industry integrates manufacturing processes, information systems and communications technologies. In particular, Industrial Internet of Things (IIoT) and Industrial Augmented Reality (IAR) are key for the Industry 4.0 paradigm [1].

In addition, cyber-physical systems enable the interconnection between the real and virtual worlds. Although it is not a new term [2], digital twins [3] have experienced an increase in interest in recent years. In the case of the shipbuilding industry, processes are constantly evolving by introducing new technologies to adapt to Industry 4.0.

The aim of this paper is to demonstrate in a practical scenario the capabilities of Industry 4.0 for shipbuilding by mixing three key technologies (digital twin, IAR and IIoT) with the objective of optimizing maintenance, production and operator training tasks. To this end, an application has been developed for Microsoft Hololens Augmented Reality glasses [4]. It consists of a digital twin of a cooler and it allows the visualization of animations and the interaction with the model in a virtual way. In addition, the application displays real-time information obtained from sensors embedded in the cooler.

2. Design of the System

The architecture of the designed system is depicted in Figure 1, where the multiple modules of the system can be distinguished clearly. Both the AR/MR and IoT layers make use of the Service Layer to communicate with each other. In addition, the Service Layer is in charge of coordinating all the processes as well as managing the different protocols used by the heterogeneous devices involved in the system.

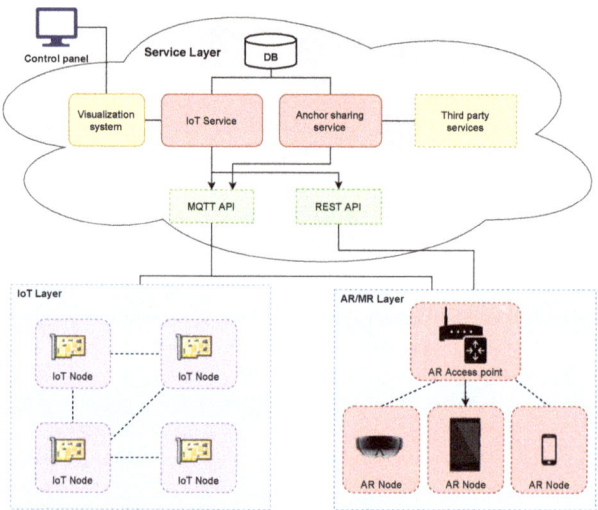

Figure 1. Diagram of the architecture of the system.

In order to show the capabilities of the proposed system, an application was developed for Microsoft HoloLens smartglasses. Such an application allows for visualizing the 3D model of a cooler, as well as to receiving indications on repair and maintenance processes and operating parameters measured in real time by embedded sensors. The application is shown in Figure 2, which has been captured by one of the users, who watches in real time how the other user interacts with the digital twin of the cooler. Thus, both users share the same collaborative experience.

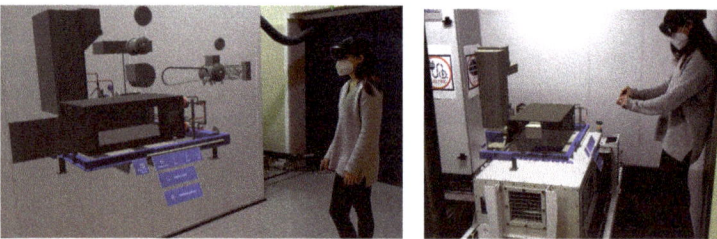

Figure 2. Expanded view of the parts of the digital twin of the cooler (**left**) and user performing a repair procedure on the real cooler, being guided by the developed AR application (**right**).

3. Experiments

In order to measure the performance of the system, a series of tests were carried out in a real environment. Taking advantage of the fact that Unity [5] allows the development of applications for different environments and operating systems, a mock-up version of the IAR application was developed to emulate its behavior when running multiple instances on a computer. Thus, a desktop computer can perform operations as if it were multiple users using the IAR application. In this way, the network load can be simulated in a realistic scenario without needing to purchase multiple pairs of HoloLens smart glasses.

The performed test cases were carried out for scenarios with 5, 10, 15 and 20 simultaneous clients. Average latencies were measured using 2.4 GHz and 5 GHz IEEE 802.11 ac networks. In all cases, the measured latencies included the processing and rendering times of the information contained in the packets. In other words, the latency is measured since a packet is generated at the source device and until it is processed and the information is rendered on the screen of the destination device. This includes waiting times related to the frame rate limits imposed by the smart glasses graphics engine. Measuring times in such a way ensures that the results provide an accurate representation of the waiting times that would be experienced by a real user that executes the application.

The average obtained latencies are shown in Table 1. As it can be observed, latency increases with the number of users. Additionally, the variance is notably low, especially for a lower number of users, due to network stability (i.e., users generate less interference). The differences between the 2.4 GHz and 5 GHz networks are approximately 3–5 ms, always higher in the case of the 2.4 GHz network due to the saturation of the spectrum in terms of the frequency and the characteristics of the physical layer.

Table 1. The 2.4 GHz and 5 GHz average latency measured for a device on the network (ms).

Clients	Average	Standard Deviation	Variance
5	24.0804	13.4883	0.25171
10	40.777	20.925	0.53113
15	61.4403	30.2245	1.02500
20	86.0936	38.2146	1.61572

4. Discussion

The developed digital twin application was created and tested to develop shipyard assembly instructions and support. The proposed features allow for the detailed visualization of virtual elements in their full size, positioned precisely in the location where the real elements would be positioned. Moreover, the proposed application facilitates IIoT real-time interactions, collaborative training, and assistance tasks, all of which help to speed up manufacturing operations.

Funding: This work was supported by the Plant Information and Augmented Reality research line of the Navantia-UDC Joint Research Unit (IN853B-2018/02). The authors would like to thank CITIC for its support. CITIC, a research center accredited by Galician University System, is funded by "Consellería de Cultura, Educación e Universidades from Xunta de Galicia", with 80% of funds coming from ERDF Funds, ERDF Operational Programme Galicia 2014-2020, and the remaining 20% from "Secretaría Xeral de Universidades" (Grant ED431G 2019/01).

Conflicts of Interest: The authors declare no conflict of interest.

References

1. Fraga-Lamas, P.; Fernández-Caramés, T.M.; Blanco-Novoa, O.; Vilar-Montesinos, M. A review on industrial augmented reality systems for the industry 4.0 shipyard. *IEEE Access* **2018**, *6*, 13358–13375. [CrossRef]
2. Shafto, M.; Conroy, M.; Doyle, R.; Glaessgen, E.; Kemp, C.; LeMoigne, J. *DRAFT Modeling, Simulation, Information Technology & Processing Roadmap*; Technology Area 11; NASA—National Aeronautics and Space Administration: Washington, DC, USA, 2010.
3. Qi, Q.; Tao, F. Digital Twin and Big Data Towards Smart Manufacturing and Industry 4.0: 360 Degree Comparison. *IEEE Access* **2018**, *6*, 3585–3593. [CrossRef]
4. Microsoft HoloLens Official Web Page. Available online: https://www.microsoft.com/en-us/hololens (accessed on 31 July 2021).
5. Unity 3D Development Platform Official Web Page. Available online: https://unity.com/ (accessed on 31 July 2021).

Proceeding Paper

E-Voting System Using Hyperledger Fabric Blockchain and Smart Contracts [†]

Javier Díaz-Santiso [1] and Paula Fraga-Lamas [1,2,*]

[1] Department of Computer Engineering, Faculty of Computer Science, Universidade da Coruña, 15071 A Coruña, Spain; javier.diazs@udc.es

[2] Centro de Investigación CITIC, Universidade da Coruña, 15071 A Coruña, Spain

* Correspondence: paula.fraga@udc.es; Tel.: +34-981167000 (ext. 6051)

[†] Presented at the 4th XoveTIC Conference, A Coruña, Spain, 7–8 October 2021.

Abstract: The emergence of the current pandemic has led to a new reality in which bureaucratic formalities have been affected in terms of health security, procedures, resource management, among others. Specifically, in the electoral processes, where the difficulty of fulfilling the social distance and the mobility restrictions reopen the debate on the implementation of other more advanced and modern alternatives, such as electronic voting (e-voting). This article presents the design and implementation of a decentralized e-voting system that has the potential to provide a higher level of transparency, security, and cost-efficiency. Hyperledger Fabric blockchain and smart contracts are used to cast votes, which are then recorded in an immutable way, giving voters anonymity and trust in the fairness of the election process. In addition, promising results of the performance of the e-voting system in terms of latency and transaction load are presented.

Keywords: blockchain; e-voting; Hyperledger Fabric; Hyperledger Caliper; decentralized systems

1. Introduction

The inexorable advance of the Internet and technology is changing our habits and the way we interact with each other. Despite the countless technological innovations in today's society, there are still processes that employ obsolete and inefficient mechanisms, as is the case of voting, which is mostly done through paper ballots. This article arises from this problem, with the aim of creating an electronic voting (e-voting) application that guarantees immutability and improves the current electoral systems in terms of performance and reliability. To meet this premise, an e-voting system based on blockchain technology is implemented. Specifically, the Hyperledger Fabric platform [1] is used since it allows for the implementation of permissioned networks and is widely accepted in business environments. Thus, this technology is used to develop a decentralized and scalable e-voting system for both public institutions and private business consortiums.

2. Design and Implementation

The proposed e-voting system makes use of a blockchain network implemented through the Hyperledger Fabric platform. Nodes are stored in replicated ledgers on CouchDBs. Data inside the different blocks are secured by cryptographic hashing using the SHA-256 algorithm and are also chained using hash to guarantee the immutability of votes. In addition, the blockchain implemented through Fabric ensures the integrity of transactions through TLS 1.2 certificates for communication between nodes and PKI-based X.509 certificates for node and user authorization.

Figure 1 shows the proposed architecture. This network consists of three organizations, each with a peer node (the one in charge of hosting a copy of the ledger and updating it) and an associated certificate authority. To manage the network communication and to

build and distribute the transaction blocks, a cluster of orderers was implemented, with a certification authority independent of the organizations associated to this cluster.

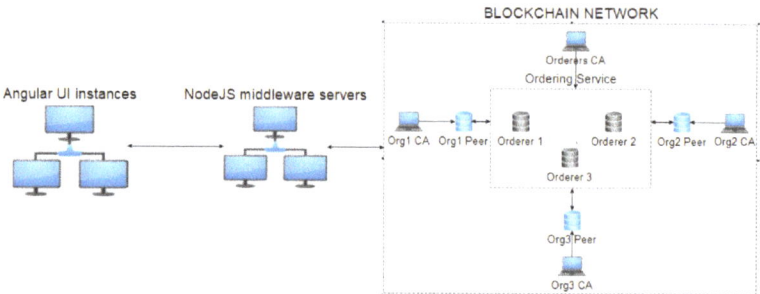

Figure 1. Architecture of the proposed e-voting system.

Two smart contracts were deployed on the Fabric network: one to perform voter validation and another that function as a ballot box, in order to guarantee secrecy and voter anonymity. Additionally, to ensure the authenticity of the network participants, X.509 certificates were used through the Fabric Membership Service Provider component [2]. Such a component is used to abstract the mechanisms and protocols required for the management of these certificates. The generation and validation of the cryptographic material was performed by simulating certificate authorities through the Fabric framework.

In order to support the functionalities of the smart contracts, multiple servers were used in Node.js, with the purpose of guaranteeing the decentralized philosophy of blockchain, specifically on Express. These operations are exposed through an API REST, following the procedure shown in rfc2616. This layer of the application is responsible for managing the authorization within the platform, through the integration of JSON Web Tokens, an open source standard for the generation of access tokens proposed by the IETF in rfc5719. The environment proposed to allow consuming this API consists of a user interface implemented on Angular. It should be noted that this layer of the system has navigation and functionalities restricted according to the role of the user, being the administrators the ones in charge of integrating new data into the system and its monitoring, and the voters are the ones enabled to participate in electoral processes and visualize the results.

Finally, as a complement to the described system, two tools provided by the Hyperledger platform, Explorer and Caliper, were integrated. Regarding the former, it was the entry point for the graphical visualization of the operation of the network blockchain, both in terms of the blocks indexed to the blockchain and the transactions they contain, and in terms of the network participants. Regarding the latter, it is a benchmark tool that allows for analyzing the tolerance of the blockchain network in terms of latency and supported congestion, allowing to verify that the system supports a high load of concurrent transactions without penalizing performance.

3. Results

Analyzing the performance metrics shown in Figure 2, it is worth noting the low latency of the blockchain read operations and the high transaction load supported by the vote casting and total vote listing operations.

Name	Succ	Fail	Send Rate (TPS)	Max Latency (s)	Min Latency (s)	Avg Latency (s)	Throughput (TPS)
Create ballot	997	0	50.1	9.86	2.10	6.75	34.9
List all ballots	1000	0	50.1	0.13	0.01	0.03	50.0
List all voters	1000	0	50.1	0.09	0.01	0.02	50.0
Find voter by dni	1000	0	50.1	0.05	0.01	0.01	50.0
List ballot voters	1000	0	50.1	0.09	0.01	0.02	50.0
Get ballot result	1000	0	50.1	0.13	0.01	0.03	50.0
Get ballot by id	2500	0	298.4	8.37	0.16	3.94	284.3
Vote	2500	0	298.5	7.90	0.14	3.75	283.3

Figure 2. Performance of the e-voting blockchain platform developed.

This high transaction load is linked to a high latency, so a study on the number of transactions, shown in Figure 3, was carried out to obtain an optimal performance in terms of latency. As a result, the inflection point from which the e-voting system starts to deteriorate its performance was obtained.

Name	Succ	Fail	Send Rate (TPS)	Max Latency (s)	Min Latency (s)	Avg Latency (s)	Throughput (TPS)
Get ballot result	2500	0	100.0	0.06	0.01	0.01	100.0
Get ballot by id	2500	0	150.1	0.10	0.01	0.01	150.0
Vote	2500	0	200.1	0.28	0.01	0.01	200.0

Figure 3. Transactions for optimal performance of the e-voting blockchain platform.

4. Discussion

Regarding the implementation of blockchain solutions, Hyperledger presents problems with concurrency management due to its Multiversion Concurrency Control (MVCC) system, by means of which an entity cannot be modified in concurrent transactions, making it necessary to store composite keys for concurrent changes.

Additionally, although Fabric nodes support 2500 concurrent transactions, the Hyperledger Caliper platform only allows 500 simultaneous transactions, preventing the analysis of the maximum performance of the Hyperledger blockchain.

5. Conclusions

The proposed e-voting system was designed and tested with the aim of studying the feasibility of a decentralized solution capable of supporting the most demanding requirements of both public environments and private business consortiums. In view of the preliminary results, it is clear that blockchain fulfilled requirements for e-voting schemes like transparency, consistency, and resiliency. In addition, it is undeniable the breakthrough that blockchain technology provides in terms of automating processes in an immutable and secure way.

Hyperledger's platform is a relatively new framework that has certain improvable aspects such as concurrency management on the same entity or the early stage of development of complementary frameworks to the blockchain network.

In order to deploy this system in a real-world environment, additional performance tests and audits need to be performed to ensure scalability and robustness in large-scale elections.

Conflicts of Interest: The authors declare no conflict of interest.

References

1. The Linux Foundation, Hyperledger Fabric. Available online: https://www.hyperledger.org/use/fabric (accessed on 3 August 2021).
2. Membership Service Provider. Available online: https://hyperledger-fabric.readthedocs.io/en/release-2.2/msp.html (accessed on 3 August 2021).

Proceeding Paper

Embedding ROS and AI-Based Perception Capabilities in a Novel Low-Cost Assistive Robotic Platform †

Jaime Mas-Santillán *, Francisco Javier Acevedo-Rodríguez and Roberto Javier López-Sastre

GRAM, Department of Signal Theory and Communications, University of Alcalá, 28805 Alcalá de Henares, Spain; javier.acevedo@uah.es (F.J.A.-R.); robertoj.lopez@uah.es (R.J.L.-S.)
* Correspondence: jaime.mas@edu.uah.es
† Presented at the 4th XoveTIC Conference, A Coruña, Spain, 7–8 October 2021.

Abstract: This paper describes how we developed a novel low-cost assistive robotic platform, with AI-based perception capabilities, able to navigate autonomously using Robot Operating System (ROS). The platform is a differential wheeled robot, equipped with two motors and encoders, which are controlled with an Arduino board. It also includes a Jetson Xavier processing board on which we deploy all AI processes, and the ROS architecture. As a result of the work, we have a fully functional platform, able to recognize actions online, and navigate autonomously through environments whose map has been preloaded.

Keywords: assistive robotics; artificial intelligence; ROS; RVIZ; Arduino; computer vision; navigation; online action detection

1. Introduction

Research in assistive robotics is experiencing a tremendous boom. More and more robotic platforms are emerging to assist people with functional diversity or the elderly (e.g., [1–3]). This is all due to major advances in robotics and artificial intelligence in recent years. However, despite all the advances, most of these commercial platforms are quite expensive.

In this work, we focus on the development of a low-cost assistive robotic platform, with advanced navigation and AI-based perception capabilities. For us, there is no doubt that cost-effectiveness must be considered in the context of assistive technology, because the final deployment of robots to end-users usually results in an expense paid by families or health services. Therefore, the main contribution of this work is the construction of a novel low-cost assistive robot. We have been able to develop a fully functional robotic platform, capable of navigating autonomously and recognizing the actions of its users, where all the functionalities are integrated into a Robot Operating System (ROS) architecture.

2. Low-Cost Robotic Platform

2.1. Hardware Description

The platform is a differential wheeled robot, equipped with two motors and their corresponding encoders, which are controlled with an Arduino board. The internal structure is constructed of wood and metal. The outer shell, imitating a person wearing a tuxedo, was made entirely by 3D printing. The complete platform measures approximately 800 mm, slightly higher than a table. As for the sensors, the platform has: one LIDAR, a touch screen, and a frontal camera. The LIDAR takes the measurements of the obstacles used for navigation and localization purposes. Finally, we have a Jetson Xavier board with ROS integration. Figure 1a shows a picture of the robot.

(a)

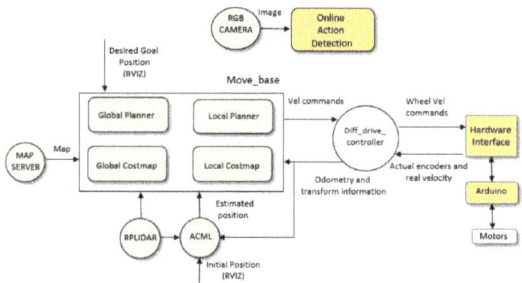

(b)

Figure 1. (**a**) Picture of our novel low-cost robotic platform and (**b**) ROS Architecture implemented.

2.2. ROS Based Software Architecture

The system architecture is based on ROS Melodic. Figure 1b shows a diagram with the complete ROS architecture we have implemented, mainly using Python. Green nodes represent distributed software ROS packages, and orange nodes are those ROS nodes, entirely developed by us, to integrate ROS into our platform.

The core of the navigation system is based on the ROS Navigation Stack, that is fed with: a map provided by the map server, the odometry source from the wheels, the LIDAR information, and the estimated position, provided in our case by the Adaptive Monte Carlo Localization (AMCL) package. The interface with the user is done by means of RVIZ. This ROS package provides a visual environment where the map and the estimated robot position are shown. The user can indicate an initial position to help the robot to localize itself and can order the robot to move to a desired position, specifying yaw rotation. RVIZ will send ROS messages to the move_base core package which generates the linear and angular velocity commands needed to move the robot to the desired position. All these commands, and their parameters, are continuously updated with the information of new possible obstacles, the odometry, and the estimated localization.

In order to fully embed ROS in our robotic platform, we have developed the Hardware Interface package that: (1) translates ROS commands to the Arduino board; and (2) sends, back to the ROS system, the messages with the specific format needed to complete the communication loop with the Arduino. The Arduino package in Figure 1b includes the developed libraries to establish the communication between the engines of the platform and ROS, using a serial port. In particular, we have designed a communication protocol with commands that allow us to read the data from the encoders, and to generate a sequence of speed commands to be transmitted to each wheel.

As for the AI perception capabilities, the architecture integrates a specific node for the Online Action Detection (OAD), see Figure 1b. In this node we have deployed a 3D convolutional neural network model [4], which is able to recognize the actions performed by the user of the platform. All this processing is integrated in the ROS architecture, which means that the OAD system can run on an external node. In tests in the laboratory, we have tried to run the OAD node on a workstation, so that the Jetson board is relieved of all the intensive processing required by this AI functionality.

3. Experiments

We have tested the platform in the building of the Polytechnic School of the University of Alcalá. For doing so, we have created a set of maps of different floors of this building, which can be used with the RVIZ application.

In the experiments, we have started the robot from different departure positions, with different target locations, and various orientations. We have also tested how the platform interacts with dynamic obstacles during the navigation. Based on the results, we have observed that in most of the cases the platform manages to reach its objective, and with the correct orientation. Moreover, in all cases the platform never collided with objects or people. For a 10-m run, our robot can take about a minute and a half, but it depends on how many obstacles it has encountered during the trajectory. Sometimes, we have observed that when driving in very open spaces, when the LiDAR does not detect obstacles or walls, the platform needs to stop to recalculate its position, turning on itself. Figure 2a shows RVIZ interface when our robot is navigating. We have recorded a video of the platform navigating: https://youtu.be/qjXZxAmTKXk, accessed on 29 September 2021.

Figure 2. (**a**) Our robotic platform navigating using RVIZ and (**b**) Qualitative results of the OAD system.

For the OAD, we have embedded in our platform, a model trained using the UCF-101 dataset [5], which exhibits an average clip accuracy of 72.4% for *all* the 101 action categories in the test set of *Split 1* of UCF-101. Figure 2b shows OAD qualitative results.

4. Conclusions

We have developed a low-cost assistive robotic platform that is able to navigate autonomously, detecting dynamic obstacles and following an optimal trajectory. Our robot is also able to recognize actions online, processing the images acquired by an RGB camera. All these processes are fully integrated into an ROS architecture. Future work will be to develop some applications that will allow the platform to interact and help people with functional diversity.

Author Contributions: Conceptualization, all; methodology, R.J.L.-S., F.J.A.-R.; software, J.M.-S., F.J.A.-R.; validation, all; investigation, all; writing—original draft preparation, all; writing—review and editing, all; supervision, R.J.L.-S.; project administration, R.J.L.-S.; funding acquisition, R.J.L.-S. All authors have read and agreed to the published version of the manuscript.

Funding: This research was funded by: (a) project AIRPLANE, with reference PID2019-104323RB-C31, of Spain's Ministry of Science and Innovation; and (b) project CM/JIN/2019-022 of the University of Alcalá.

Institutional Review Board Statement: Not applicable.

Informed Consent Statement: Not applicable.

Data Availability Statement: This research uses the publicly available UCF-101 dataset [5].

Conflicts of Interest: The authors declare no conflict of interest. The funders had no role in the design of the study; in the collection, analyses, or interpretation of data; in the writing of the manuscript, or in the decision to publish the results.

References

1. Lamas, C.M.; Bellas, F.; Guijarro-Berdiñas, B. SARDAM: Service Assistant Robot for Daily Activity Monitoring. *Proceedings* **2020**, *54*, 3. [CrossRef]
2. Martinez-Martin, E.; Costa, A.; Cazorla, M. PHAROS 2.0—A PHysical Assistant RObot System Improved. *Sensors* **2019**, *19*, 4531. [CrossRef] [PubMed]
3. Zlatintsi, A.; Dometios, A.; Kardaris, N.; Rodomagoulakis, I.; Koutras, P.; Papageorgiou, X.; Maragos, P.; Tzafestas, C.; Vartholomeos, P.; Hauer, K.; et al. I-Support: A robotic platform of an assistive bathing robot for the elderly population. *Robot. Auton. Syst.* **2020**, *126*, 103451. [CrossRef]
4. Baptista-Ríos, M.; López-Sastre, R.J.; Caba Heilbron, F.; Van Gemert, J.C.; Acevedo-Rodríguez, F.J.; Maldonado-Bascón, S. Rethinking Online Action Detection in Untrimmed Videos: A Novel Online Evaluation Protocol. *IEEE Access* **2019**, *8*, 5139–5146. [CrossRef]
5. Soomro, K.; Zamir, A.R.; Shah, M. UCF101: A Dataset of 101 Human Actions Classes From Videos in The Wild. *arXiv* **2012**, arXiv:cs.CV/1212.0402.

Proceeding Paper

RGen: Data Generator for Benchmarking Big Data Workloads [†]

Rubén Pérez-Jove [1,*], Roberto R. Expósito [2] and Juan Touriño [2]

1 Grupo RNASA-IMEDIR, CITIC, Universidade da Coruña, 15071 A Coruña, Spain
2 Computer Architecture Group, CITIC, Universidade da Coruña, 15071 A Coruña, Spain; rreye@udc.es (R.R.E.); juan@udc.es (J.T.)
* Correspondence: ruben.perez.jove@udc.es
† Presented at the 4th XoveTIC Conference, A Coruña, Spain, 7–8 October 2021.

Abstract: This paper presents RGen, a parallel data generator for benchmarking Big Data workloads, which integrates existing features and new functionalities in a standalone tool. The main functionalities developed in this work were the generation of text and graphs that meet the characteristics defined by the 4 Vs of Big Data. On the one hand, the LDA model has been used for text generation, which extracts topics or themes covered in a series of documents. On the other hand, graph generation is based on the Kronecker model. The experimental evaluation carried out on a 16-node cluster has shown that RGen provides very good weak and strong scalability results. RGen is publicly available to download at https://github.com/rubenperez98/RGen, accessed on 30 September 2021.

Keywords: Data generator; MapReduce; HDFS; Apache Hadoop; Java; Big Data; Benchmarking

1. Introduction

One of the main problems that arise in those fields where huge amounts of data are managed is the necessity of having datasets that settle all the requirements in terms of volume, type and truthfulness. Overall, this kind of data can be extracted from preprocessed sources or generated synthetically. Specifically, the benchmark suites used to characterize the performance of Big Data frameworks and workloads generally rely on third-party tools for generating each type of input data that is needed, as there is no other option providing all of them. In this context, RGen has been developed as a parallel data generator for benchmarking Big Data workloads. RGen brings together a twofold task of integrating existing features and developing new functionalities in a standalone generator tool. The initial requirements for developing such tool are those specified by the data generation necessities of the Big Data Evaluator (BDEv) benchmark suite [1], which provides support for multiple representative Big Data workloads.

The main objective is the development of a parallel and scalable tool that gathers the necessary functionalities for BDEv without having to depend on third-party software to generate data for a great variety of workloads. Additionally, the performance evaluation and scalability of the data generator has been carried out both in a local environment and in a high-performance cluster. Different configurations have been evaluated considering both the number of nodes used and the amount of data to be generated in parallel.

2. Design and Implementation

RGen was developed under the MapReduce programming paradigm [2], more specifically on top of the Apache Hadoop framework [3], supporting the generation of data directly on the Hadoop Distributed File System (HDFS) [4].

The first step was the study of the state of the art regarding data generation topic. This research concluded with the choice of DataGen, the data generator tool integrated in the HiBench suite [5], as the base platform for our tool. The next step consisted in integrating some existing generation features not provided by DataGen from native classes of the Hadoop and Mahout frameworks.

The following phases were the development of two new generation methods, being the first one the text generation. To create new text that can preserve the characteristics of existing realistic data, the Latent Dirichlet Allocation (LDA) model [6] was selected, as it is one of the most widespread topic models. The implementation in RGen is able to generate text taking an LDA model as an input parameter, keeping the original characteristics of a pre-analyzed set of documents. Similarly to the previous method, the graph generation was tackled by using the Kronecker model [7], which allows keeping the most important characteristics of a set of nodes and vertexes and generating from such information new graphs that preserve its original constitution.

3. Experimental Evaluation

To analyze the scalability of the tool when generating data in a parallel way, multiple experiments were carried out, focused on evaluating the new features implemented in RGen: the text and graph generation based on the LDA and Kronecker models, respectively. Along with them, the experiments were also executed for random text generation and using PageRank for graph generation as baseline for comparison purposes.

Scalability is the capability of a parallel code to keep its performance when the computational resources and/or the problem size are increased. There are two ways of measuring this metric: (1) weak scalability, where the number of CPU cores is increased while keeping constant the workload per core (i.e., both the number of cores and the problem size are increased); and strong scalability, where the resources are increased while the total workload remains the same (i.e., the workload per core is reduced). Weak scalability tests the capability of addressing larger problems in the same time by increasing the resources in a proportional way. On the other hand, strong scalability focuses on minimizing the runtime needed for solving the same problem by adding more resources.

Table 1 shows the configuration of the experiments conducted to analyze weak and strong scalability. The experiments were executed on the Pluton cluster of the Computer Architecture Group, where each node provides 16 physical CPU cores, 64 GB of memory and 1 TB local disk intended for HDFS storage. Additionally, all the nodes are interconnected via InfiniBand FDR (56 Gbps). As can be seen in Table 1, the experiments were conducted varying the number of nodes from two up to 16.

Table 1. Configuration of the experiments carried out on a high-performance cluster.

#Nodes	Text Data Volume		Graph Data Volume	
	Weak Scalability	Strong Scalability	Weak Scalability	Strong Scalability
2	40 GB	320 GB	67 M nodes	536 M nodes
4	80 GB	320 GB	134 M nodes	536 M nodes
8	160 GB	320 GB	268 M nodes	536 M nodes
16	320 GB	320 GB	536 M nodes	536 M nodes

4. Results and Conclusions

Figures 1 and 2 show the results for text and graph generation, respectively. Each plot presents both weak and strong scalability for the new generation methods (single lines) and for those used as baseline (marked lines). The runtimes for weak scalability are shown in green lines against the left axis, while the red lines present the runtimes for strong scalability against the right axis. The first conclusion that can be drawn is that the new generation methods take more time to execute for the same experiment than those used as baseline. This is an expected behavior as the computational complexity of these methods for generating data based on the LDA and Kronecker models is significantly higher than generating text randomly or using PageRank for graph generation.

When analyzing these results further, it can be concluded that RGen provides good scalability overall. In the case of text generation (see Figure 1), almost constant runtimes are obtained for weak scalability, which means that RGen provides similar runtimes when the number of resources and the workload are increased proportionally. Regarding strong scalability, it can be seen a significant reduction in runtime when generating text using the LDA model. This means that the same amount of text (320 GB) is generated much faster when increasing the computational resources. The results show almost linear strong scalability for LDA-based text generation, powered by combining MapReduce with HDFS (only *Map* tasks are executed in this case).

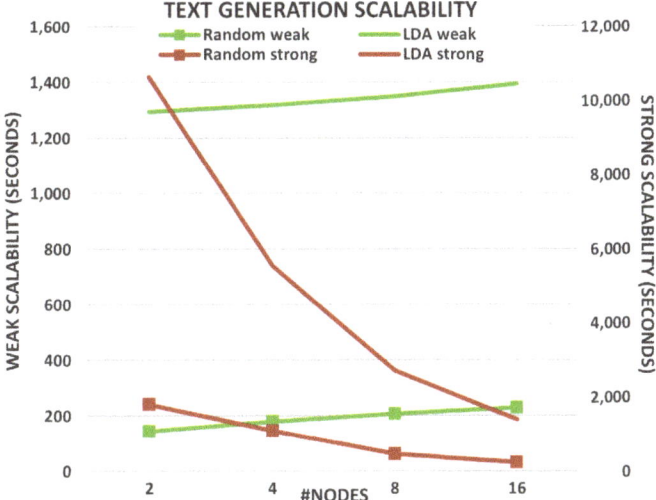

Figure 1. Scalability results for text.

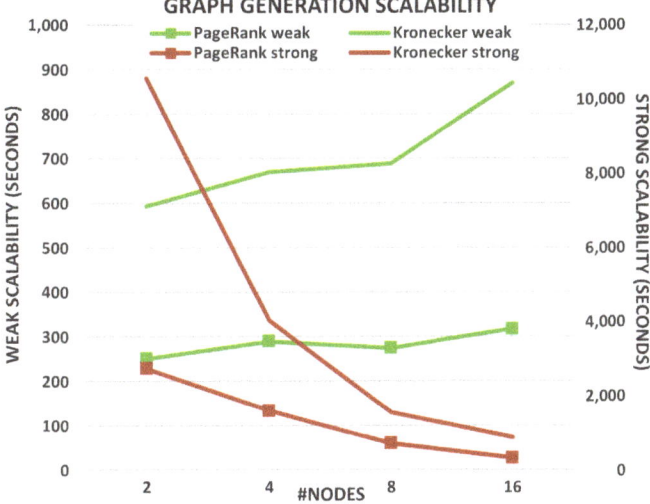

Figure 2. Scalability results for graphs.

The results for graph generation show a similar trend (see Figure 2). On the one hand, weak scalability presents a more irregular pattern for both data generation methods when compared to text generation. However, these results can be explained taking into account that the Kronecker method executes two MapReduce jobs instead of only one, and they also require to execute *Reduce* tasks. Both facts can hinder scalability as the cluster network performance now plays a key role, especially when using 16 nodes. On the other hand, the strong scalability provided by the Kronecker model is even more noticeable than in the PageRank implementation.

Author Contributions: Conceptualization, R.P.-J., R.R.E. and J.T.; methodology, R.P.-J., R.R.E. and J.T.; implementation, R.P.-J.; validation, R.P.-J.; writing—original draft preparation, R.P.-J.; writing—review and editing, R.R.E. and J.T. All authors have read and agreed to the published version of the manuscript.

Funding: CITIC, as Research Center accredited by Galician University System, is funded by "Consellería de Cultura, Educación e Universidade from Xunta de Galicia", supported in an 80% through ERDF, ERDF Operational Programme Galicia 2014–2020, and the remaining 20% by "Secretaría Xeral de Universidades (Grant ED431G 2019/01). This project was also supported by the "Consellería de Cultura, Educación e Ordenación Universitaria" via the Consolidation and Structuring of Competitive Research Units—Competitive Reference Groups (ED431C 2018/49 and 2021/30).

Conflicts of Interest: The authors declare no conflict of interest.

References

1. Veiga, J.; Enes, J.; Expósito, R.R.; Touriño, J. BDEv 3.0: Energy Efficiency and Microarchitectural Characterization of Big Data Processing Frameworks. *Future Gener. Comput. Syst.* **2018**, *86*, 565–581. [CrossRef]
2. Dean, J.; Ghemawat, S. MapReduce: Simplified Data Processing on Large Clusters. *Commun. ACM* **2008**, *51*, 107–113. [CrossRef]
3. The Apache Software Foundation. Apache Hadoop. Available online: https://hadoop.apache.org (accessed on 30 July 2021).
4. Shvachko, K.; Kuang, H.; Radia, S.; Chansler, R. The Hadoop Distributed File System. In Proceedings of the IEEE 26th Symposium on Mass Storage Systems and Technologies (MSST'2010), Incline Village, NV, USA, 3–7 May 2010; pp. 1–10.
5. Huang, S.; Huang, J.; Dai, J.; Xie, T.; Huang, B. The HiBench Benchmark Suite: Characterization of the MapReduce-based Data Analysis. In Proceedings of the IEEE 26th International Conference on Data Engineering Workshops (ICDEW'2010), Long Beach, CA, USA, 1–6 March 2010; pp. 41–51.
6. Blei, D.M.; Ng, A.Y.; Jordan, M.I. Latent Dirichlet Allocation. *J. Mach. Learn. Res.* **2003**, *3*, 993–1022.
7. Leskovec, J.; Chakrabarti, D.; Kleinberg, J.; Faloutsos, C.; Ghahramani, Z. Kronecker Graphs: An Approach to Modeling Networks. *J. Mach. Learn. Res.* **2010**, *11*, 985–1042.

Proceeding Paper

Survey on Preprocessing Techniques for Big Data Projects †

Ignacio D. Lopez-Miguel

Centro de Postgrado, Universidad Internacional Menéndez Pelayo, C/ Isaac peral, 23, 28040 Madrid, Spain; lopezmiguelignacio@posgrado.uimp.es
† Presented at the 4th XoveTIC Conference, A Coruña, Spain, 7–8 October 2021.

Abstract: In the era of big data, a vast amount of data are being produced. This results in two main issues when trying to discover knowledge from these data. There is a lot of information that is not relevant to the problem we want to solve, and there are many imperfections and errors in the data. Therefore, preprocessing these data is a key step before applying any kind of learning algorithm. Reducing the number of features to a relevant subset (feature selection) and reducing the possible values of continuous variables (discretisation) are two of the main preprocessing techniques. This paper will review different methods for completing these two steps, focusing on the big data context and giving examples of projects where they have been applied.

Keywords: preprocessing; big data; feature selection; discretisation

1. Introduction

With the irruption of the "big data" phenomenon, massive amounts of data are generated daily. These data are normally available in a raw format and need to be treated before acquiring any knowledge from them. This step in the big data chain is usually referred to as preprocessing and there exists a wide range of techniques [1].

The main approaches to preprocess big data are discretisation and feature selection. The former transforms continuous data to a limited set of values. Feature selection aims to reduce the number of attributes [1,2].

The remainder of this paper is organised as follows: Section 2 introduces the different preprocessing techniques, dividing them into feature selection and discretisation. For each of these techniques, a classification with different examples for each category is presented. Section 3 concludes the paper and suggests a future line of research.

2. Data Preprocessing

Different feature selection and discretisation techniques are presented in this section based on big data projects where they have been applied.

2.1. Feature Selection

The different feature selection techniques for big data mining can be classified into filter methods, wrapper methods, and embedded methods [1].

2.1.1. Filter Methods

Features are selected according to the value of different metrics, usually certain statistical criteria.

In the context of text mining, it is common to use the bag-of-words approach so that each word is taken as a unique feature. Chi-squared was used to filter the most relevant terms in a text mining algorithm to estimate credit score at Deutsche Bank [3].

In relation to text mining as well, in [4] tweets are analysed in order to figure out the impact of their sentiment on stock market movements. The authors also use a filter method to select the most relevant features—Fisher score.

Citation: Lopez-Miguel, I.D. Survey on Preprocessing Techniques for Big Data Projects. *Eng. Proc.* **2021**, *7*, 14. https://doi.org/10.3390/engproc2021007014

Academic Editors: Joaquim de Moura, Marco A. González, Javier Pereira and Manuel G. Penedo

Published: 7 October 2021

Publisher's Note: MDPI stays neutral with regard to jurisdictional claims in published maps and institutional affiliations.

Copyright: © 2021 by the author. Licensee MDPI, Basel, Switzerland. This article is an open access article distributed under the terms and conditions of the Creative Commons Attribution (CC BY) license (https://creativecommons.org/licenses/by/4.0/).

Based on Chi-squared and the GUIDE regression tree, Loh [5,6] presents a technique to perform feature selection in a large genomic dataset.

Other filter methods include Information Gain [7], correlation [8], variance similarity [9], and Dispersion ratio [10].

Some work has been done to adapt these methods to the big data context, such as in [11], where a framework to parallelise and scale some of these algorithms is introduced.

2.1.2. Embedded Methods

Feature selection is performed in the process of fitting a model to a given dataset.

SVM-RFE (Supported Vector Machine Recursive Feature Elimination), introduced in [12] to analyse DNA microarrays has shown its power in several applications, such as in bioinformatics [13].

The Feature Selection-Perceptron (FS-P) [14] technique has been used in a proton (^{1}H) magnetic resonance spectroscopy (MRS) database to select features that could better predict brain tumours.

Based on a more complex neural network, the embedded method BlogReg is introduced in [15], where it is applied to data collected from the sensors of a robot.

2.1.3. Wrapper Methods

Wrapper methods refer to an iterative process in which a subset of features is evaluated at a time.

A wrapper method based on the decision tree C4.5 has been used for many years [16]. However, developments based on this method are still ongoing, such as the one from [17], which is applied to healthcare data (Medical Internet of Things).

Another wrapper method is based on the SVM algorithm [18]. It has been widely used since its creation, such as in [19], predicting arrhythmias from cardiac data.

FSSEM (Feature Subset Selection wrapped around EM clustering) [20] is also a wrapped method, and a popular stepwise approach for regression problems [21].

2.2. Discretisation

Discretisation is the step where continuous variables are transformed into categorical ones [2]. There exist multiple classifications for discretization techniques, but here one of unsupervised and supervised discretisation is chosen [2].

2.2.1. Unsupervised

Unsupervised discretisation methods do not take into account the target of the learning algorithm when the features are discretised.

Equal width interval discretisation and equal frequency interval discretisation need to be adapted in the context of big data streaming as done in [22].

In [23], k-means [24] discretisation is used to transform the target for road detection.

Other methods based on k-means algorithm have been proposed, such as Cokmeans and Bikmeans, used in [25] in the context of microarrays.

2.2.2. Supervised

Supervised discretisation does take into account the target of the learning algorithm. One of the most popular methods is based on entropy [26]. This algorithm was parallelised in [27].

Chi-squared is the basis for ChiMerge [28], ChiSplit [29], and Khiops [30]. They were parallelised in [31] to work for big data problems.

The previously presented approaches are univariate, but there also exist supervised multivariate discretisation (SMD) techniques, such as the one in [32].

3. Conclusions

Due to extension limitations, this paper has only given some feature selection and discretisation techniques, mentioning some up-to-date examples of where they are used. There is growing interest in adapting these techniques so that they can perform efficiently in the big data context. In this direction, a future line of work is to create a comprehensive and complete taxonomy of the up-to-date feature selection and discretisation techniques, performing experimental results in the big data context.

Funding: This research received no external funding.

References

1. Bolón-Canedo, V.; Sánchez-Maroño, N.; Alonso-Betanzos, A. Recent advances and emerging challenges of feature selection in the context of big data. *Knowl.-Based Syst.* **2015**, *86*, 33–45. [CrossRef]
2. Dash, R.; Paramguru, R.; Dash, R. Comparative analysis of supervised and unsupervised discretization techniques. *Int. J. Adv. Sci. Technol.* **2011**, *2*, 29–37.
3. Hristova, D.; Probst, J.; Eckrich, E. Ratingbot: A text mining based rating approach. *ICIS* **2017**, *8*, 1–20.
4. Abbes, H. Tweets Sentiment and Their Impact on Stock Market Movements. Master's Thesis, École de gestion de l'Université de Liège, Liège, Belgium, 2016.
5. Loh, W.Y. Regression trees with unbiased variable selection and interaction detection. *Stat. Sin.* **2002**, *12*, 361–386.
6. Loh, W.Y. Variable Selection for Classification and Regression in Large p, Small n Problems. In *Probability Approximations and Beyond*; Springer: New York, NY, USA, 2012; Volume 205, pp. 135–159.
7. Azhagusundari, B.; Thanamani, A.S. Feature selection based on information gain. *Int. J. Innov. Technol. Explor. Eng. (IJITEE)* **2013**, *2*, 18–21.
8. Hall, M. Correlation-Based Feature Selection for Machine Learning. Ph.D. Dissertation, University of Waikato Hamilton, Hamilton, New Zealand, 1999.
9. Nassuna, H.; Eyobu, O.S.; Kim, J.H.; Lee, D. Feature selection based on variance distribution of power spectral density for driving behavior recognition. In Proceedings of the 2019 14th IEEE Conference on Industrial Electronics and Applications (ICIEA), Xi'an, China, 19–21 June 2019; pp. 335–338.
10. Fong, S.; Biuk-Aghai, R.P.; Si, Y.W. Lightweight feature selection methods based on standardized measure of dispersion for mining big data. In Proceedings of the 2016 IEEE International Conference on Computer and Information Technology, Nadi, Fiji, 8–10 December 2016; pp. 553–559.
11. Morán-Fernández, L.; Bolón-Canedo, V.; Alonso-Betanzos, A. Centralized vs. distributed feature selection methods based on data complexity measures. *Knowl.-Based Syst.* **2017**, *117*, 27–45. [CrossRef]
12. Guyon, I.; Weston, J.; Barnhill, S.; Vapnik, V. Gene selection for cancer classification using support vector machines. *Mach. Learn.* **2002**, *46*, 389–422. [CrossRef]
13. Lin, X.; Li, C.; Zhang, Y.; Su, B.; Fan, M.; Wei, H. Selecting feature subsets based on svm-rfe and the overlapping ratio with applications in bioinformatics. *Molecules* **2018**, *23*, 52. [CrossRef]
14. Mejia-Lavalle, M.; Sucar, L.; Arroyo-Figueroa, G. Feature selection with a perceptron neural net. In Proceedings of the International Workshop on Feature Selection for Data Mining, Hong Kong, China, 18–22 December 2006; pp. 131–135.
15. Kaya, E.; Morani, K. The Improvement Achieved Using Blogreg Feature Selection Algorithm in a Developed Artificial Neural Network Classification. *Int. J. Sci. Res. Eng. Technol. (IJSET)* **2019**, *13*, 28–31.
16. Langley, P. Selection of relevant features in machine learning. *Proc. AAAI Fall Symp. Relev.* **1994**, *97*, 245–271.
17. Lee, S.J.; Xu, Z.; Li, T.; Yang, Y. A novel bagging c4.5 algorithm based on wrapper feature selection for supporting wise clinical decision making. *J. Biomed. Informat.* **2018**, *78*, 144–155. [CrossRef] [PubMed]
18. Maldonado, S.; Weber, R. A wrapper method for feature selection using support vector machines. *Inf. Sci.* **2009**, *179*, 2208–2217. [CrossRef]
19. Mustaqeem, A.; Anwar, S.; Majid, M.; Khan, R. Wrapper method for feature selection to classify cardiac arrhythmia. In Proceedings of the 2017 39th Annual International Conference of the IEEE Engineering in Medicine and Biology Society (EMBC), Jeju, Korea, 11–15 July 2017; Volume 2017, pp. 3656–3659.
20. Dy, J.G.; Brodley, C.E. Feature subset selection and order identification for unsupervised learning. In Proceedings of the Seventeenth International Conference on Machine Learning, San Francisco, CA, USA, 2 October 2000; pp. 247–254.
21. Pace, N.; Briggs, W. Stepwise logistic regression. *Anesthesia Analgesia* **2009**, *109*, 285–286. [CrossRef]
22. Sisovic, S.; Brkic Bakaric, M.; Matetic, M. Reducing data stream complexity by applying count-min algorithm and discretization procedure. In Proceedings of the 2018 IEEE Fourth International Conference on Big Data Computing Service and Applications (BigDataService), Bamberg, Germany, 26–29 March 2018; pp. 221–228.
23. Xiao, L.; Dai, B.; Liu, D.; Zhao, D.; Wu, T. Monocular road detection using structured random forest. *Int. J. Adv. Robot. Syst.* **2016**, *13*, 101. [CrossRef]

24. MacQueen, J. Some methods for classification and analysis of multivariate observations. In *Proceedings of the Fifth Berkeley Symposium on Mathematical Statistics and Probability*; University of California Press: Berkeley, CA, USA, 1967; pp. 281–297.
25. Li, Y.; Liu, L.; Bai, X.; Cai, H.; Ji, W.; Guo, D.; Zhu, Y. Comparative study of discretization methods of microarray data for inferring transcriptional regulatory networks. *BMC Bioinform.* **2010**, *11*, 520. [CrossRef] [PubMed]
26. Fayyad, U.; Irani, K. Multi-interval discretization of continuous-valued attributes for classification learning. *IJCAI* **1993**, *13*, 1022–1027.
27. Ramírez-Gallego, S.; García, S.; Mourino-Talin, H.; Martinez, D. Distributed entropy minimization discretizer for big data analysis under apache spark. In Proceedings of the 2015 IEEE Trustcom/BigDataSE/ISPA, Helsinki, Finland, 20–22 August 2015; pp. 33–40.
28. Kerber, R. Chimerge: Discretization of numeric attributes. In Proceedings of the Tenth National Conference on Artificial Intelligence, AAAI'92, San Jose, CA, USA, 12–16 July 1992; pp. 123–128.
29. Bertier, P.; Bouroche, J.M. *Analyse des données Multidimensionnelles*; PUF: Paris, France, 1975.
30. Boulle, M. Khiops: A statistical discretization method of continuous attributes. *Mach. Learn.* **2004**, *55*, 53–69. [CrossRef]
31. Zhang, Y.; Yu, J.; Wang, J. *Parallel Implementation of chi2 Algorithm in Mapreduce Framework*; Springer: Cham, Switzerland, 2014; pp. 890–899.
32. Jiang, F.; Zhao, Z.; Ge, Y. A supervised and multivariate discretization algorithm for rough sets. In *Rough Set and Knowledge Technology*; Yu, J., Greco, S., Lingras, P., Wang, G., Skowron, A., Eds.; Springer: Berlin/Heidelberg, Germany, 2010; pp. 596–603.

Proceeding Paper

The Influence of Brain Activity on the Interactive Process through Biofeedback Mechanisms in Virtual Reality Environments †

Rita Costa [1,‡], Paulo Veloso Gomes [2,*,‡], António Correia [2,‡], António Marques [2,‡] and Javier Pereira [3,‡]

1. LabRP-CIR, Psychosocial Rehabilitation Laboratory, Center for Rehabilitation Research, School of Engineering, Polytechnic Institute of Porto, 4200-072 Porto, Portugal; 1171445@isep.ipp.pt
2. LabRP-CIR, Psychosocial Rehabilitation Laboratory, Center for Rehabilitation Research, School of Health, Polytechnic Institute of Porto, 4200-374 Porto, Portugal; amsc@ess.ipp.pt (A.C.); ajmarques@ess.ipp.pt (A.M.)
3. CITIC, Research Center of Information and Communication Technologies, Talionis Research Group, Universidade da Coruña, 15008 A Coruña, Spain; javier.pereira@udc.es

* Correspondence: pvg@ess.ipp.pt
† Presented at the 4th XoveTIC Conference, A Coruña, Spain, 7–8 October 2021.
‡ These authors contributed equally to this work.

Abstract: This work focuses on the development of a software link interface tool between the Looxid Link Device coupled to the HTC Vive Pro VR HeadSets and the Unity platform, to generate real-time interactivity in virtual reality applications. The software incorporates a dynamic and parameterizable algorithm to be used as a core-engine in the real-time Biofeedback process, recognizing the values of the biological signals registered in each of the EEG channels of the Looxid Link device. The values of EEG frequencies detected in real time can be used to generate elements of interactivity, with different frequencies and intensities.

Keywords: biofeedback; immersive environments; electroencephalography; virtual reality

1. Introduction

Exposure to immersive environments creates different sensations with different intensities in participants. The participant's responses to the stimuli sent by the virtual environment reflect the effect it causes. During exposure, the participant's brain activity is stimulated and changes in this activity can be measured by electroencephalography. The analysis of the results of the registered signals reflects the effect provoked on the participant [1,2].

Since the changes in brain activity are a participant's response, usually involuntary, to the stimuli sent by the system, the interest in using them as an element of interaction becomes relevant. If the system can detect and interpret these values, it can use them to become more interactive, adapting its behavior to the participant's reactions. Stimuli trigger emotions and emotions generate reactions. The inclusion of interactivity during the experience by real-time Biofeedback mechanisms increases the feeling of presence in the virtual environment [3].

The real-time data obtained on the user's physiological aspects allows for determining how the stimuli affect him. On the other hand, when the user receives information in real time about a certain aspect of his physiology, he can determine how his mental changes can influence his state [4].

The introduction of biofeedback systems in the design of a simple immersive environment transform it into an Emotionally Adaptive Immersive Environment, where the user experience can be optimized through the continuously adaptation of stimuli to the user emotional state. The quantity and intensity of the stimuli are determined through an adaptive affective algorithm, which collect, interpret, and convert the user's physiological data [5].

The main objective of this project is to develop a software tool that incorporates a dynamic and parameterizable algorithm to be used as a core engine in the real-time Bio-feedback process, this software tool is the element responsible for making the connection between the Looxid Link device coupled to VR HeadSet and the unity platform that manages the immersive environment.

2. Materials and Methods

2.1. Materials

Table 1 describes the hardware and software used to develop the project. For a non-evasive electroencephalogram device (Looxid Link™ Mask for VIVE) coupled with VR Headsets HTC Vive Pro™, the software was developed using the C# programming language.

Table 1. Hardware and software used to develop and implement the project.

Equipment	Specifications
Computer	CPU: Intel® Core™ i7-9700K (3.60 GHz–4.90 GHz)
	Graphic card: NVIDIA® GeForce® RTX 2080 Ti
	Memory: 64 GB RAM
VR Headset HTC Vive Pro™	High resolution Dual AMOLED 3.5″ diagonal screens
	1440 × 1600 pixels per eye (2880 × 1600 pixels combined)
	Refresh rate: 90 Hz; Field of view: 110 degrees
	Integrated microphones with 3D Spatial Audio
	Four SteamVR Base Station 2.0: 10 m × 10 m
	VIVE Wireless Adapter
Looxid Link™ Mask for VIVE	EEG sensors; Looxid Link Hub
	6 channels: AF3, AF4, AF7, AF8, Fp1, Fp2
	1 reference: FPz at extended 10–10 system
	Dry electrodes on flexible PCB; Sampling rate: 500 Hz
	Resolution: 24 bits per channel (with 1 LSB = 0.27 µV)
	Filtering: digital notch filters at 50 Hz and 60 Hz, 1–50 Hz
	Digital bandpass; Real-time data access
	Raw EEG data: 500 Hz (with/without filter options)
	Feature indexes (alpha, beta, gamma, theta, delta): 10 Hz
	Mind indexes (attention, relaxation, balance): 10 Hz
Software	Unity Personal 2020.3 LTS
	C# programming language

2.2. Methods

Unity3D software was used as a development and interconnection platform between the Looxid Link device coupled to VR HeadSet and the VR application. Using the C# programming language, an algorithm was developed to create a real-time Bio-feedback core-engine generator.

The algorithm recognizes the values of the biological signals registered in each of the EEG channels of the Looxid Link device; these values reflect the participant's states of relaxation and attention, allowing the definition of value intervals, with the attribution to each one of interactive variables that can be used in the Biofeedback process.

The development of the algorithm included five aspects. Access the values of the EEG signals detected by the Looxid Link device through sensors AF3, AF4, AF7 AF8, Fp1, and Fp2, and Fpz. Group the values detected by each of the sensors into frequency ranges aggregating these values into two indicators, relaxation and attention. Assign an interaction variable to each frequency range. Assign the desired functions to each interaction variable.

Parameterize the period between readings of the values of the interaction variables allows for determining the desired degree of interactivity.

3. Results

The software incorporates a dynamic and parameterizable algorithm to be used as a core-engine in the real-time biofeedback process. The algorithm recognizes the values of the biological signals registered in each of the EEG channels of the Looxid Link device, identifying the participant's states of relaxation and attention and allowing the definition of value intervals, with an interaction variable attributed to each one that can be used in the Biofeedback process by VR applications.

4. Discussion and Conclusions

One of the applications of the developed core-engine can focus on the participant's states of relaxation and attention. The Looxid Link device determines these two states in real time during exposure, allowing them to be used as an interactive element. The algorithm uses these values and, according to predefined intervals, readjusts the intensity of the stimuli generated by the system or triggers new stimuli.

This feature has two important advantages. It increases the level of interactivity generated by the application, as this results from the real-time reading of the participant's brain activity that was generated by the emitted stimuli, with the new stimuli generated adapting to the participant's real reactions. The other advantage is the interoperability of the algorithm, which can be adapted to different virtual reality applications, simply by parameterizing the intervals according to the desired amount and sensitivity of the system. After this parameterization, it is possible to assign which stimuli are intended for each interaction variable.

Author Contributions: Conceptualization, R.C., P.V.G.; methodology, R.C., P.V.G.; validation, P.V.G.; investigation, R.C.; writing—original draft preparation, R.C.; writing—review and editing, R.C., P.V.G.; visualization, R.C., P.V.G.; supervision, A.M., J.P.; project administration, R.C. All authors have read and agreed to the published version of the manuscript.

Funding: This research received no external funding.

Institutional Review Board Statement: Not applicable.

Informed Consent Statement: Not applicable.

Acknowledgments: This research was carried out and used the equipment of the Psychosocial Rehabilitation Laboratory (LabRP) of the Research Center in Rehabilitation of the School of Allied Health Technologies, Polytechnic Institute of Porto.

References

1. Tori, R.; Kirner, C.; Siscoutto, R. *Fundamentos e Tecnologia de Realidade Virtual e Aumentada*; Editora SBC: Porto Alegre, Brazil, 2006. ISBN 85-7669-068-3.
2. Sá, C.; Gomes, P.V.; Marques, A.; Correia, A. The Use of Portable EEG Devices in Development of Immersive Virtual Reality Environments for Converting Emotional States into Specific Commands. *Proceedings* **2020**, *54*, 43. [CrossRef]
3. Kumar, A.; Killingsworth, M.A.; Gilovich, T. Waiting for Merlot: Anticipatory Consumption of Experiential and Material Purchases. *Psychol. Sci.* **2014**, *25*, 1924–1931. [CrossRef] [PubMed]
4. Barandas, M.; Gamboa, H.; Fonseca, J.M. A Real Time Biofeedback System Using Visual User Interface for Physical Rehabilitation. *Procedia Manuf.* **2015**, *3*, 823–828. [CrossRef]
5. Gomes, P.V.; Marques, A.; Donga, J.; Sá, C.; Correia, A.; Pereira, J. Adaptive model for biofeedback data flows management in the design of interactive immersive environments. *Appl. Sci.* **2021**, *11*, 5067. [CrossRef]

Detection of DoS Attacks in an IoT Environment with MQTT Protocol Based on Intelligent Binary Classifiers [†]

Álvaro Michelena [1,*,‡], Francisco Zayas-Gato [2,‡], Esteban Jove [1,2,‡] and José Luis Calvo-Rolle [1,2,‡]

1. Campus de Elviña, Universidade da Coruña, CITIC, 15071 A Coruña, Spain; esteban.jove@udc.es (E.J.); jlcalvo@udc.es (J.L.C.-R.)
2. Departamento de Ingeniería Industrial, Universidade da Coruña, CTC, 15405 Ferrol, Spain; f.zayas.gato@udc.es
* Correspondence: alvaro.michelena@udc.es
† Presented at the 4th XoveTIC Conference, A Coruña, Spain, 7–8 October 2021.
‡ These authors contributed equally to this work.

Abstract: The present work deals with the problem of detecting Denial of Service attacks in an IoT environment. To achieve this goal, a dataset registered in an MQTT protocol network is used, applying dimension reduction techniques combined with classification algorithms. The final classifiers presents successful results.

Keywords: MQTT; IoT; DoS; logistic regression; KNN; decision trees; deep neural networks

1. Introduction

Use of the IoT (Internet of Things) paradigm has increased during recent years; this technology has become an essential pillar for a wide variety of processes, in industrial, home, and telecommunications applications, among others. This new concept contributes to encourage connectivity between physical devices, such as controllers, sensors, and actuators, looking for a greater flexibility and process optimisation [1].

However, the significant increase in the flow of communications has resulted a rise in vulnerability, caused by different attacks that put at risk the system's integrity. According to the nature of each attack, different consequences are possible, such as appearance of malware that may harm the equipment, unauthorised access to network information, or DoS (Denial of Service) attacks [2].

In this context, the implementation of algorithms capable of detecting these attacks plays a significant role to ensure the integrity of an IoT environment. Accordingly, this work proposes the use of different intelligent techniques to face the task of detecting DoS attacks in an MQTT network. This document is structured as follows: After the present section, the description of the dataset is carried out in the case of study section. Then, the used techniques are detailed, followed by the experiments and results section. Finally, the conclusions are exposed in the last section.

2. Materials and Methods

2.1. Dataset Description

The MQTT (Message Queuing Telemetry Transport) protocol works at the application level of the TCP (Transmission Control Protocol). This environment is one of the most used in IoT systems [3]. It is based on a star architecture, which pivots on a central broker that manages the network messages. The message procedure follows a publication/subscription approach, where the messages are characterised as a string implementing a nested structure.

To generate the dataset, a server with an Aedes library acted as broker. An ESP 8266 device was in charge of establishing a connection with the several sensors and actuators.

However, the broker was vulnerable to DoS attacks through port MQTT 1883. An MQTT-malaria program was in charge of performing these operations.

The traffic registered during the experiments contained a total number of 94624 samples, with 65 variables containing network information and a label indicating whether the instance is "normal" or "attack". After an initial analysis of the original dataset, the repeated samples were removed, and the constant variables deleted. Furthermore, the categorical variables were transformed following a natural coding criteria. Finally, the data presented 39 variables, 49910 normal instances, and 9429 attacks.

2.2. Used Techniques

2.2.1. Principal Component Analysis

This dimension reduction technique aims to find the directions of higher variability in a dataset, known as principal components [4]. This is performed through the calculation of the eigenvalues of the correlation matrix. Then, using the eigenvectors, the initial set can be linearly transformed into lower dimension space.

2.2.2. Classification Techniques

Logistic Regression

The Logistic Regression (LR) classification technique makes use of a sigmoid function to calculate the class membership probability, whose values are fitted following a gradient descent criteria [5].

K Nearest Neighbours

This classification method uses the data density to label a new instance. To estimate the class membership, it evaluates the K Nearest Neighbours (KNN) and counts the number of samples of each class [5].

Decision Trees

A Decision Tree (DT) algorithm is implemented by repeatedly splitting the dataset using a criteria that maximises the sample separation. At each split, the entropy decrease should be maximised due to the own split [5].

Deep Neural Networks

The Deep Neural Networks (DNN) are based on an architecture made of multiple layers, whose neurons are connected with the neurons of adjacent layers. The weight of each connection, and the parameters of activation functions are tuned during the training process following a minimising error criteria [5].

3. Experiments and Results

3.1. Experimental Setup

Different experiments were carried out to obtain the best classifier. First, with the aim of minimising the computation times and improve the classifier performance, a dimension reduction was carried out using PCA. In this case, two types of reduction were considered: two components and five components. A 10-fold cross-validation was developed, measuring the accuracy, F1 score, precision, recall, specificity, and the Area Under the Receiving Operating Curve (AUC) [6]. This last measure is the one selected to determine the best classifier, because it is nonsensitive to class distribution.

3.2. Results

First, an initial analysis of the PCA result was conducted. From the results achieved in Figure 1, the number of components selected were two and five. With this configuration, the four classification techniques were tested, leading to the final results shown in Figure 2.

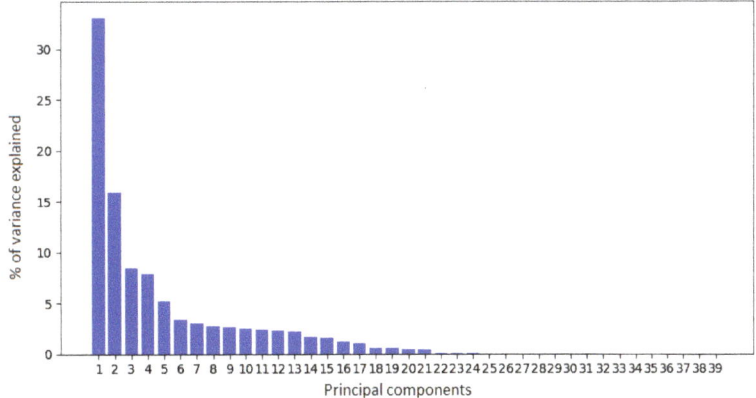

Figure 1. Result of PCA.

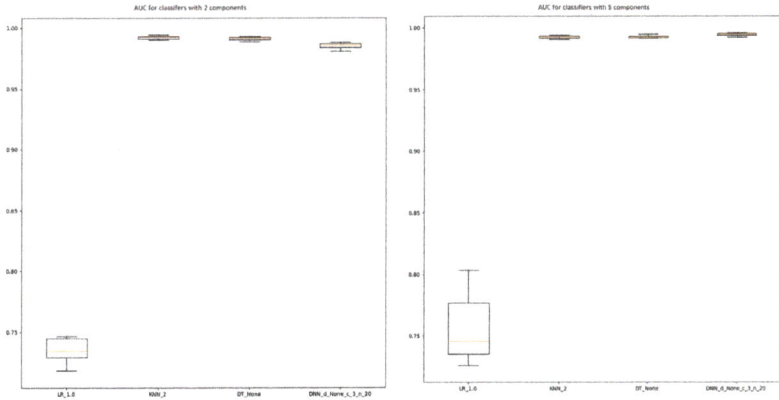

Figure 2. Boxplot representing AUC results for 2 and 5 components.

4. Conclusions

The present papers deals with the detection of DoS attack by means of intelligent classifiers. LR classifiers do not achieve as good a performance as the rest of the techniques. Furthermore, using two and five components does not affect significantly the classifiers performance. The implementation of this approach could entail significant benefits for IoT environments with MQTT protocols.

Acknowledgments: CITIC, as a Research Center of the University System of Galicia, is funded by Consellería de Educación, Universidade e Formación Profesional of the Xunta de Galicia through the European Regional Development Fund (ERDF) and the Secretaría Xeral de Universidades (Ref. ED431G 2019/01).

References

1. Lee, J.; Kao, A. Industry 4.0 Factory in Big Data Environment. tec. News. *HARTING's Technol. Newsl.* **2014**, *26*, 8–9.
2. Zhang, X.; Upton, O.; Beebe, N.L.; Choo, K.K.R. IoT Botnet Forensics: A Comprehensive Digital Forensic Case Study on Mirai Botnet Servers. *Forensic Sci. Int. Digit. Investig.* **2020**, *32*, 300926. [CrossRef]
3. Liu, J.; Kantarci, B.; Adams, C. Machine learning-driven intrusion detection for Contiki-NG-based IoT networks exposed to NSL-KDD dataset. In Proceedings of the 2nd ACM Workshop on Wireless Security and Machine Learning, Linz, Austria, 13 July 2020; pp. 25–30.
4. Martinez, A.M.; Kak, A.C. Pca versus lda. *IEEE Trans. Pattern Anal. Mach. Intell.* **2001**, *23*, 228–233. [CrossRef]

5. Dreiseitl, S.; Ohno-Machado, L. Logistic regression and artificial neural network classification models: A methodology review. *J. Biomed. Informat.* **2002**, *35*, 5–6. [CrossRef]
6. Jove, E.; Gonzalez-Cava, J.M.; Casteleiro-Roca, J.L.; Méndez-Pérez, J.A.; Reboso-Morales, J.A.; Pérez-Castelo, F.J.; de Cos Juez, F.J.; Calvo-Rolle, J.L. Modelling the hypnotic patient response in general anaesthesia using intelligent models. *Log. J. IGPL* **2019**, *27*, 189–201. [CrossRef]

Proceeding Paper

Nonparametric Inference for Mixture Cure Model When Cure Information Is Partially Available [†]

Wende Clarence Safari [1,2,*], Ignacio López-de-Ullibarri [2] and María Amalia Jácome [1,2]

[1] Centro de Investigación en Tecnologías de la Información y las Comunicaciones (CITIC), Universidade da Coruña, 15071 A Coruña, Spain
[2] MODES Group, Department of Mathematics, Universidade da Coruña, 15071 A Coruña, Spain; ilu@udc.es (I.L.-d.-U.); majacome@udc.es (M.A.J.)
* Correspondence: wende.safari@udc.es
[†] Presented at the 4th XoveTIC Conference, A Coruña, Spain, 7–8 October 2021.

Abstract: We introduce nonparametric estimators to estimate the conditional survival function, cure probability and latency function in the setting of a mixture cure model when the cure status is partially known. For the sake of illustration, we present an application concerning patients hospitalized with COVID-19 in Galicia (Spain) during the first outbreak of the epidemic.

Keywords: COVID-19; ICU; kernel estimators; mixture cure model; survival analysis

1. Introduction

Survival analysis arises in many applications where we want to reason about the amount of time until the considered event happens. A common assumption in standard survival modeling is that all individuals can experience the event if observed for a sufficient amount of time. Cure models [1] have been developed because there might be situations where the standard survival model is not true, for example, in the event of a recurrence in some diseases or death from some types of cancer. One challenge with time-to-event data is that the event is not always observed (censored observations). Standard cure models typically make inferences based on the assumption that the cure status information is an unobserved (latent) variable as the event is only known for the uncensored (uncured) subjects, but it is unknown for the censored observations whether it is cured or not. There are situations where cure status information is known for some of the censored individuals as they can be identified to be insusceptible to the considered event, that is, known to be cured. For example, when a medical test ascertains that a disease has entirely disappeared after treatment.

In this paper, we present kernel methods to estimate the conditional survival function, cure probability and latency function in the presence of cure status information. The proposed approach contributes to state-of-the-art in time-to-event data, as it extends previous works in the mixture cure model.

2. Estimation When the Cure Status Is Partially Available

Let Y be the time until the event of interest, X is a vector of covariates and $F(t \mid \mathbf{x}) = P(Y \leq t \mid \mathbf{X} = \mathbf{x})$ is the distribution function of Y conditional on $\mathbf{X} = \mathbf{x}$. In follow-up studies, the event of interest may not be observed due to, for example, the end of the study or loss to follow up, which occurs at censoring time C^* with conditional distribution function $G(t \mid \mathbf{x}) = P(C^* \leq t \mid \mathbf{X} = \mathbf{x})$. As a consequence, instead of observing Y, only the possibly censored survival time $T^* = \min(Y, C^*)$ and the indicator of the event $\delta = \mathbf{1}(Y < C^*)$ can be observed. The random variables Y and C^* are assumed to be conditionally independent given $\mathbf{X} = \mathbf{x}$, which is a widely used assumption in most studies. We set $Y = \infty$ if the subject will not experience the event and so is cured. Let $\nu = \mathbf{1}(Y = \infty)$

be the indicator of being cured. Note that ν is partially observed because the individual is known not to be cured ($\nu = 0$) when the event is observed ($\delta = 1$), but in the general situation, ν is unknown when $\delta = 0$. When the cure status is partially known, some censored individuals are identified to be cured, so $\nu = 1$ is observed.

To accommodate the cure status information, we include an additional random variable ξ, which indicates whether the cure status ν is known ($\xi = 1$) or not ($\xi = 0$). Furthermore, let the censoring distribution be an improper distribution function $G(t \mid \mathbf{x}) = (1 - \pi(\mathbf{x}))G_0(t \mid \mathbf{x})$. Thus, with probability $\pi(\mathbf{x})$, the censoring variable is $C^* = \infty$, and with probability $1 - \pi(\mathbf{x})$ the value of the censoring variable C^* corresponds to the value of a random variable C with proper continuous distribution function $G_0(t \mid \mathbf{x})$. A cured individual is identified with probability $P(\xi = 1 \mid \nu = 1, \mathbf{X} = \mathbf{x}) = P(C^* = \infty \mid \mathbf{X} = \mathbf{x}) = \pi(\mathbf{x})$. In this setup, the data actually observed are $\{(\mathbf{X}_i, T_i, \delta_i, \xi_i, \xi_i \nu_i) : i = 1, \ldots, n\}$, where the observed time is $T_i = \min(Y_i, C_i^*) = T_i^*$, except for those identified as cured which is $T_i = C_i$. Hence, the observations $\{(\mathbf{X}_i, T_i, \delta_i, \xi_i, \xi_i \nu_i) : i = 1, \ldots, n\}$ can be classified into three groups: (a) the individual is observed to have experienced the event and, therefore, is known to be uncured $(\mathbf{X}_i, T_i = Y_i, \delta_i = 1, \xi_i = 1, \xi_i \nu_i = 0)$; (b) the lifetime is censored and the cure status is unknown $(\mathbf{X}_i, T_i = C_i, \delta_i = 0, \xi_i = 0, \xi_i \nu_i = 0)$; and (c) the lifetime is censored and the individual is known to be cured $(\mathbf{X}_i, T_i = C_i, \delta_i = 0, \xi_i = 1, \xi_i \nu_i = 1)$. In standard cure models where the cure status is unknown for all the censored observations, only groups (a) and (b) are considered.

The probability of cure is $1 - p(\mathbf{x}) = P(Y = \infty \mid \mathbf{X} = \mathbf{x})$, and the conditional survival function of the uncured individuals, also known as latency, is $S_0(t \mid \mathbf{x}) = P(Y > t \mid Y < \infty, \mathbf{X} = \mathbf{x})$. The mixture cure model specifies the survival function $S(t \mid \mathbf{x}) = P(Y > t \mid \mathbf{X} = \mathbf{x})$ as the following.

$$S(t \mid \mathbf{x}) = 1 - p(\mathbf{x}) + p(\mathbf{x}) S_0(t \mid \mathbf{x}). \tag{1}$$

Assuming model (1) and the availability of a suitable estimator of the $S(t \mid x)$, estimators of the cure probability and the latency can be derived by considering the following relationships.

$$1 - p(x) = \lim_{t \to \infty} S(t \mid x) > 0, \quad S_0(t \mid x) = \frac{S(t \mid x) - \{1 - p(x)\}}{p(x)}. \tag{2}$$

Safari et al. [2] proposed the generalized product-limit estimator of the conditional survival function $S(t \mid x)$ when the cure status is partially known, which is the following:

$$\widehat{S}_h^c(t \mid x) = \prod_{i=1}^n \left(1 - \frac{\delta_{[i]} B_{h[i]}(x) \mathbf{1}\left(T_{(i)} \leq t\right)}{\sum_{j=i}^n B_{h[j]}(x) + \sum_{j=1}^{i-1} B_{h[j]}(x) \mathbf{1}\left(\xi_{[j]} \nu_{[j]} = 1\right)}\right), \tag{3}$$

where $X_{[i]}, \delta_{[i]}, \xi_{[i]}$, and $\nu_{[i]}$ are the concomitants of the ordered observed times $T_{(1)} \leq \ldots \leq T_{(n)}$, and $B_{h[i]}(x)$ is the Nadaraya–Watson (NW) weight of the following:

$$B_{h[i]}(x) = \frac{K_h\left(x - X_{[i]}\right)}{\sum_{j=1}^n K_h\left(x - X_j\right)},$$

$K_h(\cdot) = K(\cdot/h)/h$ is a kernel function $K(\cdot)$ rescaled with bandwidth h. The corresponding estimator of the cure rate $1 - p(x)$ [3] is the following:

$$1 - \widehat{p}_h^c(x) = \widehat{S}_h^c\left(T_{(n)}^1 \mid x\right), \tag{4}$$

where $T_{(n)}^1$ is the largest uncensored observed time. Here, in light of (3), (4), and the relation in (2), a nonparametric estimator of the latency function is given by the following.

$$\widehat{S}^c_{0,h_1,h_2}(t \mid x) = \begin{cases} \dfrac{\widehat{S}^c_{h_2}(t \mid x) - (1 - \widehat{p}^c_{h_1}(x))}{\widehat{p}^c_{h_1}(x)} & \text{if } 0 \leq t \leq T^1_{(n)} \text{ and } \widehat{S}^c_{h_2}(t \mid x) > 1 - \widehat{p}^c_{h_1}(x) \\ 0 & \text{otherwise.} \end{cases} \quad (5)$$

The optimal bandwidth for $\widehat{S}^c_h(t \mid x)$ in (3) is not necessarily the optimal bandwidth for $1 - \widehat{p}^c_h(x)$ in (4); therefore, the estimator in (5) is a more general estimator that uses two different bandwidths for estimating $S(t \mid x)$ and $1 - p(x)$. Note that if $h = h_1 = h_2$, then the estimator in (5) reduces to the following estimator.

$$\widehat{S}^c_{0,h}(t \mid x) = \dfrac{\widehat{S}^c_h(t \mid x) - (1 - \widehat{p}^c_h(x))}{\widehat{p}^c_h(x)}.$$

3. Application to COVID-19 Data

For illustration of the nonparametric estimators stated in Section 2, we present an application concerning patients hospitalized with COVID-19 in Galicia (Spain) during the first outbreak of the epidemic. We have a medical database of 10,454 COVID-19 patients reported by the Galician Healthcare Service between 6 March and 7 May 2020. This database contains some information on sex, age, and the dates of different medical outcomes such as admission to the intensive care unit (ICU), discharge, or death. The aim was to estimate the time from hospital ward until admission to ICU while adjusting for age and sex. In our analysis we included only 2380 patients who had been hospitalized for at least a day. Among them, 8.3% were admitted to ICU and 91.7% were censored. In the censored group, 68.8% patients were discharged from the hospital alive and without the need for ICU, and 13.8% died without entering the ICU. Therefore, these patients were identified to be "cured" from the event of interest, which is admission to ICU. Note that in this example, "being cured" means being free of experiencing admission to ICU and not being cured in medical terms.

Acknowledgments: This work has been supported by MINECO grant MTM2017-82724-R and the Xunta de Galicia (Grupos de Referencia Competitiva ED431C-2016-014) and we wish to acknowledge the support received from the Centro de Investigación de Galicia "CITIC" funded by Xunta de Galicia and the European Union (European Regional Development Fund Galicia 2014–2020 Program) by grant ED431G 2019/01. The authors are grateful to Andrés Paz-Ares Rodríguez (General Director of Public Health), Xurxo Hervada Vidal (General Deputy Director of Information on Health and Epidemiology), and Benigno Rosón Calvo (general deputy director of the SERGAS information system) for providing the COVID-19 data.

Institutional Review Board Statement: Not applicable.

Informed Consent Statement: Not applicable.

Data Availability Statement: Not applicable.

References

1. Peng, Y.; Yu, B. *Cure Models: Methods, Applications, and Implementation*; Chapman and Hall/CRC: Boca Raton, FL, USA, 2021.
2. Safari, W.C.; López-de-Ullibarri, I.; Jácome, M.A. A product-limit estimator of the conditional survival function when cure status is partially known. *Biometr. J.* **2021**, *63*, 984–1005. [CrossRef] [PubMed]
3. Safari, W.C.; López-de-Ullibarri, I.; Jácome, M.A. Nonparametric Kernel Estimation of the Probability of Cure in a Mixture Cure Model When the Cure Status Is Partially Observed. Submitted. 2021. Available online: https://dm.udc.es/preprint/main_paper_cure_rate_Safari_et_al.pdf (accessed on 29 September 2021).

Proceeding Paper

Design, Implementation and Validation of a Bluetooth 5 Real-Time Monitoring System for Large Indoor Environments [†]

Iván Froiz-Míguez [1,2,*], Paula Fraga-Lamas [1,2] and Tiago M. Fernández-Caramés [1,2]

1. Department of Computer Engineering, Faculty of Computer Science, Universidade da Coruña, 15071 A Coruña, Spain; paula.fraga@udc.es (P.F.-L.); tiago.fernandez@udc.es (T.M.F.-C.)
2. Centro de Investigación CITIC, Universidade da Coruña, 15071 A Coruña, Spain
* Correspondence: ivan.froiz@udc.es
† Presented at the 4th XoveTIC Conference, A Coruña, Spain, 7–8 October 2021.

Abstract: The progress of LPWAN technologies in recent years has increased their use in various types of environments as well as increased the applications in which they are used. However, due to the duty cycle limitations of license-free based technologies, they have a considerable limitation for applications with frequent data transmission or real-time data. In this regard, technologies working in the 2.4 GHz band are a compelling option to consider but their main problem concerns their limited range. Fortunately, the new Bluetooth 5 standard has a new feature (Long Range mode) that is especially useful in long distance or large indoor environments. This paper describes a practical study on this new technology for indoor environments. The performed experiments evaluate reception range, communications quality, channel occupancy, response times, and power consumption. The obtained results indicate that a three-floor building of more than 4200 m^2 may be covered with a stable signal with only two Bluetooth 5 nodes.

Keywords: Bluetooth 5; LPWAN; IoT; LE coded; real-time monitoring

1. Introduction

LPWAN technologies have undergone constant evolution in the last years and have become widespread in many environments. However, they do have limitations in certain types of applications, one of which concerns the restrictions on transmission due to the duty cycle. In this aspect, 2.4 GHz license-exempt ISM-band technologies are the main alternative. However, such a band has worse propagation than sub-1 GHz bands and a high occupancy in many environments, thus it is normally used only for certain IoT scenarios. There are 2.4 GHz technologies like Bluetooth that have proven to provide a good data transfer power consumption ratio, while others based on the IEEE 802.15.4 standard (e.g., XBee, Thread, and ANT) offer a better sensitivity [1].

Commonly, Bluetooth is used for scenarios that require short-range communications, but with the arrival of the new Bluetooth 5 standard, studies have shown that it has improved consumption and response time [2], as well as an improved range. This is achieved thanks to a new long-range mode (LE-coded PHY) that allows for adding extra sensitivity, with respect to the legacy version of the Bluetooth 4.x standard, by lowering the data rate to 125 Kbps, which makes it a rival of IEEE 802.15.4 standard technologies in terms of range; for this reason, it is compelling for indoor use considering the additional range [3]. This new feature not only improves the communications range but also makes it more stable in environments with electromagnetic interference.

2. Materials and Methods

In order to test the performance of the Bluetooth 5 in realistic indoor scenarios, two Nordic Semiconductor development kits were used (nRF52840-DK [4]), which can transmit at a maximum power of 8 dBm and have a sensitivity of −103 dBm in the LE-coded mode.

The tests were carried out in the Scientific Area Building of the University of A Coruña (Spain), which occupies an area of roughly 4200 m^2 and is divided into three 1400 m^2 floors.

For the deployed architecture, the following considerations were taken into account. On the one hand, as one of the advantages of the system is unrestricted transmission, we decided to test the system with fast transmissions in order to estimate its performance for real-time applications. On the other hand, although Bluetooth has several topologies, we decided to use a star topology with nodes operating in the long-range mode and at maximum power, with the aim of using the smallest number of nodes to cover the largest distances as possible.

Considering the mentioned experimental setup, we decided to implement two different devices: a GATT peripheral and a GATT central that make use of the LE-coded PHY. The GATT peripheral node was located in a fixed position, updating a predefined characteristic value every 500 ms. The GATT central node was placed at different positions and, after connecting to the peripheral, read its characteristic and stored the collected information for later analysis. The positions and orientations of the deployed nodes are shown in Figure 1.

Figure 1. Bluetooth 5 node distribution for the three floors (blue: server node; red: clients).

3. Results

Table 1 shows the results in terms of the error rate of the received packets as well as the minimum, maximum, and average Receive Signal Strength Indicator (RSSI) values when transmitting 200 packets for each point. As it can be observed, good error rates were obtained for eight of the fourteen clients in spite of using a single-server node positioned in the second floor. In points B, D, F, and N, the maximum RSSI was less than −93; thus, considering that the theoretical sensitivity in Legacy (LE 1M) for the nodes was −96 dBm, it is logical that these were the points with the higher packet error rates. Additionally, it was at these extreme points where the use of the LE-coded mode allowed for a sensible decrease in the packet error rate.

Table 1. Error rate and RSSI values obtained at the different measurement points.

Parameter/Point	A	B	C	D	E	F	G	H	I	J	K	L	M	N
Error rate (%)	1	71	0	41	0	94	0	19	22	7	2	41	4	74
Min. RSSI (dBm)	−90	−94	−84	−98	−98	−98	−80	−99	−97	−98	−95	−99	−99	−98
Max. RSSI (dBm)	−80	−99	−62	−93	−81	−95	−63	−81	−82	−84	−87	−84	−89	−94
Avg. RSSI (dBm)	−84.9	−96.2	−67.8	−95.3	−86.3	−96.6	−69.6	−87.7	−86	−91.8	−90.2	−91.5	−92.9	−95.7

4. Discussion

It is important to consider that while the use of the LE-coded mode to increase the sensitivity was good for the considered indoor environment, it is also necessary to keep in mind that increasing the airtime can also saturate the channel, especially for advertisements, which are emitted in only three channels. Thus, Figure 2a,b compare the energy consumption and length of two advertisement events: one in the LE-coded mode (Figure 2a) and the other one in Legacy mode (Figure 2b). As it can be observed, the LE-coded event required roughly 3 ms more than in the Legacy mode, thus the latter almost doubles the former in length. This longer airtime also increases power consumption.

Figure 2c shows the channel occupation for the three advertisement channels (in green), wherein the values in gray show the average occupation of the channel. The tests were performed for four nodes that sent advertisements every 20 ms (the minimum value allowed) at 8 dBm within a 2 m range. Although it is an extreme case used just for testing the limits of the system, significant channel saturation can be observed.

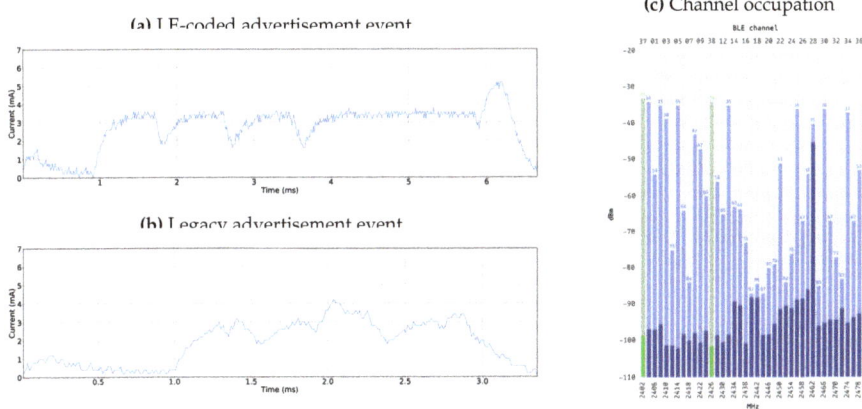

Figure 2. Airtime and channel occupation analysis.

In view of these results, it can be concluded that the system would benefit from the use of a second server node, as well as from determining the optimal position for the nodes. Moreover, the use of omni-directional antennas instead of the tested integrated directional PCB antennas would be beneficial in the evaluated indoor environment due to the reflections and would also provide full coverage to the entire building.

5. Conclusions

The purpose of this work was to analyze the coverage and performance provided by Bluetooth 5 in a large IoT indoor environment. The performed experiments show that the LE-coded mode offers notably better results than the Legacy version indoors due to the increased sensitivity. In terms of data propagation and reception, the covered distances considerably improve those obtained by most 2.4 GHz band technologies. Nonetheless, traditional 2.4 GHz technologies cannot be compared to LPWAN technologies as their unrestricted transmissions make them more suitable for the evaluated use case. The main concern to consider is to not abuse the advertisement events in the LE-coded mode, as they can saturate the available channels.

References

1. Dementyev, A.; Hodges, S.; Taylor, S.; Smith, J. Power Consumption Analysis of Bluetooth Low Energy, ZigBee and ANT Sensor Nodes in a Cyclic Sleep Scenario. In Proceedings of the IEEE International Wireless Symposium (IWS), Beijing, China, 14–18 April 2013; pp. 1–4.
2. Bulić, P.; Kojek, G.; Biasizzo, A. Data Transmission Efficiency in Bluetooth Low Energy Versions. *Sensors* **2019**, *19*, 3746. [CrossRef] [PubMed]
3. Zhang, C.; Yan, Y. Experimental Performance Evaluation of Bluetooth 5 for In-building Networks. In Proceedings of the 11th International Conference on Network of the Future, Bordeaux, France, 12–14 October 2020; pp. 115–119.
4. Nordic nRF52840-DK, Datasheet. Available online: https://infocenter.nordicsemi.com/pdf/nRF52840_OPS_v0.5.pdf (accessed on 5 August 2021).

Proceeding Paper

The Effect of Music on Brain Activity an Emotional State [†]

Joana Cunha [1,‡], Paulo Veloso Gomes [1,*,‡], António Marques [1,‡] and Javier Pereira [2,‡]

1. LabRP-CIR, Psychosocial Rehabilitation Laboratory, Center for Rehabilitation Research, School of Health, Polytechnic Institute of Porto, 4200-465 Porto, Portugal; 10160312@ess.ipp.pt (J.C.); ajmarques@ess.ipp.pt (A.M.)
2. CITIC, Research Center of Information and Communication Technologies, Talionis Research Group, Universidade da Coruña, 15071A Coruña, Spain; javier.pereira@udc.es

* Correspondence: pvg@ess.ipp.pt
† Presented at the 4th XoveTIC Conference, A Coruña, Spain, 7–8 October 2021.
‡ These authors contributed equally to this work.

Abstract: This study explores the potential of music as a therapy element in digital therapy programs to improve mental health and well-being. Music induces an emotional component in the individual that translates into changes in their brain activity, which can be monitored through electroencephalography. A scoping review was conducted to identify the most recent relevant publications related to the effect of music on brain activity and emotional state in digital therapy programs. From 585 identified publications, six relevant publications were selected that meet all the requirements defined in the study.

Keywords: music; emotions; brain activity; electroencephalography

1. Introduction

The influence of music on brain activity and emotional state is a topic that has gained relevance due to its potential application in therapeutic programs with clear benefits for patients. The sound, rhythm, time, intensity, and frequency of the music can induce different types of positive or negative emotions. Music can generate positive and negative emotions, and its effect may vary from person to person [1].

The emotional impact provided by music can be gauged by performing measurements of brain signals through the EEG, allowing us to relate the emotions felt to the music that triggered them [2].

A scoping review was carried out to identify the most recent relevant publications related to the effect of music on brain activity and emotional state in digital therapies programs, selecting a set of studies from the last 5 years.

2. Materials and Methods

The present scoping review was conducted in conformity with the Joanna Briggs Institute (JBI) and PRISMA method guidelines to identify the most recent relevant publications related to the effect of music on brain activity and emotional state in digital therapies programs. To ensure a comprehensive number of documents with significant evidence for the intended analysis, the research equation was elaborated: music AND (electroencephalography OR electroencephalogram OR EEG) AND emotion* AND ("digital therapies" OR "digital therapy" OR "digital treatment"). The research was carried out in scientific databases B-On, Google Scholar and Semantic Scholar, during May of 2021.

3. Results

The study flow diagram is presented in Figure 1. Initially, a sample of 585 documents were collected, and after removing the duplicates, 570 documents were obtained. After analyzing each document based on the theme and summary, the sample was reduced to

180 selected articles. Subsequently, and after applying the inclusion criteria, a sample of six articles were obtained to be mapped.

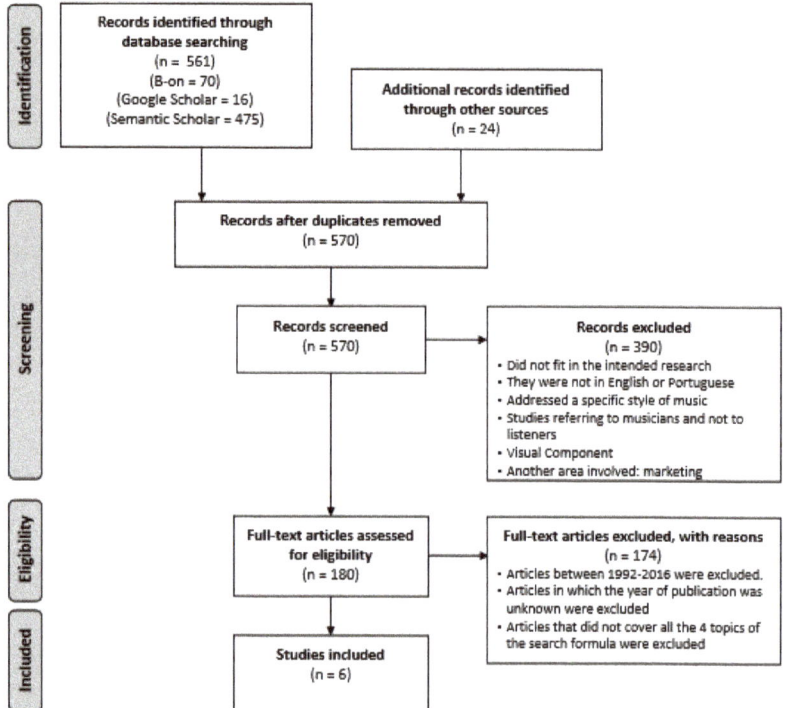

Figure 1. Preferred Reporting Items for Systematic Reviews and Meta-Analyses (PRISMA) flow diagram for the scoping review process. Adapted from Moher D, Liberati A, Tetzlaff J, Altman DG: The PRISMA Statement. PLoS Med 6(7): e1000097. https://doi.org/10.1371/journal.pmed.1000097.

From Table 1, it is possible to analyze the selected documents that correspond to all the requirements defined in the research process.

Table 1. Mapping of scientific articles based on requirements defined in the study.

Reference	Abstract
Dutta et al., 2020 [3]	The electroencephalogram allows to understand the impact of music, through the emotions felt and the registered signal. The prolonged influence of negative emotions leads to mental illnesses such as anxiety or depression. This article allowed to develop a music playlist.
Lee et al., 2020 [4]	This article implements a music recommendation system to provide users with a list of emotions according to different symptoms. Through a combination of algorithms, is possible to carry out a survey of different types of music, to achieve a music therapy system aimed at treating depression.

Table 1. *Cont.*

Reference	Abstract
Ramirez et al., 2018 [5]	This article evaluated, based on an electroencephalographic recording, the emotional response of patients with end-stage cancer to a music therapy (MT) intervention in a randomized clinical trial. Subsequently, emotional indicators were extracted to quantify the overall effect of MT on patients compared to controls and the relative effect of the different MT techniques applied during each session.
Schaefer, 2017 [6]	This article investigated the emotions evoked by music, and their potential as a therapy. The tomographies performed allowed to understand which areas of the brain are activated by musical stimuli.It was also discovered that the blocking of a specific class of receptors can be a mechanism for the treatment of certain psychiatric or neurological diseases associated with music, with neurochemical studies being an aspect to be considered.
Soontreekulpong et al., 2018 [7]	This article investigated the relationship between the effects of three musical beats: slow, normal and fast, with the major mode and the electroencephalogram beta index for negative emotion reduction. Stroop color tests were used to induce stress in some participants. The results shows when the musical rhythm was normal, it was more effective in decreasing beta activity in the right frontal region compared to the others, proving that music is one of the resources for reducing negative emotion.
Turrell et al., 2019 [8]	In this study, after subjecting some individuals to electroencephalographic recording while listening to music, to have a direct effect on people's emotions, it was possible to verify that there was significant activity in five different regions of the brain.

4. Discussion and Conclusions

In this scoping review, the authors identified six recent and relevant publications related to the effect of music on brain activity and emotional state in digital therapy programs. To cover the concepts that involve the subject of the study, four research terms were defined: "Music", "Electroencephalography", "Emotion" and "Digital Therapies".

This study identified relevant publications that describe very revealing studies on the importance of music as a therapeutic element in mental health and well-being areas.

Author Contributions: Conceptualization, J.C., P.V.G.; methodology, J.C., P.V.G.; validation, P.V.G.; investigation, J.C.; writing—original draft preparation, J.C.; writing—review and editing, J.C., P.V.G.; visualization, J.C., P.V.G.; supervision, A.M., J.P.; project administration, J.C. All authors have read and agreed to the published version of the manuscript.

Funding: This research received no external funding.

Acknowledgments: This research was carried out and used the equipment of the Psychosocial Rehabilitation Laboratory (LabRp) of the Research Center in Rehabilitation of the School of Allied Health Technologies, Polytechnic Institute of Porto.

Conflicts of Interest: The authors declare no conflict of interest.

References

1. Hausmann, M.; Hodgetts, S.; Eerola, T. Music-induced changes in functional cerebral asymmetries. *Brain Cogn.* **2016**, *104*, 58–71. [CrossRef] [PubMed]
2. Daly, I.; Williams, D.; Hallowell, J.; Hwang, F.; Kirke, A.; Malik, A.; Nasuto, S.J. Music-induced emotions can be predicted from a combination of brain activity and acoustic features. *Brain Cogn.* **2015**, *101*, 1–11. [CrossRef] [PubMed]
3. Dutta, E.; Bothra, A.; Chaspari, T.; Ioerger, T.; Mortazavi, B.J. Reinforcement Learning using EEG signals for Therapeutic Use of Music in Emotion Management. In Proceedings of the 2020 42nd Annual International Conference of the IEEE Engineering in Medicine & Biology Society (EMBC), Montreal, QC, Canada, 20–24 July 2020; pp. 5553–5556.

4. Lee, S.; Chen, T.; Hsien, Y.; Cao, L. A Music Recommendation System for Depression Therapy Based on EEG. In Proceedings of the 2020 IEEE International Conference on Consumer Electronics—Taiwan (ICCE-Taiwan), Taoyuan, Taiwan, 28–30 September 2020.
5. Ramirez, R.; Planas, J.; Escude, N.; Mercade, J.; Farriols, C.; Kenny, D.T. EEG-Based Analysis of the Emotional Effect of Music Therapy on Palliative Care Cancer Patients. *Front. Psychol.* **2018**, *9*, 1–7. [CrossRef] [PubMed]
6. Schaefer, H. Music-Evoked Emotions—Current Studies. *Front. Neurosci.* **2017**, *11*, 1–27. [CrossRef] [PubMed]
7. Soontreekulpong, N.; Jirakittayakorn, N.; Wongsawat, Y. Investigation of Various Manipulated Music Tempo for Reducing Negative Emotion Using Beta EEG Index. In Proceedings of the 2018 International Electrical Engineering Congress (IEECON), Krabi, Thailand, 7–9 March 2018; pp. 1–4.
8. Turrell, A.; Halpern, A.R.; Javadi, A. When tension is exciting: An EEG exploration of excitement in music. *bioRxiv* **2019**, [CrossRef]

Proceeding Paper

Training of Machine Learning Models for Recurrence Prediction in Patients with Respiratory Pathologies [†]

Ainhoa Molinero Rodríguez [1,*], Carla Guerra Tort [1,*], Victoria Suárez Ulloa [2], José M. López Gestal [3], Javier Pereira [1] and Vanessa Aguiar Pulido [4]

1. CITIC-Research Center of Information and Communication Technologies, University of A Coruña, 15071 A Coruña, Spain; javier.pereira@udc.es
2. Institute for Biomedical Research of A Coruña (INIBIC)-Fundación Profesor Novoa Santos, 15006 A Coruña, Spain; victoria.suarez.ulloa@sergas.es
3. Instituto Médico Quirúrgico San Rafael, 15009 A Coruña, Spain; jlopez@imqsanrafael.es
4. Computational Biology, University of Miami, Miami, FL 33136, USA; vaguiarpulido@gmail.com
* Correspondence: a.molinero@udc.es (A.M.R.); c.gtort@udc.es (C.G.T.)
† Presented at the 4th XoveTIC Conference, A Coruña, Spain, 7–8 October 2021.

Abstract: Information extracted from electronic health records (EHRs) is used for predictive tasks and clinical pattern recognition. Machine learning techniques also allow the extraction of knowledge from EHR. This study is a continuation of previous work in which EHRs were exploited to make predictions about patients with respiratory diseases. In this study, we will try to predict the recurrence of patients with respiratory diseases using four different machine learning algorithms.

Keywords: electronic health record (EHR); machine learning; linear discriminant analysis; quadratic discriminant analysis; k-nearest neighbors; decision trees

1. Introduction

The electronic health record (EHR) is an electronic version of patient's medical history and demographic, clinical and administrative data are included in them [1,2]. The EHR was created to improve the efficiency of health systems; however, it has several applications in clinical informatics and epidemiology. Specifically, EHR have been used for patient clustering, disease prediction and pattern recognition [3].

The analysis of clinical data associated to EHRs is based in statistical and Artificial Intelligence (AI) procedures. Recently, machine learning and deep learning algorithms have been successfully used to extract informative and useful patterns from the EHRs [4].

The present study is a continuation of previous work [5] in which EHRs were exploited to make predictions about patients with respiratory diseases. In this project, we propose the use of Machine Learning to predict the recurrence of patients with respiratory diseases in less than 6, 12 or 18 months (depending on diagnosis). For this task, four machine learning algorithms were used: linear discriminant analysis (LDA), quadratic discriminant analysis (QDA), k-nearest neighbors (kNN) and decision trees.

2. Materials and Methods

2.1. Data Set Description

Anonymous patient data were extracted from the San Rafael Hospital database. Records range from January 2000 to January 2020. The data set consisted consisted of 996 records and 40 variables. A total of 47.19% of patients suffered a relapse in less than six months, whilst 52.81% had not relapsed in that period of time.

2.2. Machine Learning Algorithms

2.2.1. Linear Discriminant Analysis

Linear discriminant analysis (LDA) is generally used to classify patterns between two classes [6]. LDA models differences among samples assigned to certain groups, in order to maximize the ratio of the between-group variance and the within-group variance.

2.2.2. Quadratic Discriminant Analysis

Quadratic discriminant analysis (QDA) is used when it is known that individual classes show distinct covariances. In this method, individual covariance matrix is estimated for every class of observations.

2.2.3. K-Nearest Neighbors

The k-nearest neighbor classifiers (k-NNCs) assumes that similar features will form a different cluster in feature space with multiple data points. The classifier takes k-nearest neighbors to find similarities between the test data and the features of a different class.

2.2.4. Decision Trees

Decision trees (DTs) are used for classification and regression. The DT predicts the value of a target variable by learning simple decision rules inferred from the data features.

3. Results and Discussion

Figure 1 shows the results obtained for the four models. The accuracy is expressed as the ratio of correctly predicted observation to the total observations; sensitivity, ratio of true positives to actual positives; and specificity, ratio of true negatives to total negatives in the data.

	LDA		QDA		KNN		Decision Trees	
	Train	Test	Train	Test	Train	Test	Train	Test
Accuracy	63.27	59.87	64.12	61.54	57.53		93.26	60.54
Sensitivity	67.12	65.19	74.46	75.95	62.66		94.84	62.03
Specificity	58.97	53.9	50.76	45.39	51.77		91.49	58.87

Figure 1. Results obtained for the four models.

The overall accuracy for the four models is 60%; however, the accuracy value must be greater than 80% to be considered good.

The differences between sensitivity and specificity indicate that these models have a better performance predicting non-relapses than relapses. As expected, the accuracies reported by this study were lower than the ones we would expect. In this study, we used a dataset which did not have input and output parameters for a specific disease diagnostic. Clinical records from San Rafael included information about diagnosis, procedures or health system, but it did not include parameters to diagnose a respiratory disease. With aim to make better predictions, data sets need to include more useful information such as whether the patient is smoker or not, air quality or physical activity. The use of machine learning for health predictions is growing in popularity, although some challenges lie ahead.

Author Contributions: Conceptualization, A.M.R., C.G.T., J.P.; methodology, A.M.-R.; writing, A.M.R; supervision, V.S.U., J.M.L.G., V.A.P. All authors have read and agreed to the published version of the manuscript.

Funding: Centro de Investigación de Galicia CITIC and Campus Innova (agreement I+D+ 2019-20) is funded by Consellería de Educación, Universidade e Formación Profesional from Xunta de Galicia and European Union (European Regional Development Fund - FEDER Galicia 2014-2020 Program) by grant ED431G 2019/01 and Universidade da Coruña. Partially supported by the Spanish Ministry of Science (Challenges of Society 2019) PID2019-104323RB-C33.

Conflicts of Interest: The authors declare no conflict of interest.

References

1. Pham, T.; Tran, T.; Phung, D.; Venkatesh, S. Predicting healthcare trajectories from medical records: A deep learning approach. *J. Biomed. Inform.* **2017**, *69*, 218–229. [CrossRef] [PubMed]
2. Yadav, P.; Steinbach, M.; Kumar, V.; Simon, G. Mining Electronic Health Records (EHRs): A Survey. *ACM Comput. Surv.* **2018**, *50*, 85:1–85:40. [CrossRef]
3. Luo, Y.; Szolovits, P.; Dighe A.S. Using machine learning to predict laboratory test results. *Am. J. Clin. Pathol.* **2016**, *145*, 778–788. [CrossRef]
4. Shickel, B.; Tighe, P.J.; Bihorac, A.; Rashidi, P. Deep EHR: A Survey of Recent Advances in Deep Learning Techniques for Electronic Health Record (EHR) Analysis. *IEEE J. Biomed. Health Inform.* **2018**, *22*, 1589–1604. [CrossRef] [PubMed]
5. Guerra Tort, C.; Aguiar Pulido, V.; Suárez Ulloa, V.; Docampo Boedo, F.; López Gestal, J.M.; Pereira Loureiro, J. Electronic Health Records Exploitation Using Artificial Intelligence Techniques. *Proceedings* **2020**, *54*, 60. [CrossRef]
6. Izenman A.J. *Linear Discriminant Analysis. In: Modern Multivariate Statistical Techniques*. Springer Texts in Statistics; Springer: New York, NY, USA, 2013.

Proceeding Paper

Development of Dual Activities with Micro:Bit for Interventions in People with Cerebral Palsy [†]

Ainhoa Molinero-Rodríguez [1,*], Rubén Carneiro-Medín [2], Carmen Miranda-Duro [1], Laura Nieto-Riveiro [1], Paula M. Castro [3] and Adriana Dapena [3]

[1] CITIC, Talionis Group, Universidade da Coruña, 15071 A Coruña, Spain; carmen.miranda@udc.es (C.M.-D.); laura.nieto@udc.es (L.N.-R.)
[2] Aspace Coruña, Sada, 15160 A Coruña, Spain; ruben.cm@aspacecoruna.org
[3] CITIC, GTEC Group, Universidade da Coruña, 15071 A Coruña, Spain; paula.castro@udc.es (P.M.C.); adriana.dapena@udc.es (A.D.)
* Correspondence: a.molinero@udc.es
[†] Presented at the 4th XoveTIC Conference, A Coruña, Spain, 7–8 October 2021.

Abstract: Several studies have shown that video games help to motivate users in different kinds of therapies. Therefore, in this work we developed a tool that includes dual activities for therapy, as well as a data system for the specialist to follow the evolution of the user. The aim of dual activities is to train cognitive and aerobic capacities at the same time. The interaction between the user and the game is made through two Micro:Bits. Once the user finishes the game, the therapist can follow the evolution of the user through some parameters included in the activities.

Keywords: cerebral palsy; Micro:Bit; gamification; dual therapies

1. Introduction

Cerebral palsy (CP) is a group of disorders that affect a person's ability to move and maintain balance and posture [1]. CP is caused by damage to the brain or abnormal development. Since symptoms vary from person to person, there is not a specific treatment for all children with cerebral palsy.

Nowadays, the search for low-cost and more effective treatments has resulted in the incorporation of new information and telecommunication technologies (ICT) in the field of rehabilitation, for instance telerehabilitation [2]. In this context of telerehabilitation, systems that incorporate video games play an important role. Several studies have shown that playing video games can improve attention, memory and overall performance [3,4].

The aim of this project is to develop a tool that includes dual activities for rehabilitation, as well as a data-system for the specialists to track the evolution of the user. These activities are controlled by the Micro:Bit board, which includes sensors that collect environmental information such as acceleration, temperature or light. These games have the same purpose: to train motor activity and cognitive skills simultaneously. To complete the game, the user must pedal a stationary bike, whilst solving matching, mathematical and memory challenges.

2. Materials and Methods

The Micro:Bit is a board [5] developed by the BBC, designed to encourage children to get involved with computing and programming. This type of device can be programmed using simple graphical interfaces. Programs can be created with Microsoft MakeCode, its own programming environment, but environments such as Scratch, Tynker or Code.org are used to develop projects with this type of device.

This project was developed in Kittenblock, based in Scratch. This platform supports the programming of two Micro:bits. We used two Micro:bit boards, one version 1.5 and the other v.2. The communications with the Micro:bit v2 are through Bluetooth and with the v1.5 board are through a USB.

We created three games, shown in Figure 1, which have the same purpose: to train aerobic and cognitive skills.

- Maths. The aim is to solve addition and subtraction problems.
- Memory. The user must memorize a pattern of objects.
- Shape matching. Different objects are shown and the user must match them with their shape.

Some variables were defined in order to represent the user's progress. Kittenblock saves these variables and after each session with the user, the therapist can save the progress and store it in a csv file. The structure and an example of the CSV file are shown below: [Username], [date], [time], [score], [speed of game], [level of dificult].

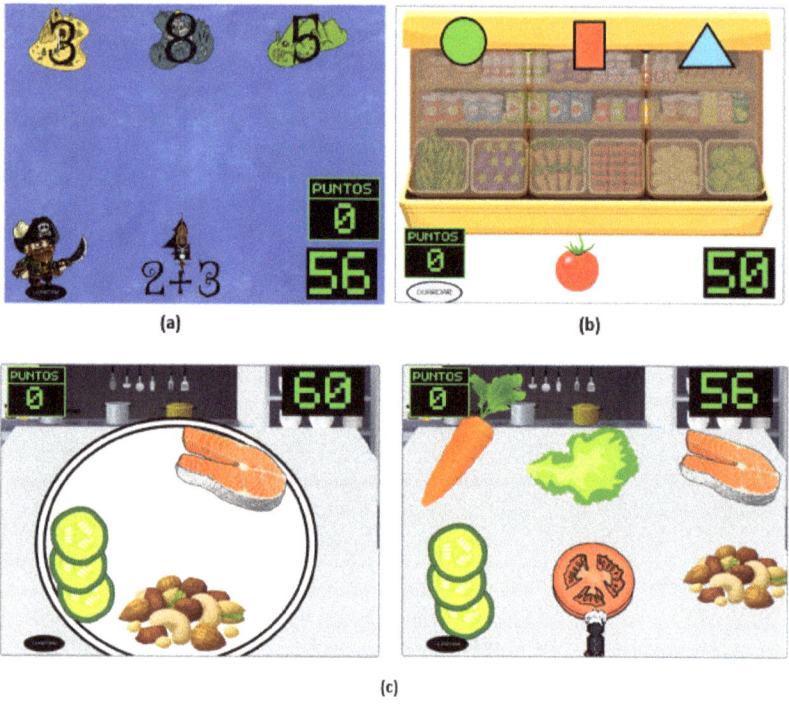

Figure 1. Developed games: (**a**) Math, (**b**) shape matching and (**c**) memory games.

3. Future Work

Some tasks and tests have been left for the future due to time constraints and pandemic-derived problems, restricting access to the Aspace facility and its users. In the future, the tool will be tested with real users in order to measure its effectiveness. Moreover, a platform is being developed using Django, a Python Web framework. Through this app the therapist can graphically analyze the results collected by the tool, track each user's progress and facilitate data recollection.

Author Contributions: Conceptualization, R.C.-M.; methodology, A.M.-R.; software, A.M.-R.; writing, A.M.-R.; supervision, C.M.-D., L.N.-R., P.M.C. and A.D. All authors have read and agreed to the published version of the manuscript.

Funding: Centro de Investigación de Galicia CITIC and Campus Innova (agreement I+D+ 2019-20) is funded by Consellería de Educación, Universidade e Formación Profesional from Xunta de Galicia and European Union (European Regional Development Fund—FEDER Galicia 2014-2020 Program) by grant ED431G 2019/01 and Universidade da Coruña. Partially supported by the Spanish Ministry of Science (Challenges of Society 2019) PID2019-104323RB-C33.

Institutional Review Board Statement: Not applicable.

Informed Consent Statement: Not applicable.

Conflicts of Interest: The authors declare no conflict of interest.

References

1. Bax, M.; Goldstein, M.; Rosenbaum, P.; Leviton, A.; Paneth, N.; Dan, B.; Jacobsson, B.; Damiano, D. Executive Committee for the Definition of Cerebral Palsy. Proposed definition and classification of cerebral palsy, April 2005. *Dev. Med. Child Neurol.* **2005**, *47*, 571–576. [CrossRef] [PubMed]
2. Cano-de la Cuerda, R.; Muñoz-Hellín, E.; Alguacil-Diego, I.M.; Molina-Rueda, F. Telerrehabilitación y neurología. *Rev. Neurol.* **2010**, *51*, 49–56. [CrossRef] [PubMed]
3. Susi, T.; Johannesson, M.; Backlund, P. *Serious Games: An Overview*; Technical Report HS- IKI -TR-07-001; School of Humanities and Informatics University of Skövde: Skövde, Sweden, 2007.
4. Rego, P.; Moreira, P.M.; Reis, L.P. Serious games for rehabilitation: A survey and a classification towards a taxonomy. In Proceedings of the 5th Iberian Conference on Information Systems and Technologies, Santiago de Compostela, Spain, 16–19 June 2010; pp. 1–6.
5. Microes.org. Qué es micro:bit—Microes.org—Comunidad micro:bit en España. 2021. Available online: http://microes.org/que-es-microbit.php (accessed on 20 July 2021).

Proceeding Paper

Deep Multi-Segmentation Approach for the Joint Classification and Segmentation of the Retinal Arterial and Venous Trees in Color Fundus Images [†]

José Morano [1,2,*], Álvaro S. Hervella [1,2], Jorge Novo [1,2] and José Rouco [1,2]

1. Centro de Investigación CITIC, Universidade da Coruña, 15001 A Coruña, Spain; a.suarezh@udc.es (Á.S.H.); jnovo@udc.es (J.N.); jrouco@udc.es (J.R.)
2. VARPA Research Group, Instituto de Investigación Biomédica de A Coruña (INIBIC), Universidade da Coruña, 15001 A Coruña, Spain
* Correspondence: j.morano@udc.es
† Presented at the 4th XoveTIC Conference, A Coruña, Spain, 7–8 October 2021.

Abstract: The analysis of the retinal vasculature represents a crucial stage in the diagnosis of several diseases. An exhaustive analysis involves segmenting the retinal vessels and classifying them into veins and arteries. In this work, we present an accurate approach, based on deep neural networks, for the joint segmentation and classification of the retinal veins and arteries from color fundus images. The presented approach decomposes this joint task into three related subtasks: the segmentation of arteries, veins and the whole vascular tree. The experiments performed show that our method achieves competitive results in the discrimination of arteries and veins, while clearly enhancing the segmentation of the different structures. Moreover, unlike other approaches, our method allows for the straightforward detection of vessel crossings, and preserves the continuity of the arterial and venous vascular trees at these locations.

Keywords: medical imaging; vessel segmentation; artery and vein classification; deep learning

1. Introduction

The analysis of the retinal vasculature represents a crucial stage in the diagnosis of several diseases, such as diabetes, age-related macular degeneration (AMD) and glaucoma [1]. This is due to the presence of these diseases causing changes in the retinal vessels. An exhaustive analysis of the retinal vasculature involves segmenting the vascular tree and classifying their vessels into veins and arteries. Despite its utility, this type of analysis is rarely applied in clinical practice, as performing it manually is arduous, and often leads to partly subjective results. For this reason, several automatic methods have been proposed. Early methods addressed these tasks into two sequential steps [2]. However, this approach causes the classification results to be highly conditioned by the segmentation results. To overcome this issue, the current state of the art (SOTA) addresses both tasks as a single multi-class semantic segmentation problem [3–6].

In this work, we present an accurate approach, based on deep neural networks, for the joint segmentation and classification of the retinal arteries and veins (JSCAV) from color fundus images. This approach, differently to SOTA, decomposes the joint task into three subtasks: the segmentation of arteries, veins and the whole vascular tree. In the following sections, we discuss this approach and its associated advantages.

2. Materials and Methods

The current SOTA formulates the JSCAV task as a single multi-class semantic segmentation problem. However, this approach leads to incomplete segmentation maps for veins and arteries, and does not directly provide vasculature segmentation maps.

As an alternative, we present an approach that decomposes the joint task into three segmentation subtasks [7]. Each of these subtasks addresses the segmentation of one of three classes of interest: arteries, veins and the whole vascular tree. To implement this multi-segmentation (MS) approach, a deep neural network is trained end-to-end using a novel loss function: BCE3. This loss function computes the loss as the sum of the individual segmentation losses of the aforementioned classes. Each individual loss is computed as the binary cross-entropy (BCE) between the predicted probability map and the manually annotated segmentation map. This setting allows for the intuitive handling of vessel crossings, and directly provides precise and complete segmentation maps of the various vascular trees. It also allows for the direct detection of vessel crossings through the element-wise product of the predicted artery and vein maps.

To train and evaluate the networks in the JSCAV task, we employed the publicly available RITE dataset [8], which is composed of 40 color fundus images and their corresponding arteries, veins and vasculature segmentation masks. To facilitate training of the networks, we used the image preprocessing technique specified in [3], as well as online data augmentation. To validate our method, a U-Net network [9] was trained, using both the traditional and the MS approaches.

3. Results and Conclusions

Figure 1 shows an example of an RITE retinography and its arteries, veins, vessels and crossings segmentation maps predicted by a model trained using the MS approach. Figure 2 shows the details of the arteries, veins and vessels segmentation maps of the same retinography predicted by a model trained using the MS and the traditional approaches.

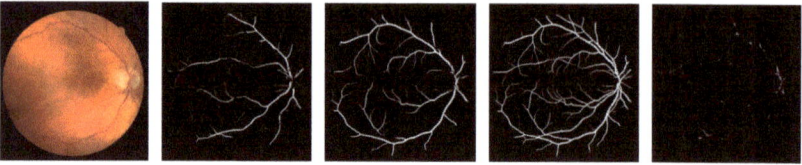

Figure 1. Example segmentation maps predicted by a model trained using the MS approach. From left to right: arteries, veins, vessels and crossings.

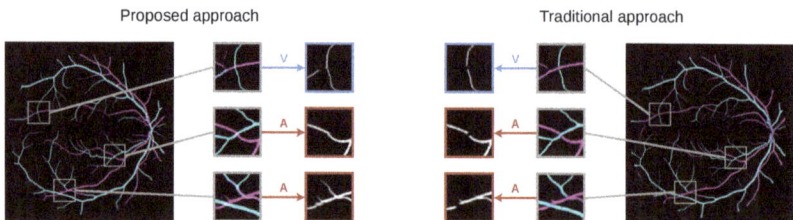

Figure 2. Examples of arteries, veins and vessels probability maps (in RGB) predicted by the models trained using the MS and the traditional approaches.

The ablation study performed in the RITE dataset shows that our method provides an adequate performance, especially in the segmentation of the different structures. Notably, the MS approach achieves a mean accuracy of 89.24 ± 0.73 in the classification of arteries and veins, and an AUC-ROC of 98.33 ± 0.04 in the segmentation of vessels; for its part, the traditional approach achieves 88.78 ± 0.53 and 98.07 ± 0.04, respectively.

In addition, the comparison with the SOTA works in the same dataset, depicted in Figure 3, clearly demonstrates that the presented method achieves competitive results in the discrimination of arteries and veins, while significantly enhancing the vascular segmentation.

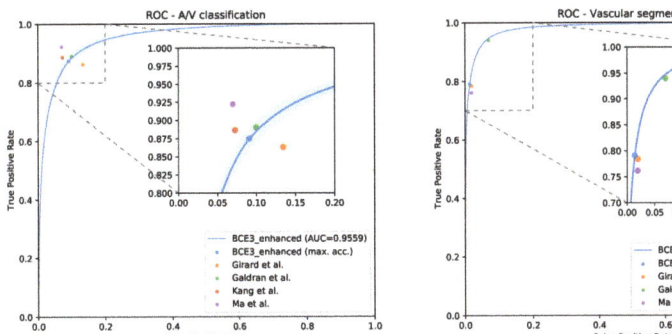

Figure 3. ROC curves in the RITE dataset for the MS approach along with the point representations of the SOTA approaches for artery/vein classification (**left**) and vascular segmentation (**right**).

Therefore, the presented deep multi-segmentation method allows for the detection of more vessels and to better segment the different structures, while achieving competitive classification results. Furthermore, unlike previous approaches, the method allows for the straightforward detection of vessel crossings, as well as preserving the continuity of the arterial and venous vascular trees at these locations (see Figure 2).

Author Contributions: Conceptualization, Á.S.H., J.N. and J.R.; methodology, Á.S.H. and J.M.; software, Á.S.H. and J.M.; validation, Á.S.H. and J.M.; formal analysis, Á.S.H. and J.M.; investigation, J.M.; resources, J.N. and J.R.; data curation, Á.S.H. and J.M.; writing—original draft preparation, J.M.; writing—review and editing, J.M. and J.N.; visualization, J.M.; supervision, J.N. and J.R.; project administration, J.N. and J.R.; funding acquisition, J.N. and J.R. All authors have read and agreed to the published version of the manuscript.

Funding: This work was funded by Instituto de Salud Carlos III, Government of Spain, and the European Regional Development Fund (ERDF) of the European Union (EU) through the DTS18/00136 research project; Ministerio de Ciencia e Innovación, Government of Spain, through the RTI2018-095894-B-I00 and PID2019-108435RB-I00 research projects; Axencia Galega de Innovación (GAIN), Xunta de Galicia, ref. IN845D 2020/38; Xunta de Galicia and European Social Fund (ESF) of the EU through the predoctoral grant contracts ED481A-2017/328 and ED481A 2021/140; Consellería de Cultura, Educación e Universidade, Xunta de Galicia, through Grupos de Referencia Competitiva, grant ref. ED431C 2020/24; CITIC, Centro de Investigación de Galicia ref. ED431G 2019/01, is funded by Consellería de Educación, Universidade e Formación Profesional, Xunta de Galicia, through the ERDF (80%) and Secretaría Xeral de Universidades (20%).

Conflicts of Interest: The authors declare no conflict of interest.

References

1. Kanski, J.J.; Bowling, B. *Clinical Ophthalmology: A Systematic Approach*, 7th ed.; Elsevier Health Sciences: New York, NY, USA, 2011.
2. Staal, J.; Abràmoff, M.D.; Niemeijer, M.; Viergever, M.A.; van Ginneken, B. Ridge-based vessel segmentation in color images of the retina. *IEEE Trans. Med. Imaging* **2004**, *23*, 501–509. [CrossRef] [PubMed]
3. Girard, F.; Kavalec, C.; Cheriet, F. Joint segmentation and classification of retinal arteries/veins from fundus images. *Artif. Intell. Med.* **2019**, *94*, 96–109. [CrossRef] [PubMed]
4. Galdran, A.; Meyer, M.; Costa, P.; MendonÇa; Campilho, A. Uncertainty-Aware Artery/Vein Classification on Retinal Images. In Proceedings of the 2019 IEEE 16th International Symposium on Biomedical Imaging (ISBI 2019), Venice, Italy, 8–11 April 2019; pp. 556–560. [CrossRef]
5. Ma, W.; Yu, S.; Ma, K.; Wang, J.; Ding, X.; Zheng, Y. Multi-task Neural Networks with Spatial Activation for Retinal Vessel Segmentation and Artery/Vein Classification. In *Medical Image Computing and Computer Assisted Intervention—MICCAI 2019*; Shen, D., Liu, T., Peters, T.M., Staib, L.H., Essert, C., Zhou, S., Yap, P.T., Khan, A., Eds.; Springer International Publishing: Cham, Switzerland, 2019; pp. 769–778. [CrossRef]
6. Kang, H.; Gao, Y.; Guo, S.; Xu, X.; Li, T.; Wang, K. AVNet: A retinal artery/vein classification network with category-attention weighted fusion. *Comput. Methods Programs Biomed.* **2020**, *195*, 105629. [CrossRef] [PubMed]

7. Morano, J.; Hervella, Á.S.; Novo, J.; Rouco, J. Simultaneous segmentation and classification of the retinal arteries and veins from color fundus images. *Artif. Intell. Med.* **2021**, *118*, 102116. [CrossRef] [PubMed]
8. Hu, Q.; Abràmoff, M.D.; Garvin, M.K. Automated Separation of Binary Overlapping Trees in Low-Contrast Color Retinal Images. In *Medical Image Computing and Computer-Assisted Intervention—MICCAI 2013*; Mori, K., Sakuma, I., Sato, Y., Barillot, C., Navab, N., Eds.; Springer: Berlin/Heidelberg, Germany, 2013; pp. 436–443. [CrossRef]
9. Ronneberger, O.; Fischer, P.; Brox, T. U-Net: Convolutional Networks for Biomedical Image Segmentation. In *Medical Image Computing and Computer-Assisted Intervention—MICCAI 2015*; Navab, N., Hornegger, J., Wells, W.M., Frangi, A.F., Eds.; Springer International Publishing: Cham, Switzerland, 2015; pp. 234–241. [CrossRef]

Proceeding Paper

Multiple-Choice Question Answering Models for Automatic Depression Severity Estimation [†]

Jorge Gabín *, Anxo Pérez and Javier Parapar

Information Retrieval Lab, Centro de Investigación en Tecnoloxías da, Información e as Comunicacións (CITIC), Universidade da Coruña, 15071 A Coruña, Spain; anxo.pvila@udc.es (A.P.); javier.parapar@udc.es (J.P.)
* Correspondence: jorge.gabin@udc.es; Tel.: +34-881-01-12-76
† Presented at the 4th XoveTIC Conference, A Coruña, Spain, 7–8 October 2021.

Abstract: Depression is one of the most prevalent mental health diseases. Although there are effective treatments, the main problem relies on providing early and effective risk detection. Medical experts use self-reporting questionnaires to elaborate their diagnosis, but these questionnaires have some limitations. Social stigmas and the lack of awareness often negatively affect the success of these self-report questionnaires. This article aims to describe techniques to automatically estimate the depression severity from users on social media. We explored the use of pre-trained language models over the subject's writings. We addressed the task "Measuring the Severity of the Signs of Depression" of eRisk 2020, an initiative in the CLEF Conference. In this task, participants have to fill the Beck Depression Questionnaire (BDI-II). Our proposal explores the application of pre-trained Multiple-Choice Question Answering (MCQA) models to predict user's answers to the BDI-II questionnaire using their posts on social media. These MCQA models are built over the BERT (Bidirectional Encoder Representations from Transformers) architecture. Our results showed that multiple-choice question answering models could be a suitable alternative for estimating the depression degree, even when small amounts of training data are available (20 users).

Keywords: depression prediction; social media; pre-trained language models; multiple-choice question answering

1. Introduction

The World Health Organization (WHO) [1] placed mental health as one of the most relevant components of health. Depression is one of the most common mental disorders. By itself, it affects more than 270 million people. Despite having many harmful effects, there are some effective known treatments. The main problem relies on providing early and effective risk detection.

One of the most reliable and frequent methods to measure depression severity is the Beck Depression Inventory-II (BDI-II) [2]. Although significant evidence exists regarding its performance, some aspects often affect the results of these questionnaires.

These days, health organizations are publishing these questionnaires so that users can fill them in by themselves. However, people with mental disorders usually do not dare to visit those web pages and fill in the questionnaires. In this new communication era, people use social networks to share their feelings and emotions. Hence, these platforms are a great way to collect data to identify disorders like depression [3].

In this context, we describe an approach to improve the automatic estimation of the degree of depression from users on social media. Our study presents the use of pre-trained language models [4] to predict the depression degree of subjects. We evaluated these models for the task "Measuring the Severity of the Signs of Depression" of the CLEF 2020 eRisk Track [5]. Our results achieved moderate performance among all the participants of the task.

2. Experiments

2.1. Datasets

In this study, we use the datasets provided by eRisk 2019 and 2020 for the task "Measuring the Severity of the Signs of Depression" [5,6]. Each dataset contains the history of 20 and 70 users, respectively, providing the users' actual responses to the questionnaire and its complete history of postings. We used the 2019 dataset as training data and the 2020 dataset for testing.

We also used RACE (Large-scale ReAding Comprehension Dataset From Examinations) [7] and SWAG (Large-Scale Adversarial Dataset for Grounded Commonsense Inference) [8], two general-purpose multiple-choice question answering datasets. After some preliminary comparisons, we selected the RACE dataset to perform the first fine-tune over BERT as the results obtained were slightly better.

2.2. Beck Depression Inventory-II (BDI-II)

Beck Depression Inventory-II (BDI-II) is a questionnaire formed by 21 items to measure the depression severity. For each item, the BDI-II provides four options (except items 15 and 17, which provide seven options) and sentences to explain their meanings. These options represent a scale from the absence of the symptom to a total identification.

2.3. Models

We used a modified BERT [9] model for Multiple-Choice Question Answering (MCQA). This model was built over the pre-trained bert-base-uncased model, modifying it to allow multiple-choice question answering. In [4], we can see the process followed to build the model and its comparison with other baseline models.

We also tried to pre-train the MCQA models provided by the Hugging Face library (such as RoBERTa for multiple-choice), but the results obtained were much worse than those obtained using the adaptation mentioned.

2.4. Our Approach

Pre-trained language models are usually trained on a large text corpus and then fine-tuned on a downstream task. Following this approach, in the training phase, we fine-tuned a pre-trained model using the RACE dataset. We additionally fine-tuned the model using training data from the 2019 eRisk task. For that, we built a custom dataset that contains every post from each user combined with each question from the BDI-II questionnaire with all its options (0–3), and the label which represents the actual option was chosen by the user. After analyzing the results obtained, we decided to filter the training data as there was too much noise. Therefore, we calculated the post and question embeddings and used only the top 50 posts more similar to each question as training data in the fine-tuning process.

To run both fine-tunings, we used a batch size of eight (four, when fine-tuning with the seven options dataset), a maximum sequence length of 320, a learning rate of 5×10^{-5}, two epochs, and two gradient accumulation steps.

To carry out inference, we feed the model with every post from each user combined with each question from the BDI-II questionnaire with all its options. As a result, we will receive the model's confidence on each option for each pair of post-questions. Given that confidence, we can extract the inferred answer for each paired user-question by selecting the option with the most appearances.

In this phase, we used the following parameters: a batch size of 48, a maximum sequence length of 320, and a minimum option probability of 0.4 (0.2 for seven options questions). We subtract 0.01 from the minimum probability if no posts achieve that minimum probability.

Finally, to facilitate the whole inference process, we built another dataset using the test data from the 2020 task and following the same approach as explained before.

3. Results and Discussion

In Table 1, we show the results obtained following the explained approach.

Table 1. Results of our model, along with the best baselines of eRisk 2020. Bold values correspond to the best result for each metric.

Model	AHR (%)	ACR (%)	ADODL (%)	DCHR (%)
BioInfo@UAVR [10]	**38.30**	69.21	76.01	30.00
ILab [11]	37.07	**69.41**	81.70	27.14
Prhlt-Upv [12]	34.56	67.44	80.63	**35.71**
Relai [13]	36.39	68.32	**83.15**	34.29
MCQA Model	25.03	57.76	75.58	31.43

On the one hand, we can see in the results table that we get good results in both ADODL and DCHR metrics. However, on the other hand, the results obtained in AHR and ACR metrics were poor compared with the best results of the 2020 task.

Inspecting the model's answers to the BDI-II, we could see that it overestimates depression severity. This is likely because both the train and test data are still noisy. With this in mind, in future work, we plan to design more effective data filtering processes on both the training and test data.

4. Conclusions

In this article, we studied the application of pre-trained multiple-choice question answering models to automatically estimate the depression severity of users on social media. The results obtained are promising and a good starting point to continue researching this type of model.

Acknowledgments: This work was supported by projects RTI2018-093336-B-C22 (MCIU & ERDF), GPC ED431B 2019/03 (Xunta de Galicia & ERDF) and CITIC, which is financial supported by Consellería de Educación, Universidade e Formación Profesional of the Xunta de Galicia through the ERDF (80%) and Secretaría Xeral de Universidades (20%), (Ref ED431G 2019/01).

References

1. World Health Organization. Health & Environmental Research Online (HERO). In *Proceedings of the Preamble to the Constitution of the World Health Organization as Adopted by the International Health Conference, New York, NY, USA, 19–22 June 1946*; World Health Organization: Geneva, Switzerland, 1948.
2. Beck, A.T.; Steer, R.A.; Brown, G.K. *Beck Depression Inventory (BDI–II)*; Pearson: London, UK, 1996; Volume 10.
3. De Choudhury, M.; Counts, S.; Horvitz, E. Social media as a measurement tool of depression in populations. In Proceedings of the 5th Annual ACM Web Science Conference, Paris, France, 2–4 May 2013; pp. 47–56.
4. Xu, K.; Tin, J.; Kim, J. A BERT based model for Multiple-Choice Reading Comprehension. *Passages* **2019**, *6*, 362.
5. Losada, D.E.; Crestani, F.; Parapar, J. eRisk 2020: Self-harm and depression challenges. In Proceedings of the European Conference on Information Retrieval, Lisbon, Portugal, 14–17 April 2020; Springer: Berlin/Heidelberg, Germany, 2020; pp. 557–563.
6. Losada, D.E.; Crestani, F.; Parapar, J. Overview of erisk 2019 early risk prediction on the internet. In Proceedings of the International Conference of the Cross-Language Evaluation Forum for European Languages, Lugano, Switzerland, 9–12 September 2019; Springer: Berlin/Heidelberg, Germany, 2019; pp. 340–357.
7. Lai, G.; Xie, Q.; Liu, H.; Yang, Y.; Hovy, E. Race: Large-scale reading comprehension dataset from examinations. *arXiv* **2017**, arXiv:1704.04683.
8. Zellers, R.; Bisk, Y.; Schwartz, R.; Choi, Y. Swag: A large-scale adversarial dataset for grounded commonsense inference. *arXiv* **2018**, arXiv:1808.05326.
9. Vaswani, A.; Shazeer, N.; Parmar, N.; Uszkoreit, J.; Jones, L.; Gomez, A.N.; Kaiser, L.; Polosukhin, I. Attention Is All You Need. *CoRR* **2017**, *2017*, 5998–6008.
10. Oliveira, L. BioInfo@ UAVR at eRisk 2020: On the use of psycholinguistics features and machine learning for the classification and quantification of mental diseases. In Proceedings of the CEUR Workshop Proceedings, Thessaloniki, Greece, 22–25 September 2020; Volume 2696; CLEF (Working Notes).

11. Martínez-Castaño, R.; Htait, A.; Azzopardi, L.; Moshfeghi, Y. Early risk detection of self-harm and depression severity using BERT-based transformers: iLab at CLEF eRisk 2020. In Proceedings of the CEUR Workshop Proceedings, Thessaloniki, Greece, 22–25 September 2020; Volume 2696; CLEF (Working Notes).
12. Uban, A.S.; Rosso, P. Deep learning architectures and strategies for early detection of self-harm and depression level prediction. In Proceedings of the CEUR Workshop Proceedings, Thessaloniki, Greece, 22–25 September 2020; CLEF (Working Notes); Sun SITE Central Europe: Aachen, Germany, 2020; Volume 2696, pp. 1–12.
13. Maupomé, D.; Armstrong, M.D.; Belbahar, R.M.; Alezot, J.; Balassiano, R.; Queudot, M.; Mosser, S.; Meurs, M.J. Early Mental Health Risk Assessment through Writing Styles, Topics and Neural Models. In Proceedings of the CEUR Workshop Proceedings, Thessaloniki, Greece, 22–25 September 2020; Volume 2696; CLEF (Working Notes).

Proceeding Paper

Applicability of Clinical Decision Support in Management among Patients Undergoing Cardiac Surgery in Intensive Care Unit: A Systematic Review [†]

Patricia Concheiro-Moscoso [1,2,*], Miguel Pereira [3,4], Francisco José Martínez-Martínez [5], Thais Pousada [1,2] and Javier Pereira [1,2]

1. CITIC, TALIONIS Group, Elviña Campus, University of A Coruña, 15071 A Coruña, Spain; thais.pousada.garcia@udc.es (T.P.); javier.pereira@udc.es (J.P.)
2. Faculty of Health Sciences, Oza Campus, University of A Coruña, 15071 A Coruña, Spain
3. Service of Anesthesiology, Resuscitation, Intensive Care, Álvaro Cunqueiro Hospital, Sergas, 36213 Vigo, Spain; miguel.angel.pereira.loureiro@sergas.es
4. CITIC, RNASA-IMEDIR Group, Computer Science Faculty, University of A Coruña, Elviña, 15071 A Coruña, Spain
5. Biomedicine Institute of Valencia (CSIC), 46019 Valencia, Spain; f.martinezm@udc.es
* Correspondence: patricia.concheiro@udc.es; Tel.: +34-881-015-870
† Presented at the 4th XoveTIC Conference, A Coruña, Spain, 7–8 October 2021.

Abstract: Advances achieved in recent decades regarding cardiac surgery have revealed a new risk that goes beyond surgeons' dexterity; post-operative hours are crucial in these patients and are usually spent at intensive care units (ICUs), where they need to be continuously monitored to adjust the treatments. Clinical decision support systems (CDSS) have been developed to take this real-time information and provide clinical suggestions to physicians, so as to reduce medical errors and increase patient recovery ratio. In this review, an initial total of 666 papers were considered, finishing with 23 of them after the researchers' filter, which included the deletion of duplications and exclusion if the title and abstract were not of real interest. The review of these papers concludes the applicability and extends the CDSS offer to both doctors and patients. Better prognosis and recovery rate are achieved by using this technology, which also has high acceptance among most physicians. However, despite the evidence that well-designed CDSS are effective, they still need to be refined to offer the best assistance as possible, which may still take time, despite the promising models that have already been applied in real ICUs.

Keywords: clinical decision support; computerized physician order entry; intensive care units; cardiac surgery

1. Introduction

Patients who need heart surgery require long stays in intensive care units (ICU), compared to other types of surgery, due to their complications. These patients demand the use of broad resources during their stay, such as high vigilance, quick analysis of parameters or adjustments in their medical treatment. The assistance of vital support for the patients is made through the maintenance of vital signs in a target range, the coordination of early therapy directed by objectives in a cardiogenic shock, and the hemodynamic stabilization of LCOS. These techniques can speed up post-operative recovery, decrease hospital stays or the use of mechanical ventilation, and reduce ICU days. At the ICU, the health experts must carry out the control of these parameters, care for the subjects' needs, and prevent complications by ensuring the optimal state of the patients. The use of clinical decision support (CDS) can be very appropriate, supporting the doctor to improve the clinical progress of the patient. The Computerized Physician Order Entry (CPOE) offers support to avoid errors in the dosages and improve the adjustment according to the patient's comorbidities. Databases are also an important system in the ICU, because they can enhance learning about the knowledge of the evolution and prevent or act in each clinical situation. Knowing the impact of these tools can improve the health care of cardiac patients in the ICU. This review aims to determine the impact of clinical decision systems on cardiac patients in ICUs.

2. Materials and Methods

2.1. Design of the Study

The authors conducted this review between 2019 and 2020. This review was guided following the Preferred Reporting Items for Systematic Reviews and Meta-Analyses (PRISMA) statement. Relevant studies were selected and analyzed regarding clinical decision support.

2.2. Search Strategy

A search was conducted to find relevant literature published related to alert systems and cardiac patients in the ICU (2010–current). The search was performed on three databases: Pubmed, Web of Science, EBCOS host. This review include only those studies that (1) studied ICU patients of any age with cardiac pathologies and associated problems; (2) analyzed the use of EHRs, CPOE, or MIMIC-III in the data systems' inpatient follow-up; (3) described the combination of CDSSs with previous systems for the improvement of healthcare; (4) provided predictive values for the implementation of these tools in ICUs.

2.3. Study Selection

A total of 666 results were obtained in the literature search, including 629 from the search and 37 from the bibliographies of other studies. After eliminating duplicates, two authors read the titles and abstracts generated by the search strategy independently, but at the same time, for identifying eligible articles and maintaining the consistency in the review. Overall, 283 articles were selected in the first review, whereas 48 were collected in the second review, and finally, 22 results were included.

2.4. Statistical Analysis

Each study was classified according to whether it was a CDSS, CPOE, EHR, or database system, as well as a combination of these decision support systems. On the contrary, the studies were grouped by the measurement of the results.

3. Results

Twenty-two studies met our inclusion criteria. Thirteen studies evaluated the functionality of CDSS in ICUs, three examined the applicability of databases in ICUs, one each studied the usefulness of HER, and CPOE; and four analyzed the function of combination CDSS/CPOE, CDSS/database and CDSS/EHR. The publication dates of these studies ranged from 2006–2018. Eight studies focused on the development and validation of information systems, four studies used retrospective analysis, two studies conducted an experimental design and a controlled trial, and the remaining each were a prospective cohort, performance study, multicenter study, observational cohort research. The results were grouped into six main blocks:

Development forecast: Five studies examined the use of CDSSs as a tool to predict the evolution that patients may have after heart surgery.

Medication errors: Four studies focused on the analysis of the performance of support systems, specifically on the tools applied to CPOE systems in the prevention of errors in the pharmacological treatment of patients in ICUs.

Warning systems: Four studies analyzed the incorporation of CDSSs into surveillance and continuous analysis, to allow the fast detection of clinical alterations.

Standardization and compliance with protocols: Three studies examined the applicability of these tools to help in the implementation of protocols and complex diagnostics.

Precise adjustment to objectives: Six studies analyzed the application of CDSS in clinical practice and how it makes it possible to maintain a constant within a more precise target range.

Cost reduction: Three studies analyzed how the CDSS can contribute to improving the quality and efficiency of patient care and improving patient outcomes, promoting the reduction of health costs.

Acceptance: Four studies report the high acceptance of these support systems in different fields of both treatment and diagnostic acceptance.

4. Discussion and Conclusions

As seen in this review, CDSS have proved themselves to be a complementary tool for treatment that improves life expectancy in a remarkable way. With the decreasing time physicians has for every patient, CDSS may even become substitutes of these professionals when it comes to assist the nursing staff in the tactical decisions, as long as they have been trained successfully through real qualified clinicians' decisions. At intensive care units, this improvement and assistance become fundamental, as one bad decision might have fatal consequences for the patients therein. Besides medical benefits, costs reduction due to CDSS implementation also allows the investment in hospital equipment and the recruitment of more health care workers, which in turn, improves the assistance received by the patients, thus creating a positive feedback in which both workers and patients benefit. However, as with all emerging technologies, these systems need to be tested and refined to offer a life-saving assistance that is as accurate as possible. This still may take some time, but the current available systems suggest the potential of these technologies for health improvement [1].

Author Contributions: The authors contributed to this research article in the following ways: conceptualization, M.P., P.C.-M. and J.P.; methodology, M.P. and P.C.-M.; formal analysis, M.P., P.C.-M., F.J.M.-M., T.P. and J.P.; investigation, M.P., P.C.-M., F.J.M.-M. and J.P.; writing—original draft preparation, M.P., P.C.-M. and F.J.M.-M.; writing—review and editing: T.P. and J.P.; visualization and supervision, all authors; funding acquisition, P.C.-M. All authors read and agreed to the published version of the manuscript.

Funding: The authors disclosed receipt of the following financial support for the research, authorship, and/or publication of this article: All the economic costs involved in the study will be borne by the research team. This work was supported in part by some grants from the European Social Fund 2014–2020. CITIC (Research Centre of the Galician University System) and the Galician University System (SUG) obtained funds through Regional Development Fund (ERDF) with 80%, Operational Programme ERDF Galicia 2014–2020 and the remaining 20% by the Secretaría Xeral de Universidades of the Galician University System (SUG). Specifically, the author PCM obtained a scholarship (Ref.ED481A-2019/069) to develop the PhD thesis. On the other hand, the diffusion and publication of this research was funded by the CITIC, Research Centre of the Galician University System, with the support previously mentioned (Ref ED431G 2019/01).

Institutional Review Board Statement: Not applicable.

Informed Consent Statement: Not applicable.

Data Availability Statement: The study's data are available to any researcher who contacts the corresponding author, Patricia Concheiro-Moscoso (patricia.concheiro@udc.es).

Conflicts of Interest: The authors declare no conflict of interest.

Reference

1. Pereira, M.; Concheiro-Moscoso, P.; López-Álvarez, A.; Baños, G.; Pazos, A.; Pereira, J. Applicability of Clinical Decision Support in Management among Patients Undergoing Cardiac Surgery in Intensive Care Unit: A Systematic Review. *Appl. Sci.* **2021**, *11*, 2880. [CrossRef]

Proceeding Paper

SQoF-WEAR Project. The Use of Wearable Devices to Identify the Impact of Stress on Workers' Quality of Life [†]

Patricia Concheiro-Moscoso [1,2,*], Betania Groba [1,2], Sílvia Monteiro-Fonseca [3], Nereida Canosa [1,2] and Cristina Queirós [3]

[1] CITIC, TALIONIS Group, Elviña Campus, University of A Coruña, 15071 A Coruña, Spain; b.groba@udc.es (B.G.); nereida.canosa@udc.es (N.C.)
[2] Faculty of Health Sciences, Oza Campus, University of A Coruña, 15071 A Coruña, Spain
[3] Faculty of Psychology and Education Sciences, University of Porto, 4200-135 Porto, Portugal; s.monteirofonseca@gmail.com (S.M.-F.); cqueiros@fpce.up.pt (C.Q.)
* Correspondence: patricia.concheiro@udc.es; Tel.: +34-881-015-870
[†] Presented at the 4th XoveTIC Conference, A Coruña, Spain, 7–8 October 2021.

Abstract: (1) Background: Stress is a major public health problem due to its relevant health, social and economic repercussions. Moreover, stress can be associated with work; when stress increases over time, burnout can occur, an occupational phenomenon recognized by the WHO in 2019. There is interest in the use of wearable devices to monitor and control stressors and their influence on the condition of workers. This study aims to identify the level of job stress and its influence on the quality of life of workers. (2) Methods:This longitudinal study was carried out between the end of May and mid-July 2021. Three assessment tools along with a daily and a weekly questionnaire were computerized through the RedCap platform. The participants had to fill out the diary and weekly questionnaires and wear a Xiaomi Mi Band 5 during the project. (3) Results and discussion: Thirty-six workers from the University of Coruña and from the University of Porto participated in the project. This study promotes the awareness of workers regarding their work stress and the influence of this factor on their quality of life using physiological (e.g., activity, sleep, and heart rate) and psychological indicators (self-report questionnaires in different moments).

Keywords: Xiaomi Mi Smart Band 5; burnout; occupational balance; occupational therapy; participatory health; wearable technology; work stress; sleep

1. Introduction

Work and working conditions can influence health status and quality of life. Work can be influenced by different factors such as work overload, lack of support, etc. The increase in these factors can cause work stress in the worker. When work stress is prolonged and worsened over time, it can lead to burnout situations. Burnout is an occupational phenomenon was recognized by the World Health Organization (WHO) in 2019.

Occupational stress has become one of the most frequent health problems in workers. It is estimated that approximately 3 million workers suffer from occupational stress and that it's 50–60% of the cases of absenteeism and presenteeism. In addition, it is estimated that burnout affects 10% of workers. In the last year, these data have been increased because of the current pandemic situation. Since working conditions have been significantly damaged due to the new forms of work organization and sociolabor relations.

Epidemiological studies report that workers with high levels of stress suffer from anxiety or fatigue, and in several situations, may develop depression. Some studies also consider occupational stress as a triggering factor for cardiovascular and respiratory diseases and physical or cognitive fatigue. Some studies refer to the importance and care of the components' workers' lives, with sleep being one of the most important factors for workers' life. Likewise, the balance between the activities of daily life and work is relevant to obtain the workers' satisfaction and well-being.

Due to the aforementioned, institutions associated with occupational health and work, must promote the workers' quality of life, which gained priority during the pandemic situation, considering the news work demands and the situation of the workers. Thus, the development of studies that provide us with information on the situation of workers in order to create strategies and plans for detecting and monitoring stress and associated factors with the aim of promoting their quality of life and occupational performance. Nowadays, wearable devices are becoming more and more popular in society, being devices used in some researches due to the data they provide on some physiological parameters such as sleep, activity and heart rate. The information of this wearable can be used to know a person's stress and helps to raise awareness of stress and quality at work. In this study, the levels of of work stress and its influence on sleep, daily activity, and quality of life were evaluated. For this purpose, the Xiaomi Mi Band 5 and specific scales and questionnaires were used to measure the different aspects that influence the quality of life of workers.

2. Materials and Methods

2.1. Design of the Study

A cross-sectional study was conducted among workers belonging to the University of Coruña (Spain) and the University of Porto (Portugal), between the end of May and mid-July 2021. Prior to starting the study, all participants gave their informed consent for participating. Also, the study protocol was approved by the A Coruña-Ferrol Research Ethics Committee (code: 2019/249) and by the Ethics Committee of the Faculty of Psychology and Education Science of the University of Porto (code: 2021/06-03). In addition, the study was conducted following the Helsinki Statement for human research ethics. The researchers maintained the confidentiality of all data collected and the anonymity of each participant. Thus, the project respected the Spanish 2016/679 and European Organic 95/46/E.C. Law on the protection of personal data at all times.

2.2. Data Collection and Analysis

In this study, the Xiaomi Mi Band 5 wearable device and different computerized scales were used. To obtain biometric data, participants wore the Xiaomi Mi Band 5 for one month. This device collected minute-by-minute activity and heart rate data, and daily sleep data. In addition, the Research Electronic Data Capture Consortium (REDCap) program was used to computerize the different assessment tools used in the project. Participants had to complete a sociodemographic questionnaire at the beginning of the study; three assessment tools associated with quality of life, sleep quality, and stress perception at the beginning and end of the study; and a daily and weekly questionnaire with questions associated with sleep, stress, physical activity, and occupational balance.

2.3. Statistical Analysis

The project data are obtained in raw form using .csv files, so it is necessary to clean, organize, describe and process them to perform statistical analysis. For the statistical analysis, the IBM SPSS Statistic version 22 program was used. The different numerical variables (age, sex, etc.) will be expressed as mean, standard deviation, taking into account the maximum and minimum ranges. Pearson and Spearman's Rho tests will be used for the association between the variables.

3. Results

36 workers participated in the study. A total of 58.3% belonged to the University of A Coruña, were women (53.8%), and were under 30 years of age (30.8%). Most of the participants (61.9%) had moderate work-related stress and considered that their stress level had increased somewhat to quite a lot due to the COVID-19 situation.

In daily questionnaires, most of the participants came to work in person (67.9%), and felt somewhat frustrated (27.6%) and exhausted (22.4%). In the weekly questionnaires, 39.1% considered that they had been overloaded with tasks during the week.

Averages scores of PSQI and daily questionnaires show that participants had slight difficulties falling asleep and low sleep quality (39.9%). By contrast, wearable reported that participants attained optimal sleep habits. Data from wearable Xiaomi Mi Band 5 show that participants walked on average 5780 steps. Regarding sleep, participants slept 60 min of deep sleep and 233 min light sleep.

4. Discussion and Conclusions

This project contributes to know the influence of occupational stress on the quality of life in university workers, using physiological (e.g., activity, sleep, and heart rate) and psychological indicators (self-report questionnaires in different moments). The increasing use of wearable devices encourages to obtain real-time biomedical data available for people, promoting participatory medicine and knowledge of people's health status. Thus, in this project, workers have been able to have an insight and be aware of their stress level, different stressors, and other parameters related to their activity, sleep, and heart rate. This data can help the worker to improve in their routines and habits and add strategies to reduce their stress level and improve their quality of life [1].

Author Contributions: Conceptualization, P.C.-M., B.G., S.M.-F., N.C. and C.Q.; methodology, P.C.-M., B.G., S.M.-F. and C.Q.; investigation, P.C.-M., B.G., S.M.-F. and C.Q.; writing–original draft preparation, P.C.-M. and S.M.-F.; writing–review and editing, B.G., N.C. and C.Q.; visualization, P.C.-M. and S.M.-F.; supervision, B.G., N.C. and C.Q.; project administration, B.G., N.C. and C.Q.; funding acquisition, P.C.-M. All authors have read and agreed to the published version of the manuscript.

Funding: The authors disclosed receipt of the following financial support for the research, authorship, and/or publication of this article: All the economic costs involved in the study will be borne by the research team. This work was supported in part by some grants from the European Social Fund 2014–2020. CITIC (Research Centre of the Galician University System) and the Galician University System (SUG) obtained funds through Regional Development Fund (ERDF) with 80%, Operational Programme ERDF Galicia 2014–2020 and the remaining 20% by the Secretaría Xeral de Universidades of the Galician University System (SUG). Specifically, the author PCM obtained a scholarship (Ref ED481A-2019/069) to develop the PhD thesis. On the other hand, the diffusion and publication of this research was funded by the CITIC, Research Centre of the Galician University System with the support previously mentioned (Ref ED431G 2019/01).

Institutional Review Board Statement: This study was approved by the Research Ethics Committee of A Coruña-Ferrol (ref. 2019/249) and Ethics Committee of the Faculty of Psychology and Education Science of the University of Porto (code: 2021/06-03).

Informed Consent Statement: Informed consent was obtained from all participants involved in the study. Written informed consent has been obtained from the participants to publish this paper.

Conflicts of Interest: The authors declare no conflict of interest.

Reference

1. Concheiro-Moscoso, P.; Groba, B.; Martínez-Martínez, F.J.; Miranda-Duro, M.d.C.; Nieto-Riveiro, L.; Pousada, T.; Queirós, C.; Pereira, J. Study for the Design of a Protocol to Assess the Impact of Stress in the Quality of Life of Workers. *Int. J. Environ. Res. Public Health* **2021**, *18*, 1413. [CrossRef]

Proceeding Paper

Address Space Layout Randomization Comparative Analysis on Windows 10 and Ubuntu 18.04 LTS [†]

Raquel Vázquez Díaz [1], Martiño Rivera-Dourado [1,2,*], Rubén Pérez-Jove [1,2], Pilar Vila Avendaño [1,2,3] and José M. Vázquez-Naya [1,2]

[1] Grupo RNASA-IMEDIR, Departamento de Ciencias de la Computación y Tecnologías de la Información, Facultade de Informática, Universidade da Coruña, Elviña, 15071 A Coruña, Spain; raquel.vazquez1@udc.es (R.V.D.); ruben.perez.jove@udc.es (R.P.-J.); pilar.vila@forensic-security.com (P.V.A.); jose@udc.es (J.M.V.-N.)

[2] Centro de Investigación CITIC, Universidade da Coruña, Elviña, 15071 A Coruña, Spain

[3] Forensic & Security, 15190 A Coruña, Spain

* Correspondence: martino.rivera.dourado@udc.es

[†] Presented at the 4th XoveTIC Conference, A Coruña, Spain, 7–8 October 2021.

Abstract: Memory management is one of the main tasks of an Operating System, where the data of each process running in the system is kept. In this context, there exist several types of attacks that exploit memory-related vulnerabilities, forcing Operating Systems to feature memory protection techniques that make difficult to exploit them. One of these techniques is ASLR, whose function is to introduce randomness into the virtual address space of a process. The goal of this work was to measure, analyze and compare the behavior of ASLR on the 64-bit versions of Windows 10 and Ubuntu 18.04 LTS. The results have shown that the implementation of ASLR has improved significantly on these two Operating Systems compared to previous versions. However, there are aspects, such as partial correlations or a frequency distribution that is not always uniform, so it can still be improved.

Keywords: ASLR; memory; comparative analysis; Windows; Ubuntu

1. Introduction

One of the main jobs performed by an Operating System is memory management. From a security perspective, there are plenty of attacks that leverage in the determinism of the memory space's layout to access and modify some parts of the memory. As an example of the most widespread ones, buffer overflow and string format must be mentioned.

In this context, ASLR (*Address Space Layout Randomization*) is a memory security mechanism which adds randomness into the virtual memory address space of a process. The aim of this technique is not to implement a patch to some specific problem, but making more difficult to exploit existing or future vulnerabilities.

The evolution and perfection of ASLR is notable during the last years. However, there exist an important amount of reports and studies that question the effectivity and solidity of this technique, even for the most recent Windows and Linux Operating Systems. In [1] Whitehouse performs a complete and detailed analysis of Windows Vista and, in its results, it reveals implementation errors that make the system not completely protected, situation that attackers can take advantage of to exploit memory vulnerabilities.

The main objective of this work was to base the methodology and transparerency on the Whitehouse study to obtain results of the real protection that offers ASLR, by comparing the behaviours and implementations on two recent distributions of Windows and Linux: Windows 10 and Ubuntu 18.04 LTS.

2. Materials and Methods

This section includes the methodology of the performed comparative analysis on the presented Operating Systems. Both the code and methodology are based on [1], but adapted to the modern versions of Windows and the specific features available on Linux.

2.1. Developed Code

The developed code [2], written in C for Linux and Windows, prints a log of the assigned memory addresses in each of the different areas of the process itself. With these logs, some bash scripts were crafted for the iterated execution of the tool, storing the memory addresses of each area in a CSV file. It is noteworthy that, for the compilation of the C programs, both Linux GCC and Windows WinGW compilers need concrete flags for ASLR to work.

In order to develop a comparative analysis for Windows and Linux, the code for both Operating Systems include almost identical verifications for memory addresses, from higher positions to lower ones: (1) stack, regarding variables inside a function; (2) heap, containing dynamic memory assignments; (3) BSS, where the uninitialized variables are kept; (4) data, regarding initialized static variables; (5) code.

In the case of Windows, the heap is verified by three means: creating a new heap, allocating memory in the heap and by using the malloc() function. Besides, the code for Windows also gets the PEB (*Process Environment Block*) address, which is a structure not existing in Linux. On the other hand, in Linux the code gets the heap address directly with the malloc() function. In the same way the Windows code gets the PEB address, the Linux code also gets addresses for some specific Linux memory parts like the VDSO (*Virtual Dynamic Shared Object*), as well as brk() and mmap() libraries.

2.2. Execution and Analysis

For the execution of the iterations, some batch and bash scripts were developed for Windows and Linux respectively, which are also available at [2]. These executions were performed in a PC with the following characteristics: AMD Athlon 64 ×2 4400+ with 4 GB de RAM. Regarding the specific releases of the Operating Systems, the tests were executed on Windows 10 10.0.17763 version and Ubuntu 18.04.2 LTS. In both of them, the scripts were run in two ways: continuously with 5 million iterations based on the work of Marco and Ripoll in [3]; and with system reboots each 100 iterations until reaching 500,000, considering a reasonable execution time and a significant number of repetitions, widely increased compared to the previous work of Whitehouse in [1].

Regarding the analysis, the logs resulting from the executions were pre-processed with the Pandas python library and then imported in Power BI Desktop, used as the main tool. The work is focused in the analysis of the level of entropy of the memory addresses, and the possible alterations compared with a desirable uniform distribution. For this purpose, we have used some techniques like pattern detection, correlations among areas, percentage of duplicated values and frequency distribution analysis.

3. Results and Conclusions

The first conclusion of this work is that the difference in the size of the user memory addressing space it is a determining factor in the behavioral differences between both Operating Systems. In Ubuntu, memory addresses present more entropy bits than in Windows, it presents a lower percentage of duplicated values and there exist fewer correlations among the different memory areas. In Windows, due to its memory addressing size, correlations seem not to be avoidable. Even though the addressing space in Ubuntu should be enough to avoid the correlations, they exist and in some cases are quite marked.

Regarding the frequency distribution in both systems, it tends to be uniform. It represents an improvement with respect to previous versions, as analyzed in Windows [1,4] and Linux [3,5]. However, in Windows the stack and PEB presents a bias towards lower memory addresses and in Linux, the percentage of repeated addresses in the VDSO is high.

Finally, the ratio of duplicated address values between the test without reboots and the test with reboots is higher in Ubuntu than in Windows. This factor can be understood as the impact of a reboot in the randomness of the addresses, and presents an unexpected behaviour. As shared libraries in Ubuntu are compiled as PIC, they take different virtual memory addresses in each process, in contrast with Windows where the values are equal between processes. Consequently, the impact of a reboot in Ubuntu should be lower on this matter in comparison with Windows. However, the results are higher in Ubuntu, maybe because of a specific characteristic in the implementation of ASLR in this Operating System.

In conclusion, ASLR has a better behaviour in Linux than in Windows, following the historical trend: it presents more entropy bits, less correlations and a better frequency distribution. However, considering its current memory addressing space, there are aspects that could be improved, like better correlation avoidance among the memory areas. In Windows, the correlation among memory areas is higher. In Windows 10, it would be convenient that the user memory addressing space was increased, for ASLR to be able to use more entropy bits and, in this way, the majority of the correlations would be avoided.

Author Contributions: Conceptualization, R.V.D., P.V.A. and J.M.V.-N.; methodology, R.V.D. and J.M.V.-N.; software, R.V.D.; validation, P.V.A. and J.M.V.-N.; investigation, R.V.D., P.V.A. and J.M.V.-N.; resources, P.V.A. and J.M.V.-N.; writing—original draft preparation, M.R.-D. and R.P.-J.; writing—review and editing, M.R.-D., R.P.-J. and J.M.V.-N.; supervision, P.V.A. and J.M.V.-N. All authors have read and agreed to the published version of the manuscript.

Funding: We wish to acknowledge the support received from the Centro de Investigación de Galicia "CITIC". CITIC, as Research Center accredited by Galician University System, is funded by "Consellería de Cultura, Educación e Universidade from Xunta de Galicia", supported in an 80% through ERDF, ERDF Operational Programme Galicia 2014–2020, and the remaining 20% by "Secretaría Xeral de Universidades" (Grant ED431G 2019/01). This work was also supported by the "Consellería de Cultura, Educación e Ordenación Universitaria" via the Consolidation and Structuring of Competitive Research Units—Competitive Reference Groups (ED431C 2018/49) and the COST Action 17124 DigForAsp, supported by COST (European Cooperation in Science and Technology, www.cost.eu, (accessed on 20 July 2021)).

Conflicts of Interest: The authors declare no conflict of interest.

Abbreviations

The following abbreviations are used in this manuscript:
PEB   Process Environment Block
VDSO   Virtual Dynamic Shared Object

References

1. Whitehouse, O. An Analysis of Address Space Layout Randomization on Windows Vista™. Symantec Advanced Threat Research, Tech. Rep. 2007. Available online: https://infocon.org/cons/Black%20Hat/Black%20Hat%20Europe/Black%20Hat%20Europe%202007/Presentations/bh-eu-07-whitehouse-WP-1.pdf (accessed on 20 July 2021).
2. rjetyk/aslr: Analysis and Comparative Study of Address Space Layout Randomization on Windows 10 and Ubuntu 18.04 LTS. Available online: https://github.com/rjetyk/aslr (accessed on 20 July 2021).
3. Ripoll-Ripoll, I.; Marco-Gisbert, H. Exploiting Linux and PaX ASLR's Weaknesses on 32- and 64-bit Systems. Black Hat 2016. Available online: https://paper.bobylive.com/Meeting_Papers/BlackHat/Asia-2016/asia-16-Marco-Gisbert-Exploiting-Linux-And-PaX-ASLRS-Weaknesses-On-32-And-64-Bit-Systems-wp.pdf (accessed on 21 July 2021).
4. Herrera Aristizabal, D.; Mora Rodríguez, D.; Yepes Guevara, R. Measuring ASLR Implementations on Modern Operating Systems. 2013 47th International Carnahan Conference on Security Technology (ICCST). Available online: https://ieeexplore.ieee.org/document/6922073 (accessed on 22 July 2021).
5. Ganz, J.; Peisert, S. ASLR: How Robust Is the Randomness? 2017 IEEE Cybersecurity Development. Available online: https://ieeexplore.ieee.org/abstract/document/8077804 (accessed on 22 July 2021).

Proceeding Paper

Towards a Semi-Automated Data-Driven Requirements Prioritization Approach for Reducing Stakeholder Participation in SPL Development [†]

María Isabel Limaylla *, Nelly Condori-Fernandez and Miguel R. Luaces

Database Lab. Elviña, Fac. Informática, Universidade da Coruña, CITIC, 15071 A Coruña, Spain; n.condori.fernandez@udc.es (N.C.-F.); miguel.luaces@udc.es (M.R.L.)
* Correspondence: maria.limaylla@udc.es
† Presented at the 4th XoveTIC Conference, A Coruña, Spain, 7–8 October 2021.

Abstract: Requirements prioritization (RP), part of Requirements engineering (RE), is an essential activity of Software Product-Lines (SPL) paradigm. Similar to standard systems, the identification and prioritization of the user needs are relevant to the software quality and challenging in SPL due to common requirements, increasing dependencies, and diversity of stakeholders involved. As prioritization process might become impractical when the number of derived products grows, recently there has been an exponential growth in the use of Artificial Intelligence (AI) techniques in different areas of RE. The present research aims to propose a semi-automatic multiple-criteria prioritization process for functional and non-functional requirements (FR/NFR) of software projects developed within the SPL paradigm for reducing stakeholder participation.

Keywords: multiple-criteria prioritization; Software Product Line; Artificial Intelligence (AI) techniques

1. Introduction

Requirements prioritization (RP) is an important activity of requirements management, however, this activity can become a complex process in a family of products projects, due to common requirements, increasing dependencies, and diversity of stakeholders involved. In most prioritization method, such as Hundred Dollar, MoSCoW and Numerical Assignment Technique (NAT), the participation of stakeholders are essential to provide the prioritization criteria based on their expertise [1]. In this respect, Hujainah et al. [2] suggest the exclusion of users from tasks that can be automated, and include them only in important tasks that generate value.

In the latest years, the application of AI techniques in several stages in Software Engineering has been increasing and will continue growing [3]. We argue that it is possible to take advantage of these techniques to exploit information and discover new criteria, to decrease the stakeholder's participation.

In this paper, we focus mainly on those activities that can be automated for identifying a set of prioritization criteria and generating a list of ranked requirements. We also analyzed the available datasets and discuss their main limitations. In the next section, the proposed process is shown in detail.

2. A Semi-Automated Data-Driven Requirements Prioritization Process

The proposed process consists of two phases, Criteria Identification Phase and Requirements Prioritization Phase. A summary of the proposal is shown in Figure 1.

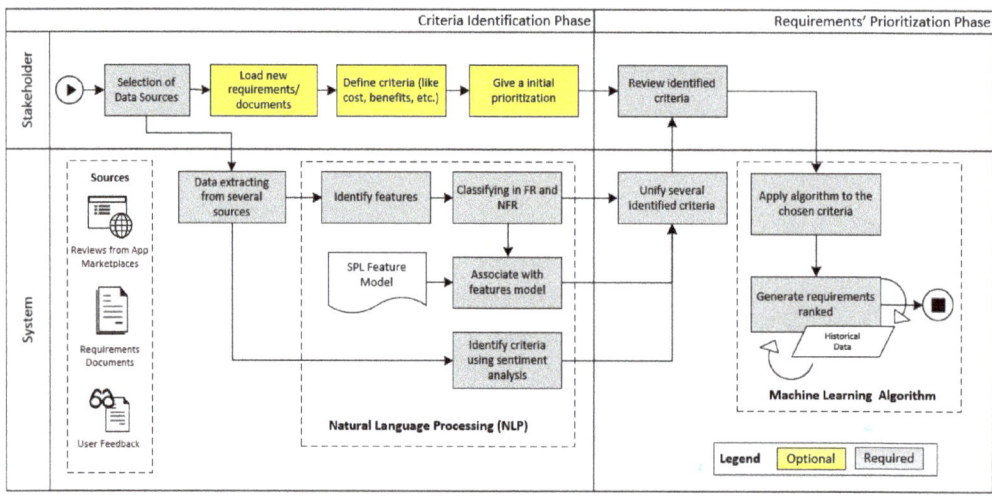

Figure 1. Data sources and AI techniques used for prioritizing requirements of SPL projects.

2.1. Criteria Identification Phase

In this first phase, multiple prioritization criteria are identified with the minimum stakeholder participation. This phase starts with the data sources selection carried out by the analyst, and, optionally, loading new requirements and criteria. Then, the data is automatically collected by extracting and analyzing data from several sources, like reviews from App Marketplaces and requirements' formal documents. After collection, Natural Language Processing (NLP) techniques can be used to identify features (features are distinctive characteristics or properties of a family of systems) and associating them with existing features in feature models. Feature models are diagrams in SPL projects that show features in a hierarchical structure and conceptual relationships among features [4]. These features can be previously prioritized and new prioritization criteria can be obtained when associating the new features with the existing ones. Moreover, thanks to the use of sentiment analysis, we aim to identify sentiment and deontic in user reviews, which can provide another type of prioritization criteria. A (supervised or non-supervised) classification algorithm is used to perform the classification in FR/NFR. This classification can be used as other criteria, due to the importance of some NFRs like security or performance, considered crucial to the quality of systems. All these criteria can be obtained automatically, without the participation of stakeholders.

2.2. Requirements Prioritization Phase

In the Second Phase, a requirements prioritization is performed based on criteria previously identified. All these criteria require to be unified and summarized in order to provide more understandable information. At this point, stakeholders can review the prioritization criteria, by confirming those that are relevant for the project. Once the criteria are selected, the prioritization is performed automatically by means of a machine learning algorithm. Algorithms such as Machine-Learned ranking, classification algorithms like Decision Tree or Random Forest, and even Deep Learning algorithms in combination with others algorithms can be used in this process. Finally, the output of this process is a list of ranked requirements. This will be saved as historical data for future use.

2.3. Datasets

Datasets are an essential component of any machine learning model. PROMISE [5] is a dataset used in most of the research for FR/NFR classification. This dataset has 625 requirement sentences, with 255 identified as functional and 370 as non-functional requirements. The NFR is labeled with the following types: Availability, Legal, Look and feel, Maintainability, Operational, Performance, Scalability, Security, Usability, Fault tolerance, and Portability. However, it presents unbalanced data in the categories of NFR. The unbalanced data can affect the precision and recall metrics of several classification algorithms, and generate a biased model. There are several ways to address this problem. Down-sampling in the majority classes is one technique, but it could lose valuable data. Synthetic data generation (Up-sampling) is another technique, that using some algorithms to create data that follow the tend of the minority classes. Balanced ensemble learning refers to the use of multiple learning machines and combines their outputs to obtain a better prediction.

For requirements prioritization methods based on supervised algorithms, RALIC [6] is a dataset used for some research. RALIC dataset contains several data about ratings and recommendations of requirements by stakeholders. This dataset is used in traditional methods and in machine learning methods for predicting the value of a rating from stakeholders.

Both datasets are in the English language. These datasets are good references but more datasets, especially in Spanish, are needed. This implies collecting historical requirements and carrying out their labeling, get balanced and standardized data and ensure enough quantity for training, testing and validation.

3. Conclusions

In this article, we presented a data-driven requirements prioritization process that can be used in SPL projects. The proposed prioritization process aims to reduce mainly the stakeholder participation through the identification of additional criteria to avoid some risks like disagreement between stakeholders and lack of time. We rely on AI techniques, like NLP and Machine Learning algorithms, to optimize mainly the criteria identification by exploiting information from different data sources. We also review two datasets that are used for FR/NFR classification and for requirements prioritization. As a result of this review, some of their limitations (e.g., imbalanced datasets), and the necessity of new datasets were identified.

Institutional Review Board Statement: Not applicable.

Informed Consent Statement: Not applicable.

Data Availability Statement: Publicly available PROMISE dataset [7] and RALIC dataset [6] were analyzed in this study.

References

1. Hudaib, A.; Masadeh, R.; Qasem, M.H.; Alzaqebah, A. Requirements Prioritization Techniques Comparison. *Mod. Appl. Sci.* **2018**, *12*, 62. [CrossRef]
2. Hujainah, F.; Bakar, R.B.A.; Abdulgabber, M.A.; Zamli, K.Z. Software Requirements Prioritisation: A Systematic Literature Review on Significance, Stakeholders, Techniques and Challenges. *IEEE Access* **2018**, *6*, 71497–71523. [CrossRef]
3. Barenkamp, M.; Rebstadt, J.; Thomas, O. Applications of AI in classical software engineering. *AI Perspect.* **2020**, *2*, 1–15. [CrossRef]
4. Lee, K.; Kang, K.C.; Lee, J. Concepts and guidelines of feature modeling for product line software engineering. In *Lecture Notes in Computer Science, Proceedings of the International Conference on Software Reuse, Austin, TX, USA, 15–19 April 2002*; Springer: Berlin/Heidelberg, Germany, 2002; pp. 62–77.
5. Sayyad Shirabad, J.; Menzies, T. *The PROMISE Repository of Software Engineering Databases*; School of Information Technology and Engineering, University of Ottawa: Ottawa, ON, Canada, 2005.
6. Lim, S.L.; Finkelstein, A. StakeRare: Using social networks and collaborative filtering for large-scale requirements elicitation. *IEEE Trans. Softw. Eng.* **2012**, *38*, 707–735. [CrossRef]
7. Cleland-Huang, J.; Mazrouee S.; Huang L.; Port, D. *nfr [Data Set]*; Zenodo: Geneva, Switzerland, 2007. [CrossRef]

Proceeding Paper

Bootstrap Selector for the Smoothing Parameter of Beran's Estimator [†]

Rebeca Peláez Suárez [1,*], Ricardo Cao Abad [2] and Juan M. Vilar Fernández [2]

[1] Research Group MODES, Department of Mathematics, CITIC, University of A Coruña, 15071 A Coruña, Spain
[2] Research Group MODES, Department of Mathematics, CITIC, University of A Coruña and ITMATI, 15071 A Coruña, Spain; ricardo.cao@udc.es (R.C.A.); juan.vilar@udc.es (J.M.V.F.)
* Correspondence: rebeca.pelaez@udc.es
[†] Presented at the 4th XoveTIC Conference, A Coruña, Spain, 7–8 October 2021.

Abstract: This work proposes a resampling technique to approximate the smoothing parameter of Beran's estimator. It is based on resampling by the smoothed bootstrap and minimising the bootstrap approximation of the mean integrated squared error to find the bootstrap bandwidth. The behaviour of this method has been tested by simulation on several models. Bootstrap confidence intervals are also addressed in this research and their performance is analysed in the simulation study.

Keywords: Beran's estimator; survival analysis; bootstrap; bandwidth selector; confidence intervals

1. Introduction

Let $\{(X_i, Z_i, \delta_i)\}_{i=1}^n$ be a simple random sample of (X, Z, δ) with X being the covariate, $Z = \min\{T, C\}$ the observed variable and $\delta = I_{T \leq C}$ the uncensoring indicator. Usually, T is the time until the occurrence of an event and C is the censoring time. The generalised product-limit estimator of the conditional survival function proposed in [1] is given by

$$\widehat{S}_h^B(t|x) = \prod_{i=1}^n \left(1 - \frac{I_{\{Z_i \leq t, \delta_i = 1\}} w_{n,i}(x)}{1 - \sum_{j=1}^n I_{\{Z_j < Z_i\}} w_{n,j}(x)}\right) \quad (1)$$

where

$$w_{n,i}(x) = \frac{K((x - X_i)/h)}{\sum_{j=1}^n K((x - X_j)/h)}$$

with $i = 1, \ldots, n$ and $h = h_n$ is the bandwidth for the covariable. This estimator depends on a smoothing parameter which is, in practice, unknown. Therefore, finding a method for automatic selection of this bandwidth is truly interesting and very helpful in the analysis of real data subject to censoring. Bootstrap confidence intervals of $S(t|x)$ are also proposed.

2. Bandwidth Selector

Let $rI_h \subset \mathbb{R}$ be an appropriate pilot bandwidth. The bootstrap resampling algorithm consists of generating $U_i \sim U(0,1)$ and $V_i \sim K$ and obtaining

$$X_i^* = X_{[nU_i]+1} + rV_i,$$

$$Z_i^* = Z_{[nU_i]+1},$$

$$\delta_i^* = \delta_{[nU_i]+1},$$

for each $i = 1, \ldots, n$. The bootstrap sample is formed as $\{(X_i^*, Z_i^*, \delta_i^*)\}_{i=1}^n$.

The optimal smoothing parameter is the bandwidth that minimizes the mean integrated squared error given by:

$$MISE_x(h) = E\left(\int \left(\widehat{S}_h(t|x) - S(t|x)\right)^2 dt\right).$$

Then, the bootstrap bandwidth is obtained by minimizing the Monte Carlo approximation of the bootstrap MISE defined as follows

$$MISE_x^*(h) \simeq \frac{1}{B}\sum_{j=1}^{B}\left(\int \left(\widehat{S}_h^{*(j)}(t|x) - \widehat{S}_r(t|x)\right)^2 dt\right),$$

where $\widehat{S}_r(t|x)$ is the Beran survival estimation with pilot bandwidth r using the original sample $\{(X_i, Z_i, \delta_i)\}_{i=1}^n$, $\widehat{S}_h^{*(j)}(t|x)$ is the Beran survival estimation with bandwidth h using the bootstrap resample $\{(X_i^{*(j)}, Z_i^{*(j)}, \delta_i^{*(j)})\}_{i=1}^n$, and B the number of bootstrap resamples.

3. Bootstrap Confidence Intervals

Let $h \in I_h \subset \mathbb{R}$ be an appropriate smoothing parameter and fixed values $(t, x) \in [a, b] \times I$, the bootstrap confidence interval for a confidence level of $1 - \alpha$ is given by

$$\left(\widehat{S}_r(t|x) - \frac{p_{1-\alpha/2}}{\sqrt{nh}}, \widehat{S}_r(t|x) - \frac{p_{\alpha/2}}{\sqrt{nh}}\right),$$

where $\widehat{S}_r(t|x)$ is the Beran estimation with the pilot bandwidth r that is used in the bootstrap resampling, and $p_{\alpha/2}$ and $p_{1-\alpha/2}$ are the $100\alpha/2$ and $100(1-\alpha/2)$ percentiles of the resampling distribution of $\sqrt{nh}(\widehat{S}_h^*(t|x) - \widehat{S}_r(t|x))$, being $\widehat{S}_h^*(t|x)$ the Beran survival estimation of the bootstrap resample.

4. Simulation Study

A simulation study is carried out to analyse the behaviour of the bootstrap algorithm previously described. Several models with different conditional probabilities of censoring were considered. Figure 1 shows the bootstrap estimations of the conditional survival function in two of these scenarios: Model 1 considers the Weibull distribution for life and censoring times and Model 2 considers exponential life and censoring times. Both models have a conditional probability of censoring equal to 0.5. Figure 2 shows the bootstrap confidence intervals in one sample from Models 1 and 2.

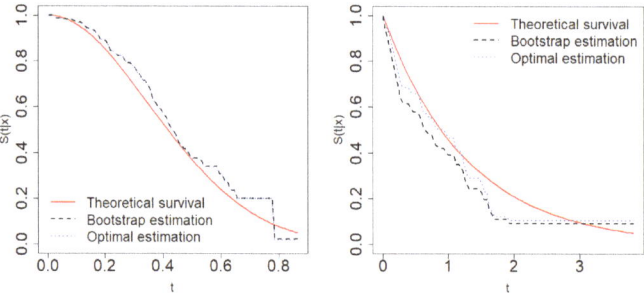

Figure 1. Theoretical survival function $S(t|x)$ (solid line), Beran's estimation with optimal bandwidth (dotted line) and Beran's estimation with bootstrap bandwidth (dashed line) for Model 1 (**left**) and Model 2 (**right**).

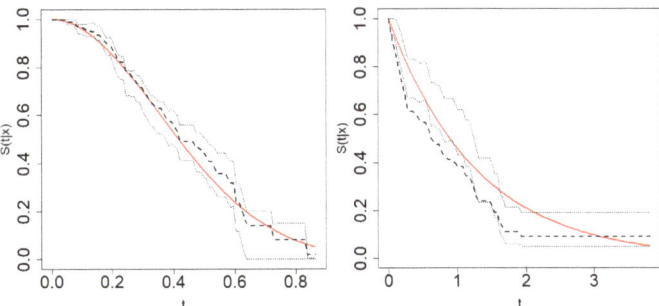

Figure 2. Theoretical survival function (solid line), Beran's estimator with bootstrap bandwidth (dashed line) and the bootstrap confidence intervals (dotted line) for each t in a grid of size $n_t = 100$ in Model 1 (**left**) and Model 2 (**right**).

5. Conclusions

The results of the simulations show that this bootstrap algorithm provides adequate smoothing parameters to estimate the survival function in this context. The bootstrap bandwidths obtained are similar to the optimal ones and the estimation errors of both are quite similar. Bootstrap confidence intervals have a reasonable behaviour.

Future lines of work focus on developing a method for choosing the bidimensional smoothing parameters involved in the doubly smoothed Beran estimator presented in [2]. In addition, we deal with the construction of confidence intervals for the conditional survival function based on the doubly smoothed Beran estimator.

Funding: This research has been supported by MINECO Grant MTM2017-82724-R, and by the Xunta de Galicia (Grupos de Referencia Competitiva ED431C-2016-015 and Centro Singular de Investigación de Galicia ED431G/01), all of them through the ERDF.

References

1. Beran, R. *Nonparametric Regression with Randomly Censored Survival Data*; Technical Report; University of California: Los Angeles, CA, USA, 1981.
2. Peláez Suárez, R.; Cao Abad, R.; Vilar Fernández, J.M. Nonparametric Estimation of the Conditional Survival Function with Double Smoothing. *SORT* **2021**, *45*.

Proceeding Paper

Succinct Data Structures in the Realm of GIS [†]

Nieves R. Brisaboa, Pablo Gutiérrez-Asorey, Miguel R. Luaces and Tirso V. Rodeiro *

Database Lab. Elviña, CITIC, Universidade da Coruña, 15071 A Coruña, Spain; nieves.brisaboa@udc.es (N.R.B.); pablo.gutierrez@udc.es (P.G.-A.); miguel.luaces@udc.es (M.R.L.)
* Correspondence: tirso.varela.rodeiro@udc.es
[†] Presented at the 4th XoveTIC Conference, A Coruña, Spain, 7–8 October 2021.

Abstract: Geographic Information Systems (GIS) have spread all over our technological environment in the last decade. The inclusion of GPS technologies in everyday portable devices along with the creation of massive shareable geographical data banks has boosted the rise of geoinformatics. Despite the technological maturity of this field, there are still relevant research challenges concerning efficient information storage and representation. One of the most powerful techniques to tackle these issues is designing new Succinct Data Structures (SDS). These structures are defined by three main characteristics: they use a compact representation of the data, they have self-index properties and, as a consequence, they do not need decompression to process the enclosed information. Thus, SDS are not only capable of storing geographical data using as little space as possible, but they can also solve queries efficiently without any previous decompression. This work introduces how SDS can be successfully applied in the GIS context through several novel approaches and practical use cases.

Keywords: data structures; geoinformatics; geographic information systems

1. Introduction

Since the dawn of mankind, we have been trying to capture the geography that surrounds us in an attempt to establish order in nature. From the very beginning of our species, we were forced to memorize important locations in order to survive; little by little we improved our cartographic skills until the current degree of sophistication. Currently, Geographic Information Systems (GIS) are still one of the most important tools in our society. Almost every gadget tracks its position or uses some kind of map. The rise of modern GIS can be understood via two main reasons:

- The improvements to Global Positioning Systems (GPS) technologies that enable all kinds of devices to geolocate any object with the highest precision.
- The popularization of massive geographic data banks.

On the one hand, advances in GPS techniques have allowed accurate sensors to become cheaper and disseminated all over the technological ecosystem. On the other hand, it was also necessary to design and implement shareable geographic data banks in order to represent within them the information of interest gathered by GPS (e.g., points, trajectories, etc.).

These new features translated directly to a constant production of large amounts of data that can be exploited in order to optimize a wide range of tasks and ease our daily life (e.g., package tracking, food delivery, etc.). Accordingly, an interest in programs able to handle trajectories and geographical information systems has grown in recent years, giving birth to all kinds of algorithms and systems that are able to locate mobile objects in real time or recover any past trajectory, attending to some user-defined criteria.

2. Succinct Data Structures

One of the most effective techniques to fight against the exponential growth of big data scenarios is compression. A vast amount of compression algorithms have been proposed in almost every context of computer science, trying to reduce as much as possible the space used. However, the aim of this field is not just to store information by reducing the space used but also to avoid interactions with secondary memory as much as possible. Usually, the information used in computers is too large to fit in primary memory, so it is necessary to load it by parts, one part at a time; this loading process is so slow that it would be preferable to perform more operations (e.g., decompression) in the main memory than to load more data from the disk.

The most common approach to achieving compression is based on *repetitiveness*. Usually, compression algorithms search for repeated chunks of data and store them as few times as possible. Sometimes, repetitiveness is not found in an individual bank of data by itself, but it does appear when compared with others. For example, DNA strands are not particularly repetitive themselves; however, different samples of the same species' genome are so similar to one another that they can be represented by their similarities and differences with respect to reference DNA.

In recent years, a new branch in the compression field has attracted a lot of attention: Succinct Data Structures (SDS). These structures tackle the space usage issue, but, in opposition to traditional approaches, they are autoindexes. Thus, the ultimate goal of SDS is to store information in a compact way while still being able to use the compacted data, i.e., perform queries without any decompression process, or at least a minimal decompression.

3. Trips over Public Transport Networks

Inhabitants of large cities increasingly choose public transport (bus, train, etc.) as their first option to move around the city. Common public transport systems should provide users with basic information about the available offerings (at least timetables, lines and stops). One of the main challenges of these systems is matching the available offerings with the historical passengers' demand. For this purpose, they need to gather information regarding how users move along the network. With the increasing use of passenger tracking technology on public transport networks (e.g., smart cards), it is now becoming possible to assemble (or accurately estimate) the actual trips a given user made along a network.

We introduced in [1] a new flexible representation based on efficient indexes [2] that support the analysis of the historical demand in real transport networks. A naive approach to represent the trips of each passenger would be to store the sequence of the traversed stops, e.g., $< S1, S5, S8, S9 >$. However, as all passengers of a bus are traversing the same stops at the same times, we just need to store that a user boards or leaves a vehicle following the journey j of line l at a given stop s, as a triple (s, l, j). Since we want to represent a user trip as a sequence of such stages, and it holds that the final stop of a stage and the starting stop of the next stage are the same (or close in walking distance), it is not necessary to explicitly represent the final stop of each stage, except for the final stop.

This solution requires less than half the space compared to a plain (not indexed) representation, while also being capable of directly solving queries about users' movement patterns such as *how many users start their trips at stop X and end at stop Y* or any of its combinations (e.g., filtering by line, only using initial stops, etc.).

4. Free Trajectories of Ships Furrowing the Sea

Millions of vessels sail across the oceans almost without movement constraints, i.e., describing free trajectories. Once again, this is a big data scenario with geographic information involved. The easiest way to apply compression techniques is to find a repetitive sequence in those arbitrary movements. Our work [3] focuses on speed and direction. The aim is to exploit the fact that in many applications, trajectories tend to be similar to others, wholly or piecewise. Thus, instead of storing all the real geographical positions measured by the GPS devices as traditional solutions, our work stores *snapshots* of the positions of all the objects at regular time intervals and the sequence of relative movements between snapshots (*logs*). As the trajectory of a vessel is not likely to perform sharp turns, the direction and the speed of the boat will remain constant for a while, translating into a sequence of repeated directions. One efficient way to capture these logs is spiral encoding, that is, using a grid with its center cell representing the vessel position in a particular snapshot and the surrounding cells representing reachable areas, each one with a different identifier (e.g., the log of a vessel traveling at slow speed to the east during two time instants and then turning to the southeast would be represented as $<1,1,2>$). Accordingly, the snapshots are saved in efficient spatial indexes, while well-known compression techniques [4] can be applied over the logs.

Our proposal can efficiently solve a wide range of queries (time-slice, time-interval and k-nearest neighbor queries) while reducing the raw data to 4–7% of its original size (two orders of magnitude less space than traditional spatio-temporal indexes).

5. Indoor Trajectories in a Nursing Home

Health care facilities are the perfect environment to track repetitive trajectories. As all the movement happens inside a building, the map where all the trajectories take place turns out to be a graph, each node/cell of the graph being a particular room [5]. Usually, the residents do not have much path diversity, so they need to roam through the same rooms throughout the day, generating massive repetitive trajectories. For example, it is likely that all residents perform the sequence *bedroom–bathroom–dining room* every single day.

Thus, in our last work [6], we presented a new approach to deal with these repetitive trajectories based on enhanced compression techniques. We designed and implemented a whole system capable of tracking the daily movements of residents and caregivers. The actual positioning data are gathered through Bluetooth Low-Energy (BLE) strategically placed all over the nursing home. Essentially, we use the sequence of room identifiers as the trajectory of a particular user. Then, our structure stores this information in a compact way, avoiding repetitiveness without resorting to random access.

Our solution reaches compression ratios of 1.44% with high-repetitive datasets, surpassing even well-known solutions such as *gzip* or *7zip* (both without random access capabilities). Furthermore, our proposal can perform random subtrajectory retrieval (30 position window) in roughly 25 µs.

6. Conclusions and Future Work

Despite the maturity level of the current Geographic Information Systems, there is still room for improvements, specifically regarding data storage and data management. In this paper we have introduced several success stories in different contexts where Succinct Data Structures and Geographic Information Systems work together to achieve higher efficiency.

For future work, we will pay attention not only to storage capabilities and retrieval performance but also to transmission times, in an attempt to send a smaller number of points of a geometry through aggregation.

Funding: This work is partially funded by the CITIC research center funded by Xunta/FEDER-UE 2014-2020 Program, ED431G 2019/01. MICINN(PGE/ERDF) [EXTRA-Compact: PID2020-114635RB-I00].

Institutional Review Board Statement: Not applicable.

Informed Consent Statement: Not applicable.

References

1. Brisaboa, N.R.; Fariña, A.; Galaktionov, D.; Rodeiro, T.V.; Rodríguez, M.A. New Structures to Solve Aggregated Queries for Trips over Public Transportation Networks. In Proceedings of the String Processing and Information Retrieval 25th International Symposium, (SPIRE), Lima, Perú, 9–11 October 2018; pp. 88–101.
2. Sadakane, K. New text indexing functionalities of the compressed suffix arrays. *J. Algorithms* **2003**, *48*, 294–313. [CrossRef]
3. Brisaboa, N.R.; Gómez-Brandón, A.; Navarro, G.; Paramá, J.R. GraCT: A Grammar-based Compressed Index for Trajectory Data. *Inf. Sci.* **2019**, *483*, 106–135. [CrossRef]
4. Larsson, N.J.; Moffat, A. Offline dictionary-based compression. In Proceedings of the Data Compression Conference, (DCC99), Snowbird, Utah, 29–31 March 1999; pp. 296–305.

5. IndoorGML OGC. Available online: www.indoorgml.net (accessed on 26 July 2021).
6. Fariña, A.; Gutiérrez-Asorey, P.; Ladra, S.; Penabad, M.R.; Rodeiro, T.V. A Compact Representation of Indoor Trajectories. *IEEE Pervasive Comput.* under review.

Proceeding Paper

Numerical Simulations and Modal Analysis to Investigate the Defects in a Coating Process [†]

David Barreiro-Villaverde [1,2,*], Marcos Lema [1] and Anne Gosset [3]

1. CITIC Research, Campus de Elviña, Universidade da Coruña, 15071 A Coruña, Spain; marcos.lema@udc.es
2. Von Karman Institute for Fluid Dynamics, Waterloosesteenweg 72, B-1640 Sint-Genesius-Rode, Belgium
3. Technological Research Center (CIT), Campus de Esteiro, Universidade da Coruña, 15403 Ferrol, Spain; anne.gosset@udc.es
* Correspondence: david.barreiro1@udc.es
† Presented at the 4th XoveTIC Conference, A Coruña, Spain, 7–8 October 2021.

Abstract: This work investigates the hydrodynamics of jet wiping, a coating process in which a thin slot gas jet impinges on a coating film dragged by a moving strip; thus, reducing the coating thickness and developing a run-back flow. The interaction between the liquid film and the gas jet is highly unsteady, producing long-wavelength defects on the final product known as undulations. We perform Computational Fluid Dynamics (CFD) simulations of the process using High-Performance Computing (HPC) resources. A multi-scale modal analysis is then applied to decrypt the mechanism of wave formation. The main undulation pattern features two-dimensional waves and is correlated with a large-scale motion of the gas jet.

Keywords: computational fluid dynamics (CFD); high-performance computing (HPC); numerical simulations; multi-scale modal analysis; coating process; multiphase flows

1. Introduction

Jet wiping is a contactless coating technique used to control the thickness of a thin film. It is intensively used in hot-dip galvanization, where the steel substrate is dipped into a molten zinc bath at 460 °C, dragging a coating layer on its surface as it is withdrawn vertically from the bath. The film thickness is reduced and controlled by a slot gas jet normally impinging on the liquid film; thus, acting as an air knife. The final coating mass applied on the substrate is a function of several process parameters represented in Figure 1: the nozzle to substrate stand-off distance, Z, the nozzle slot opening, d, the substrate speed, U_p, and the gas jet velocity, U_j.

Over a large portion of the process operational window, the final coating film displays long-wavelength patterns that alter the quality of the product (Figure 1). In a recent experimental study, the liquid film and gas flows were characterized simultaneously for several wiping conditions [1]. The spectral matching observed between the gas jet and the liquid flow suggested that the undulations are produced by a two-phase coupling instability, although the complete mechanism could not be captured. The present work aims at understanding the two-phase interaction that, ultimately, leads to undulation, using Computational Fluid Dynamics (CFD) simulations and a multi-scale modal analysis.

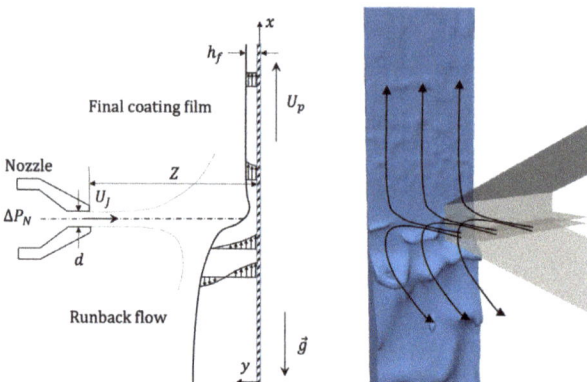

Figure 1. Two-dimensional sketch of the jet wiping process (**left**) and rendering of the flow patterns in the film for laboratory wiping conditions (**right**).

2. Methodology

We performed high-fidelity simulations of the jet wiping process in laboratory scale conditions, as described in Mendez et al. [1]. For that purpose, the incompressible two-phase flow solver InterFoam of the CFD open-source libraries OpenFOAM wass used. The numerical model was based on the Volume of Fluid (VOF) technique, to account for the two-phase nature of the problem, and Large Eddy Simulation (LES) for the treatment of turbulence in the gas jet. Its complete validation has recently been published [2].

The mesh features 10–12 M computational nodes, and the time step ranges between 1.5×10^{-6} and 7×10^{-7} s. The flow governing equations were solved numerically using 288 Intel E5-2680v3 CPUs at the Centro de Supercomputación de Galicia (CESGA), consuming a total of 3M CPU hours of priority access granted by the Spanish Supercomputing Network (RES). The flow datasets were post-processed using Modal Analysis, which consists in splitting the data as a linear combination of elementary contributions (modes). The multi-scale Proper Orthogonal Decomposition (mPOD) [3] is a data-driven decomposition—which means that the basis is built from the data itself—that classifies the modes according to their energy and frequency content; thus, featuring structures that are coherent in time and space. In this work, the mPOD was applied for the analysis of the final film flow in order to isolate the main undulation patterns. In a next step, an extended mPOD was implemented to detect the structures in the gas jet that were strictly linked to the formation of the undulation. The latter was based on the projection of the gas fields onto the temporal basis of the dominant modes of the film flow.

3. Results and Discussion

The modal decomposition of the high-fidelity simulations revealed the most relevant scales in the two-phase mechanism of wave formation. Figure 2 shows a comparison between the original and the mPOD filtered spatial normalized thickness distribution for one time step. This approximation featured a two-dimensional travelling wave pattern built from two of the most energetic modes with comparable energy and delayed $\pi/2$ in both space and time. It was remarkable how well the film flow was approximated using only a pair of mPOD modes.

The filtered gas velocity fields in Figure 3 were retrieved using the extended mPOD. The small scales observed in the original velocity fields were clearly uncorrelated with the coating waves and, therefore, were irrelevant for the mechanism of wave formation. In contrast, the undulations were well correlated with a large-scale deflection of the lower side jet, induced by the passage of large waves on the run-back flow.

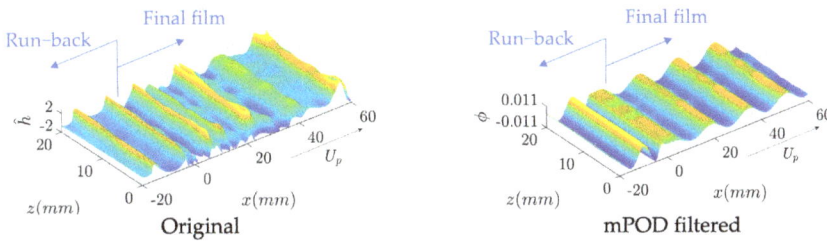

Figure 2. Snapshot of the original and mPOD filtered normalized thickness distributions.

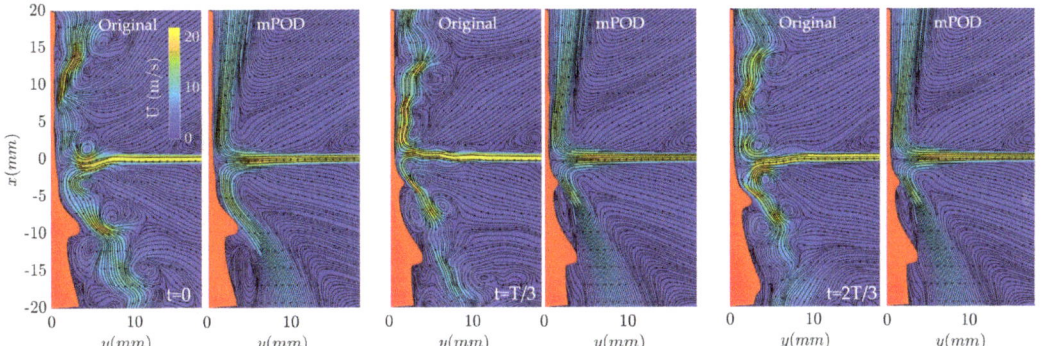

Figure 3. Snapshots of the original and mPOD filtered velocity fields for three time steps in a period T of wave formation. The instantaneous liquid film is represented in red.

4. Conclusions

The combination of high-fidelity CFD simulations and a multi-scale modal analysis allowed decrypting the main mechanism at the origin of undulation defects in jet wiping. For the wiping configuration under study, the final coating exhibited two-dimensional wave patterns originating at the location of the jet impact, due to the unsteady confinement produced by the passage of waves in the run-back flow. The mPOD is an excellent tool to identify coherent patterns in fluid flows; the filtered datasets retained the most relevant features of the flow with only two modes, achieving a compression rate of 1000.

Author Contributions: Conceptualization, D.B.-V. and A.G.; methodology, D.B.-V.; software, D.B.-V.; validation, D.B.-V. and A.G.; formal analysis, M.L.; investigation, A.G.; resources, M.L.; data curation, D.B.-V.; writing—original draft preparation, D.B.-V.; writing—review and editing, M.L. and A.G.; visualization, D.B.-V.; supervision, M.L. and A.G.; project administration, M.L.; funding acquisition, M.L. All authors have read and agreed to the published version of the manuscript.

Funding: The research project was funded by Arcelor-Mittal and D.Barreiro-Villaverde was financially supported by Xunta de Galicia with the pre-doctoral grant "Programa de axudas á etapa predoutoral" (ED481A-2020/018).

Data Availability Statement: The data that support the findings of this study are available on request from the corresponding author. The data are not publicly available due to privacy restrictions.

Acknowledgments: The authors also wish to thank the "Red Española de Supercomputación" for the attribution of special computational resources at FinisTerrae II (CESGA) and Tirant (UV) (FI-2018-3-0040, FI-2019-1-0044).

Conflicts of Interest: The authors declare no conflict of interest. The funders had no role in the design of the study; in the collection, analyses, or interpretation of data; in the writing of the manuscript, or in the decision to publish the results.

References

1. Mendez, M.A.; Gosset, A.; Buchlin, J.M. Experimental analysis of the stability of the jet wiping process, part II: Multiscale modal analysis of the gas jet-liquid film interaction. *Exp. Therm. Fluid Sci.* **2019**, *106*, 48–67. [CrossRef]
2. Barreiro-Villaverde, D.; Gosset, A.; Mendez, M. On the dynamics of jet wiping: Numerical simulations and modal analysis. *Phys. Fluids* **2021**, *33*, 062114. [CrossRef]
3. Mendez, M.A.; Balabane, M.; Buchlin, J.M. Multi-scale proper orthogonal decomposition of complex fluid flows. *J. Fluid Mech.* **2019**, *870*, 988–1036. [CrossRef]

Proceeding Paper

Simulation of the Fluid–Structure Interaction in Fishing Nets [†]

Sergio Roget [1],*, Marcos Lema [1] and Anne Gosset [2]

1. CITIC Research, Universidade da Coruña, Campus de Elviña, 15071 A Coruña, Spain; marcos.lema@udc.es
2. Technological Research Center (CIT), Universidade da Coruña, Campus de Esteiro, 15403 Ferrol, Spain; anne.gosset@udc.es
* Correspondence: sergio.roget@udc.es
† Presented at the 4th XoveTIC Conference, A Coruña, Spain, 7–8 October 2021.

Abstract: The main objective of this work is the development of a Computational Fluid Dynamics model coupled with a structural code for the simulation and optimization of fishing gears. As fishing nets are highly deformable structures under the influence of incident water, the use of merely empirical correlations for hydrodynamic forces, such as those used in many structural codes, does not provide precise predictions for their behaviour. The coupling between the structural problem and the hydrodynamic effects makes it necessary to tackle the problem through a new "fluid–structure interaction" approach, which is described here. Preliminary results obtained with the CFD model are also presented.

Keywords: computational fluid dynamics (CFD); fluid–structure interaction (FSI); porous media; trawl nets

1. Introduction

The fishing industry involves activity that is fundamental to supplying quality food to the world's population, and it constitutes a very important livelihood in coastal areas. Industrial fishing is carried out mainly by trawling gear, which consists of a bag-shaped net, towed by one or more boats, that captures the species that are in its path.

Currently, the fishing industry faces two challenges: the improvement of its energy efficiency and the elimination of discards. The best way to face these challenges is to reduce the drag coefficient of the nets and improve their selectivity.

Designing selective fishing gear is a very complex process, and it is mainly based on the expertise of fishermen and marine biologists, together with expensive tests in the open sea or in towing tanks. Nowadays, the design of gear cannot rely on Computational Fluid Dynamics (CFD) simulations of complete fishing nets because of their complex geometry and the high computational power required. With the idea to develop a simplified approach with a reduced computational cost, Patursson et al. [1] and Zhao et al. [2] propose the idea of modeling a net as a porous medium to simulate the hydrodynamic behaviour of the water flow in the structure using CFD computations.

On the other hand, the deformation of fishing nets during their operation affects their hydrodynamic behaviour. Therefore, the accurate simulation of a trawl also needs to account for structure deformation. Two-way coupling between hydrodynamic and structural models requires the implementation of a co-simulation method between a CFD model and a Finite Element Method (FEM) model of the net, following a fluid–structure interaction (FSI) approach. Zou et al. [3] propose a first approximation with one-way simulations, in which the net deformation is computed based on the hydrodynamic forces applied to the flat net. In this work, we simulate the implementation of two-way coupling between the net structure and the fluid by establishing data communication between a CFD and an FEM model. It is carried out in two steps:

- The development of a CFD model based on the use of porous surfaces for the simulation of the hydrodynamic behaviour of a fishing net.

- The implementation of co-simulation between the CFD and FEM models of a net.

2. Methodology

For the hydrodynamic model, open-source CFD libraries OpenFoam are used, which are based on the finite volume method. As for the FEM model, the choice of data is still pending further tests. The development of the final two-way coupled tool involves a series of milestones:

- The development of a CFD model based on the use of porous surfaces for the hydrodynamic behaviour of fishing net modeling, which includes the estimation of the appropriate porosity coefficients and validation of the results with experimental and numerical data.
- The implementation of co-simulation between the CFD model and an FEM model providing two-way solutions:
  - The implementation of a communication protocol between the CFD model and the FEM model.
  - The establishment and implementation of a calculation strategy based on a computational cost/accuracy ratio.

3. Preliminary Results

We are currently working on the development of the CFD model. The idea is to firstly simulate a net sample with highly detailed geometry, and validate the predictions in terms of drag and lift forces with data from the literature. This step requires a long testing procedure, in which the solver parameters are calibrated, and the minimum level of geometric details is determined in order to obtain precise results. Once the numerical results are available, we will start to develop a method to obtain the porosity parameters that lead to the same drag and lift forces as the complete net. This methodology allows the number of experiments to be reduced, leaving them only for the final validation stage.

In the first simulations, the net was idealized as a set of cylinders and spheres arranged in the shape of a cross, as described in the study by Lader et al. [4], and shown in Figure 1. Currently, two of the five configurations studied experimentally by Lader et al. [4] were simulated for a single flow velocity (0.6 m/s). The results are shown in Figure 2, where configuration 1 refers to a net without knots, and configuration 3 to a net with medium-sized knots. According to Figure 2, the CFD predictions are in good agreement with the experimental results for configuration 1. In contrast, the drag forces generated by the knot and the upper cylinder are underestimated for configuration 3. We intend to improve the numerical results by refining the mesh and adjusting the turbulence models with different wall roughnesses.

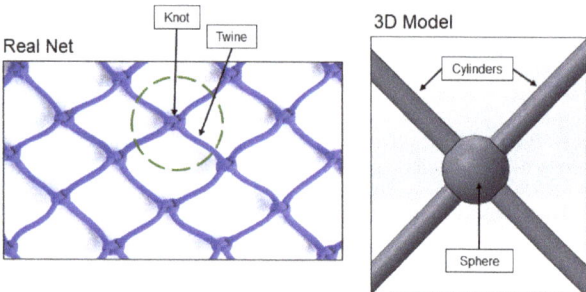

Figure 1. Real net (**left**) and idealization with cylinders and spheres (**right**).

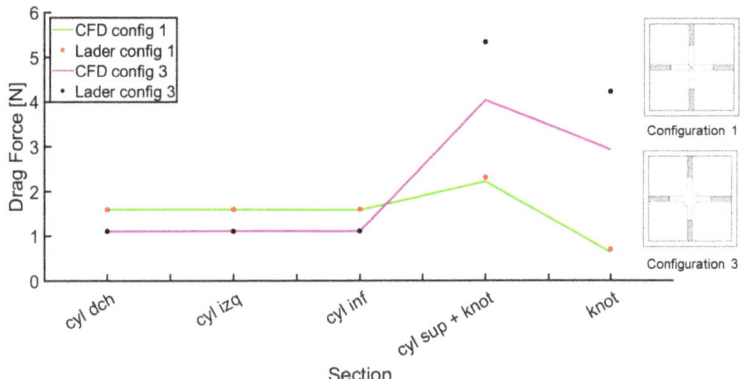

Figure 2. Results obtained by numerical simulations based on the experiments carried out by Lader et al. [4].

These simulations will be refined until a consistent relationship is achieved between the complexity of the net geometry and the accuracy of the data, since it is essential to obtain a reliable numerical model that provides the correct drag and lift forces of the net. These forces are essential data in order to obtain the porosity parameters that will allow the geometry of the net to be replaced with a porous surface.

Author Contributions: Conceptualization, S.R. and A.G.; methodology, S.R.; software, S.R.; validation, S.R., A.G.; formal analysis, M.L.; investigation, A.G.; resources, M.L.; data curation, S.R.; writing—original draft preparation, S.R.; writing—review and editing, M.L. and A.G.; visualization, S.R.; supervision, M.L. and A.G.; project administration, M.L.; funding acquisition, M.L. All authors have read and agreed to the published version of the manuscript.

Funding: Sergio Roget Mourelle is financially supported by CITIC (Centro de Investigación en Tecnologías de la Información y las Comunicaciones) with contract ED431G 2019/01—CITIC MINECO.

Institutional Review Board Statement: Not applicable.

Informed Consent Statement: Not applicable.

Data Availability Statement: The data that support the findings of this study are available on request from the corresponding author. Tha data are not publicaly available due to privacy restrictions.

Acknowledgments: The authors wish to thank the "Red Española de Supercomputación" for the attribution of special computational resources at FinisTerrae II (CESGA).

Conflicts of Interest: The authors declare no conflict of interest. The funders had no role in the design of the study; in the collection, analyses, or interpretation of data; in the writing of the manuscript, or in the decision to publish the results.

References

1. Patursson, O.; Swift, M.R.; Tsukrov, I.; Simonsen, K.; Baldwin, K.; Fredriksson, D.W.; Celikkol, B. Development of a porous media model with application to flow through and around a net panel. *Ocean Eng.* **2010**, *37*, 314–324. [CrossRef]
2. Zhao, Y.P.; Bi, C.W.; Dong, G.H.; Gui, F.K.; Cui, Y.; Guan, C.T.; Xu, T.J. Numerical simulation of the flow around fishing plane nets using the porous media model. *Ocean Eng.* **2013**, *62*, 25–37. [CrossRef]
3. Zou, B. The deformation characteristics and flow field around knotless polyethylene netting based on fluid structure interaction (FSI) one-way coupling. *Aquac. Fish.* **2020**. [CrossRef]
4. Lader, P.; Enerhaug, B.; Fredheim, A.; Klebert, P.; Pettersen, B. Forces on a cruciform/sphere structure in uniform current. *Ocean Eng.* **2014**, *82*, 180–190. [CrossRef]

Proceeding Paper

Using Reinforcement Learning in the Path Planning of Swarms of UAVs for the Photographic Capture of Terrains [†]

Alejandro Puente-Castro [1,*], Daniel Rivero [1], Alejandro Pazos [1,2] and Enrique Fernandez-Blanco [1]

1. Faculty of Computer Science, CITIC, University of A Coruña, 15071 A Coruña, Spain; daniel.rivero@udc.es (D.R.); alejandro.pazos@udc.es (A.P.); enrique.fernandez@udc.es (E.F.-B.)
2. Biomedical Research Institute of A Coruña (INIBIC), University Hospital Complex of A Coruña (CHUAC), 15006 A Coruña, Spain
* Correspondence: a.puentec@udc.es
† Presented at the 4th XoveTIC Conference, A Coruña, Spain, 7–8 October 2021.

Abstract: The number of applications using unmanned aerial vehicles (UAVs) is increasing. The use of UAVs in swarms makes many operators see more advantages than the individual use of UAVs, thus reducing operational time and costs. The main objective of this work is to design a system that, using Reinforcement Learning (RL) and Artificial Neural Networks (ANNs) techniques, can obtain a good path for each UAV in the swarm and distribute the flight environment in such a way that the combination of the captured images is as simple as possible. To determine whether it is better to use a global ANN or multiple local ANNs, experiments have been done over the same map and with different numbers of UAVs at different altitudes. The results are measured based on the time taken to find a solution. The results show that the system works with any number of UAVs if the map is correctly partitioned. On the other hand, using local ANNs seems to be the option that can find solutions faster, ensuring better trajectories than using a single global network. There is no need to use additional map information other than the current state of the environment, like targets or distance maps.

Keywords: UAV swarm; path planning; reinforcement learning; Q-learning; artificial neural network; terrain

1. Introduction

There are more and more applications for the collective use of Unmanned Aerial Vehicles (UAVs), more known UAV swarms. In addition to the advantages of the individually usage of these systems, the main motivation for swam usage is the reduction of flight time and operating costs together with increased fault tolerance [1]. Advances in the creation of algorithms [2] and telecommunications [3] allow us to have collective systems that are practically autonomous in their entirety. Thus, it is not necessary to have an operator per vehicle. Currently there are few systems that solve these path planning problems in the literature oriented to agricultural and forestry use, especially dedicated to the optimization of field survey tasks. This sector can be strongly benefited by the group use of aircraft. Therefore, the main field of application of this project is field prospecting.

This objective of this paper is to develop a system for solving the Path Planning problem with 2D grid-based maps adapted to UAVs' sensors with different number of UAVs using Q-Learning techniques.

2. Materials and Methods

This section describes the calculation used for the extraction of the flight maps and the proposed method for the calculation of the flying paths, each described in its corresponding subsection.

2.1. Flight Maps

For the calculation of the flight maps, the cell size is calculated as the projection of the capture area of the sensors on the terrain based on the image size, the flight height and the lens angle of view. In order to better combine the captured data, the smallest area among all UAVs is chosen to take advantage of the overlapping of those with larger capture areas.

No previous information is extracted from the calculated grid-map to direct the calculation of the paths in order to avoid biases. However, by storing also information such as the position of the drones and the cells already visited at each moment, it is possible to provide a great amount of information in real time in order to improve the calculation of the paths.

2.2. Proposed Model

The proposed model for the calculation of the paths is a variation of the Q-Learning algorithm [4]. In this Reinforcement Learning algorithm (RL) [5] the calculation of the q-values is predicted based on an Artificial Neural Network (ANN) [6] with two fully-connected layers with sigmoid activations and the RMSprop optimizer.

To obtain better results in less time, a Hill-Climbing policy [7] is followed to update the rewards received by the UAVs as they move. A training strategy using Memory Replay [8] has also been followed.

Another inherent problem with the proposed models is their configuration with respect to UAVs. There are two possibilities: first, to use a single global ANN for all UAVs; and, second, to use an ANN for each UAV, or local ANN. The first proposal requires less computational resources, but the path calculation for one UAV can be distorted with erroneous information from the paths of the other UAVs. On the other hand, the second approach requires more computational resources, but each ANN is specialized only for each UAV.

3. Results

For the experiments, simulations were carried out in the terrain of the CITIC research center. The metric of interest is the flight time taken to find a solution as it influences the energy consumption of each UAV. Resuls are listed at Table 1.

Table 1. Table summarizing the best times for each experiment with different numbers of UAVs and ANN configurations.

	ANN Configuration	
Number of UAVs	Global ANN	One ANN per UAV
1 UAV	00:02:19	00:02:19
2 UAVs	00:02:24	00:00:58
3 UAVs	00:01:25	00:01:39
4 UAVs	00:03:00	00:01:13
5 UAVs	00:03:32	00:01:47

4. Conclusions

The calculation of flight path calculation of UAV swarms is approachable by Q-Learning with small full-connected ANNs. This makes the system faster and more efficient than others found in the literature. Thus, facilitating its use by other users. Minimizing the time taken to find each solution is a satisfactory metric that is rarely used by other authors. However, it is one of the most realistic since it is not possible to predict the battery consumption since it depends on other external factors such as the incident wind. One ANN per UAV is usually the best option. As the number of UAVs increases the time taken to find a solution does not grow much more, unlike a global ANN.

Funding: This research received no external funding.

Institutional Review Board Statement: Not applicable.

Informed Consent Statement: Not applicable.

Acknowledgments: The authors would like to thank the support from NVidia corp., which granted the GPU used in this work. They also acknowledge the support from the CESGA, where many of the preliminary tests were run.

Abbreviations

The following abbreviations are used in this manuscript:

UAV   Unmanned Aerial Vehicle
RL   Reinforcement Learning
ANN   Artificial Neural Network

References

1. Yeaman, M.L.; Yeaman, M. *Virtual Air Power: A Case for Complementing ADF Air Operations with Uninhabited Aerial Vehicles*; Air Power Studies Centre: New Delhi, India, 1998.
2. Zhao, Y.; Zheng, Z.; Liu, Y. Survey on computational-intelligence-based UAV path planning. *Knowl.-Based Syst.* **2018**, *158*, 54–64. [CrossRef]
3. Campion, M.; Ranganathan, P.; Faruque, S. A review and future directions of UAV swarm communication architectures. In Proceedings of the 2018 IEEE International Conference on Electro/Information Technology (EIT), Rochester, MI, USA, 3–5 May 2018; pp. 0903–0908.
4. Sutton, R.S.; Barto, A.G. *Reinforcement Learning: An Introduction*; MIT Press: Cambridge, MA, USA, 2018.
5. Wiering, M.; Van Otterlo, M. Reinforcement learning. *Adapt. Learn. Optim.* **2012**, *12*, 3.
6. Hopfield, J.J. Artificial neural networks. *IEEE Circuits Devices Mag.* **1988**, *4*, 3–10. [CrossRef]
7. Kimura, H.; Yamamura, M.; Kobayashi, S. Reinforcement learning by stochastic hill climbing on discounted reward. In *Machine Learning Proceedings 1995*; Elsevier: Amsterdam, The Netherlands, 1995; pp. 295–303.
8. Foerster, J.; Nardelli, N.; Farquhar, G.; Afouras, T.; Torr, P.H.; Kohli, P.; Whiteson, S. Stabilising experience replay for deep multi-agent reinforcement learning. International conference on machine learning. *PMLR* **2017**, *70*, 1146–1155.

Proceeding Paper

Tool for SPARQL Querying over Compact RDF Representations †

Delfina Ramos-Vidal [1,2,*] and Guillermo de Bernardo [1,*]

1 Centro de Investigación CITIC, Universidade da Coruña, 15071 A Coruña, Spain
2 Departmento de Inteligencia Artificial, Universidad Politécnica de Madrid, 28040 Madrid, Spain
* Correspondence: delfina.ramos@udc.es (D.R.-V.); gdebernardo@udc.es (G.d.B.)
† Presented at the 4th XoveTIC Conference, A Coruña, Spain, 7–8 October 2021.

Abstract: We present an architecture for the efficient storing and querying of large RDF datasets. Our approach seeks to store RDF datasets in very little space while offering complete SPARQL functionality. To achieve this, our proposal was built over HDT, an RDF serialization framework, and its interaction with the Jena query engine. We propose a set of modifications to this framework in order to incorporate a range of space-efficient compact data structures for data storage and access, while using high-level capabilities to answer more complicated SPARQL queries. As a result, our approach provides a standard mechanism for using low-level data structures in complicated query situations requiring SPARQL searches, which are typically not supported by current solutions.

Keywords: RDF; SPARQL; compact data structures

1. Introduction

Massive volumes of data must be efficiently gathered and processed in the era of the Internet in which we are constantly generating more information. In recent years, significant effort has been devoted to develop mechanisms to share data in standardized, machine-readable formats, leading to the so-called Web of Data. The Resource Description Framework (RDF) defines a common framework to describe resources using URIs to name associations between items. An RDF graph can be conceptually represented as a labeled graph or as a set of *triples*. The W3C also promotes SPARQL, a querying standard for RDF, which utilizes an SQL-like language. SPARQL specifies queries via graph pattern matching, imposing limitations on the resultant RDF subgraphs. At the core of SPARQL are triple patterns, which define basic matching with the collection of triples in the RDF graph.

The RDF standard only specifies a conceptual representation of data as a graph, not a specific data storage format. As a result, RDF may be stored in a variety of formats, and a slew of RDF storage solutions, or *RDF* stores, have surfaced in recent years. Several full-featured RDF query engines, such as Virtuoso and Jena, provide full SPARQL support and can handle large RDF datasets [1]. However, in recent years, a number of solutions based on compact data structures have arisen, with the goal of reducing the storage space while still providing efficient querying. Even though database-like solutions function well and fully support SPARQL, compact data structures have been proven to outperform the former in several areas, particularly for simpler query operations such as basic triple-pattern searches.

Compact data structures designed to store RDF usually divide the problem into two parts. On the one hand, there is a Triples component, which stores each RDF triple (s, p, o) assuming that its components are integer identifiers (IDs). On the other hand, a dictionary component holds the mapping from the original strings of the RDF dataset to IDs, allowing the conversion from string to ID and versa. This leads to extremely specialized string dictionaries, such as libCSD [2] and specialized methods for storing RDF triples encoded as integer IDs, such as K2-triples [3] or RDFCSA [4]. These solutions have been shown to be able to store RDF datasets in small spaces and perform very efficiently to answer basic triple-pattern and other simple queries. The HDT library [5] provides a standard framework for the common representational notion of dictionary encoding, which divides an RDF dataset into three components (header, dictionary, and triples), and provides default implementations for the dictionary and triples. The main issue with most of these solutions based on compact data structures is that they do not completely support SPARQL; instead, they are designed to efficiently serve a limited number of queries using very specialized methods. For example, some solutions may only allow triple-pattern queries or basic join patterns.

In this paper, we present an architecture for the representation of RDF datasets that aim to provide a common framework for the representation of RDF based on compact data structures. Our approach seeks to store RDF data in little space while supporting sophisticated SPARQL searches. Our proposal has immediate applications as a common testing framework for compact data structures that have never been tested in complex SPARQL query scenarios.

2. Our Proposal

We propose an architecture that combines fully fledged RDF engines' high-level capabilities with the compression performance of low-level compact data structures. We developed a prototype tool as an extension of the HDT Java library, a solution that proposes a relatively compact representation of RDF and provides SPARQL support through an integration with Apache Jena and Jena ARQ. We take advantage of this SPARQL support and aim to avoid the main drawback of this library: the data structures used for the dictionary and triples, while reasonably efficient, are much larger than other alternatives such as K2-triples. Our tool extends this framework to allow the utilization of different underlying representations for the storage of the RDF dictionary and triples components. This way, our tool provides a simple mechanism to incorporate and test different data structures using a common framework involving SPARQL queries. Particularly, our solution provides a simple mechanism to integrate existing solutions implemented in C/C++, using Java Native Interface (JNI) to transparently incorporate these structures into our extended HDT Java framework. Currently, we have a functional prototype that integrates the K2Triples and libCSD libraries, state-of-the-art representations able to efficiently compress RDF triples and RDF dictionaries, respectively, the two main components used in the HDT framework to store RDF data. A conceptual overview of the suggested framework can be seen in Figure 1.

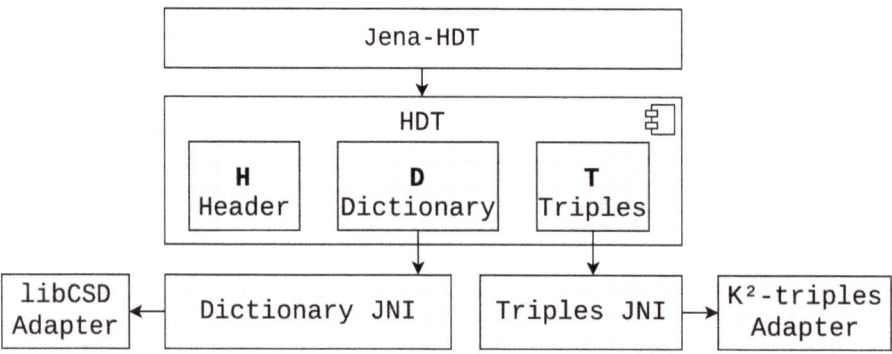

Figure 1. Architecture diagram.

The main advantage of this proposal is the possibility to integrate fully functional alternatives, commonly implemented in C or C++, alternatives that are already known for efficiently solving basic problems. These techniques are not usually applied to solve bigger problems such as SPARQL, due to the additional cost of specifically redesigning all of the

SPARQL queries processing mechanisms for each case. The proposed framework can take care of the high-level query processing, so that future integrations only need to build a specific adapter to query the desired data structure from the JNI extensions defined in our proposal, either for the dictionary or the triples component.

The proposed solution was tested with a dataset generated by the Berlin SPARQL Benchmark, containing 35 million triples. We compressed the data using the different components provided by our framework—first by using the original components given by the HDT library; secondly, by only using the component for the JNI triples and only the component for the JNI dictionary. Lastly, we compressed the dataset combining both JNI triples and dictionary components. A small sample of the results for this experiment can be seen in Table 1. The queries listed below include filters, unbound predicates, unions, result modifiers such as LIMIT, ORDER BY and DISTINCT, and the DESCRIBE operator.

Table 1. Comparison of query execution times for different compression techniques.

	HDT Components	JNITriples	JNIDictionary	JNI Components
Q1 (ms)	331	1573	349	2012
Q2 (ms)	239	202	252	270
Q3 (ms)	363	4738	356	4501
Q4 (ms)	238	214	281	265

Our JNIDictionary implementation is based on plain front coding (PFC), a technique for compressed string dictionary that is also used by the original HDT library. It can be seen that the JNIDictionary component achieves similar results to the original HDT components. Considering that both solutions use similar implementations, but JNIDictionary has the additional cost of translating from Java to C++, the competitive results suggest that the dictionary overhead can be reduced in this scenario. On the other hand, JNITriples is slower, since K^2-triples is much more compact than the solution posed by HDT but is also expected to be slower in many queries. Therefore, JNITriples is competitive in query times for the simpler queries, but significantly slower overall.

3. Conclusions and Future Work

Our proposal is currently a fully functional prototype, but we intend to improve it further in order to provide a competitive and flexible framework in the future. Upgrades in the scalability of the underlying compact data structures at construction time, as well as performance overheads owing to the usage of JNI, are currently possible. We also want to test a variety of state-of-the-art compact representations that should be simple to integrate into the existing framework and might lead to specific enhancements for various SPARQL query operations for specific implementations. As a result, our approach provides a standard framework for evaluating the performance of low-level data structures for RDF representation, as well as potential improvements.

Funding: This research was funded by Xunta de Galicia/FEDER grant ED431G 2019/01, Xunta de Galicia/FEDER-UE grant IN852A 2018/14; Ministerio de Ciencia, Innovación y Universidades grants [TIN2016-78011-C4-1-R; PID2019-105221RB-C41]; Consellería de Cultura, Educación e Universidade/Consellería de Economía, Empresa e Innovación/GAIN/Xunta de Galicia grant ED431C 2021/53; and by MICINN (PGE/ERDF) grant PID2020-114635RB-I00.

Institutional Review Board Statement: Not applicable.

Informed Consent Statement: Not applicable.

Data Availability Statement: Berlin SPARQL Benchmark http://wifo5-03.informatik.uni-mannheim.de/bizer/berlinsparqlbenchmark/.

References

1. Nitta, K.; Savnik, I. Survey of RDF storage managers. In Proceedings of the Advances in Databases, Knowledge, and Data Applications (DBKDA), Chamonix, France, 20 April 2014; pp. 148–153.
2. Martínez-Prieto, M.A.; Brisaboa, N.R.; Cánovas, R.; Claude, F.; Navarro, G. Practical compressed string dictionaries. *Inf. Syst.* **2016**, *56*, 73–108. [CrossRef]
3. Álvarez-García, S.; Brisaboa, N.R.; Fernández, J.D.; Martínez-Prieto, M.A.; Navarro, G. Compressed vertical partitioning for efficient RDF management. *Knowl. Inf. Syst.* **2015**, *44*, 439–474. [CrossRef]
4. Cerdeira-Pena, A.; Fariña, A.; Fernández, J.; Martínez-Prieto, M.A. Self-indexing RDF archives. In Proceedings of the Data Compression Conference (DCC), Snowbird, UT, USA, 30 March–1 April 2016; pp. 526–535.
5. Fernández, J.D.; Martínez-Prieto, M.A.; Gutierrez, C.; Polleres, A.; Arias, M. Binary RDF representation for publication and exchange (HDT). *J. Web Semant.* **2013**, *19*, 22–41. [CrossRef]

Proceeding Paper

Performance Optimization of a Parallel Error Correction Tool [†]

Marco Martínez-Sánchez *, Roberto R. Expósito and Juan Touriño

Computer Architecture Group, CITIC, Universidade da Coruña, 15071 A Coruña, Spain; rreye@udc.es (R.R.E.); juan@udc.es (J.T.)
* Correspondence: marco.msanchez@udc.es
† Presented at the 4th XoveTIC Conference, A Coruña, Spain, 7–8 October 2021.

Abstract: Due to the continuous development in the field of Next Generation Sequencing (NGS) technologies that have allowed researchers to take advantage of greater genetic samples in less time, it is a matter of relevance to improve the existing algorithms aimed at the enhancement of the quality of those generated reads. In this work, we present a Big Data tool implemented upon the open-source Apache Spark framework that is able to execute validated error-correction algorithms at an improved performance. The experimental evaluation conducted on a multi-core cluster has shown significant improvements in execution times, providing a maximum speedup of 9.5 over existing error correction tools when processing an NGS dataset with 25 million reads.

Keywords: high performance computing; Big Data; bioinformatics; Next Generation Sequencing

1. Introduction

In recent years, the development of effective and fast techniques for processing large volumes of genetic data has gained relevance due to the need of counting on these reads for the evolution of biology-related scientific fields. As a direct consequence of this necessity, new approaches to solve this problem have been presented throughout the last decade under the name of Next Generation Sequencing (NGS) [1]. However, even though these technologies are able to read amounts of genetic samples that are orders of magnitude larger than the previous alternatives [2], they still do not have an insignificant error rate for their generated reads. Hence, multiple algorithms have been proposed in the literature to correct these mistakes in the samples and make up higher quality reads. Among them, CloudEC [3] is a Big Data tool built upon the Apache Hadoop framework [4] that is able to perform corrections to genetic datasets by running multiple steps of alignments of the input samples, and replacing the bases with the lowest qualities of all those aligned samples with another representations of higher quality.

At the same time, significant progress has also been made in the Big Data field, where for many years some of the main approaches were based on the MapReduce paradigm [5], a programming model proposed by Google that defines multiple programmable and non-programmable phases to decouple the data transformation logic from the communication and load distribution tasks. However, some alternatives have also been proposed with this goal in mind, as it is with the Apache Spark framework [6], that are able to relieve both the data scientists and Big Data developers from directly operating with the MapReduce framework and allow them to tackle with a higher-level API. Moreover, this programming interface also comes with some optimizations not usually found in another technologies, such as the lazy computational model and the usage of the main memory for storing the data instead of secondary storage.

In this context, it makes sense to develop a new tool aimed at solving the computational challenges introduced when correcting large NGS datasets, taking advantage of Apache Spark to improve the performance of existing error correction algorithms.

2. Development

With this work, we are proposing a parallel tool able to process input FASTQ reads, an extended unaligned sequence format, also supporting the specific format internally used by CloudEC. The overall workflow of the tool can be decomposed in the six phases shown in Figure 1, which basically consist of: two mandatory stages at the beginning and the end of the pipeline to preprocess the input and format the output, respectively; two error correction phases that implement different algorithms each one; and, finally, two filtering stages that are able to tag the input reads with auxiliary information for the error correction phases. This processing pipeline is also used in the original CloudEC tool, which has served as the underlying baseline for our Spark-based implementation.

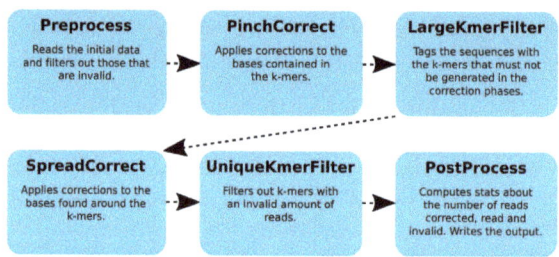

Figure 1. The six phases of the error correction tool.

For the development of our proposal, the baseline tool have been redesigned and reimplemented from scratch by replacing the Hadoop framework with Apache Spark. Since the error correction algorithms implemented by CloudEC are based on the alignment of nucleotide subsequences from the input reads, it is expected to significantly improve performance given the ability of Spark to store this temporary alignment data in the main memory instead of on a disk.

3. Experimental Evaluation

To determine the performance improvements provided by our proposal over the original CloudEC tool, the experimental evaluation has been carried out on the Pluton cluster of the Computer Architecture Group. In particular, the cluster nodes used in the experiments consist of two Intel Xeon E5-2660 octa-core processors at 2.2 GHz (i.e., 16 cores per node), 64 GiB of main memory, and one 1 TiB local SATA disk intended for intermediate data storage during the executions.

In order to provide reproducible results, the datasets used in the experiments have been obtained from SRA [7], an open repository for genomic reads. In particular, this evaluation has been conducted using two public datasets in FASTQ format whose specific features are shown in Table 1.

Table 1. Tag, SRA accessor identifier and features of the public datasets used in the experiments.

Tag	Identifier	Number of Sequences	Sequence Length
D1	SRR034509	10,353,618	202 bp
D2	SRR4291508	25,232,347	100 bp

Regarding software settings, the evaluation was undertaken with Spark 2.3.4 and Hadoop 2.9.2. Additionally, all the experiments were executed using OpenJDK 1.8.0_242. Finally, the length of the k-mers (i.e., the length of the subsequences that were used for the alignment tasks) has been set to 24 (k = 24) for both tools to ensure a fair comparison.

4. Results and Conclusions

Table 2 provides the execution times of our tool and the speedups over CloudEC for both datasets when using different number of nodes. These results show that our implementation significantly outperforms CloudEC for all the scenarios under evaluation. The maximum speedups are obtained when using 13 nodes: 2.8× and 9.5× for D1 and D2 datasets, respectively. Note that the speedups obtained are clearly higher for D2, which contains twice as many reads as D1 (see Table 1), showing the benefits of our tool when processing more compute-intensive datasets. Moreover, the scalability is improved when compared to CloudEC, as can be noted by the fact that the speedups increase monotonically with the number of nodes.

Table 2. Results of the performance evaluation of our tool. The execution times are shown in seconds for each dataset and number of cluster nodes. The speedup provided by our tool over CloudEC is shown in parentheses.

Dataset	5 Nodes	9 Nodes	13 Nodes
D1	4865 (2.4×)	1885 (2.6×)	1113 (2.8×)
D2	7473 (5.8×)	2484 (8.2×)	1511 (9.5×)

Overall, these results are very encouraging, proving that the Spark-based implementation is able to handle realistically sized NGS datasets, providing results in bounded times that are even lower than the execution times of another tools of the state of the art.

Author Contributions: Conceptualization, R.R.E. and J.T.; methodology, M.M.-S., R.R.E. and J.T.; implementation, M.M.-S.; validation, M.M.-S.; writing—original draft preparation, M.M.-S.; writing—review and editing, R.R.E. and J.T. All authors have read and agreed to the published version of the manuscript.

Funding: This research was funded by the Ministry of Science and Innovation of Spain (PID2019-104184RB-I00/AEI/10.13039/501100011033), and by Xunta de Galicia and FEDER funds of the European Union (Centro de Investigación de Galicia accreditation 2019-2022, ref. ED431G2019/01; Consolidation Program of Competitive Reference Groups, ref. ED431C 2021/30).

Institutional Review Board Statement: Not applicable.

Informed Consent Statement: Not applicable.

Conflicts of Interest: The authors declare no conflict of interest.

References

1. Sang Tae, P.; Jayoung, K. Trends in Next-Generation Sequencing and a new era for Whole Genome Sequencing. *Int. Neurol. J.* **2016**, *20* (Suppl. S2), S76–S83.
2. McCombie, W.R.; McPherson, J.D.; Mardis, E.R. Next-Generation Sequencing technologies. *Cold Spring Harb. Perspect. Med.* **2019**, *9*, a036798. [CrossRef] [PubMed]
3. Chung, W.; Ho, J.; Lin, C.; Lee, D.T. CloudEC: A MapReduce-based algorithm for correcting errors in next-generation sequencing Big Data. In Proceedings of the 2017 IEEE International Conference on Big Data, Boston, MA, USA, 11–14 December 2017; pp. 2836–2842.
4. O'Driscoll, A.; Daugelaite, J.; Sleator, R.D. 'Big data', Hadoop and cloud computing in genomics. *J. Biomed. Inf.* **2013**, *46*, 774–781. [CrossRef] [PubMed]
5. Dean, J.; Ghemawat, S. MapReduce: Simplified data processing on large clusters. *Commun. ACM* **2008**, *51*, 107–113. [CrossRef]
6. Zaharia, M.; Xin, R.S.; Wendell, P.; Das, T.; Armbrust, M.; Dave, A.; Meng, X.; Rosen, J.; Venkataraman, S.; Franklin, M.J.; et al. Apache Spark: A unified engine for Big Data processing. *Commun. ACM* **2016**, *59*, 56–65. [CrossRef]
7. Leinonen, R.; Sugawara, H.; Shumway, M. The Sequence Read Archive. *Nucleic Acids Res.* **2010**, *39* (Suppl. 1), D19–D21. [CrossRef] [PubMed]

Proceeding Paper

COVID-19 Digital Vaccination Passport Based on Blockchain with Its Own Cryptocurrency as a Reward and Mobile App for Its Use [†]

Mauro Alberto de los Santos Nodar [1,*] and Tiago Manuel Fernández Caramés [1,2,*]

1. Department of Computer Engineering, Faculty of Computer Science, Universidade da Coruña, 15071 A Coruña, Spain
2. Centro de Investigación CITIC, Universidade da Coruña, 15071 A Coruña, Spain
* Correspondence: mauro.delossantos@udc.es (M.A.d.l.S.N.); tiago.fernandez@udc.es (T.M.F.C.)
† Presented at the 4th XoveTIC Conference, A Coruña, Spain, 7–8 October 2021.

Abstract: Due to the recent outbreak of the COVID-19 pandemic, everybody's lives have changed dramatically and society went through new stages accompanied by new needs. This article details a solution for one of these needs, since it provides a system of digital certificates for the secure storage and sharing of medical data related to COVID-19, with the goal of demonstrating immunity or lack of viral infection in a unequivocal, unbreakable and secure way. The proposed system is based on Blockchain and its inherent benefits, developing also a decentralized, mobile and multiplatform app for its use and an incentive system with a customized cryptocurrency in order to reward the users who use it.

Keywords: blockchain; smart contract; Ethereum; cryptocurrency; COVID-19; digital vaccination passport; immunity certificate; distributed mobile application; kotlin mobile multiplatform

1. Introduction

Due to the global health emergency of COVID-19, declared by the WHO (World Health Organization) in 2020, a series of new stages and problems have appeared in our society that have to be faced. In particular, this paper describes a solution for one of them: the storage and use of all medical information regarding COVID-19. This solution consists of a decentralized blockchain-based secure system with automated intelligence for the storage of the most relevant COVID-19 medical information (vaccines and tests) and includes a cross-platform mobile decentralized app (Dapp) to make use of the system and a cryptocurrency to offer a way to incentivize the users who employ the system. The purpose of the project is to benefit all parties involved in its use and to improve the current pandemic situation from a public health perspective by providing a means to demonstrate immunity or lack of viral infection in order to alleviate or eliminate certain social constraints caused by the pandemic. It will also benefit health authorities by creating a compact, unbreakable and homogenous system for storing all COVID-19 information, with a high degree of scalability and potential for future exploitation. Finally, it will benefit businesses whose normal operations are affected by the pandemic (e.g., restaurants, hotels, pubs) by creating sanitary-safe environments and by providing a greater economic gain from the easing of restrictions (e.g., increased seating spots and opening hours), as well as by implementing its own commerce system that can be used as an incentive to be exploited by both parties, customers and business.

To the knowledge of the authors, the proposed solution, as described, has not been previously proposed in the literature, although similar projects are available that implement different parts of the system, such as different approaches to provide COVID-19 certificates [1], the use of blockchain-based medical information and incentives [2] or the management of private blockchains, smart contracts and cryptocurrencies [3,4].

2. Design and Implementation

Figure 1 depicts a diagram of the communications architecture of the proposed system, showing the main modules together with their components and the relationships among them. Specifically, the following modules, implemented parts and their respective technologies can be distinguished:

- A private Ethereum blockchain created with Geth. The configuration of the system was performed with a JSON file that defines its Genesis Block. It was deployed along with several mining nodes that accept different types of transactions.
- Smart contracts. These were developed in Solidity with the Remix online IDE. Smart contracts implement all the functionality of the system. It is worth highlighting the following: the medical record contract, which was devised to consult the information of medical records or to write and/or to update such data; the cryptocurrency smart contract, which enables the creation of an incentive system that also allows trading; and finally, the Faucet smart contract, created to supply the demand of Ether to the different users of the system.
- Two cross-platform mobile Dapps developed with Kotlin in KMM (Kotlin Mobile Multiplatform) to modularize the project and divide the functionality on the Blockchain: reading for patients and writing for CDCs (Centers for Disease Control).

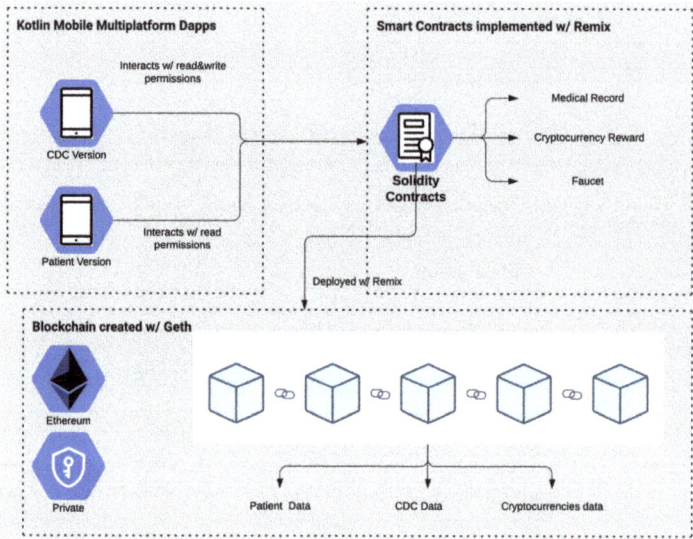

Figure 1. Architecture of the proposed project.

The development work is available on GitHub [5] under the Open Source license GNU GPLv3.

3. Examples of Use

Figure 2 shows an example of the flow of different interactions of the proposed system. Four use cases are illustrated sequentially: (1) A patient accesses a CDC for the first time after downloading the app, joins the system from the CDC app and his/her medical record is created and (2) updated with his new inoculation dose, receiving the corresponding incentive. Then, she/he will be able to (3) trade with the cryptocurrency to, for instance, send it to other users (e.g., in a bar, a hotel or transferring it to a friend). Finally, (4) the patient will be able to consult her/his medical information, also receiving her/his corresponding incentive and allowing access to her/his COVID-19 medical data for the user who read her/his passport.

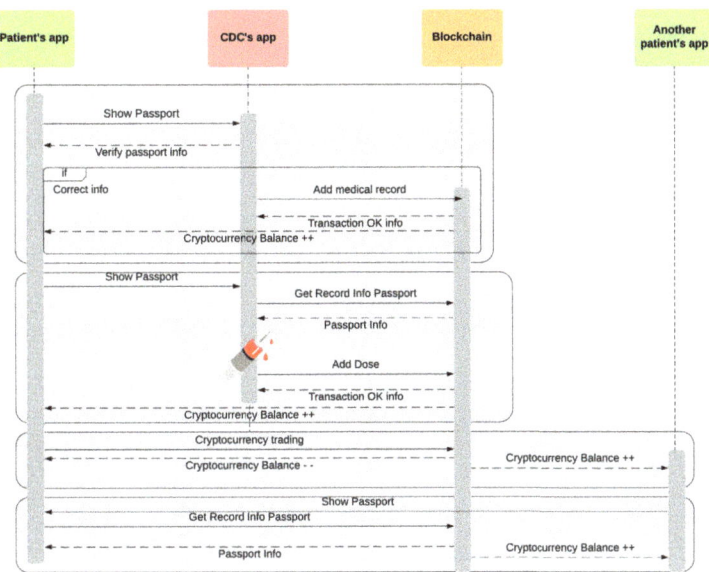

Figure 2. Sequence diagram that illustrates four use cases.

4. Discussion and Future Work

This paper described a digital passport system for COVID-19 consisting of two modules: one concerning blockchain and the other one related to the development of two cross-platform mobile Dapps. After the combination of both, the aim was to create a powerful system that improves and solves certain current situations of the COVID-19 pandemic, both from a technological perspective (as a new COVID-19 information storage system), as well as medical (favoring the creation of low health risk situations) and social (waiving restrictions as well as economically benefiting both customers and companies). These features can be provided thanks to the use of novel and disruptive technologies such as blockchain or KMM, which has been in alfa version since the end of 2020. In addition, the proposed system has social utility, since it provides a solution to one of the current problems that is being widely investigated worldwide. Finally, it is worth mentioning that future research lines will include the development of a native iOS app in KMM. In addition, further analysis will address how to enhance the management of network connections and how to provide advanced management features, such as granting or auditing CDC accounts, or controlling the restrictions to obtain incentives by the patients. To conclude, it must be emphasized that the dissemination, growth and improvement of the project, motivated by the Open Source nature of the product, will be key for the real and large-scale hypothetical future use of it.

Funding: This research received no external funding

Conflicts of Interest: The authors declare no conflict of interest.

References

1. European Commission. Coronavirus: Commission Proposes a Digital Green Certificate. Available online: https://ec.europa.eu/commission/presscorner/detail/en/IP_21_1181 (accessed on 31 July 2021).
2. Fernández-Caramés, T.M.; Froiz-Míguez, I.; Blanco Nóvoa, O.; Fraga Lamas, P. Enabling the internet of mobile crowdsourcing health things: A mobile fog computing, Blockchain and IoT based continuous glucose monitoring system for diabetes mellitus research and care. *Sensors* **2019**, *19*, 3319. [CrossRef] [PubMed]

3. Bitterli, F. Building a Private Ethereum Blockchain in a Box. Available online: https://wwz.unibas.ch/fileadmin/user_upload/wwz/00_Professuren/Schaer_DLTFintech/Lehre/Bitterli_2020.pdf (accessed on 31 July 2021).
4. Frega, N. Ethereum-Medical-Records. Available online: https://github.com/NFhbar/Ethereum-Medical-Records/tree/master/contracts (accessed on 31 July 2021).
5. COVID-19 Passport GitHub Repository. Available online: https://github.com/maurodelossantos/coronapassport.git (accessed on 8 October 2021).

Proceeding Paper

On the Adaptive Numerical Solution to the Darcy–Forchheimer Model [†]

María González * and Hiram Varela *

Departamento de Matemáticas and CITIC, Universidade da Coruña, Campus de Elviña s/n, 15071 A Coruña, Spain
* Correspondence: maria.gonzalez.taboada@udc.es (M.G.); hiram.varela@udc.es (H.V.)
† Presented at the 4th XoveTIC Conference, A Coruña, Spain, 7–8 October 2021.

Abstract: We considered a primal-mixed method for the Darcy–Forchheimer boundary value problem. This model arises in fluid mechanics through porous media at high velocities. We developed an a posteriori error analysis of residual type and derived a simple a posteriori error indicator. We proved that this indicator is reliable and locally efficient. We show a numerical experiment that confirms the theoretical results.

Keywords: Darcy–Forchheimer; mixed finite element; a posteriori error estimates

1. Introduction

The Darcy–Forchheimer model constitutes an improvement of the Darcy model which can be used when the velocity is high [1]. It is useful for simulating several physical phenomena, remarkably including fluid motion through porous media, as in petroleum reservoirs, water aquifers, blood in tissues or graphene nanoparticles through permeable materials. Let Ω be a bounded, simply connected domain in $\mathbb{R}^2$ with a Lipschitz-continuous boundary $\partial\Omega$. The problem reads as follows: given known functions $\mathbf{g}$ and f, find the velocity $\mathbf{u}$ and the pressure p such that

$$\begin{cases} \frac{\mu}{\rho}K^{-1}\mathbf{u} + \frac{\beta}{\rho}|\mathbf{u}|\mathbf{u} + \nabla p = \mathbf{g} & \text{in } \Omega, \\ \nabla \cdot \mathbf{u} = f & \text{in } \Omega, \\ \mathbf{u} \cdot \mathbf{n} = 0 & \text{on } \partial\Omega, \end{cases} \quad (1)$$

where μ is the dynamic viscosity, ρ denotes the fluid density, β is the *Forchheimer number* K denotes the permeability tensor, $\mathbf{g}$ represents gravity, f is compressibility, and $\mathbf{n}$ is the unit outward normal vector to $\partial\Omega$.

We make use of the finite element method to approximate the solution of problem (1). We present the approach by Girault and Wheeler [1], who introduced the primal formulation, in which the term $\nabla \cdot \mathbf{u}$ undergoes weakening by integration by parts. It is shown in [1] that problem (1) has a unique solution in the space $X \times M$, where $X := [L^3(\Omega)]^2$ and $M := W^{1,3/2}(\Omega) \cap L^2_0(\Omega)$ (we use the standard notations for Lebesgue and Sobolev spaces).

2. Discrete Problem

To pose a discrete problem, we can use a family $\{\mathcal{T}_h\}_{h>0}$ of conforming triangulations to divide the domain $\bar{\Omega}$ such that $\bar{\Omega} = \bigcup_{T \in \mathcal{T}_h} T$, $\forall h$, where $h > 0$ represents the mesh

size. Here we follow [2] and choose the following conforming discrete subspaces of X and M, respectively:

$$X_h := \left\{ \mathbf{v}_h \in [L^2(\Omega)]^2; \forall T \in \mathcal{T}_h, \mathbf{v}_h|_T \in [\mathbb{P}_0(T)]^2 \right\} \subset X,$$

$$M_h := Q_h^1 \cap L_0^2(\Omega) \subset M,$$

where $Q_h^1 := \left\{ q_h \in \mathcal{C}^0(\overline{\Omega}); \forall T \in \mathcal{T}_h, q_h|_T \in \mathbb{P}_1(T) \right\}$.

Then, the discrete problem consists in finding $(\mathbf{u}_h, p_h) \in X_h \times M_h$ such that

$$\begin{cases} \int_\Omega \left(\frac{\mu}{\rho} K^{-1} \mathbf{u}_h + \frac{\beta}{\rho} |\mathbf{u}_h| \mathbf{u}_h \right) \cdot \mathbf{v}_h \, dx + \int_\Omega \nabla p_h \cdot \mathbf{v}_h \, dx = \int_\Omega \mathbf{g} \cdot \mathbf{v}_h \, dx, & \forall \mathbf{v}_h \in X_h, \\ \int_\Omega \nabla q_h \cdot \mathbf{u}_h \, dx = -\int_\Omega q_h f \, dx, & \forall q_h \in M_h. \end{cases} \quad (2)$$

It is shown in [2] that problem (2) has a unique solution and that the sequence $\{(\mathbf{u}_h, p_h)\}_h$ converges to the exact solution of problem (1) in $X \times M$. Furthermore, under additional regularity assumptions on the exact solution, some error estimates were derived in [2].

3. Novel Error Estimator and Adaptive Algorithm

We denote by $\mathcal{E}_\Omega$, $\mathcal{E}_{\partial\Omega}$ and $\mathcal{E}_T$, respectively, the sets of edges e belonging to the interior domain, the boundary and the element T; h_e denotes the length of a particular edge e; and h_T is the diameter of a given element T. We denote by $\mathbb{J}_e(v)$ the jump of v across the edge e in the direction of $\mathbf{n}_e$, a fixed normal vector to side e. Finally, we use the operator $\widetilde{\mathcal{A}}(\mathbf{u}_h, p_h) := \frac{\mu}{\rho} K^{-1} \mathbf{u}_h + \frac{\beta}{\rho} |\mathbf{u}_h| \mathbf{u}_h + \nabla p_h - \mathbf{g}$.

On every triangle $T \in \mathcal{T}_h$, we propose the following a posteriori error indicator:

$$\theta_T = \left(h_T^2 \|\widetilde{\mathcal{A}}(\mathbf{u}_h, p_h)\|_{[L^2(T)]^2}^2 + \|\nabla \cdot \mathbf{u}_h - f\|_{L^2(T)}^2 + \frac{1}{2} \sum_{e \in \mathcal{E}_\Omega \cap \partial T} h_T^{-1} \|\mathbb{J}_e(\mathbf{u}_h \cdot \mathbf{n})\|_{L^2(e)}^2 + \sum_{e \in \mathcal{E}_{\partial\Omega} \cap \partial T} h_T^{-1} \|\mathbf{u}_h \cdot \mathbf{n}\|_{L^2(e)}^2 \right)^{1/2}$$

We also define the global a posteriori error indicator $\theta := \left(\sum_{T \in \mathcal{T}_h} \theta_T^2 \right)^{1/2}$.

Theorem 1. *For the primal-mixed method* (2), *there exists a positive constant C_1, independent of h, and a positive constant C_2, independent of h and T, such that*

$$\|(\mathbf{u} - \mathbf{u}_h, p - p_h)\|_{X \times M} \leq C_1 \theta,$$

$$\theta_T \leq C_2 \|(\mathbf{u} - \mathbf{u}_h, p - p_h)\|_{[L^3(w_T)]^2 \times W^{1,3/2}(w_T)}, \quad \forall T \in \mathcal{T}_h,$$

where $w_T = \bigcup_{\mathcal{E}_T \cap \mathcal{E}_{T'} \neq \emptyset} T'$.

We propose an adaptive algorithm based on the a posteriori error indicator θ. Given an initial mesh, we follow the iterative procedure described in Figure 1. Each new mesh is generated as suggested in [3].

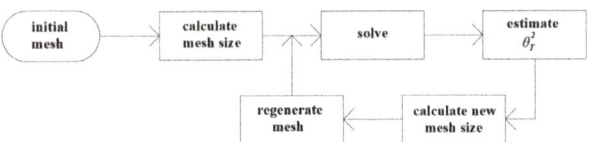

Figure 1. Adaptive algorithm flux diagram.

4. Numerical Experiment

We performed several simulations in FreeFem++ [4], validating the theoretical results. Here we select an example on an L-shaped domain, $\Omega = (-1,1)^2 \setminus [0,1]^2$, and focus on the data f and **g** so that the exact solution is

$$p(x,y) = \frac{1}{x-1.1}, \quad \mathbf{u}(x,y) = \begin{pmatrix} \exp(x)\sin(y) \\ \exp(x)\cos(y) \end{pmatrix}. \tag{3}$$

Thus the solution has a singularity in pressure close to the line $x = 1$. Figure 2 shows the mesh refinement by the adaptive algorithm. Figure 3, bottom, represents the evolution with respect to degrees of freedom (DOF) of error and indicator; on the right, we can observe the evolution of the efficiency index with DOF.

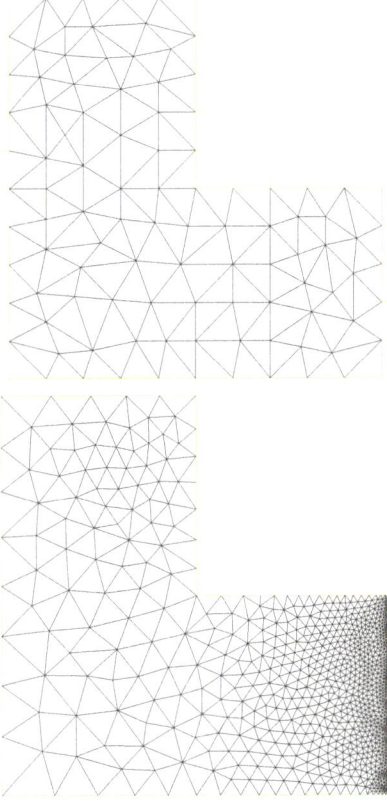

Figure 2. Example 1. Initial mesh (270 DOF) on the (**top**); intermediate adapted mesh with 1512 DOF on the (**bottom**).

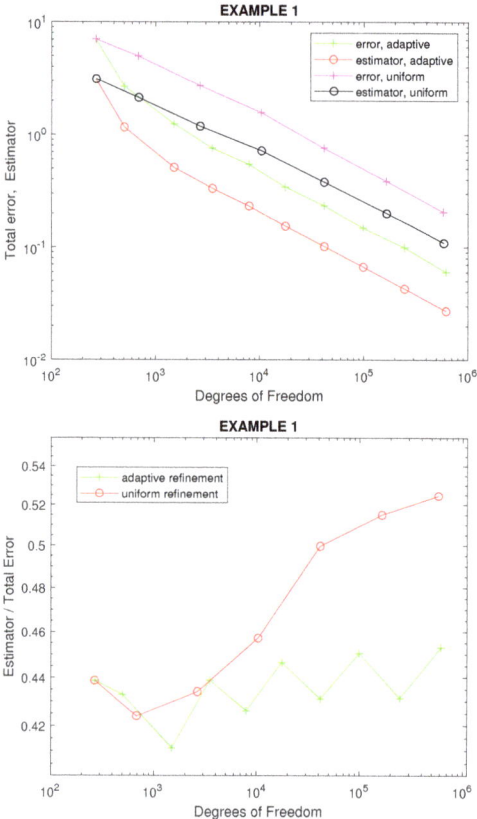

Figure 3. Example 1. (**Top**): Error and indicator evolution vs. DOF. (**Bottom**): Efficiency index vs. DOF.

5. Discussion

The adaptive algorithm was tested on an example with a singularity. From Figure 2 we can observe that the algorithm refined the mesh near the singularity, as expected. Since it is an academic example with a known solution, we could compute the exact error. The graphs in Figure 3 confirm that the error was lower for the adaptive refinement. Additionally, since the exact error and estimator followed close to parallel lines, we confirm that the indicator gives a consistent measure of the error. This could also be checked by the efficiency index, which is the ratio of indicator to exact total error.

Funding: The authors acknowledge the support of CITIC (FEDER Program and grant ED431G 2019/01). The research of M.G. is partially supported by Xunta de Galicia Grant GRC ED431C 2018-033. The research of H.V. is partially supported by Ministerio de Educación grant FPU18/06125.

Institutional Review Board Statement: Not applicable.

Informed Consent Statement: Not applicable.

Conflicts of Interest: The authors declare no conflict of interest.

References

1. Girault, V.; Wheeler, M.F. Numerical Discretization of a Darcy-Forchheimer Model. *Numer. Math.* **2008**, *110*, 161–198. [CrossRef]
2. Salas, J.J.; López, H.; Molina, B. An analysis of a mixed finite element method for a Darcy-Forchheimer model. *Math. Comput. Model.* **2013**, *57*, 2325–2338. [CrossRef]
3. Borouchaki, H.; Hecht, F.; Frey, P. Mesh gradation control. *Int. J. Numer. Meth. Eng.* **1998**, *43*, 1143–1165. [CrossRef]
4. Hetch, F. FreeFEM Documentation, Release 4.6. 2020. Available online: https://doc.freefem.org/pdf/FreeFEM-documentation.pdf (accessed on 13 October 2021).

Proceeding Paper
Detection of Chocolate Properties Using Near-Infrared Spectrophotometry †

Brais Galdo *, Enrique Fernandez-Blanco and Daniel Rivero

Faculty of Computer Science, CITIC, University of A Coruna, 15071 A Coruna, Spain; enrique.fernandez@udc.es (E.F.-B.); daniel.rivero@udc.es (D.R.)
* Correspondence: brais.cgaldo@udc.es
† Presented at the 4th XoveTIC Conference, A Coruña, Spain, 7–8 October 2021.

Abstract: Knowing the chemical composition of a substance provides valuable information about it. That is why numerous techniques have been developed to try to obtain it. One of them is the Near Infrared Spectrometry technique, a non-destructive technique that analyzes the electromagnetic spectrum in search of waves of a certain length. The aim of this project is to combine this technology with machine learning techniques to try to detect the presence of milk, as well as the level of cocoa present in an ounce of chocolate. This has given satisfactory results in both cases, so it is considered that the combination of these techniques offers great possibilities.

Keywords: near infrared spectroscopy; machine learning; artificial neural networks; intensity; absorbance; reflectance; chocolate; milk; cocoa

1. Introduction

Near-infrared spectrophotometry [1] is a technique whith which we can measure the chemical compositions of substances, and its main object of measurement is carbon. This technique is non-destructive, which gives the possibility of repeating the analysis.

The devices used for this analysis are usually very large and are housed in laboratories dedicated to this type of analysis. It is for this reason that portable spectrophotometers of reduced size and accuracy were developed. In this way, the device can be moved and measurements can be taken in the field.

Chocolate [2] is a food that is the result of the combination of various ingredients. These can vary, from nuts to different additives. Among the possible ingredients, two main ones stand out, milk and cocoa.

The aim of this work is to detect different properties in chocolate, such as the presence of milk or the level of cocoa contained in an ounce, using machine learning [3].

2. Related Work

A large number of articles can be found, in which different types of food, including chocolate, are analyzed using NIR technology. They try to find different relevant properties in chocolate, such as cocoa. It is necessary to mention at this point that the measurements performed on the different substances have been carried out using laboratory spectrophotometers. These tools have a higher precision and a longer range than the device used to carry out the data collection.

The article [4] determines sugar in chocolate using NIR technology. In this case, the temperature of the sample was raised to 40 °C and transferred to a spectrophotometry cell prior to analysis.

Noteworthy are also the articles [5,6], which try to detect some characteristics such as sugar, dairy products or moisture in chocolate, among others, using Fourier transform. The work of [7], which tries to identify whether the lard contained in the sample is adulterated, also stands out in this field.

3. Materials and Methods

The collected database has been integrated into the repository Data Mendeley and can be accessed on the site: https://data.mendeley.com/v1/datasets/xr4cct5fc7/draft?preview=1 (accessed on 28 July 2021).

The different data obtained were then analyzed. Differences can be seen in the three variables provided by the spectrophotometer: intensity, absorbance and reflectance. It is therefore considered possible to try to solve the proposed problem using ANN [8].

In this work, first of all, the detection of milk in each of the measurements is addressed. Subsequently, we have tried to tackle the problem of the cocoa level. For this purpose, it was decided to divide the tablets according to the cocoa level, with a low level being less than 50%, a medium–low level between 50% and 75%, a medium–high level between 75% and 90%, and a high level with a content above 90%.

4. Results

The results offered for each of the different problems will be presented below. The main models to be taken into account will be shown. For this purpose, 34 models of neuron networks with different configurations have been developed and trained 50 times each, with cross-validation [9]. As an objective measure, the average accuracy of these 50 trainings as well as the standard deviation will be used. Tables 1 and 2 show relevant information about the main models, such as the network architecture, the features trained with or the optimizer used in addition to the performance metrics.

Table 1. Milk detection results.

Hidden Layers	Optimizer	Characteristic	Accuracy	Standard Deviation
64–32	Adamax	Absorbance	86.31%	0.1444
128–64	Adamax	Absorbance	86.62%	0.1432
16	Adamax	Reflectance	92.12%	0.0955
128–64	Adamax	Reflectance	92.15%	0.1003

Table 2. Cocoa detection results.

Hidden Layers	Optimizer	Characteristic	Accuracy	Standard Deviation
128	Adamax	Reflectance	80.30%	0.0860
128	Adam	Reflectance	80.33%	0.0881
16–8	Adamax	Reflectance	80.82%	0.0879
64–32	Adam	Reflectance	81.66%	0.0932

4.1. Detection of Milk in Chocolate Ounces

The first problem to be addressed is related to the detection of milk in different chocolate samples. The models with the best results can be seen in Table 1. The model composed of 128 neurons in the first hidden layer and 64 in the second one, using the Adamax optimizer [10], stands out. This model obtains an accuracy of over 92% with a standard deviation of 0.1.

4.2. Detection of Cocoa Level in Ounces of Chocolate

The second problem to be addressed is related to the detection of the cocoa level in the different chocolate samples. The best models can be seen in Table 2. In this case, the model composed of 64 neurons in the first hidden layer and 32 in the second one, using the optimizer Adam [10], stands out. This model obtains an accuracy of over 81% with a standard deviation of 0.1.

5. Discussion

The use of NIR technology to try to solve the two proposed problems seems appropriate. This technology offers a good quality of the data collected and gives very valuable information that can be exploited by machine learning techniques.

ANNs are a great resource when working with this type of signals. While it is true that better results can be obtained in both problems once the data are analyzed in greater depth, it is considered a good first approach for the work to be done.

6. Conclussions

Due to the high accuracy provided by NIR technology, it is considered a very useful resource in the treated sector, providing a simple and fast way to discover different properties of various foods, such as chocolate, in this case. Good results have been obtained in the classification of both types of problems, exceeding 90% accuracy in the milk detection problem and 80% in the classification problem for cocoa levels.

7. Future Work

As for the domain, there are numerous future works that can be done in this area. It should be noted that a larger volume of measurements would be necessary for the application of regression. Some examples of future work could be related to the application of regression for detecting the percentage of cocoa, detecting the amount of sugar or detecting the presence of palm oil.

Author Contributions: Conceptualization, B.G.; methodology, B.G.; software, B.G.; validation, B.G.; formal 64 analysis, B.G.; investigation, B.G.; resources, B.G., D.R., E.F.-B.; data curation, B.G.; writing—original draft preparation, 65 B.G., D.R., E.F.-B.; writing—review and editing, B.G., D.R., E.F.-B.; visualization, B.G.; supervision, B.G., D.R., E.F.-B.; project 66 administration, B.G.; funding acquisition, B.G., D.R., E.F.-B. All authors have read and agreed to the published version of the manuscript.

Funding: This work was partially funded by the Galician goverment and EFRD funds (ED431G/01).

Institutional Review Board Statement: Not applicable.

Informed Consent Statement: Not applicable.

Data Availability Statement: Data could be donwloaded in https://github.com/braiscgaldo/NIR-Lab-2.0 (accessed on 28 July 2021).

Acknowledgments: The authors would like to thank the support from RNASA-IMEDIR group.

Conflicts of Interest: The authors declare no conflict of interest.

Abbreviations

The following abbreviations are used in this manuscript:

NIR   Near Infrared Spectroscopy
ANN   Artificial Neural Networks

References

1. Siesler, H.W.; Ozaki, Y.; Kawata, S.; Heise, H.M. *Near-Infrared Spectroscopy: Principles, Instruments, Applications*; John Wiley & Sons: Hoboken, NJ, USA, 2008.
2. Afoakwa, E.O. *Chocolate Science and Technology*; John Wiley & Sons: Hoboken, NJ, USA, 2016.
3. Mohammed, M.; Khan, M.B.; Bashier, E.B.M. *Machine Learning: Algorithms and Applications*; CRC Press: Boca Raton, FL, USA, 2016.
4. da Costa Filho, P.A. Rapid determination of sucrose in chocolate mass using near infrared spectroscopy. *Anal. Chim. Acta* **2009**, *631*, 206–211. [CrossRef] [PubMed]
5. Tarkošová, J.; Čopíková, J. Fourier Transform near Infrared Spectroscopy Applied to Analysis of Chocolate. *J. Near Infrared Spectrosc.* **2000**, *8*, 251–257. [CrossRef]
6. Copikova, J.; Novotna, M.; Smidova, I.; Synytsya, A.; Cerna, M. Application of Near Infrared Spectroscopy in Chocolate Analysis. *Chem. Listy* **2003**, *97*, 571–575.

7. Che Man, Y.B.; Syahariza, Z.A.; Mirghani, M.E.S.; Jinap, S.; Bakar, J. Analysis of potential lard adulteration in chocolate and chocolate products using Fourier transform infrared spectroscopy. *Food Chem.* **2005**, *90*, 815–819. [CrossRef]
8. Goodfellow, I.; Bengio, Y.; Courville, A. *Deep Learning*; MIT Press: Cambridge, MA, USA, 2016.
9. Browne, M.W. Cross-validation methods. *J. Math. Psychol.* **2000**, *44*, 108–132. [CrossRef] [PubMed]
10. Kingma, D.P.; Ba, J. Adam: A method for stochastic optimization. *arXiv* **2014**, arXiv:1412.6980.

Proceeding Paper

Development of a Server for the Implementation of Data Processing Pipelines and ANN Training [†]

Brais Galdo *, Daniel Rivero and Enrique Fernandez-Blanco

Faculty of Computer Science, CITIC, University of A Coruna, 15071 A Coruña, Spain; daniel.rivero@udc.es (D.R.); enrique.fernandez@udc.es (E.F.-B.)
* Correspondence: brais.cgaldo@udc.es
† Presented at the 4th XoveTIC Conference, A Coruña, Spain, 7–8 October 2021.

Abstract: Data processing and the use of machine learning techniques make it possible to solve a wide variety of problems. The great disadvantage of using this type of technology is the enormous amount of computation involved. This is why we have tried to develop an architecture that makes the best possible use of the resources available on each machine. The growth of cloud computing and the rise of virtualization techniques have led to a development that allows these tasks to be carried out in a more optimized way.

Keywords: machine learning; Artificial Neural Networks; deep learning; data processing; web server; virtualization; docker

1. Introduction

The use of data processing techniques [1] and machine learning [2] is based on trying to detect patterns in a set of data in order to provide an estimate on the data. This technology is experiencing a great boom due to the optimization of the different algorithms and the notable increase in the computational capacity of the different systems.

Both database processing and the training of machine learning models are very complex and computationally expensive tasks. When this is added to the processing of very large databases or the development of complex models, it is common to have specific hardware to speed up these tasks. Otherwise, this task would take a long time to be performed on a conventional computer, even breaking some of its components due to the stress caused by computational volume.

In addition, defining different processing pipelines or different models can be very complex for people who are not experts in the field. To alleviate these deficiencies, there are tools that allow this task to be carried out visually. This would be the case of Weka [3], which allows performing these tasks in a simple way. However, this application does not allow its execution on different machines.

With these points in mind, namely ease of use and scalability, the architecture of a distributed system for database processing and training of machine learning models is proposed. In this way, the resources of the machine on which the different processes are executed will be specifically dedicated to this task.

2. Materials and Methods

The boom of the different virtualization technologies [4] makes them ideal for the construction of a system of this style. They allow the developed system to be independent of the machine on which it is executed, which provides great versatility and flexibility. In addition, these technologies allow an exclusive use of the resources, allowing them to contain only the necessary modules. One of the most powerful and versatile technologies in this field is *Docker* [5], which allows an easy definition of systems with their characteristics to be taken into account. This, in addition to efficiency when carrying out the tasks, would

provide greater security since the machine will only contain the services necessary to perform the task entrusted to it.

The architecture developed must also allow the management of different users and databases. This is not such a costly task, so it will be included in the same module to optimize the architecture resources.

3. Results

Thanks to this architecture, load balancing [6] of the different training and data processing processes can be carried out exclusively. This implies that the nodes will be activated on demand and will have all the resources dedicated to the work they want to perform without taking into account other functionalities such as user authentication or the management of the different files that would consume a series of resources unnecessarily. Likewise, the architecture of the system would be as shown in the Figure 1.

It is necessary to mention that the current development is based on the ANN technique, which allows the implementation of deep learning models [7].

This architecture can be divided into a front-end part based on an MVC pattern [8] and a back-end part composed of three large modules. These modules are divided according to their expected workload. Firstly, there is a Data Processing module [1], whose objective is to perform the operations indicated by the user on the data. Secondly, a model training module [2] has been detected, which is in charge of generating the models indicated by the user and performing the training with the required database. Finally, a Facade module [9] is needed, in charge of acting as a facade and performing the less expensive operations such as user management and management of the different files on the server.

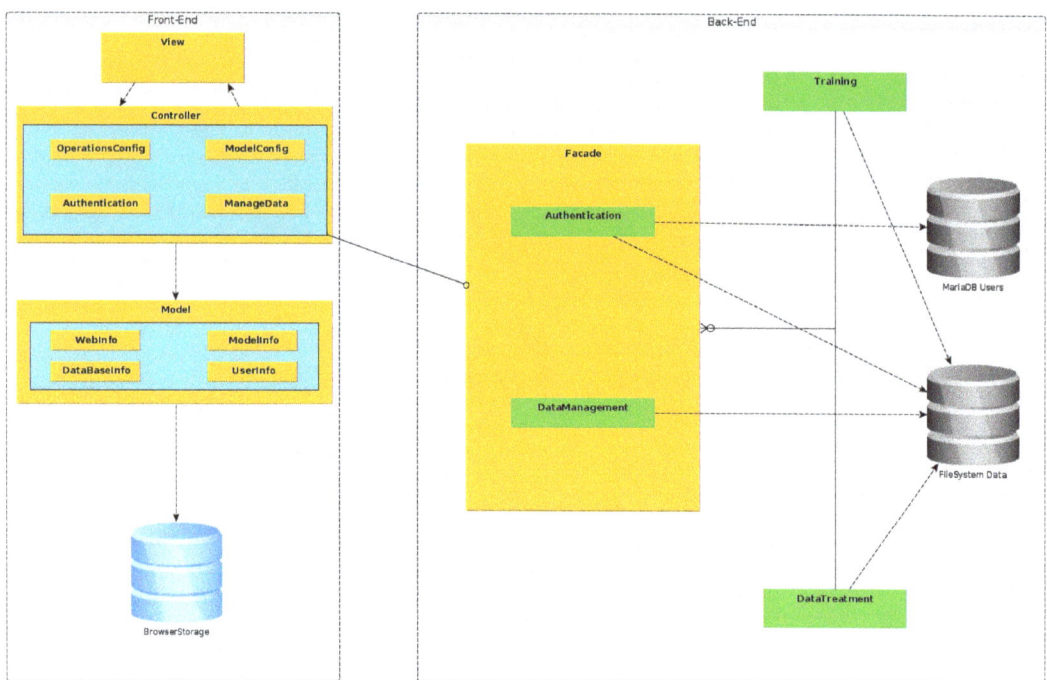

Figure 1. Data processing and model training server architecture.

A possible implementation of this architecture can be found on the GitHub repository https://github.com/braiscgaldo/NIR-Lab-2.0 (accessed on 3 July 2021).

4. Discussion

A scheme has been defined for a server capable of performing the data processing and model training tasks in a distributed and on-demand manner. This offers a number of advantages over other systems such as Weka. The latter performs these tasks in a single instance, which causes the resources of the machine in which it is executed to be depleted due to the fact that it must manage all the functionalities present in the system.

This approach offers the possibility of running on cloud services such as AWS [10], Azure [11], or Google Cloud [12]. This architecture enables the replication of nodes as needed for the execution of data processing or model training in a unique way, which offers a great advantage over desktop applications whose only source of computational power is the computer itself.

5. Future Work

This project presents numerous avenues for future work. One of these possible developments is motivated by the extension of the type of machine learning models. It would be straightforward to extend the set of models composed only of ANN to other algorithms such as SVM, KNN, RF, or LDA.

It is also necessary to highlight the possibility of interactive data processing, visualizing at each point how the different variables defined by the user behave.

Author Contributions: Conceptualization, B.G.; methodology, B.G.; software, B.G.; validation, B.G.; formal 64 analysis, B.G.; investigation, B.G.; resources, B.G., D.R., E.F.-B.; data curation, B.G.; writing—original draft preparation, 65 B.G., D.R., E.F.-B.; writing—review and editing, B.G., D.R., E.F.-B.; visualization, B.G.; supervision, B.G., D.R., E.F.-B.; project 66 administration, B.G.; funding acquisition, B.G., D.R., E.F.-B. All authors have read and agreed to the published version of the manuscript.

Funding: This work was partially funded by the Galician goverment and EFRD funds (ED431G/01).

Institutional Review Board Statement: Not applicable.

Informed Consent Statement: Not applicable.

Data Availability Statement: An implementation could be found in https://github.com/braiscgaldo/NIR-Lab-2.0 (accessed on 3 July 2021).

Acknowledgments: The authors would like to thank the support from RNASA-IMEDIR group.

Conflicts of Interest: The authors declare no conflict of interest.

Abbreviations

The following abbreviations are used in this manuscript:

RNA   Redes de Neuronas Artificiales
SVM   Support Vector Machine
KNN   K-Nearest Neighbor
RF   Random Forest
LDA   Linear Discriminant Analysis

References

1. Brandt, S.; Brandt, S. *Data Analysis*; Springer: Berlin/Heidelberg, Germany, 1998.
2. Mohammed, M.; Khan, M.B.; Bashier, E.B.M. *Machine Learning: Algorithms and Applications*; CRC Press: Boca Raton, FL, USA, 2016.
3. Bouckaert, R.R.; Frank, E.; Hall, M.A.; Holmes, G.; Pfahringer, B.; Reutemann, P.; Witten, I.H. WEKA—Experiences with a Java Open-Source Project. *J. Mach. Learn. Res.* **2010**, *11*, 2533–2541.
4. Xing, Y.; Zhan, Y. Virtualization and cloud computing. In *Future Wireless Networks and Information Systems*; Springer: Berlin/Heidelberg, Germany, 2012; pp. 305–312.
5. Anderson, C. Docker [software engineering]. *IEEE Softw.* **2015**, *32*, 102-c3. [CrossRef]
6. Cardellini, V.; Colajanni, M.; Yu, P.S. Dynamic load balancing on web-server systems. *IEEE Internet Comput.* **1999**, *3*, 28–39. [CrossRef]
7. Goodfellow, I.; Bengio, Y.; Courville, A. *Deep Learning*; MIT Press: Cambridge, MA, USA, 2016.

8. Krasner, G.E.; Pope, S.T. A description of the model-view-controller user interface paradigm in the smalltalk-80 system. *J. Object Oriented Program.* **1988**, *1*, 26–49.
9. Schmidt, D.C.; Stal, M.; Rohnert, H.; Buschmann, F. *Pattern-Oriented Software Architecture, Patterns for Concurrent and Networked Objects*; John Wiley & Sons: Hoboken, NJ, USA, 2013; Volume 2.
10. Amazon, E. Amazon Web Services. 2015; p. 39. Available online: http://aws.amazon.com/es/ec2/ (accessed on 11 November 2020).
11. Chappell, D. Introducing the Azure Services Platform. White Paper, October 2008; p. 1364. Available online: http://www.davidchappell.com (accessed on 13 November 2020).
12. Geewax, J.J.J. *Google Cloud Platform in Action*; Manning: Shelter Island, NY, USA, 2018.

Proceeding Paper

Improving Medical Data Annotation Including Humans in the Machine Learning Loop †

José Bobes-Bascarán *, Eduardo Mosqueira-Rey and David Alonso-Ríos

Centro de Investigación en TIC (CITIC), Universidade da Coruña, Elviña, 15071 A Coruña, Spain; eduardo.mosqueira@udc.es (E.M.-R.); david.alonso@udc.es (D.A-R.)
* Correspondence: jose.bobes@udc.es
† Presented at the 4th XoveTIC Conference, A Coruña, Spain, 7–8 October 2021.

Abstract: At present, the great majority of Artificial Intelligence (AI) systems require the participation of humans in their development, tuning, and maintenance. Particularly, Machine Learning (ML) systems could greatly benefit from their expertise or knowledge. Thus, there is an increasing interest around how humans interact with those systems to obtain the best performance for both the AI system and the humans involved. Several approaches have been studied and proposed in the literature that can be gathered under the umbrella term of Human-in-the-Loop Machine Learning. The application of those techniques to the health informatics environment could provide a great value on prognosis and diagnosis tasks contributing to develop a better health service for Cancer related diseases.

Keywords: Human-in-the-Loop Machine Learning; Interactive Machine Learning; Machine Teaching; Iterative Machine Teaching; Active Learning

1. Introduction

The majority of Machine Learning (ML) systems require the participation of humans at several steps of the AI pipeline. With this requirement in mind, new types of interactions between humans and machine learning algorithms are being defined, which we can group under the term Human-in-the-Loop Machine Learning (HITL-ML) [1]. The goal is to make machine learning models more accurate, obtain the desired accuracy faster, and also make humans more efficient when training or using a ML model.

In the health domain (and others), due to the reduced number of datasets, traditional ML approaches suffer from insufficient training samples [2]. Using specific techniques as the ones described in this proposal could help improving both the training process and the final user performance.

2. Materials and Methods

Hybrid Intelligence Systems include several strategies with the goal of enhancing the capabilities of either the human, the machine or both of them. A taxonomy has been proposed based on the task characteristics, learning paradigm, AI-Human interaction, and Human-AI interaction [3].

We describe below several techniques that can be grouped under the term Human-in-the-Loop Machine Learning (HITL-ML), and can be applied between others, to the Cancer prognosis and diagnosis scenarios, where training samples are scarce and domain expert knowledge is expensive.

2.1. Human-in-the-Loop Techniques

Human-in-the-Loop ML has the goal of increasing the accuracy of a ML model, reaching the target performance faster, combining human and machine intelligence to maximize

accuracy, and assisting human tasks with machine learning to increase efficiency [1]. The most relevant tasks mentioned are:

- Annotating unlabeled data to create training, validation, and evaluation data.
- Sampling the most important unlabeled data items.
- Incorporating Human-Computer Interaction principles into annotation.

Depending on who is in control of the learning process, we do identify different approaches: Active Learning, Interactive Machine Learning, and Machine Teaching.

2.2. Active Learning

One of the first techniques is Active Learning (AL) [4], where the system remains in control of the learning process and treats humans as oracles to label relevant unlabeled data. It is particularly useful when the labeling example process is expensive or time-consuming, and it also applies to the scenario of scarcity of examples (e.g., cancer). AL uses an interactive/iterative process for obtaining training data, unlike passive or classical learning, where the data is provided in advance. The learner requests information from the oracle, that it selects based on different query strategies.

2.3. Interactive Machine Learning

Another approach is Interactive Machine Learning (IML), in which there is a closer interaction between users and learning systems, with people iteratively supplying information in a more focused, frequent and incremental way compared to traditional machine learning [5,6]. In this technique the learning process control is shared between the system and the users, working closely to benefit from each other.

2.4. Machine Teaching

Finally, Machine Teaching (MT) [7,8] where the idea is to focus on the teacher role a human can play to create useful information from the data available. With the aim of facilitating the construction of new models that nowadays require practitioners with deep knowledge of machine learning, this method proposes to decouple knowledge about machine learning algorithms from the process of teaching. The human would behave as a teacher guiding the learning process [9].

A particular version of MT is *Iterative* Machine Teaching (iMT) [10] whose goal is to obtain the optimal training set given a machine learning algorithm and a target model. The idea is to learn a target concept with a minimal number of iterations using the smallest dataset.

2.5. Applying and Interpreting the Results

Once the model is deployed and it is used in a production environment, we could use Explainable AI (XAI) [11] to make the results of AI systems more understandable to humans.

There are specific domains where the aforementioned methods could fulfill the targets of the expected model. As an example, ML-approaches can be of particular interest to solve issues in Health Informatics, where we are lacking big data sets, we need to deal with complex data and/or rare events, and traditional learning algorithms suffer due to insufficient training samples [2].

3. Results

To date, we explored two of the techniques exposed: Iterative Machine Teaching (iMT) and Active Learning (AL). We have analyzed how to integrate them in the learning process using common datasets: Gaussian, MNIST and Vehicles.

Our proposal to incorporate iMT and AL into the machine learning loop is to use iMT as a technique to obtain the "Minimum Viable Data (MVD)" for training a learning model, that is, a dataset that allows us to increase speed and reduce complexity in the learning process by allowing to build early prototypes.

The results of the application of the iMT and AL on known datasets can be found at [12]. There we can see that, in the iMT experiment, the results show—both in the example problems and in the real-world problem—that the algorithms trained by any of the proposed teachers obtain better results than those trained by randomly choosing the examples. In our AL experiment, we find that the greatest advantage of this approach is in the continuous improvement of the model, which enhances resilience and prevents obsolescence.

4. Discussion

The quality of the data is a key factor that can make the model to fail in certain scenarios. If our data is better our algorithms will generalize better. This is the idea of the so-called data-centric approach which is behind some of the techniques explored (i.e., Machine Teaching).

The methods described in this paper are not mutually exclusive, so they can be combined with the aim of obtaining better results. Some of the techniques apply at different stages of the ML pipeline. Furthermore they can be incrementally implemented enhancing the model at every step.

The outcomes of the experiments conducted were obtained using common datasets as inputs. Even if they are promising, we plan to apply these techniques to relevant medical databases as The Cancer Genome Atlas Program (TCGA).

As for future work, we would be interested in applying these techniques considering multi-class problems and utilize the TCGA datasets.

5. Conclusions

The techniques exposed (combined or individually) can be applied to a specific domain (Cancer diagnosis and prognosis) making Machine Learning (ML) methods accessible to subject-matter experts and improving the performance of both the system and the human (i.e., HITL-ML), obtaining semantic and interpretable ML models (i.e., Explainable AI).

Funding: This work has been supported by the State Research Agency of the Spanish Government,112grant (PID2019-107194GB-I00/AEI/10.13039/501100011033) and by the Xunta de Galicia, grant113(ED431C 2018/34) with the European Union ERDF funds. We wish to acknowledge the support114received from the Centro de Investigacin de Galicia "CITIC", funded by Xunta de Galicia and the115European Union (European Regional Development Fund- Galicia 2014-2020 Program), by grant116ED431G 2019/01.

Informed Consent Statement: Not applicable.

Conflicts of Interest: The authors declare no conflict of interest.

References

1. Munro, R. *Human-in-the-Loop Machine Learning*; Manning Publications: Shelter Island, NY, USA, 2020.
2. Holzinger, A. Interactive machine learning for health informatics: When do we need the human-in-the-loop? *Brain Inform.* **2016**, *3*, 119–131. [CrossRef] [PubMed]
3. Dellermann, D.; Calma, A.; Lipusch, N.; Weber, T.; Weigel, S.; Ebel, P. The future of human-AI collaboration: A taxonomy of design knowledge for hybrid intelligence systems. In Proceedings of the 52nd Hawaii International Conference on System Sciences, Honolulu, HI, USA, 8–11 January 2019.
4. Settles, B. *Active Learning Literature Survey*; Technical Report; Department of Computer Sciences, University of Wisconsin-Madison: Madison, WI, USA, 2009.
5. Fails, J.A.; Olsen, D.R. Interactive Machine Learning. In Proceedings of the 8th International Conference on IUI'03 Intelligent User Interfaces, Miami, FL, USA, 12–15 January 2003; Association for Computing Machinery: New York, NY, USA, 2003; pp. 39–45. [CrossRef]
6. Amershi, S.; Cakmak, M.; Knox, W.B.; Kulesza, T. Power to the People: The Role of Humans in Interactive Machine Learning. *AI Mag.* **2014**, *35*, 105–120. [CrossRef]
7. Simard, P.Y.; Amershi, S.; Chickering, D.M.; Pelton, A.E.; Ghorashi, S.; Meek, C.; Ramos, G.; Suh, J.; Verwey, J.; Wang, M.; et al. Machine Teaching: A New Paradigm for Building Machine Learning Systems. *arXiv* **2017**, arXiv:1707.06742.
8. Lindvall, M.; Molin, J.; Löwgren, J. From Machine Learning to Machine Teaching: The Importance of UX. *Interactions* **2018**, *25*, 52–57. [CrossRef]

9. Ramos, G.; Meek, C.; Simard, P.; Suh, J.; Ghorashi, S. Interactive machine teaching: A human-centered approach to building machine-learned models. *Hum.-Comput. Interact.* **2020**, *35*, 1–39. [CrossRef]
10. Liu, W.; Dai, B.; Humayun, A.; Tay, C.; Yu, C.; Smith, L.B.; Rehg, J.M.; Song, L. Iterative Machine Teaching. In Proceedings of the 34th International Conference on Machine Learning (ICML-2017), Sydney, Australia, 6–11 August 2017; Volume 70; pp. 2149–2158. Available online: http://xxx.lanl.gov/abs/1705.10470 (accessed on 15 July 2021).
11. Adadi, A.; Berrada, M. Peeking Inside the Black-Box: A Survey on Explainable Artificial Intelligence (XAI). *IEEE Access* **2018**, *6*, 52138–52160. [CrossRef]
12. Mosqueira-Rey, E.; Alonso-Ríos, D.; Baamonde-Lozano, A. Integrating Iterative Machine Teaching and Active Learning into the Machine Learning Loop. In Proceedings of the 25 International Conference on Knowledge-Based and Intelligent Information & Engineering Systems (KES-2021), Szczecin, Poland, 8–10 September 2021; Volume 192, pp. 553–562. [CrossRef]

Proceeding Paper

Close Binary Stars in Planetary Nebulae through Gaia EDR3 [†]

Iker González-Santamaría [1,2,*], Minia Manteiga [2,3] and Carlos Dafonte [1,2]

1. Department of Computer Science and Information Technology, Campus Elviña sn, Universidade da Coruña (UDC), 15071 A Coruña, Spain; carlos.dafonte@udc.es
2. CITIC, Centre for Information and Communications Technology Research, Campus de Elviña sn, Universidade da Coruña (UDC), 15071 A Coruña, Spain; manteiga@udc.es
3. Department of Nautical Sciences and Marine Engineering, Universidade da Coruña (UDC), Paseo de Ronda 51, 15011 A Coruña, Spain
* Correspondence: iker.gonzalez@udc.es
† Presented at the 4th XoveTIC Conference, A Coruña, Spain, 7–8 October 2021.

Abstract: The aim of this work is to search for evidence of close binary stars associated with planetary nebulae (ionized stellar envelopes in expansion) by mining the astronomical archive of Gaia EDR3. For this task, using big data techniques, we selected a sample of central stars of planetary nebulae from almost 2000 million sources in an EDR3 database. Then, we analysed some of their parameters, which could provide clues about the presence of close binary systems, and we ran a statistical test to verify the results. Using this method, we concluded that red stars tend to show more affinity with close binarity than blue ones.

Keywords: astrometry; binary stars; Gaia EDR3; planetary nebulae

1. Introduction

Planetary Nebulae (PNe) are the stellar objects that are generated when low- and intermediate-mass stars eject and ionize the envelope that surrounds them, reaching their final phase of evolution. In some cases, they come from a binary star system, instead of being generated by a single star. These cases are of special interest, as they can provide information about the morphology, formation and evolution of the PNe [1].

Therefore, the aim of this work is to search for binary stars in PNe, concretely close binary systems, which should have more influence in the PNe than the wide binaries. In these cases, the closeness between both stars allows for mass transfer between them, and this effect could generate a stellar structure made of gas known as a common envelope. This would be the origin of some peculiar PN morphologies, such as bipolar ones (see Figure 1).

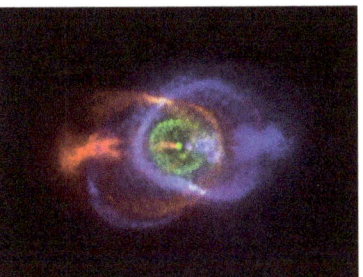

Figure 1. Common envelope between both stars in a close binary system.

To carry out this research, we relied on data provided by ESA's Gaia satellite, which was launched at the end of 2013 with the aim of making a star map of the Milky Way.

We made use of the recently published (December 2020) data archive from this mission: Gaia EDR3 (Early Data Release 3). This database contains astrometric and photometric parameters of almost 2000 million stellar objects, so its exploitation requires the use of big data techniques.

2. Materials and Methods

The first step was to select a galactic PNe sample on which to analyse the binarity of their Central Stars (CSs). To carry out this data-mining process, we created a cross-match between the PNe coordinates from the literature [2] and sources from the Gaia EDR3 archive. Through this procedure, we obtained a 2035 PNe sample with reliable CS identifications.

The detection of close binary stars is not an easy task, because the proximity between both stellar components means that they cannot be visually resolved as two separate sources. However, it is known that the presence of a companion star can influence the decrease in the astrometric data quality that Gaia measures for the CS. Consequently, to find some evidence of binarity, we analysed certain parameters of the EDR3 database that were related to this detection quality. One of these parameters was astrometric excess noise, which measures the disagreement between the observations of a source and the best-fitting standard astrometric model. Another significant parameter was the Image Parameter Determination (IPD) harmonic amplitude; this measures the deviation in the image centroid fitting. Other parameters that could be considered are uncertainties in the source coordinates, in Right Ascension (RA) and in Declination (Dec) units. We also included the Renormalised Unit Weight Error (RUWE) parameter, which is related to the goodness of fit to the models when a source is detected. As the Gaia satellite is scanning the sky constantly, it takes measurements throughout multiple epochs for each source during its mission. Therefore, the mentioned parameters were calculated by data-mining techniques, considering and processing all the data collected from different epochs.

In addition, the colour of the star could also shed light on the presence of a possible binary system. The CSPNe usually have blue colours (indicators of a high temperature, capable of ionizing the PN). Therefore, stars detected as having reddish colours could be related to the presence of a companion star that is overshadowing, and consequently reddening, the central star. Therefore, with the aim of analysing this possible effect, we decided to separate our PNe sample into two subsets: blue and red stars. Then, in order to independently analyse their relationship with binarity, we calculated the mean values of each Gaia EDR3 parameter given for each subset.

3. Results

As a result, we found that the subset of red stars tends to have higher mean values in these quality parameters than the blue stars subset. This means that the quality of measurements is worse in the case of red stars.

We obtained much more astrometric excess noise for red stars than for blue ones, while the IPD harmonic amplitude showed similar values for both subsets, in terms of mean. Regarding the coordinate uncertainties and RUWE parameter, we also obtained slightly higher values for red stars than for blue ones. Therefore, red CSPNe would have more probability of belonging to a binary system. In Table 1, the mean values for each parameter in each subset can be observed.

Furthermore, with the aim of corroborating this hypothesis, we performed a Kolmogorov–Smirnov statistical test over these parameters and between both subsets, to analyse the similarity between both samples (red and blue). The p-values and D-values obtained from this analysis are shown in Table 1. For p-values below 0.1, the null hypothesis that both samples are similar can be rejected, with a significance of 99%. If the corresponding D-value is greater than 0.153, the null hypothesis can be also rejected.

Therefore, all values (except RUWE) indicate a non-similarity between both subsets. This confirms that the subset of red stars tends to have more affinity with binarity than the subset of blue stars.

Table 1. Mean values (with uncertainties) of different detection quality parameters for both samples (blue and red stars). In addition, the obtained p-values and D-values from a Kolmogorov–Smirnov statistical test between both samples and over those parameters are provided.

Parameter	Blue Stars	Red Stars	p-Value	D-Value
Astrometric Excess Noise	0.287 (0.060)	0.393 (0.076)	0	0.358
IPD Harmonic Amplitude	0.043 (0.015)	0.043 (0.013)	0	0.217
RA error	0.047 (0.013)	0.053 (0.017)	0.001	0.177
Dec error	0.044 (0.010)	0.049 (0.015)	0.001	0.189
RUWE	1.013 (0.051)	1.059 (0.042)	0.080	0.117

4. Discussion

Using Gaia accurate astrometry and data-mining methods, we were able to collect a PNe sample with reliable CS identifications, from almost 2000 million sources in Gaia EDR3 database.

Then, using this sample, we carried out a statistical analysis of several quality parameters, which enabled us to clarify which type of star has a higher possibility of forming a close binary system. In this type of system, both components cannot be visualised as separate sources, and it may be necessary to apply a statistical method to draw any conclusions.

Next year, with the launch of Gaia DR3, a greater quantity of astrometric and photometric data are expected, with increased accuracy. This will allow us to shed more light on the close binarity in PNe.

Author Contributions: Conceptualization, M.M.; methodology, I.G.-S. and M.M.; software, I.G.-S.; investigation, I.G.-S., M.M. and C.D.; writing—original draft preparation, I.G.-S.; writing—review and editing, M.M. and C.D.; supervision, M.M. and C.D. All authors have read and agreed to the published version of the manuscript.

Funding: Funding from Spanish Ministry project RTI2018-095076-B-C22, Xunta de Galicia ED431B 2021/36, and AYA-2017-88254-P is acknowledged by the authors. IGS acknowledges financial support from the Spanish National Programme for the Promotion of Talent and its Employability grant BES-2017-083126 cofunded by the European Social Fund.

Data Availability Statement: This research has made use of data from the European Space Agency (ESA) Gaia mission, processed by the Gaia Data Processing and Analysis Consortium (DPAC): [https://gea.esac.esa.int/archive/].

Conflicts of Interest: The authors declare no conflict of interest.

References

1. Boffin, H.M.J.; Jones, D. *The Importance of Binaries in the Formation and Evolution of Planetary Nebulae*; Springer: Berlin/Heidelberg, Germany, 2019. [CrossRef]
2. Parker, Q.A.; Bojicic, I.S.; Frew, D.J. HASH: The Hong Kong/AAO/Strasbourg H_α planetary nebula database. *J. Phys. Conf. Ser.* **2016**, *728*, 032008. [CrossRef]

Proceeding Paper

Deep Learning-Based Method for Computing Initial Margin [†]

Joel Pérez Villarino * and Álvaro Leitao Rodríguez

Research Group M2NICA, Department of Mathematics, CITIC, Universidade da Coruña, Campus de Elviña, 15071 A Coruña, Spain; alvaro.leitao@udc.es
* Correspondence: joel.perez.villarino@udc.es
† Presented at the 4th XoveTIC Conference, A Coruña, Spain, 7–8 October 2021.

Abstract: Following the guidelines of the Basel III agreement (2013), large financial institutions are forced to incorporate additional collateral, known as Initial Margin, in their transactions in OTC markets. Currently, the computation of such collateral is performed following the *Standard Initial Margin Model* (SIMM) methodology. Focusing on a portfolio consisting of an interest rate swap, we propose the use of Artificial Neural Networks (ANN) to approximate the Initial Margin value of the portfolio over its lifetime. The goal is to find an optimal configuration of structural hyperparameters, as well as to analyze the robustness of the network to variations in the model parameters and swap features.

Keywords: computational finance; collateral; initial margin; deep learning

1. Introduction

Due to the financial crisis experienced in 2008, the G8 World Council promoted the regulation of stricter actions for *over-the-counter* (OTC) derivatives market, especially to reduce the counterparty credit risk. Among the mandated measures is the progressive implementation of an additional type of collateral, known as Initial Margin (IM), with the aim of acting as a "cushion" against pronounced changes in the value of the portfolio contracts.

For the IM calculation, it is standard market practice to follow the Standard Initial Margin Model (SIMM) methodology [1], promoted by International Swaps and Derivatives Association (ISDA), which only requires the sensitivities of the portfolio as input data. When the goal is to know this amount over the whole life of the portfolio, the SIMM simulation becomes challenging due to the heavy computational burden coming from nested Monte Carlo simulations and the high-dimensional nature of the problem [2].

Among the existing alternatives to brute-force simulation, there are approaches based on Deep Learning algorithms, as [2]. We aim to implement a supervised neural network for computing the IM over the considered portfolio's life, with special attention to its structure's design. In this regard, we limit our work to portfolios consisting of a single product, a vanilla interest rate swap.

2. Materials and Methods

As a Deep Learning model for the task of computing the IM, we propose to use a self-normalizing neural network (SNN) [3], adding a single unit output layer (since the IM is a scalar quantity) with a ReLu activation function and He normal kernel initialization strategy [4]. We impose that all hidden layers have the same number of units, and such hyperparameters are fixed in the later results.

A supervised training is carried out. Unlike the usual methodology, where features associated with the scenario ω and time step j tuple are considered as a single input data for training, x_j^w, with the corresponding target y_j^w; we propose to use the entire scenario as input data, x^w, with the corresponding target vector y^w. We believe that this incorporates additional information to the training, allowing the learning of intrinsic features that can improve it.

The interest rate swap portfolio's dataset is produced synthetically, on the fly, from the simulation of several interest rate scenarios under the Hull–White dynamic [5]. We establish that it is necessary to know the following quantities throughout the life of the portfolio: the swap value; the two weeks, 1 month, 3 month and 6 month cash rates; the swap par rates for the following vertices: 1 year, 2 years, 3 years, 5 years, 10 years, 15 years, 20 years, and 30 years (as input features of the model); and the IM value (as model's target), for which is necessary to know the swap sensitivities in relation to the rates mentioned above.

The methodology recommended by ISDA, termed as PV01, is chosen for the production of swap sensitivities. It consists of calculating the impact of small changes in the swap rates used to construct the zero curve.

The SIMM methodology [6], is followed for the production of IM. Based on the assumptions of working in a single currency unit and exclusively with a portfolio consisting of a swap, the following formula is obtained for the SIMM:

$$SIMM = \max\left(1, \sqrt{\frac{|\sum_k s_k|}{CT}}\right) \sqrt{\sum_k (RW_k s_k)^2 + \sum_k \sum_{l \neq k} \rho_{k,l} (RW_k s_k)(RW_l s_l)}, \quad (1)$$

where s_k, RW_k are the net sensitivity and the risk weight for the rate tenor k; $\rho_{k,l}$ is the tenor correlation and CT is the concentration threshold for the given currency. RW_k, $\rho_{k,l}$ and CT are parameters given by ISDA.

3. Results

First of all, we study the optimal choice of structural hyperparameters of our proposed neural network (depth and width). Finally, we present some experiments related to training robustness as a function of Hull–White simulation parameters and swap features (A summary of the results obtained is presented. The extended version can be found in [7]).

3.1. Numerical Experiments to Set Structural Hyperparameters

For the test in this subsection, a 1-year fixed, 6-months floating at-the-money swap with 10-year maturity is considered. We establish the theoretical values $a = 0.1$, $\sigma = 0.5\%$ for the Hull–White parameters and we choose the market forward rate, $f(0,t)$, obtained from all Eurozone governments bonds on 28 January 2021 (Source: European Central Bank (ECB)). A dataset with 5000 scenarios and 199 time steps is produced. In all tests, we use 4000 scenarios for training and 1000 for validation.

With respect to our neural network, we worked with the stochastic gradient descent optimizer and the following training hyperparameters: a bath size of 256, a learning rate of 0.001, and 1000 epochs.

3.1.1. The Depth Test

We set the total number of units to 512, which will be distributed, by means of integer division, over the following number of hidden layers: 1, 2, 3, 4, 6, 8, 10, 12, and 16. We present the results from 10 training trials due to the stochasticity of the optimization algorithm.

We can observe in Figure 1 that a moderate number of hidden layers (between 3 and 6) tend to offer a better performance than the model with two hidden layers, theoretically the one with the highest capacity. We set the number of hidden layers in our network to 4. It presents the best performance on the trials considered, with shorter execution time than its direct competitors.

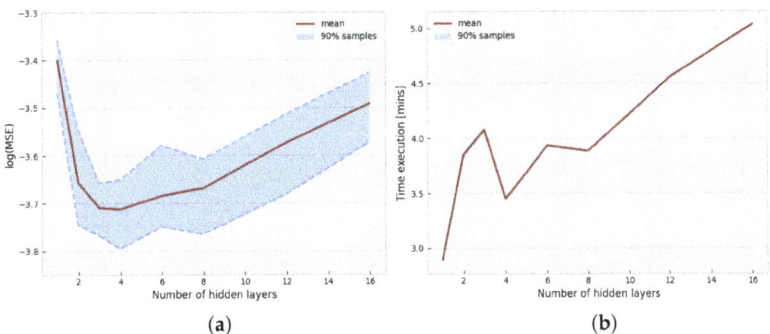

Figure 1. Results obtained for the depth test. (**a**) convergence of the MSE training set with respect to the number of hidden layers; (**b**) execution time according to the number of hidden layers.

3.1.2. The Width Test

We set the number of hidden layers to 4 and we consider the following numbers of units: 1, 2, 4, 8, 16, 24, 32, 48, 64, 96, and 128. All other specifications remain unchanged.

The test shows that, as the number of neurons per layer increases, the network performance increases, as well as the execution time required. In order to achieve a balance between network efficiency and training time, we choose to select 48 units per hidden layer.

3.2. Numerical Experiments on Network Robustness

In this subsection we used the Adam optimizer with a learning rate of 10^{-4}.

On the one hand, it has been tested how the model training responds to market situations different from the reference configuration. In general, similar results are obtained, although in situations of stressed volatility the so-called zero-inflated data problem appears. On the other hand, the influence of the swap features is analyzed. Roughly speaking, it will be necessary to have a trained model for each maturity considered, but it is feasible to use the model trained for a given frequency payments on swaps at different frequencies.

4. Conclusions and Future Research

We have found that the proposed Deep Learning model provides good approximations of IM trajectories for the simplified portfolio considered. It shows an excellent performance on our main study dataset. It is maintained for higher volatility environments. We also concluded that it is feasible to use the same model as an IM computation engine for swaps with different payment structures. However, this is not possible for different maturities. It is necessary to have a model for each case.

Future research related to this work should be focused on the scalability of the model to other interest rate products; building a model for the IM computation of other ISDA product classes, such as equity or commodity; and developing a similar neural network-based methodology to compute the IM for a real portfolio, consisting of many contracts from different product classes and driven by multiple risk factors.

Institutional Review Board Statement: Not applicable.

Informed Consent Statement: Not applicable.

Data Availability Statement: Not applicable.

References

1. ISDA. *Key Trends in the Size and Composition of OTC Derivatives Markets in the First Half of 2020*; ISDA: New York, NY, USA, 2020.
2. Ma, X.; Spinner, S.; Venditti, A.; Li, Z.; Tang, S. Initial Margin Simulation with Deep Learning. *SSRN Electron. J.* **2019**. [CrossRef]

3. Klambauer, G.; Unterthiner, T.; Mayr, A.; Hochreiter, S. Self-Normalizing Neural Networks. In *Advances in Neural Information Processing Systems 30 (NIPS 2017)*; Guyon, I., von Luxburg, U., Bengio, S., Wallach, H.M., Fergus, R., Vishwanathan, S.V.N., Garnett, R., Eds.; Curran Associates, Inc.: New York, NY, USA, 2017; pp. 971–980.
4. He, K.; Zhang, X.; Ren, S.; Sun, J. Delving Deep into Rectifiers: Surpassing Human-Level Performance on ImageNet Classification. In Proceedings of the 2015 IEEE International Conference on Computer Vision (ICCV '15), Santiago, Chile, 7–13 December 2015; pp. 1026–1034.
5. Hull, J.; White, A. Numerical Procedures for Implementing Term Structure Models I. *J. Deriv.* **1994**, 2, 7–16. [CrossRef]
6. ISDA. *ISDA SIMM Methodology*, version 2.0; ISDA: New York, NY, USA, 2017.
7. Villarino, J.P. Deep Learning-Based Method for Computing Initial Margin. Master's Thesis, University of A Coruña, A Coruña, Spain, 2021.

Proceeding Paper

A Bi-Objective Scheduling Problem in a Home Care Business [†]

Isabel Méndez-Fernández [1,2,*], Silvia Lorenzo-Freire [1,2] and Ángel Manuel González-Rueda [1,2]

1. Grupo MODES, Departamento de Matemáticas, Universidade da Coruña, 15071 A Coruña, Spain; silvia.lorenzo@udc.es (S.L.-F.); angel.manuel.rueda@udc.es (Á.M.G.-R.)
2. Centro de Investigación TIC—CITIC, Universidade da Coruña, 15071 A Coruña, Spain
* Correspondence: isabel.mendez.fernandez@udc.es
† Presented at the 4th XoveTIC Conference, A Coruña, Spain, 7–8 October 2021.

Abstract: In this work we study a routing and scheduling problem for a home care business. The problem is composed of two conflicting objectives, therefore we study it as a bi-objective one. We obtain the Pareto frontier for small size instances using the AUGMECON2 method and, for bigger cases, we developed an heuristic algorithm. We also obtained some preliminary results that show the algorithm has good behaviour.

Keywords: optimization; scheduling; heuristic algorithms; operations research

1. Introduction

Home care services aim to help elderly, sick or dependent people maintain their quality of life without having to leave their homes. The goal of a Home Care Scheduling Problem is to obtain the routes that the company's employees must follow, as well as the times at which each service has to be carried out.

In our problem, the users are the company's clients, and they require a number of services that need to be carried out, by the company's employees, throughout the week. To correctly address the users' needs it is essential that they define the characteristics of the services they request: the day of the week they belong to, their duration, a hard time window and a soft time window. These time windows are necessary because they are used to determine the schedule of each service. Hard time windows state the times within which services must be completed, to have a feasible plan. Soft time windows represent when the user prefers to be attended, even though it is not necessary to uphold them.

The caregivers are the company's employees and their work consists of visiting users at their homes to carry out the tasks required by them. Every caregiver has a contract, which states the maximum number of hours they can work during each day, and the number of hours that they are hired to work during the week. Caregivers' working days start at the beginning of the first service and end when the last one is finished. All breaks that caregivers have during the day are considered worked time, with the exception of the largest one—if it lasts two or more hours.

To maintain the users satisfaction, the company works with a list of 6 affinity levels that establish the compatibility between users and caregivers.

2. The Problem

The purpose of this work is to provide the company with the caregivers' schedules for the week. In the interest of achieving the best possible schedules, we consider two clearly differentiated objectives: the cost of the schedule and the users' welfare.

The cost of the schedule represents the expenses associated with the caregivers carrying out their routes, and it is composed of two elements:

1. The overtime of the caregivers. This is caused by allowing the caregivers to work more hours during the week than initially agreed, while still adhering to their daily maximum allowed working time, which results in an extra cost for the company.

2. The total working time of the caregivers. This is the sum of the daily working time of each caregiver according to the schedules, and by reducing them we are saving the company money while also optimizing the caregivers time.

The users' welfare represents the degree of well being and satisfaction that users present according to the schedule, and combines two elements:

1. The affinity between caregivers and the users they attend. By maximizing the affinity, we try to ensure that users will be attended by caregivers they are most comfortable with.
2. The penalization for carrying out a service before, or after, its soft time window. Minimizing this value means that the services will be scheduled as close as possible to their soft time windows.

For the schedules to be feasible, the company requires that: each service has to be carried out within its hard time window by one caregiver, the caregivers' daily scheduled time cannot surpass their maximum working hours, the largest break a caregiver has during the day will not be considered as working time.

3. Resolution Methods

The problem has two conflicting objectives, which means that there is not a single solution that optimizes both of them at the same time. In a multi-objective problem with p objectives we say that x dominates y if $f_k(x) \leq f_k(y)\ \forall k \in \{1,...,p\}$ and $f_k(x) < f_k(y)$ for at least one $k \in \{1,...,p\}$. To solve our problem we look for the Pareto frontier, which is a set composed by the non-dominated solutions.

We modelled the problem as a Mixed Integer Programming (MIP) one and used it to obtain non-dominated solutions with the AUGMECON2 method [1]. However, because this problem is a complex one, we can only solve small instances with the AUGMECON2 method. Therefore, it is necessary to develop an heuristic algorithm to generate good approximations of the non-dominated set for instances of bigger size.

The algorithm presented in this problem is divided into three steps:

Step 1 We initiate the sets by obtaining the best solutions for each of the objectives (considering a lexicographic objective function) using the Adaptive Large Neighbourhood Search (ALNS) [2].

Step 2 We obtain a set of multiple solutions with different routes. This is done by applying the ALNS to a solution chosen at random from the ones already found.

Step 3 The set of non-dominated solutions is obtained by randomly choosing a solution and then modifying its schedule in order to improve one of the objectives. In order to modify the schedule of a solution the method randomly selects a service and an objective. Then the service is advanced or delayed in order to improve the objective under consideration.

4. Results

In this section we present the preliminary computational results obtained to check the behaviour of the heuristic algorithm. The instances we solved are the ones presented in [3], which were adapted to the characteristics of our problem.

In Figures 1 and 2 we present the Pareto front obtained by the AUGMECON2 method (blue colour) as well as two approximations of the non-dominated set obtained by different configurations of the algorithm. These configurations depend of the number of iterations used, and are described in Table 1.

Table 1. Configurations of the experiments.

	Step 1	Step 2	Step 3
Configuration 1	1000	1000	10,000
Configuration 2	1000	500	100,000

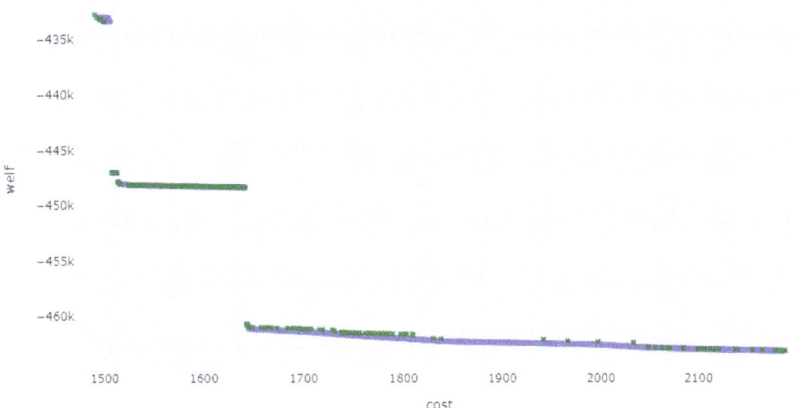

Figure 1. Approximation of the Pareto frontier—Configuration 1.

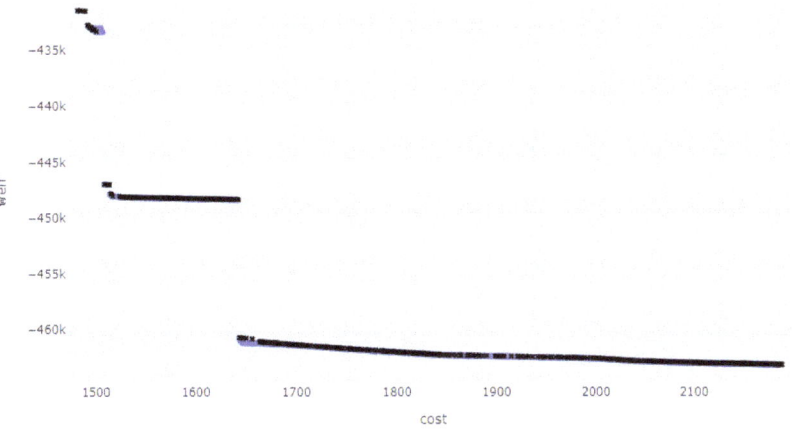

Figure 2. Approximation of the Pareto frontier—Configuration 2.

We can see that the approximation presented in Figure 2 (black) is better than the one in Figure 1 (green), because it is closer to the Pareto frontier. In fact, Figure 2 shows that our algorithm can provide good approximations of the Pareto frontier.

Author Contributions: I.M.-F., S.L.-F. and Á.M.G.-R. studied the problem and designed the algorithm; I.M.-F. implemented the algorithm and performed the experiments. All authors have read and agreed to the published version of the manuscript.

Funding: This research/work has been supported by MINECO grant MTM2017-87197-C3-1-P, and by the Xunta de Galicia through the ERDF (Grupos de Referencia Competitiva ED431C-2016-015 and ED431C-2020-14 and Centro de Investigación del Sistema universitario de Galicia ED431G 2019/01).

Institutional Review Board Statement: Not applicable.

Informed Consent Statement: Not applicable.

Data Availability Statement: Not applicable.

Conflicts of Interest: The authors declare no conflict of interest.

References

1. Mavrotas, G.; Florios, K. An improved version of the augmented ϵ-constraint method (AUGMECON2) for finding the exact pareto set in multi-objective integer programming problems. *Appl. Math. Comput.* **2013**, *219*, 9652–9669.
2. Ropke, S.; Pisinger, D. An adaptive large neighborhood search heuristic for the pickup and delivery problem with time windows. *Transp. Sci.* **2006**, *40*, 455–472. [CrossRef]
3. Solomon, M.M. Algorithms for the vehicle routing and scheduling problems with time window constraints. *Oper. Res.* **1987**, *35*, 254–265. [CrossRef]

Proceeding Paper

Virtual Reality at the Service of People with Functional Diversity: Personalized Intervention Spaces †

Manuel Lagos *, Jessica Martín, Ángel Gómez and Thais Pousada

CITIC (Centre for Information and Communications Technology Research), Elviña Campus, University of A Coruña, 15071 A Coruña, Spain; j.martin1@udc.es (J.M.); angel.gomez@udc.es (Á.G.); thais.pousada.garcia@udc.es (T.P.)
* Correspondence: m.lagos@udc.es
† Presented at the 4th XoveTIC Conference, A Coruña, Spain, 7–8 October 2021.

Abstract: Virtual reality allows to generate an environment of great realism, while achieving the immersion of the user in it. The purpose of this project is to use this technology as a complementary tool in the rehabilitation of people with functional diversity. To do this, an application is being developed that will offer different environments that simulate situations in everyday life. Through its initial menu, the professional will be able to select the virtual work environment, with different configuration options to adapt each scenario to the user's needs. This customization of the scenarios will allow such things as configuring the degree of difficulty of the activity to eventually adapting the elements of the scenario to the functional capacity of the user.

Keywords: virtual reality; immersive environment; functional diversity; unity; leap motion

1. Introduction

The rehabilitation process of people with functional diversity is complex, and during the sessions carried out by health professionals, different elements are used to configure an appropriate environment to deal with the user's difficulties. For the configuration of these environments (in a controlled way), the presence of possible physical or economic limitations is frequent. Physical, in terms of the characteristics of the space in which the sessions are held, and the difficulty of replicating different environments, especially outdoors, so that the person can put their daily life skills into practice; and economic, in terms of the outlay to be made in the acquisition of various materials, which could be used to configure the different environments.

Virtual reality is a technological resource that allows to generate spaces of great realism, while achieving the immersion of the user in them. So why not harness the potential of virtual reality in the rehabilitation of people with functional diversity?

The use of this technology makes it possible to considerably reduce the physical limitations mentioned above. Thus, custom environments can be programmed, adding any element through 3D modeling.

Therefore, the objective of this project was to use virtual reality as a complementary means of intervention in rehabilitation sessions with people with functional diversity. To achieve this objective, an application is being developed that will offer different environments that simulate everyday life situations.

2. Technologies

As for the technologies used, a virtual reality equipment HTC VIVE [1] is used, which will be in charge of creating the virtual reality experience, allowing the user to be immersed in the different scenarios developed.

It is worth highlighting the use of the Leap Motion [2] device, an optical system capable of tracking the movement of the person's hands and fingers, which allows her/him

to interact with the different environments directly, without the need for controls. The incorporation of this device was an added value in the project since, precisely, several work environments are intended to work mobility problems in the hands, which is undoubtedly carried out more effectively by avoiding the use of controls as a means of interaction with this virtual space.

Unity [3], a real-time development platform, is used as the programming environment, allowing the creation of interactive environments for multiple platforms, such as PCs, consoles, or virtual reality equipment.

3. Description of the Application

Through the main menu, the professional will be able to select the virtual work environment and its characteristics, with different configuration options to adapt each scenario to the user's needs (both physically and cognitively).

Work environments are modeled in the form of a test, with a series of objectives that the user must achieve. In this way, it is intended that the person who runs the test feels motivated to achieve the established goals, while training and progressively improving their abilities, reducing their functional limitations.

One of the scenarios under development represents a vegetable garden with different vegetables that the user must collect. This scenario can be configured to train both physical and cognitive abilities. Likewise, the level of difficulty of the activity can also be chosen, allowing the training to be adapted according to the user's progress.

In terms of physical work, the application was intended to strengthen the abdominal musculature in people using wheelchairs. To do this, one of the tasks proposed to the user was to collect tomatoes and place them in different boxes. The height of the plants can be configured in the main menu, allowing to adapt the level of difficulty to the user's abilities, as indicated above.

If the goal is to work cognitive skills, the garden will not only contain tomatoes, but a multitude of vegetables. In this case, the objective to be achieved by the user will be to complete several boxes with different combinations of vegetables.

Another of the environments being developed simulates a supermarket. This scenario is of great interest due to the number of daily life tasks that it allows us to train. Some of the activities that are under development are: Purchase of a series of items indicated in a list, selection of the products necessary to prepare a cooking recipe, or cash payment training.

All these developments are in progress, and the research team is working with professionals and persons with functional diversity to get their opinion about different features during the application of virtual scenarios. Several work meetings have been carried out to get the perspectives of future users.

4. Discussion

Currently, there are different digital distribution platforms for video games that include virtual reality applications in their catalog, such as Steam [4].

When using commercial applications as a complementary tool in rehabilitation sessions with people with functional diversity, it is possible to find several drawbacks, such as the lack of customization, since they are general-purpose applications with few configuration options. It is also common to find very complex applications, with unclear instructions and no feedback to guide the user during the game [5]. Generally, controllers are used as a means of interaction, which is a drawback for people with a functional limitation in their hands.

In a review about the application of Virtual Reality in Complex Medical Rehabilitation, authors once analyzed the literature and concluded that the use of virtual environments has proven effectiveness on the recovery of impaired motor skills in people with disabilities. However, to get the optimal results of this application, a personalized approach and monitoring registration of some physical and cognitive variables are required [6].

Therefore, the application being developed in this project is a great contribution to the use of virtual reality in the rehabilitation of people with functional diversity, allowing the adaptation of the environments to the user's needs, offering visual and auditory feedback during the execution of the game and allowing to dispense with controls, thanks to the use of the Leap Motion device.

5. Conclusions

The application presented here is a novelty development to be applied in the field of health, concretely, in the rehabilitation's intervention with people with functional diversity. The use of virtual environments, personalized to the skills of the user by rehabilitation, professionally constitutes a motivating factor to enhance him/her to actively participate and compromise in her/his progression of the treatment.

The customized virtual environments developed in the present project have clear advantages:

- The virtual reality itself supposes a potent technological tool in the rehabilitation process, offering multiple possibilities to bring a great variety of scenarios into the room of the intervention center or hospital.
- The possibility of customizing the levels of both physical and cognitive tasks presented in each scenario allows to establish specific goals and activities for each person, and to adjust them according the improvement of the user.
- The use of Leap Motion combined with the virtual reality glasses offers a greater immersive experience, avoiding the need for controls, and allowing the person to use her/his hands and fingers to improve their coordination and dexterity skills themselves.

In the future, we expect that this application will be a consistent tool showing different and motivating scenarios of daily life which has been implemented, at low cost, in rehabilitation centers.

Author Contributions: Conceptualization, Á.G. and M.L.; methodology, M.L. and T.P.; software, M.L. and Á.G.; validation, M.L.; T.P. and J.M.; formal analysis, Á.G.; investigation, M.L.; resources, T.P.; data curation, J.M.; writing—original draft preparation, M.L. and J.M.; writing—review and editing, T.P. and Á.G.; visualization, J.M.; supervision, Á.G.; project administration, Á.G. and T.P.; funding acquisition, T.P. All authors have read and agreed to the published version of the manuscript.

Funding: This research had the support for its publication by National Program of R+D+i oriented to the Challenges of Society 2019 (coordinated research) Grant number: PID2019-104323RB-C33. Ministry of science and innovation.

Institutional Review Board Statement: Not applicable.

Informed Consent Statement: Not applicable.

Data Availability Statement: Not applicable.

Acknowledgments: The development of the project is supported by CITIC as a Research Center of the Galician University System is financed by the Consellería de Educación, Universidades y Formación Profesional (Xunta de Galicia) through the ERDF (80%), Operational Program ERDF Galicia 2014–2020 and the remaining 20% by the Secretaria Xeral de Universidades (Ref. ED431G 2019/01).

Conflicts of Interest: The authors declare no conflict of interest.

References

1. HTC VIVE. Available online: https://www.vive.com/eu/product/vive/ (accessed on 23 July 2021).
2. Leap Motion. Available online: https://www.ultraleap.com/product/leap-motion-controller/ (accessed on 10 June 2021).
3. Unity. Available online: https://unity.com/es (accessed on 20 July 2021).
4. Steam. Available online: https://store.steampowered.com (accessed on 28 July 2021).

5. Miranda-Duro, M.d.C.; Concheiro-Moscoso, P.; Viqueira, J.L.; Nieto-Riveiro, L.; Domínguez, N.C.; García, T.P. Virtual Reality Game Analysis for People with Functional Diversity: An Inclusive Perspective. *Proceedings* **2020**, *54*, 20. [CrossRef]
6. Volovik, M.G.; Borzikov, V.V.; Kuznetsov, A.; Bazarov, D.; Polyakova, A.G. Virtual Reality Technology in Complex Medical Rehabilitation of Patients with Disabilities. Review. *Sovrem. Tehnol. Med.* **2018**, 10, 173. [CrossRef]

Proceeding Paper

A Parallel Tool for the Identification of Differentially Methylated Regions in Genomic Analyses [†]

Alejandro Fernández-Fraga *, Jorge González-Domínguez and Juan Touriño

Computer Architecture Group, CITIC, Universidade da Coruña, 15071 A Coruña, Spain; jgonzalezd@udc.es (J.G.-D.); juan@udc.es (J.T.)
* Correspondence: a.fernandez3@udc.es
[†] Presented at 4th XoveTIC Conference, A Coruña, Spain, 7–8 October 2021.

Abstract: Methylation is a chemical process that modifies DNA through the addition of a methyl group to one or several nucleotides. Discovering differentially methylated regions is an important research field in genomics, as it can help to anticipate the risk of suffering from certain diseases. RADMeth is one of the most accurate tools in this field, but it has high computational complexity. In this work, we present a hybrid MPI-OpenMP parallel implementation of RADMeth to accelerate its execution on distributed-memory systems, reaching speedups of up to 189 when running on 256 cores and allowing for its application to large-scale datasets.

Keywords: methylation; whole-genome bisulfite sequencing; high performance computing; MPI; OpenMP

1. Introduction

DNA methylation is a chemical modification of DNA resulting from the addition of a methyl group to a certain nucleotide. This process, which mainly occurs at cytosines within particular regions of the DNA, is associated with different biological functions, and abnormal methylation levels can indicate the presence of certain diseases. For instance, the existence of regions with different methylation levels is a common characteristic for several types of cancer. Therefore, discovering differentially methylated regions is an important research field in genomics, as it can help to anticipate the risk of suffering from some diseases. Nevertheless, the high computational cost associated with this task prevents its application to large-scale datasets.

In this work, we focus on the tool RADMeth [1], since it showed superior accuracy in terms of biological results when compared to several counterparts [2]. RADMeth is a publicly available tool to find individual differentially methylated sites and genomic regions in data from Whole-Genome Bisulfite Sequencing experiments, which is the state-of-the-art technology for obtaining a comprehensive view of DNA methylation. The tool uses beta-binomial regression for high-precision differential methylation analysis over these data, and it can handle medium-size experiments. Despite its accurate biological results, the main drawback of RADMeth is its high computational requirements that prevent its usage on large-size experiments.

The objective of this work is to develop a parallel tool for the identification of differentially methylated regions that provides exactly the same accurate biological results as RADMeth, but employs High Performance Computing (HPC) techniques to accelerate the execution. This goal has been achieved by using the Message Passing Interface (MPI) and OpenMP parallel programming standards to provide support for multiple processes and threads, respectively. This parallel implementation allows for the exploitation of the architecture of distributed-memory systems, such as multicore clusters, and then an analysis of large-size datasets by significantly reducing the execution times associated with them.

2. Parallel Implementation of RADMeth

RADMeth works with datasets that are represented as matrices, where the columns are the samples, the rows are the CpG sites (i.e., regions of the DNA where methylation mainly occurs), and each position in the matrix contains two values: one containing the number of reads associated with a certain CpG site, and another one containing the number of methylated reads. The output dataset is formatted with a row for each CpG site, which contains the p-value from the experiment associated with it. In this work, we propose a hybrid parallel tool based on the MPI message-passing library and OpenMP threads that works with the same data format as RADMeth and guarantees the same exact accurate results, but with significantly reduced execution times.

This has been achieved by applying domain decomposition to the input CpG sites. This means that the CpG sites of the input dataset are divided into blocks so that each block is processed in parallel by a different processing element. Our implementation makes use of this domain decomposition at two levels of parallelism. First, the dataset is statically distributed in blocks of the same size among MPI processes. Besides the execution time gains, this MPI parallelization enables the joint usage of the memory of several nodes. Second, the workload of each process is dynamically distributed among OpenMP threads.

Two performance optimizations have been applied to our parallel tool:

- Parallel data loading and storing, to take advantage of parallel programming not only in the critical phase of the tool but also in the input and output phases. This optimization technique not only improves the performance of the tool on its own, but it also allows the tool to load the entire dataset at once in a distributed and scalable manner, without concern about memory problems, which allows the tool to achieve an even better performance in these phases.
- Dynamic workload distribution. The time to process different CpG sites can present high variability. This may lead to workload imbalances; that is, even though the blocks of data associated with each process have the same size, one block might need more time than another one. This problem is alleviated thanks to the second level of parallelization, where the workload for each MPI process is distributed dynamically among the OpenMP threads launched by it.

3. Results and Conclusions

The experiments for the performance analysis of the parallel version of RADMeth were conducted on 16 nodes of the "Pluton" cluster, a distributed-memory system that is based on Intel Xeon processors and installed at CITIC. Each node is composed of two processors with eight cores each (16 logical threads using HyperThreading) and 64 GB of main memory. The whole system provides a total of 256 cores (512 logical threads with HyperThreading) and 1 TB of memory. In order to keep the reproducibility of the experiments, we have used two representative datasets that are publicly available, Akalin 2012 and Hansen 2014. The Akalin dataset is made of 28,670,426 CpG sites and 2 samples, whereas the Hansen dataset consists of 28,217,449 and 6 samples. In addition to those properties, it is important to mention that the Akalin dataset is a worst-case scenario in terms of workload imbalance, meaning that a high percentage of the workload is associated with a very small contiguous block of CpG sites. A parallel tool with only static data distribution is unable to accelerate the execution of this dataset, proving the dynamic workload distribution to be an outstanding performance optimization, completely compulsory for the tool to scale in critical scenarios.

Table 1 also shows the runtime and speedup (in parentheses) for different number of nodes. Regarding the parallel executions, the same configuration for each node was used, as it proved to be the most efficient one after some preliminary tests: one MPI process with 16 cores each (32 logical threads per MPI process using HyperThreading). The reason is that the dynamic distribution, necessary for high scalability, is implemented at the thread level, so the higher the threads-to-process ratio is, the better the workload balance is, and the better the performance of the parallel tool is. As can be seen in the table, the parallel version of RADMeth performs well and offers excellent scalability (execution times largely decrease when the number of cores increases). Furthermore, due to the execution time reduction, the parallel tool allows for the analysis of large-scale datasets when this method is applied.

Table 1. Dataset scalability, execution times (in seconds), and speedups (in parentheses).

	Akalin 2012	Hansen 2014
Original RADMeth	10,886.90	45,931.20
1 Node	498.65 (21.83)	2424.93 (18.94)
2 Nodes	304.76 (35.72)	1228.00 (37.40)
4 Nodes	326.55 (33.33)	803.70 (57.14)
8 Nodes	215.10 (50.61)	444.67 (103.29)
16 Nodes	121.35 (89.71)	242.97 (189.03)

Author Contributions: Conceptualization, J.G.-D. and J.T.; methodology, A.F.-F., J.G.-D. and J.T.; implementation, A.F.-F.; validation, A.F.-F.; writing—original draft preparation, A.F.-F.; writing—review and editing, J.G.-D. and J.T. All authors have read and agreed to the published version of the manuscript.

Funding: This research was funded by the Ministry of Science and Innovation of Spain (PID2019-104184RB-I00/AEI/10.13039/501100011033) and by Xunta de Galicia and FEDER funds of the EU (Centro de Investigación de Galicia accreditation 2019-2022, ref. ED431G2019/01; Consolidation Program of Competitive Reference Groups, ED431C 2021/30).

Institutional Review Board Statement: Not applicable.

Informed Consent Statement: Not applicable.

Data Availability Statement: Not applicable.

Conflicts of Interest: The authors declare that there is no conflict of interest.

References

1. Dolzhenko, E.; Smith, A.D. Using beta-binomial regression for high-precision differential methylation analysis in multifactor whole-genome bisulfite sequencing experiments. *BMC Bioinform.* **2014**, *15*, 215. [CrossRef] [PubMed]
2. Klein, H.U.; Hebestreit, K. An evaluation of methods to test predefined genomic regions for differential methylation in bisulfite sequencing data. *Briefings Bioinform.* **2016**, *17*, 796–807. [CrossRef] [PubMed]

Proceeding Paper

Quantum Arithmetic for Directly Embedded Arrays [†]

Alberto Manzano [1,*,‡], Daniele Musso [2,‡], Álvaro Leitao [1], Andrés Gómez [2], Carlos Vázquez [1], Gustavo Ordóñez [3] and María Rodríguez-Nogueiras [3]

[1] Research Group M2NICA, Department of Mathematics, CITIC, University of A Coruña, Campus de Elviña S/N, 15071 A Coruña, Spain; alvaro.leitao@udc.gal (Á.L.); carlos.vazquez.cendon@udc.es (C.V.)
[2] Centro de Supercomputación de Galicia (CESGA), Avenida de Vigo, 15705 Santiago de Compostela, Spain; daniele.musso@cesga.es (D.M.); andres.gomez.tato@cesga.es (A.G.)
[3] Global Risk Analytics, HSBC, Centenary Sq, Birmingham B1 1HQ, UK; gustavo.ordonez-sanz@hsbc.com (G.O.); maria.r.nogueiras@hsbc.com (M.R.-N.)
[*] Correspondence: alberto.manzano.herrero@udc.es
[†] Presented at the 4th XoveTIC Conference, A Coruña, Spain, 7–8 October 2021.
[‡] These authors contributed equally to this work.

Abstract: We describe a general-purpose framework to implement quantum algorithms relying upon an efficient handling of arrays. The cornerstone of the framework is the direct embedding of information into quantum amplitudes, thus avoiding hampering square roots. We discuss the entire pipeline, from data loading to information extraction. Particular attention is devoted to the definition of an efficient toolkit of basic quantum operations on arrays. We comment on strong and weak points of the proposed quantum manipulations, especially in relation to an effective exploitation of quantum parallelism. We describe in detail some general-purpose routines as well as their embedding in full algorithms. Their efficiency is critically discussed both locally, at the level of the routine, and globally, at the level of the full algorithm. Finally, we comment on some applications in the quantitative finance domain.

Keywords: quantum computing; quantum simulation

1. Introduction

Quantum hardware and software are still in their early days of development; thus, the design of quantum algorithms typically focuses on low-level operations. Although one should always keep in mind the hardware limitations, especially when describing possible near-term implementations of quantum algorithms, it is convenient to pursue higher levels of abstraction. Apart from its long-term and algorithmic interest, a more abstract and standardized approach serves practical purposes too, for example, that of making the benchmarking of quantum computer performances a more solid and transparent process. In turn, this helps pushing the research and the development in quantum computation at all levels. In the present paper, we describe a novel framework for the design of quantum algorithms on a more abstract plane. To this aim, we have three proposals [1].

2. Results

Our first proposal consists in the definition of a quantum matrix, namely a quantum state organized in two registers:

$$|\psi\rangle = \sum_{i=0}^{I-1} \sum_{j=0}^{J-1} c_{ij} |i\rangle_{n_I} \otimes |j\rangle_{n_J}. \tag{1}$$

Specifically, we interpret the first register as the index running over the rows and the second register as the index running over the columns. This way of storing the information has a common ground with that of Flexible Representation of Quantum Images (FRQI) and the Novel Enhanced Quantum Representation (NEQR) [2,3]. The main difference with FRQI and NEQR is that we encode the information of the (i,j) entry of the matrix in the quantum amplitude. Intuitively, the matrix is a bi-dimensional memory array where the amplitude encodes the information stored in the (i,j) memory location (see Figure 1).

	$\|0\rangle_{n_J}$	$\|1\rangle_{n_J}$	...	$\|j\rangle_{n_J}$	...	$\|J\rangle_{n_J}$
$\|0\rangle_{n_I}$	c_{00}	c_{01}	...	c_{0j}	...	c_{0J}
$\|1\rangle_{n_I}$	c_{10}	c_{11}	...	c_{1j}	...	c_{1J}
...	...	...	...	...	...	...
$\|i\rangle_{n_I}$	c_{i0}	c_{i1}	...	c_{ij}	...	c_{iJ}
...	...	...	...	...	...	...
$\|I\rangle_{n_I}$	c_{I0}	c_{I1}	...	c_{Ij}	...	c_{IJ}

Figure 1. Quantum matrix structure.

The second proposal is a key technical feature about how we encode the information into the quantum amplitudes, the so-called direct embedding [4]. Namely, the information to be stored into the quantum matrix is directly loaded into the amplitudes without taking square roots, as it is instead usually done in the literature. Such loading choice has several and important implications in later stages of the quantum algorithms and—most importantly—the information stored into the quantum state is handled and combined more easily, because algebraic operations are not hampered by the presence of square roots.

The third and final proposal is to give a full overview of the complete pipeline, or overall structure, of a generic algorithm admitting implementation within this framework (see Figure 2).

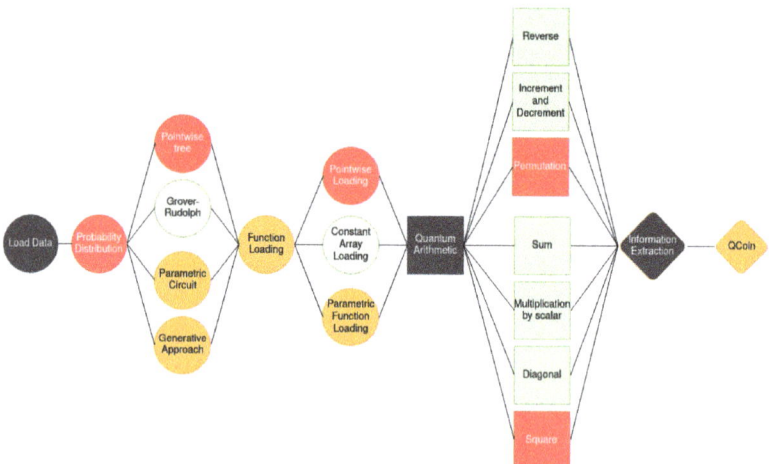

Figure 2. Structure of the pipeline. The dark gray nodes represent the three main steps; the nodes in red correspond to algorithms that are not efficient, for those in yellow the efficiency varies from case to case and, finally, the nodes in green represent efficient algorithms.

The first step of every algorithm corresponds to loading some input data. In the quantum case, it is often convenient to split this step into two sub steps:

1. Loading a probability distribution [4–6];
2. Loading a bi-dimensional function.

It is not strictly necessary to split the loading into two steps. Yet, we consider such splitting because—typically—we adopt different loading techniques for them: the probability distribution is loaded with a state preparation algorithm (e.g., a multiplexor binary tree); the function is loaded by means of another technique.

The second step of the pipeline in our framework corresponds to the implementation of various arithmetic operations, typically at the level of entire arrays or sub-arrays, and we refer to it as quantum arithmetic.

The third and last step of the pipeline corresponds to extracting the information that we have stored in the quantum state, namely the read-out of the state that encodes the result of the algorithm. There are multiple techniques for this purpose such as those appearing in [7–11].

3. Discussion

One of the advantages of organizing the pipeline as we have discussed is that it enjoys a modular structure; therefore, we can develop, analyze and improve each of the steps independently, achieving a better understanding of the problems in each domain.

In this paper, apart from introducing the framework, we provide some simple examples of arithmetic operations with finance in view. The possibility of implementing arithmetic operations has been considered in the literature since the early days of quantum computation. Apart from the quantum implementation of logical circuits corresponding to basic operations, such as the quantum adder [12,13], also the manipulation of "continuous" numbers has been studied. Let us mention some works which, at least in spirit, are closer to ours [14–17]. The difference with such approaches consists in the fact that we use a new embedding and organize the information into the matrix (1); these two aspects combined allow us to work in a transparent and simple manner.

Funding: This research was funded by the European Project NExt ApplicationS of Quantum Computing (NEASQC), funded by Horizon 2020 Program inside the call H2020-FETFLAG-2020-01(Grant Agreement 951821). Part of the computational resources for this project were provided by the Centro de Supercomputación de Galicia (CESGA).

Conflicts of Interest: The authors declare no conflict of interest.

References

1. Manzano, A.; Musso, D.; Leitao, Á.; Gómez, A.; Vázquez, C.; Ordóñez, G.; Rodríguez-Nogueiras, M. Quantum Arithmetic for Directly Embedded Arrays. *arXiv* **2021**, arXiv:2107.13872.
2. Le, P.; Iliyasu, A.; Dong, F.; Hirota, K. A flexible representation of quantum images for polynomial preparation, image compression and processing operations. *Quantum Inf. Process.* **2011**, *10*, 63–84. [CrossRef]
3. Zhang, Y.; Lu, K.; Gao, Y.; Wang, M. NEQR: A novel enhanced quantum representation of digital images. *Quantum Inf. Process.* **2013**, *12*, 2833–2860. [CrossRef]
4. Kubo, K.; Nakagawa, Y.O.; Endo, S.; Nagayama, S. Variational quantum simulations of stochastic differential equations. *arXiv* **2020**, arXiv:2012.04429.
5. Grover, L.; Rudolph, T. Creating superpositions that correspond to efficiently integrable probability distributions. *arXiv* **2002**, arXiv:quant-ph/0208112.
6. Nakaji, K.; Uno, S.; Suzuki, Y.; Raymond, R.; Onodera, T.; Tanaka, T.; Tezuka, H.; Mitsuda, N.; Yamamoto, N. Approximate amplitude encoding in shallow parameterized quantum circuits and its application to financial market indicator. *arXiv* **2021**, arXiv:2103.13211.
7. Shimada, N.H.; Hachisuka, T. Quantum Coin Method for Numerical Integration. *arXiv* **2020**, arXiv:1910.00263.
8. Brassard, G.; Hoyer, P.; Mosca, M.; Tapp, A. Quantum Amplitude Amplification and Estimation. *AMS Contemp. Math. Ser.* **2000**, *305*, 53–74. [CrossRef]
9. Suzuki, Y.; Uno, S.; Raymond, R.; Tanaka, T.; Onodera, T.; Yamamoto, N. Amplitude estimation without phase estimation. *Quantum Inf. Process.* **2020**, *19*, 75. [CrossRef]
10. Grinko, D.; Gacon, J.; Zoufal, C.; Woerner, S. Iterative Quantum Amplitude Estimation. *npj Quantum Inf.* **2021**, *7*. [CrossRef]
11. Giurgica-Tiron, T.; Kerenidis, I.; Labib, F.; Prakash, A.; Zeng, W. Low depth algorithms for quantum amplitude estimation. *arXiv* **2020**, arXiv:2012.03348.

12. Draper, T.G. Addition on a Quantum Computer. *arXiv* **2000**, arXiv:quant-ph/0008033.
13. Cuccaro, S.A.; Draper, T.G.; Kutin, S.A.; Petrie Moulton, D. A new quantum ripple-carry addition circuit. *arXiv* **2004**, arXiv:quant-ph/0410184.
14. Wang, S.; Wang, Z.; Cui, G.; Fan, L.; Shi, S.; Shang, R.; Li, W.; Wei, Z.; Gu, Y. Quantum Amplitude Arithmetic. *arXiv* **2020**, arXiv:2012.11056
15. Vedral, V.; Barenco, A.; Ekert, A. Quantum networks for elementary arithmetic operations. *Phys. Rev. A* **1996**, *54*, 147–153. [CrossRef] [PubMed]
16. Lloyd, S.; Braunstein, S.L. Quantum Computation over Continuous Variables. *Phys. Rev. Lett.* **1999**, *82*, 1784–1787. [CrossRef]
17. Xiaopeng, C.; Yu, S. *QBLAS: A Quantum Basic Linear Algebra and Simulation Library*; GitHub: San Francisco, CA, USA, 2019.

Proceeding Paper

PreLectO: An App for Cognitive Stimulation through Games in Early Childhood [†]

Pedro Nogueiras [1], Paula M. Castro [2,*] and Adriana Dapena [2]

[1] Department of Computer Engineering, University of A Coruña, 15071 A Coruña, Spain; pedro.nogueiras@udc.es
[2] CITIC Research Center, Department of Computer Engineering, University of A Coruña, 15071 A Coruña, Spain; adriana.dapena@udc.es
* Correspondence: paula.castro@udc.es
[†] Presented at the 4th XoveTIC Conference, A Coruña, Spain, 7–8 October 2021.

Abstract: The goal of this work was to develop a mobile application for Android devices, with the objective of stimulating the cognitive skills of children from 0 to 6 years old who are suffering from learning disabilities, while focusing on the most common learning impediments such as reading and writing disorders. This application is based on games specifically designed to meet the needs of this group. For this purpose, we collaborated with professionals from an organization in the area of A Coruña who established the functional requirements of the application and carried out the validation tests. The application monitored the progress of its users, thus allowing the therapists to track them and adapt the training program to each of their individual needs.

Keywords: Android; cognitive difficulties; data analysis; learning; mobile application; reading and writing skills; service-learning; stimulation through games

1. Introduction

Reading and writing are fundamental activities in our daily lives. Their acquisition and mastery are essential for the proper development of children and have a great impact on their adult life. But before being able to read and write, generally from the age of six years old, these children must first acquire a series of skills that will enable them to learn to read and write as well as prevent the appearance of future difficulties in this process. These cognitive abilities [1] are, among others, attention, decision making, learning, reasoning, perception, language abilities, or memory. Therefore, early attention provided in the first years of childhood will improve these pre-reading and pre-writing skills in children who are likely to have difficulties in this area.

This work presents the development of an Android mobile application, referred to as an *app*, which aims to help in this preventive intervention during preschool and early childhood education (0–6 years) by stimulating those early skills through games designed by the authors. These games use the ARASAAC pictograms of the Government of Aragon [2] as a vehicle of accessible communication for children with cognitive difficulties. One of the highlights of this *app* is that it allows the professional to follow the child's progress through a statistics module so that they can detect the area of difficulty and enhance the training by focusing on appropriate games.

This work is structured as follows: Section 2 details the materials and methods used; Section 3 shows the results of this work, with a functional *app* verified by the entity and its users; and finally, a discussion is presented in Section 4.

2. Materials and Methods

We used the Scrum process [3] in this work, so a total of 9 sprints of 1, 2, 3, or 4 weeks were planned, depending on the tasks to be addressed and the availability of the authors.

The total execution time was 24 weeks. In addition, this software methodology was combined with another work methodology known as service-learning [4], which provides a service to society while students acquire the necessary skills. To this end, we collaborated with a non-profit organization in the area of A Coruña, which serves, among other groups, children with learning difficulties.

Regarding material resources, an HP OMEN 15-ce0xx laptop with an Intel i7-7700HQ 2.8 GHz processor and Windows 10 was used for the development of this work. In addition, 4 mobile phones (two Xiaomi and two Samsung) and 2 tablets (one Samsung and one BQ) were used to test the developed *app* on physical devices. As for software resources, we used the following in this work: Android Studio, the official development environment for Android; IntelliJ, an integrated development environment with a "premium" version available for free through a license provided by the University of A Coruña; Kotlin, an open-source language used by Google for Android *app* development; Android, currently the most widespread open-source operating system on mobile devices; Firebase, a Google cloud platform for project creation and synchronization; Cloud Firestore, a NoSQL database hosted in the cloud; Firebase Authentication, for authentication services; ARASAAC pictograms, for accessible communication; Picasso, an open-source library for Kotlin that allows the downloading of images from a URL and uploading them to the *app* interface in real time; AnyChart, a library for JavaScript and Kotlin that represent statistical data in a wide variety of types of interactive graphics; and finally, LaTeX and Git as text composition and version control software, respectively.

3. Results

As a result, we have a functional *app* called PreLectO that allows access to both game and administration modules. Regarding the game module for users, we implemented 9 games (see image on the right side of Figure 1), allowing for the selection of the category to be trained, the number of times the game was to be played, or (if possible) the type of game, always with immediate feedback on game performance. To summarize, the nine games implemented are as follows:

- In the first game, referred to as *Relaciono*, the user selects one of the shown objects whose name begins with the given letter (see the first image on the first row of Figure 1);
- In the second game, referred to as *El intruso*, the user must identify the intruder from among four images, which is the one that does not belong to the semantic field (see the second image on the first row of Figure 1);
- In the third game, referred to as *¿Cuál falta?*, the user must select the letter that completes the given word, with an image provided as support (see the third image on the first row of Figure 1);
- In the fourth game, referred to as *Adivino sonidos*, the user must identify which image corresponds to a given sound (see the fourth image on the first row of Figure 1);
- In the fifth game, referred to as *Palabra correcta*, the user makes associations between uppercase and lowercase letters or words (see the last two images on the first row of Figure 1);
- In the sixth game, referred to as *¡A contar!*, the user practices on counting elements (see the first two images on the second row of Figure 1);
- In the seventh game, referred to as *Veo veo*, the user must use his/her visual recognition skills to find a certain object in a grid of elements (see the third and fourth images on the second row of Figure 1);
- In the eighth game, referred to as *Memorizo los sonidos*, the users work with auditory memory by identifying sound sequences (see the fifth image on the second row of Figure 1);
- Finally, in the ninth game, referred to as *Encuentro fonemas*, the user finds the object whose name includes the given sound (see the last image on the second row of Figure 1).

Figure 1. Game module menu (**left**) and some images of the games on the two rows (**right**).

For the administration module, we developed a user management system and another one for recording results during the sessions. These results can then be visualized by the specialists on graphs such as the one shown in Figure 2. On these graphs, we can see statistics such as the time required to achieve a successful outcome, or the percentage of successes, which will allow a time analysis of the child's progress according to the skills that were being worked in each game or in a set of games, subsequently recommending a therapy adapted to each scenario.

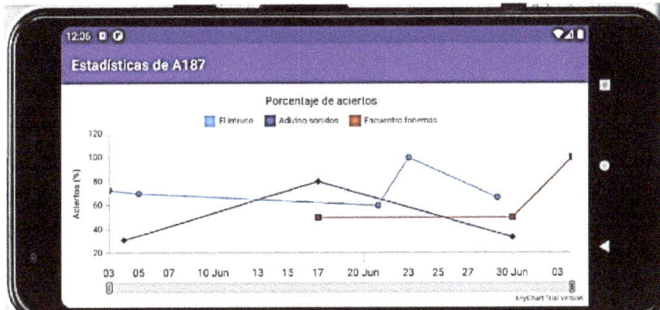

Figure 2. Example of an image of statistical results to track the child's progress.

Throughout this development, two acceptance tests were performed by the entity—one at the end of the 5th sprint and another at the end of the 7th sprint in our Scrum methodology. Both tests were satisfactorily passed and some changes were incorporated into the *app* as a result. So far, only one 6-year-old user has tested our *app*; the child adequately responded to the therapy performed after using it.

4. Discussion

As a result of this work, a functional mobile application that responds to the needs of children with reading and writing disorders is now available. This was made possible by following the indications of both required functionalities and modifications after two validation tests were carried out by a social entity in the area of A Coruña on different versions of the application.

PreLectO allows the training and monitoring of the child's progress, which is essential for therapies used by professionals in these types of entities. In addition, stimulation through games specifically designed for young children attracts the attention of the child who, in this way, learns by playing.

Author Contributions: The authors contributed equally to the work. All authors have read and agreed to the published version of the manuscript.

Funding: This work was funded by the Xunta de Galicia (through grant ED431C 2020/15, and grant ED431G 2019/01 to support the Centro de Investigación de Galicia "CITIC"), the Agencia Estatal de Investigación of Spain (through grants RED2018-102668-T and PID2019-104958RB-C42), and ERDF funds of the European Union (FEDER Galicia 2014–2020 and AEI/FEDER Programs, EU).

Conflicts of Interest: The authors declare no conflict of interest.

References

1. Kiely, K.M. Cognitive Function. In *Encyclopedia of Quality of Life and Well-Being Research*; Michalos, A.C., Ed.; Springer: Dordrecht, The Netherlands, 2014; pp. 974–978. [CrossRef]
2. ARASAAC. Pictogramas para la Comunicación Aumentativa y Alternativa. 2021. Available online: https://arasaac.org/ (accessed on 4 August 2021).
3. Sutherland, J. *SCRUM, the Art of Doing Twice the Job in Half the Time*, 1st ed.; Crown Business: New York, NY, USA, 2014.
4. Levesque-Bristol, C.; Knapp, T.D.; Fisher, B.J. The Effectiveness of Service-Learning: It's Not Always what you Think. *J. Exp. Educ.* **2011**, *33*, 208–224. [CrossRef]

Proceeding Paper

Proposal and Integration of Functionalities for an Assistive Platform in Complex Indoor Environments [†]

Victoria Noci-Luna *, Sergio Lafuente-Arroyo, Saturnino Maldonado-Bascón and Pilar Martin-Martin

GRAM, Department of Signal Theory and Communications, University of Alcalá, 28801 Alcalá de Henares, Spain; sergio.lafuente@uah.es (S.L.-A.); saturnino.maldonado@uah.es (S.M.-B.); p.martin@uah.es (P.M.-M.)

* Correspondence: victoria.noci@edu.uah.es
† Presented at the 4th XoveTIC Conference, A Coruña, Spain, 7–8 October 2021.

Abstract: The objective of this work is the proposal of a new navigation algorithm and its integration in a platform that is already designed and built, improving the functionality of the robot in order to patrol complex indoor environments. This patrol contains various features related to the navigation and the localization of the platform using a particle filter that allows the robot to move autonomously through the environment with the data obtained from an RGB-D camera and LIDAR. The navigation algorithm is adapted dynamically in real-time using the well-known CNN real-time object detector You Only Look Once (YOLOv3), which we have retrained with our own database. The platform detects standing and fallen people. Additionally, it registers people using a specific face recognition convolutional neural network. All these functionalities are controlled and centralized in a friendly user interface that appears on the robot's touch screen and a voice service model is also used.

Keywords: assistive robot; fallen people detection; self-location; friendly interface

1. Introduction

The demographic changes and the large increase of dependency rates in developed countries, together with the rising demand for professional care, pose new requirements in all aspects of society [1]. For all of these reasons, in this paper, we present an assistive patrol robot. There are several proposals related to this topic, such as [2] or [3], that propose assistive service robots that aim to support the independent living of elderly people in their own homes. However, we focus our research on navigation in complex environments, such as nursing homes or hospitals where the structure is very repetitive with so many similar corridors or halls making localization tasks very difficult.

2. Assistive Robotic Platform

As the basis of our work, we have used an updated version of our low-cost and autonomous assistance robot "LOLA," which can be seen in Figure 1. It is a differential wheeled robot, equipped with two motors and their corresponding encoders, which are all controlled with an open-source Arduino board. The complete platform measures approximately 800 mm. The sensing part is composed of an Intel RealSense D435 camera and a LIDAR. An on-board computer is used, with Ubuntu 18.04.5 LTS as the operating system, and it includes an Nvidia board Quadro RTX 5000.

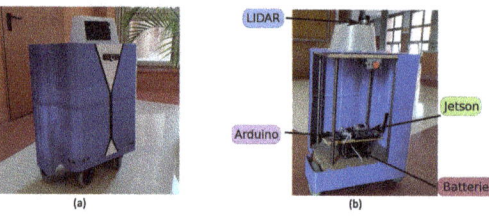

Figure 1. LOLA robotic platform. (**a**) Frontal picture. (**b**) Internal structure.

3. Functionalities Integration

Due to the mobile nature of the platform, it has the capacity to navigate in the environment. It executes other functionalities in parallel that generate information of interest about the detected objects during the route. All of them are controlled from a single user interface which is managed from a touch screen. The following sub-sections explain them in more detail.

3.1. Navigation

We propose a special method based on a particle filter, where the information to estimate the robot's position in each iteration is obtained only from the object detections that are in the surroundings of the platform. This detection is computed using YOLOv3 [4]. For this purpose, we have retrained YOLOv3, which is based on CNNs, in a fine-tuning process for some classes of interests, such as doors, windows, or persons.

The map of the environment and the middle and end-points that make up our routes are previously known and loaded, so the patrolling policy decides in each iteration, based on the estimated position calculated by the particle filter, the next movement that the platform should perform to reach the next corresponding node. The information of the LIDAR is also considered in the process of navigation in order to prevent the platform from colliding with elements of the environment.

3.2. People Registration

This utility aims to generate a record of people during the robot's navigation. Facial recognition on the images captured by the platform's camera makes it possible to identify the people registered in a database. In addition, the identity information is complemented with the time and the location of the detection on the map. Our face recognition module is based on the open-source face recognition package [5], which was built using dlib's state-of-the-art face recognition.

3.3. Fallen People Detection

This functionality is oriented to the automatic detection of fallen people based on computer vision. A retrained YOLOv3, where one of the classes is a fallen person, has been used. If a fallen person is detected, the platform asks if the person needs help. If so, or if there is no answer, the platform sounds the alarm, sending an email to the configured person and generating an audible sound. In the case where no help is needed, the platform continues with the patrolling.

3.4. Audio Generation with AWS

The platform also has the ability to convert from text to speech using Amazon Web Services [6], playing audios on and offline. The system stores the identified conversions which are already done to reduce the number of petitions to the server.

3.5. Single and Friendly Interface

All the platform's behavior is controlled by a single user interface which is displayed and managed from the touch screen. It is made up of buttons that control the different functionalities. If the interface is not being used, it shows a standby face. An example is shown in Figure 3b,c

4. Results

For the generation of the results, we have made a complete route with a platform prototype in our testing environment, which is the third floor of the Polytechnic School of the University of Alcalá.

Two examples of object detection by YOLOv3 are shown in Figures 2a and 3a. An example of people registration is shown in Figure 2b, where facial recognition has been applied to the category 'person' at the output of the detector YOLOv3. Then, the detected person's position is registered on the map as a purple cross.

Figure 2c shows the identification of all types of objects that are in our environment. They are represented by a different colour. This helps the particle filter to locate the platform with the capture made with the camera.

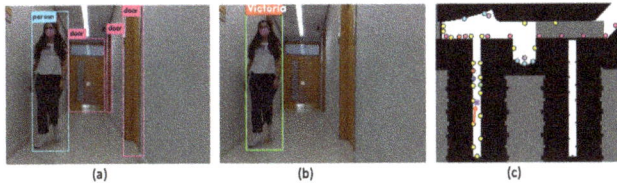

Figure 2. An example of people registration. (**a**) Detected objects by YOLO. (**b**) Face recognition in standing people. (**c**) Detected person mapped (purple cross) and estimated pose of the platform after the detection (red dot with orientation).

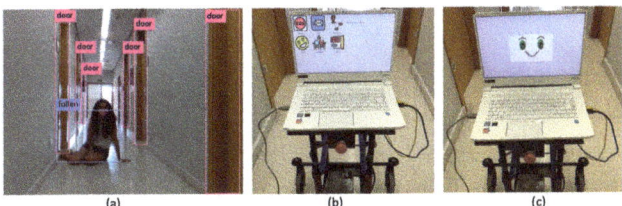

Figure 3. More functionalities examples. (**a**) Fallen person detected by YOLO. (**b**) The user interface: control menu. (**c**) The user interface: standby interface.

5. Conclusions

In this paper, we propose a new navigation algorithm and its integration with other functionalities in an assistive platform for complex indoor environments, where the structure makes location tasks very difficult. Our platform has facial recognition and the possibility of detecting fallen people. The navigation is based on a particle filter, which is used to locate the robot with the object detections made by YOLOv3 with the capture of the camera, so our patrolling policy decides the next movement. Simultaneously, a continuous check of the surroundings of the platform is carried out by the LIDAR to avoid collisions. All these functionalities are controlled by a friendly interface based on a touch screen and a voice service model.

Funding: This work was supported by the projects: (a) project AIRPLANE, with reference PID2019-104323RBC31, of Spain's Ministry of Science and Innovation; and (b) project CM/JIN/2019-022 of the University of Alcalá.

References

1. Abades Porcel, M.; Rayón Valpuesta, E. Ageing in Spain: It's a challenge or social problem? *Gerokomos* **2012**, *23*, 151–155. [CrossRef]
2. Bajones, M.; Fischinger, D.; Weiss, A.; Wolf, D.; Vincze, M.; de la Puente, P.; Körtner, T.; Weninger, M.; Papoutsakis, K.; Michel, D.; et al. Hobbit: Providing fall detection and prevention for the elderly in the real world. *J. Robot.* **2018**. [CrossRef]
3. Portugal, D.; Alvito, P.; Christodoulou, E.; Samaras, G.; Dias, J. A study on the deployment of a service robot in an elderly care center. *Int. J. Soc. Robot.* **2019**, *11*, 317–341. [CrossRef]
4. Redmon, J.; Farhadi, A. Yolov3: An incremental improvement. *arXiv* **2018**, arXiv:1804.02767.
5. Facial Recognition Package for Python. Available online: https://pypi.org/project/face-recognition/ (accessed on 28 July 2021).
6. Hashemipour, S.; Ali, M. Amazon Web Services (AWS)–An Overview of the On-Demand Cloud Computing Platform. In Proceedings of the Emerging Technologies in Computing, iCETic, London, UK, 19–20 August 2020; Volume 332, pp. 40–47. [CrossRef]

Proceeding Paper

PRACTICUM DIRECT Simulator for Decision Making during Pandemics [†]

Alejandro Puente-Castro [1,*], Brais Galdo [1], Ismael Said Criado [2], David Baltar Boileve [3], Juan R. Rabuñal [1], Alejandro Pazos [1,4] and Modesto Martínez-Pillado [5]

1. Faculty of Computer Science, CITIC, University of A Coruna, 15071 A Coruña, Spain; brais.cgaldo@udc.es (B.G.); juan.rabunal@udc.es (J.R.R.); alejandro.pazos@udc.es (A.P.)
2. Povisa Hospital, Hospital Montecelo, Pontevedra, Instituto de Investigación Sanitaria Galicia Sur (IISGS), 36071 Pontevedra, Spain; ismaelsaid@gmail.com
3. Hospital Universitario Lucus Augusti, 27003 Lugo, Spain; david.baltar@iisgaliciasur.es
4. Biomedical Research Institute of A Coruña (INIBIC), University Hospital Complex of A Coruna (CHUAC), 15006 A Coruña, Spain
5. Quality Unit, Instituto de Investigación Sanitaria Galicia Sur (IISGS), 36312 Vigo, Spain; mmartinezpil@gmail.com
* Correspondence: a.puentec@udc.es
† Presented at the 4th XoveTIC Conference, A Coruña, Spain, 7–8 October 2021.

Abstract: The past and current situation of the SARS-CoV-2 pandemic has put the entire society, and especially all hospital systems, worldwide to the test. It is essential that health system managers and decision makers optimize the management of resources, even being forced to improvise new units, divert resources usually destined to other functions and/or change the usual care modality by considerably enhancing aspects of telemedicine. Artificial Intelligence (AI) techniques and procedures are of great help in decision making in emergency environments due to severe pandemics because of their predictive capacity. This paper presents the PRACTICUM DIRECT project, which proposes the design and implementation of a tool to assist health system managers in making decisions on the early management of hospital resources. It makes use of AI techniques to identify the most critical variables in each case and build models capable of showing the possibilities and consequences of the decisions taken on resources at each moment of the emergency. It includes a simulator that shows how they would affect management. The current status is that of the selection of the most appropriate variables, taking into account those affected during the SARS-CoV-2 pandemic: infectious diseases, cardio-neuro-circulatory diseases, metabolic diseases and rehabilitative medicine.

Keywords: pandemics; artificial intelligence; simulator; resources; expert system

1. Introduction

Decision making based on prior knowledge or experience is a very common practice in medicine [1], especially because of the current situation experienced by the SARS-Cov-2 pandemic [2], where many centers, regardless of the country, have been overwhelmed by the increasing number of admissions and the scarce number of available staff and beds [3]. Some facilities or medical systems take advantage of all this lived knowledge to create reports or systematic reviews that can be used for future cases [4]. The use of prior knowledge for decision making in future situations is very common in pandemics [5]. This allows decisions to be determined more quickly and effectively, since, during the pandemic, many treatments and diagnoses, both SARS-Cov-2-dependent and independent, have been reconsidered, most of them having to be postponed or canceled [6].

This paper introduces the PRACTICUM DIRECT project. It proposes a tool to assist in decision making on the optimization of resources in the case of pandemics. This tool is supported by Artificial Intelligence (AI) techniques to have a greater predictive capacity and, thus, to have a better assistance from the tool.

2. Materials and Methods

This section describes the tool architecture and introduces the current status of the project.

2.1. Software Architecture

As architecture, we opted for the classic architecture divided into front-end and back-end (Figure 1). The front-end is in charge of visualization and user authentication. The back-end is in charge of all medical data processing.

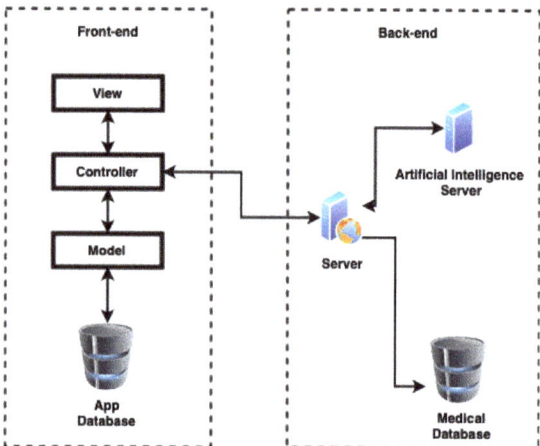

Figure 1. Simplified diagram of the tool structure. In the back-end, predictions are determined by means of AI models. The front-end is responsible for authentication and visualization of the application.

For better usability, the graphical interface will be simplified with a traffic light system to indicate how urgent the situation is and the actions to be taken. Thus, green would indicate a situation of minimal urgency, yellow would be medium urgency and red would be extreme urgency.

2.2. Proposed Model

The proposed Artificial Intelligence [7] model is a rule-based expert system [8]. In this way, knowledge can be inferred (inference engine) from the experience of the medical specialists (expert knowledge) and from all the previous information on pandemic actions collected in the center itself and in other centers (knowledge base). The combination of information allows to obtain the current information that the specialists have, while considering other known previous actions, some being from other centers (Figure 2).

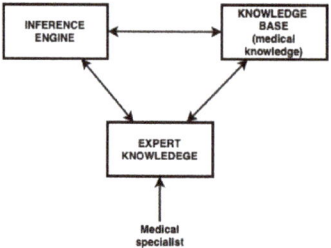

Figure 2. Basic scheme of the operation of a rule-based expert system applied in medicine. Knowledge inference is conducted in the inference engine from all the knowledge.

2.3. Medical Variables

Currently, a study is underway to select the medical variables with which to train the model and test the system. For the evaluation of the selection, four pathologies that were among the most affected during the SARS-CoV-2 pandemic due to their urgency of treatment or lethality were taken into account: infectious diseases, diseases of the circulatory system, metabolic diseases and rehabilitations.

3. Conclusions

The main conclusion is that there is a wide range of variables to be taken into account. For the initial phases of the project, it is necessary to filter and select only those most affected by the pandemic.

The development of the software tool has to guarantee security regarding access to the information of the resources and medical variables, all this while maintaining efficiency and usability.

Funding: This research was funded by the General Directorate of Culture, Education and University Management of Xunta de Galicia "PRACTICUM DIRECT" Ref. IN845D-2020/03 and the GRANT FOR THE PROGRAM FOR CONSOLIDATION AND STRUCTURING OF COMPETITIVE RESEARCH UNITS Ref. ED431C 2018/49.

Institutional Review Board Statement: Not applicable.

Informed Consent Statement: Not applicable.

Conflicts of Interest: The authors declare no conflict of interest.

Abbreviations

The following abbreviations are used in this manuscript:

SARS-CoV-2	Severe Acute Respiratory Syndrome Coronavirus 2
AI	Artificial Intelligence

References

1. Sackett, D.L.; Rosenberg, W.M.; Gray, J.M.; Haynes, R.B.; Richardson, W.S. Evidence based medicine: What it is and what it is not. *BMJ* **1996**, *312*, 71. [CrossRef] [PubMed]
2. Petersen, E.; Koopmans, M.; Go, U.; Hamer, D.H.; Petrosillo, N.; Castelli, F.; Storgaard, M.; Al Khalili, S.; Simonsen, L. Comparing SARS-CoV-2 with SARS-CoV and influenza pandemics. *Lancet Infect. Dis.* **2020**, *20*, e238–e244. [CrossRef]
3. Borasio, G.D.; Gamondi, C.; Obrist, M.; Jox, R. COVID-19: Decision making and palliative care. *Swiss Med. Wkly.* **2020**, *150*, 1314. [CrossRef] [PubMed]
4. Fretheim, A.; Brurberg, K.G.; Forland, F. Rapid reviews for rapid decision-making during the coronavirus disease (COVID-19) pandemic, Norway, 2020. *Eurosurveillance* **2020**, *25*, 2000687. [CrossRef] [PubMed]
5. Lal, A.; Ashworth, H.C.; Dada, S.; Hoemeke, L.; Tambo, E. Optimizing pandemic preparedness and response through health information systems: Lessons learned from Ebola to COVID-19. In *Disaster Medicine and Public Health Preparedness*; Cambridge University Press: Cambridge, MA, USA, 2020; pp. 1–8.
6. Chang, H.; Yu, J.Y.; Yoon, S.Y.; Hwang, S.Y.; Yoon, H.; Cha, W.C.; Sim, M.S.; Jo, I.J.; Kim, T. Impact of COVID-19 Pandemic on the Overall Diagnostic and Therapeutic Process for Patients of Emergency Department and Those with Acute Cerebrovascular Disease. *J. Clin. Med.* **2020**, *9*, 3842. [CrossRef] [PubMed]
7. Russel, S.; Norvig, P. *Artificial Intelligence: A Modern Approach*; Prentice Hall: Hoboken, NJ, USA, 2003; Volume 178.
8. Clancey, W.J. The epistemology of a rule-based expert system—A framework for explanation. *Artif. Intell.* **1983**, *20*, 215–251. [CrossRef]

Proceeding Paper

Developing a Simulation Model for Autonomous Driving Education in the Robobo SmartCity Framework †

Daniel Juanatey, Martin Naya, Tamara Baamonde and Francisco Bellas *

GII, CITIC Research Center, Campus de Elviña, 15008 A Coruña, Spain; daniel.juanatey@udc.es (D.J.); martin.naya@udc.es (M.N.); tamara.bardao@udc.es (T.B.)
* Correspondence: francisco.bellas@udc.es
† Presented at the 4th XoveTIC Conference, A Coruña, Spain, 7–8 October 2021.

Abstract: This paper focuses on long-term education in Artificial Intelligence (AI) applied to robotics. Specifically, it presents the Robobo SmartCity educational framework. It is based on two main elements: the smartphone-based robot Robobo and a real model of a smart city. We describe the development of a simulation model of Robobo SmartCity in the CoppeliaSim 3D simulator, implementing both the real mock-up and the model of Robobo. In addition, a set of Python libraries that allow teachers and students to use state-of-the-art algorithms in their education projects is described too.

Keywords: intelligent robotics; educational robots; self-driving cars; robotic simulation; computer vision

Citation: Juanatey, D.; Naya, M.; Baamonde, T.; Bellas, F. Developing a Simulation Model for Autonomous Driving Education in the Robobo SmartCity Framework. *Eng. Proc.* **2021**, *7*, 49. https://doi.org/10.3390/engproc2021007049

Academic Editors: Joaquim de Moura, Marco A. González, Javier Pereira and Manuel G. Penedo

Published: 23 October 2021

Publisher's Note: MDPI stays neutral with regard to jurisdictional claims in published maps and institutional affiliations.

Copyright: © 2021 by the authors. Licensee MDPI, Basel, Switzerland. This article is an open access article distributed under the terms and conditions of the Creative Commons Attribution (CC BY) license (https://creativecommons.org/licenses/by/4.0/).

1. Introduction

This work is focused on an educational framework for teaching intelligent robotics in secondary school or university, developed at the University of Coruña: the Robobo SmartCity. This framework is based on two main elements: (1) the smartphone-based robot Robobo [1], and a (2) model of a smart city, considering both simulation-based and real formats. In this framework, many different challenges and lessons on intelligent robotics can be carried out, mainly focused on the field of self-driving vehicles. It allows teachers to propose challenges dealing with basic problems in robotics, such as control navigation and obstacle avoidance, but also more complex ones that require computer vision, such as traffic sign detection and object identification. The idea of using autonomous driving and smart cities as environments for robotics teaching is becoming quite popular. For example, the authors of [2] proposed a modular and integrated approach towards teaching autonomous driving. Another relevant approach is the autoauto platform [3], which utilizes the concept of self-driving cars for teaching robotics and AI to young students. Costa et al. [4] presented an autonomous driving simulator to gain the attention of and prepare the students to compete in the Portuguese National Robotic Festival (PNRT), especially in the Autonomous Driving Competition (ADC). A very similar approach to the one proposed here is Duckietown [5], an online MOOC for teaching AI and robotics based on self-driving cars, with which the authors have created a whole educational environment, with different city layouts, traffic signals, etc.

2. City Model and Libraries

The smart city used in this project is a scaled model of a city neighborhood (Figure 1 left) represented by a rectangular city layout of 3.5 m × 4 m. This layout is made up of an external two-way road, surrounding a central part that contains a roundabout, where four two-way road sections intersect. There are four areas in the layout containing two buildings, one parking area and one green zone. The main elements related to robotics teaching are the traffic signs (Figure 1 right) that must be detected to control the movement along the city, the lanes that must be followed to avoid running out of the road, and other elements that can be in the city, such as other Robobos or small figures that simulate humans or animals at scale.

Figure 1. Left: A general overview of the real Robobo SmartCity layout. **Right**: A snapshot of two different traffic signs with an ArUco marker.

As the school's budget is limited and they may encounter several difficulties both in acquiring and in mounting a real city model like the one presented above, a simulation of it has been created. The model replicates the real smart city mock-up and the real Robobo robot, providing the possibility to transfer the simulation result to the real robot directly. Developing and testing initial solutions in the simulated models and then switching them to real ones using the real Robobo is a highly efficient methodology for most schools.

The model runs under the CoppeliaSim simulator [6]. It is realistic and powerful simulator, especially in terms of the possibilities that the user has to control the scene, the physics, and the dynamics of the simulation. This simulation model is suitable for intermediate and advanced students with digital skills in terms of 3D design and programming. Only Python is supported, and the bridge for using the CoppeliaSim model and the real Robobo is straightforward, which is documented on the Robobo wiki [7].

To allow Robobo to move, sense, or interact with the environment in Robobo SmartCity, a series of libraries with different functionalities have been developed in the scope of this work. The aim of these libraries is to help and guide students in performing realistic programs while learning robotics and intelligence systems through autonomous driving. These libraries are [8]:

- Lane detection. It allows Robobo to detect the lanes of the city model, both the continuous and discontinuous ones. Its implementation is based on the Canny algorithm for edge detection and uses the Hough transformation line detection.
- Object recognition. It allows Robobo to identify the different objects that it may encounter during navigation. These objects can be other Robobos or objects found on the road, such as human-like dolls crossing in a pedestrian crossing, or pet-like dolls. The object recognition system employs a pre-configured artificial neural network (ANN) based on Mobilenet [9] as a recognition algorithm. Although it is possible to download it already pre-trained with a series of objects, it was trained from scratch using the machine learning framework Tensorflow with a set of specific objects relevant for this framework.
- ArUco detection. This library allows ArUco fiducial markers detection, which can be used as artificial landmarks for robot location, or in this case, to identify traffic signs.
- Traffic sign recognition. It allows detecting the vertical traffic signs using the camera, without relying upon ArUco or QR tags. This library is based on a multilayer perceptron ANN and a dataset of real traffic signs.

3. Education Project Example

This section is dedicated to presenting one specific project carried out by a student in his final undergraduate project at the Industrial Engineering school of the University of Coruña, to show the potential of the Robobo SmartCity for teaching advanced concepts in intelligent robotics.

The main objective was to improve the object detection library commented above. First, he had to test the real-time response of the library while taking images from the python stream. This functionality was tested in various situations within the city. For example, the student verified how the library allowed Robobo to avoid collision with other Robobos in the scene, as displayed in the left image of Figure 2. Moreover, to go deeper into his training about deep learning techniques, the student was assigned the task of training the original MobileNet model with new objects. Some of them were images of traffic lights (green, yellow, and red), used to improve the realism of the autonomous circulation of the robot in the city (Figure 2 right).

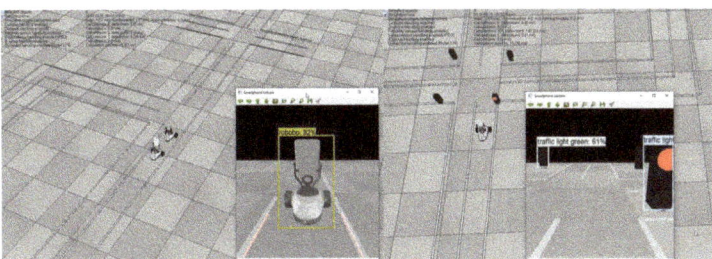

Figure 2. Left: Object recognition library detecting other Robobos on the scene. **Right**: Traffic sign detection library identifying the traffic lights on the scene.

4. Conclusions

A simulated model of the Robobo SmartCity education framework has been presented, together with some libraries developed to support intelligent robotics teaching at different levels. The model's abilities have been presented through a specific project carried out by a university student, showing the potentiality of the framework for teaching different concepts of robotics and AI that have impacts in real life.

Author Contributions: Conceptualization, M.N., F.B.; methodology, M.N., F.B.; software, D.J.; validation, M.N., D.J.; formal analysis, F.B.; resources, T.B.; writing, M.N., F.B.; visualization, T.B. All authors have read and agreed to the published version of the manuscript.

Institutional Review Board Statement: Not applicable.

Informed Consent Statement: Not applicable.

Data Availability Statement: Link to data.

Acknowledgments: This work has been partially funded by the Ministerio de Ciencia, Innovación y Universidades of Spain/FEDER (grant RTI2018-101114-B-I00), the Erasmus+ Programme of the European Union through grant number 2019-1-ES01-KA201-065742, and the Centro de Investigación de Galicia "CITIC", funded by Xunta de Galicia and the European Union (European Regional Development Fund—Galicia 2014-2020 Program), by grant ED431G 2019/01.

Conflicts of Interest: The authors declare no conflict of interest. The funders had no role in the design of the study; in the collection, analyses, or interpretation of data; in the writing of the manuscript, or in the decision to publish the results.

References

1. Bellas, F.; Naya, M.; Varela, G.; Llamas, L.; Prieto, A.; Becerra, J.C.; Duro, R. The Robobo Project: Bringing Educational Robotics Closer to Real-World Applications. In *Advances in Intelligent Systems and Computing*; Springer: Cham, Switzerland, 2017; Volume 630, pp. 226–237.
2. Tang, J.; Shaoshan, L.; Pei, S.; Zuckerman, S.; Chen, L.; Shi, W.; Gaudiot, J.-L. Teaching autonomous driving using a modular and integrated approach. In Proceedings of the 2018 IEEE 42nd Annual Computer Software and Applications Conference (COMPSAC), Tokyo, Japan, 23–27 July 2018; Volume 1, pp. 361–366.
3. Autoauto Platform. Available online: https://www.autoauto.ai (accessed on 24 June 2021).

4. Costa, V.; Rossetti, R.; Sousa, A. Simulator for teaching robotics, ROS and autonomous driving in a competitive mindset. *Int. J. Technol. Hum. Interact.* **2017**, *13*, 19–32. [CrossRef]
5. Tani, J.; Paull, L.; Zuber, M.T.; Rus, D.; How, J.; Leonard, J.; Censi, A. Duckietown: An Innovative Way to Teach Autonomy. In *Advances in Intelligent Systems and Computing*; Alimisis, D., Moro, M., Menegatti, E., Eds.; Springer: Cham, Switzerland, 2016; Volume 560.
6. Coppelia Simulation Platform. Available online: https://www.coppeliarobotics.com (accessed on 1 August 2021).
7. Robobo Wiki. Available online: https://github.com/mintforpeople/robobo-programming/wiki/CoppeliaSim (accessed on 1 August 2021).
8. Robobo SmartCity Documentation. Available online: https://github.com/mintforpeople/robobo-programming/wiki/RoboboSmartCity (accessed on 1 August 2021).
9. MobileNet Library. Available online: https://github.com/tensorflow/models/tree/master/research/slim/nets/mobilenet (accessed on 1 August 2021).

Proceeding Paper

Monitoring of Older Adults' Daily Activity and Sleep with Xiaomi Mi Band 2 †

María del Carmen Miranda-Duro [1,2,*], Laura Nieto-Riveiro [1,2], Betania Groba [1,2] and Nereida Canosa [1,2]

1 CITIC (Centre for Information and Communications Technology Research), TALIONIS Group, Elviña Campus, University of A Coruña, 15071 A Coruña, Spain; llaura.nieto@udc.es (L.N.-R.); bb.groba@udc.es (B.G.); nnereida.canosa@udc.es (N.C.)
2 Faculty of Health Sciences, Oza Campus, University of A Coruna, 15071 A Coruña, Spain
* Correspondence: carmen.miranda@udc.es
† Presented at the 4th XoveTIC Conference, A Coruña, Spain, 7–8 October 2021.

Abstract: Nowadays, the use of wearable devices is still emerging. Monitoring with wearable sensors is an easy and non-intrusive approach to encourage preventive care for older adults. Wearable devices are becoming an assessment tool for evaluating physical activity and sleep, among other biomedical parameters. The objective of the present study is to explore the daily activity and sleep of older adults from three nursing homes, as measured by Xiaomi Mi Band 2. The results showed that people with a greater number of steps (representing daily activity) could be related to a lower probability of risk of falling, dependency on basic activities of daily living, and mobility problems. Regarding sleep, the results suggest that people at risk of falling tend to be awake longer at night. Independent people get more deep sleep, while people who identify problems in their usual activities have a lower total sleep time. Finally, people who identify pain or discomfort have less light sleep and sleep in total.

Keywords: wearable technology; remote monitoring; occupational therapy

1. Introduction

The use of wearable technology has been developed in uncontrolled and free-living environments instead of clinical settings. Wearable devices can register physiological parameters, physical activity, sleep quality, gait structures, or plantar pressures and shear, among others. Additionally, the key advantage of wearable sensors is that there is no need for a professional who has to perform tests to obtain clinical data. In addition, monitoring people in a daily living environment and over continuous periods may become more feasible and ecological. The evidence shows that the main wearable devices used in older adults' populations were wristbands, activity monitors, or accelerometers. The main objectives of using these devices are: (1) to explore the relationship between sleep behavior and gait performance; (2) to validate the devices by step count; (3) to evaluate the feasibility and efficacy of the device; (4) to determine the validity of a device compared to Actigraph; or (5) to understand the use of wristbands by older adults by conducting qualitative or mixed studies. Accordingly, this study aims to analyze the utility of the Xiaomi Mi Band 2 to assess older adults' daily activity and sleep [1].

2. Materials and Methods

A cross-sectional study was conducted between March 2017 and December 2019. The participants were people aged over 65 years old residing in or attending a nursing home or day center. The participants had to wear the Xiaomi Mi Band 2 during 30 days/24 h.

The main parameters analysed from the Xiaomi Mi Band 2 were the number of steps taken (daily activity) and sleep quality (daily deep sleep, daily shallow sleep, total daily sleep, and awake time in bed during the night). Additionally, from institutional data, we analyzed the most recent Barthel Index score, Tinetti Index score, and the presence or absence of cognitive impairment. The Barthel Index measures the level of dependency in B.A.D.L., such as feeding, bathing, grooming, dressing, bowel control, bladder control, toilet use, transfers, mobility on level surfaces, and mobility up and down stairs. In the Barthel Index, the score can range between 0 and 100 points; 100 is considered independency in basic activities of daily living (B.A.D.L.), and >100 is considered any level of dependency in B.A.D.L. The Tinetti Scale assesses the risk of falling based on gait and balance. The total score for the Tinetti Scale can range between 0 and 28; a score ≥ 24 is considered to indicate no risk of falling, and a score <24 indicates the risk of falling.

Moreover, we analyzed the quality of life of the older adults with EuroQol-5D-5L. This assessment evaluates four elements. The first element consists of a descriptive system of five dimensions: mobility (walking ability), self-care (washing or dressing), usual activities (i.e., work, study, household chores, family activities, or leisure time activities), pain/discomfort, and anxiety/depression. These are assessed as: (1) no problems, (2) slight problems, (3) moderate problems, (4) severe problems, or (5) extreme problems/inability. In this case, we considered those having any problem or no problem to analyze. The second element was a visual analog scale (VAS), in which the participant rates his/her perceived health from 0 (the worst imaginable health) to 100 (the best imaginable health). Finally, the third and fourth elements (the EQ-5D-5L Index and the Severity Index, respectively) are two indexes calculated from the descriptive system's scores. The EQ-5D-5L Severity Index score ranges from 0 (absence of problems) to 100 (more severity), and the EQ-5D-5L Index ranges from 0 (state of health similar to death) to 1 (better health status).

Data analysis was carried out with IBM SPSS version 25, including a descriptive and inferential analysis. The present study was approved by an ethics committee and is registered in clinical trials (NCT03504813, NCT04592796).

3. Results and Discussion

The main findings obtained were that a greater number of steps and distance could indicate a lower probability of presenting a risk of falling, dependency in B.A.D.L., or perception of mobility problems. Nowadays, there is no agreement on what dose of physical activity should be performed to maintain a person's functional independence. However, it is known that with moderate physical activity levels, there can be significant results. Likewise, the relationship between staying physically active and engaging in regular physical activity, with health benefits, particularly in fall rate reduction, has been well documented for decades [1].

Considering participants that did not perceive mobility problems, were without risk of falling and were independent in B.A.D.L, the number of daily steps ranged from 2500 to 6000 steps, approximately. Similar data were obtained in the O'Brien study, in which the intermediate steps of older adults were 2500–4000. However, according to Tudor-Locke et al., this range fits a sedentary profile. These authors suggested that below 6000 daily steps could not provide health benefits [1].

Daily steps are a modifiable factor intrinsically related to the objective assessment of daily physical activity. They have a strong impact on health in any population, but especially in older adults. It affects their level of independence and quality of life, taking into account the repercussions of falls. This study suggested that wearable devices, like Xiaomi Mi Band 2, may be used for appropriate assessments, which can help to identify people with daily activity and sleep problems [1].

Regarding sleep, in this study, we observed that daily awake time at night was weakly associated with the risk of falling ($p = 0.013$, F = 0.127). Although the data were not supported by strong associations, the data showed an important aspect of using wearable devices. Wearable devices continuously monitor the person, which provides the approximate time that the person has been awake at night, and, therefore, they can help to understand their needs [1].

The existing literature has supported a relationship between short sleep duration and injury from falling. In addition, maintaining daily routines was associated with a reduced rate of insomnia in older adults. In the present study, 54.83 percent of the participants slept less than 420–480 min, which is the adequate range of sleep per day, while participants with a risk of falling slept 360 ± 118 min per day. This is in comparison with those with no risk of falling, who slept 421 ± 85 min per day. These findings indicate that people who are not at risk of falling tend to sleep more and have sleep levels that are within the appropriate range, although it was not possible to conclude a significant relationship [1].

4. Conclusions

Wristbands may be an effective and fast way to evaluate people without requiring extended time for professionals to determine their day-to-day needs. It will now be useful in the COVID situation to observe how this situation has affected people's physical activity and sleep levels.

Funding: The authors disclosed the receipt of the following financial support for the research, authorship, and/or publication of this article: The research team will bear all the economic costs involved in the study with the support of the C.I.T.I.C., as the research center accredited by Galician University System, which is funded by "Consellería de Cultura, Educación e Universidades from Xunta de Galicia," which provided 80 percent of funds through E.R.D.F. Funds, E.R.D.F. Operational Programme Galicia 2014–2020. The remaining 20 percent was provided by "Secretaría Xeral de Universidades" [Grant ED431G 2019/01]. Moreover, M.D.C.M. obtained a scholarship [Ref.ED481A-2019/069] and M.D.C.M. [Ref.ED481A 2018/205] gained a scholarship to develop a Ph.D. In addition, this work is also supported in part by the Ministerio de Ciencia e Innovación R+D+I projects in the framework of the national programs of knowledge generation and scientific and technological strengthening of the R+D+I system and the challenges of society's oriented R+D+I 2019 call (PID2019-104323RB-C33).

Institutional Review Board Statement: Two protocols were approved by the Autonomic Research Ethics of Galicia, one with the protocol code IN852A 2016/10 and registered in Clinical Trials with the identifier NCT03504813, and another project with ethics protocol code 2018/473 and registered in Clinical Trials with the identifier NCT04592796.

Informed Consent Statement: All participants consent the divulgation of data.

Data Availability Statement: Not applied.

Conflicts of Interest: The authors declare no conflict of interest. The funders had no role in the design of the study; in the collection, analyses, or interpretation of data; in the writing of the manuscript, or in the decision to publish the results.

Reference

1. Miranda-Duro, M.d.C.; Nieto-Riveiro, L.; Concheiro-Moscoso, P.; Groba, B.; Pousada, T.; Canosa, N.; Pereira, J.T. Analysis of Older Adults in Spanish Care Facilities, Risk of Falling and Daily Activity Using Xiaomi Mi Band 2. *Sensors* **2021**, *21*, 3341. [CrossRef] [PubMed]

Proceeding Paper
Applying Artificial Intelligence for Operating System Fingerprinting †

Rubén Pérez-Jove [1,2,*], Cristian R. Munteanu [1,2,3], Alejandro Pazos Sierra [1,2,3] and José M. Vázquez-Naya [1,2]

1. Grupo RNASA-IMEDIR, Departamento de Ciencias de la Computación y Tecnologías de la Información, Facultade de Informática, Universidade da Coruña, Elviña, 15071 A Coruña, Spain; c.munteanu@udc.es (C.R.M.); alejandro.pazos@udc.es (A.P.S.); jose@udc.es (J.M.V.-N.)
2. Centro de Investigación CITIC, Universidade da Coruña, Elviña, 15071 A Coruña, Spain
3. IKERDATA S.L., ZITEK, University of Basque Country UPVEHU, Rectorate Building, 48940 Leioa, Spain
* Correspondence: ruben.perez.jove@udc.es
† Presented at the 4th XoveTIC Conference, A Coruña, Spain, 7–8 October 2021.

Abstract: In the field of computer security, the possibility of knowing which specific version of an operating system is running behind a machine can be useful, to assist in a penetration test or monitor the devices connected to a specific network. One of the most widespread tools that better provides this functionality is Nmap, which follows a rule-based approach for this process. In this context, applying machine learning techniques seems to be a good option for addressing this task. The present work explores the strengths of different machine learning algorithms to perform operating system fingerprinting, using for that, the Nmap reference database. Moreover, some optimizations were applied to the method which brought the best results, random forest, obtaining an accuracy higher than 96%.

Keywords: operating systems; fingerprinting; Nmap; machine learning

1. Introduction

The aim of operating system (OS) fingerprinting is to identify which family and version of OS is running behind a device analyzing the network traffic it generates. Knowing the specific details of the system controlling a machine is interesting in the way that it can support the detection of unauthorized devices in a network or assist in determining the vulnerability of a target host. One of the most known and spread tools to perform this task is Nmap [1], which can carry out active OS detection, as well as XProbe2 [2]. On the other hand, passive OS detection can be performed with the tool P0f [3].

Traditionally, the way of performing this task is a rule-based approach, followed by Nmap in its IPv4 analysis [4]. The process can be summed up in three steps: sending specific probes to the target, recollecting and parsing the responses, executing a set of tests onto these responses in order to generate a characteristic signature, and finally comparing that stamp with every single entry of its database of preprocessed signatures in turn.

The main aim of the present project is to develop a PoC of an operating system fingerprinting model based on the latest Nmap database, analyzing which classical machine learning algorithms provide better results. In fact, this approach, based on the logistic regression technique, is already followed by the tool in its IPv6 scan.

2. Materials and Methods

The process followed in this work can be split into two well distinguished phases, starting with the extraction and preparation of the data in a suitable format for the second stage, where the training and testing tasks were performed.

2.1. Dataset Preparation

The OS database of the latest version of Nmap (7.9) [5] was downloaded as the base point to construct our dataset. This file contained all of the fingerprints gathered by the community and grouped by Nmap, since 1998, in text format. A specific fingerprint consists of the collection of the results of the predefined tests that Nmap executes against the responses received of a particular known OS.

In order to simplify our approach, we filtered those fingerprints by only selecting those from a group of OS families representing the most widespread systems in use nowadays: Android, BSD, Linux, Solaris, Windows, iOS, and macOS. All these features represent different types of information, such as numerical or boolean values, as well as specific categories. For all these types, a codification keeping the idea of transforming the data to numerical values was chosen. In this way, the null or absent values were codified as -1.

Besides, a condition between more than one value could be specified, expressed as a combination of any of these operators: boolean OR, range of values, "more than" or "less than". We represented the OR operator as a lineal combination between the possible values of all the features of a single fingerprint, creating a new row for every alternative that would have produced less than 100,000 new combinations. On the other hand, the range operator was represented as a random value generated between both the limits of the range for every single row of the same fingerprint. The "more than" and "less than" operators were ignored because of the almost absence of them in the database. In order to obtain better results in the next stage, some preprocessing of this dataset, such as removing duplicated values and near zero variance features, was done. This process finished with a dataset of 264,852 cases and 233 features.

2.2. Machine Learning Modeling

Once we had a suitable dataset that represented, in a simplified manner, the knowledge of the Nmap database, the modeling process was performed. The first step consisted of splitting randomly the dataset in a training and test set, following a proportion of 90/10, respectively, leaving the same number of cases for each class in both groups. The dataset was imbalanced, as there were not the same number of examples for every OS family. To fix this, a vector with the class weights was calculated and passed as a parameter to the training algorithms.

The set of classic machine learning algorithms tested was: Gaussian Naive Bayes (GNB), linear discriminant analysis (LDA), logistic regression (LR), multilayer perceptron classifier (MLPC), decision tree (DT), random forest (RF), and bagging classifier (Bag). For each model created with these methods, the accuracy, precision, recall, and f1-score metrics were calculated in order to compare them.

In a second improvement phase, a hyperparameter optimization was performed using the grid search cross validation method. The base algorithm used in this process was the one which raised the best results in the previous stage. We chose a list of values for a selection of the available parameters of this method and executed the grid search fitting three-fold for each candidate.

3. Results and Discussion

The metrics calculated on the models generated during this work (see Table 1) point to several potential options when it comes to performing fingerprinting of operating systems with classic machine learning methods. Specifically, the model that was developed more deeply was RF, since it yielded the best results in the first approach with an accuracy value of 0.96055. However, all of the tested models, with the exception of GNB and LR, offered prediction results higher than 90%. In fact, even choosing the RF algorithm in the second improvement stage because of its results, we could have chosen the LDA method, as, in terms of complexity, it is much simpler, meaning it could execute the category prediction faster.

Table 1. Machine Learning algorithm validation results.

Method	Accuracy	Precision	Recall	F1-Score
GaussianNB	0.10764	0.62907	0.10764	0.05814
LinearDiscriminantAnalysis	0.95734	0.96275	0.95734	0.95857
LogisticRegression	0.11013	0.78129	0.11013	0.07955
MLPClassifier	0.93147	0.94640	0.93147	0.91723
DecisionTreeClassifier	0.95216	0.95168	0.95216	0.95185
RandomForestClassifier	**0.96055**	**0.96360**	**0.96055**	**0.95844**
BaggingClassifier	0.95794	0.96102	0.95794	0.95782

After choosing RF as the best option for this problem, we attempted to improve its results carrying out some optimizations. The grid search method applied generated 648 different models, where the concrete parameters of the best generated model was: bootstrap = False; max_depth = 20; max_features = auto; min_samples_leaf = 1; min_samples_split = 5; n_estimators = 50. This progress allowed us to get an accuracy of 0.96096. Besides, some ideas can be concluded from the confusion matrix of this latest model. In general, the solution responds correctly to the classification of every category, but it has some problems in distinguishing between Android and Linux, as well as between iOS and macOS. Taking into account that Android is in its basis a Linux system, and that iOS and macOS are both the mobile and laptop operating systems of Apple, these results show that the model is capable of learning the generalizations and main differences between families of operating systems without being over-fitted to all the specific cases of each cases.

This work was an initial approach to the problem of fingerprinting operating systems using machine learning. With restrictions, in terms of execution time and the amount of computational resources, a simplified dataset was created, and some basic models were generated. In spite of being a prototype, the obtained results evidence that this kind of work can be successfully conducted with classical machine learning techniques, with an acceptable grade of complexity of the process. In this researching line, there are plenty of improvements and other different approaches that can be performed in order to get more effective models, such as balancing the dataset, improving the codification of the features, scaling its values, or attempting to apply autoML or deep learning to the problem. It is worth mentioning that the code developed during this work is publicly available in the following GitHub repository: https://github.com/rubenperezudc/osfingerprintingia (accessed on 25 October 2021).

Author Contributions: Conceptualization: R.P.-J., C.R.M., and J.M.V.-N.; methodology: R.P.-J., C.R.M., and J.M.V.-N.; software: R.P.-J. and C.R.M.: formal analysis: R.P.-J. and C.R.M.; investigation, R.P.-J. and C.R.M.; resources: R.P.-J., C.R.M., A.P.S. and J.M.V.-N.; data curation: R.P.-J. and C.R.M.; writing—original draft preparation: R.P.-J.; writing—review and editing: R.P.-J., C.R.M., A.P.S., and J.M.V.-N.; visualization, R.P.-J. and C.R.M.; supervision, C.R.M., A.P.S., and J.M.V.-N. All authors have read and agreed to the published version of the manuscript.

Funding: CITIC, as a research center accredited by the Galician University System, is funded by "Consellería de Cultura, Educación e Universidade from Xunta de Galicia", supported—80% through ERDF, ERDF Operational Programme Galicia 2014–2020, and the remaining 20% by "Secretaría Xeral de Universidades (Grant ED431G 2019/01). This project was also supported by the "Consellería de Cultura, Educación e Ordenación Universitaria" via the Consolidation and Structuring of Competitive Research Units–Competitive Reference Groups (ED431C 2018/49) and the COST Action 17124 DigForAsp, supported by COST (European Cooperation in Science and Technology, www.cost.eu, (accessed on 25 October 2021)).

Conflicts of Interest: The authors declare no conflict of interest.

References

1. Nmap: The Network Mapper—Free Security Scanner. Available online: https://nmap.org/ (accessed on 31 July 2021).
2. XProbe2—Linux Man Page. Available online: https://linux.die.net/man/1/xprobe2 (accessed on 31 July 2021).
3. p0f. Available online: https://lcamtuf.coredump.cx/p0f3/ (accessed on 31 July 2021).
4. Chapter 8. Remote OS Detection Nmap. Available online: https://nmap.org/book/osdetect.html (accessed on 31 July 2021).
5. Operating Systems Fingerprint Database (version 7.9) Nmap. Available online: https://svn.nmap.org/nmap-releases/nmap-7.90/nmap-os-db (accessed on 31 July 2021).

Proceeding Paper

PICTOTEMPO: An App for Personal Organization in Autism Spectrum Disorders [†]

Noé Vila-Muñoz [1], Paula M. Castro [2] and Óscar Fresnedo [2,*]

1. University of A Coruña, 15001 A Coruña, Spain; noe.vila@udc.es
2. CITIC Research Center, Department of Computer Engineering, University of A Coruña, 15001 A Coruña, Spain; paula.castro@udc.es
* Correspondence: oscar.fresnedo@udc.es
† Presented at the 4th XoveTIC Conference, A Coruña, Spain, 7–8 October 2021.

Abstract: In this work, we develop a mobile application which allows to create digital schedules for children with autism spectrum disorder. These schedules comprise a sorted sequence of tasks or activities which facilitates children to understand and anticipate the upcoming events, thus reducing their stress and frustration. For that, the activities are identified and described with the help of visual supports (pictograms) which can be visualized on the screen of any mobile device. The developed application also allows to gather valuable information about the performance and interests of the children from their interactions with it, helping to refine and define more appropriate routines or support therapies for the children. In this way, the aim of this work is to contribute to improve the lives of people with functional and cognitive diversity, especially children with these disorders, and also their families.

Keywords: data analysis; diversity support; mobile application; service-learning; social digitization

1. Introduction

The Autism Spectrum Disorder (ASD) is a neurodevelopmental disorder which usually shows up during the first years of a person's life. The use of suitable software tools and adapted technology can become a differential factor by accentuating the positive impact of the professional interventions on their preparation and application, and also on organization of daily routine of people with ASD, thus changing the way they interact with relatives [1]. This disorder includes some common characteristics such as the presence of difficulties in the nature and quality of social and communicative interactions, very restricted interests and difficulty in facing unanticipated changes in their daily routine [2]. In this sense, the use of pictograms helps these people to understand and assimilate those actions, instead of using oral or written instructions [3].

In this work, we present a mobile application, referred to as app in the following, and termed as PICTOTEMPO, which allows to create in a simple and systematic way digital daily schedules for children with ASD or with any other type of functional or cognitive diversity. These schedules comprise the sequence of tasks and/or activities sorted and associated with the corresponding temporal slot in which they must be completed by the child. In this way, the user (child) can check the task/activity at every time interval, which is shown through pictograms that facilitate the child's comprehension. These digital schedules hence replace the "manual" ones which are traditionally used to work with these groups, thus optimizing time and resources. Another important novelty of this app is that it allows the collection of information for the monitoring of the tasks completed by the children with the aim of improving the therapeutic interventions.

2. Materials and Methods

The chosen methodology for the work was Scrum, because it is characterized by being an agile methodology with an incremental and iterative development. According to this, we initially define a set of high-level requirements for the app and split its development into six iterations or sprints with a same length of two weeks.

In addition, this software methodology was combined with another work methodology known as Service-Learning (SL) [4]. SL emerges as an excellent mechanism to integrate the development of socially responsible and committed citizens during student's formal education. Considering this methodology, this work was carried out with the collaboration of a social entity devoted to children with different types of disorders, including ASD, reading and writing disorders or other functional diversities. This collaboration involves the definition of app requirements, the realization of some tests to evaluate visual design and app functionalities, and also the tests in real scenarios with children affected by ASD, which greatly helped to improve the final product.

3. Results

In this section we present the app, which is divided into two clearly different modules: one for the users, i.e. children with some type of ASD, and another one for educators or relatives that work with them.

Regarding the user's module, the app is oriented to show, depending on date and time, the task/activity to be performed by the user in that moment. As observed in Figure 1, this module is designed and adapted to facilitate the interaction with the child. In this sense, the aim was to provide a simple, friendly, clear and uncluttered interface without distracting elements.

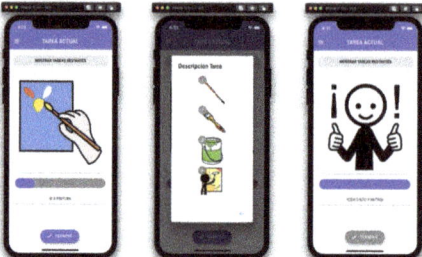

Figure 1. Examples of some views in the child's module.

As before, the educator's module is adapted to simplify the main actions such as create tasks and routines, manage users or obtain and visualize statistical results.

Figure 2 shows some illustrative examples corresponding to the app's view for the creation of routines and tasks. An administrator of this app (relatives, educators, professionals) could create routines with their corresponding tasks/activities, which must be allocated to a specific available temporal slot.

Another relevant functionality in the educator's module is the visualization of statistics as a result of data register. This functionality allows to interactively visualize useful information about the completed tasks (see Figure 3). These statistics show whether the tasks were completed or not, the percentage of time used with respect to the time initially planned for the completion of a task, and the success or not about its completion. The statistics are a key point for education in the context of the ASD since educators will be able to obtain valuable information about children performances according to work areas or their preferences and interests, for example. This information can hence be used to adapt routines or therapies to each child.

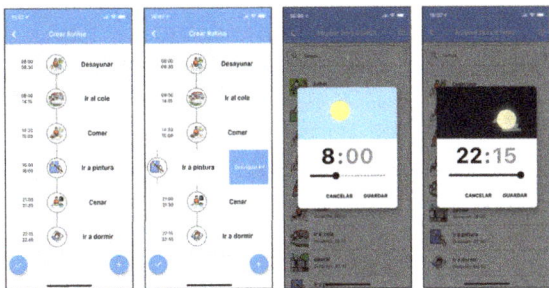

Figure 2. Examples of some views for the creation of routines/tasks in the educator's module.

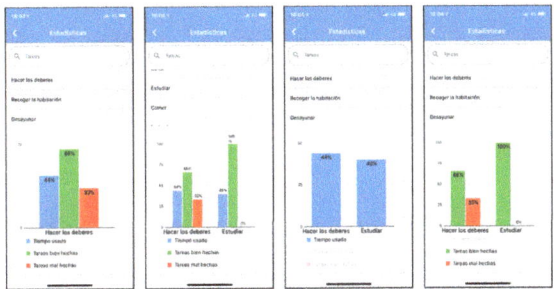

Figure 3. Examples of same views of statistics in the educator's module.

4. Discussion

The aim of this work was to improve the lives of people with functional and cognitive diversity, especially children with ASD, and also their families. Considering the feedback from the collaborator entity, we can conclude that a complete and functional mobile application has been developed since it meets its needs and those of its users. Therefore, it could be employed by those entities, educational environments or families of children with ASD. Finally, it is worth noting that in the current pandemic situation, this type of developments allow to remotely monitor and provide support to these more vulnerable groups avoiding risks of a face-to-face service, which is often not possible.

Author Contributions: The authors contributed equally to the work. All authors have read and agreed to the published version of the manuscript.

Funding: This work has been funded by the Xunta de Galicia (by grant ED431C 2020/15, and grant ED431G 2019/01 to support the Centro de Investigación de Galicia "CITIC"), the Agencia Estatal de Investigación of Spain (by grants RED2018-102668-T and PID2019-104958RB-C42) and ERDF funds of the EU (FEDER Galicia 2014-2020 & AEI/FEDER Programs, UE).

Institutional Review Board Statement: Not applicable.

Informed Consent Statement: Informed consent was obtained from all subjects involved in the study.

Conflicts of Interest: The authors declare no conflict of interest.

Abbreviations

The following abbreviations are used in this manuscript:

ASD   Autism Spectrum Disorder
SL   Service-Learning

References

1. Charitaki, G. The effect of ICT on emotional education and development of young children with Autism Spectrum Disorder. *Procedia Comput. Sci.* **2015**, *65*, 285–293. [CrossRef]
2. Kodak, T.; Bergmann, S. Autism spectrum disorder: Characteristics, associated behaviors, and early intervention. *Pediatr. Clin. N. Am.* **2020**, *67*, 525–535. [CrossRef] [PubMed]
3. Herrera, G.; Casas, X.; Sevilla, J.; Rosa, L.; Pardo, C.; Plaza, J.; Jordan, R.; Le Groux, S. Pictogram room: Natural interaction technologies to aid in the development of children with autism. *Annu. Clin. Health Psychol.* **2012**, *8*, 39–44.
4. Levesque-Bristol, C.; Knapp, T.D.; Fisher, B.J. The Effectiveness of Service-Learning: It's Not Always what you Think. *J. Exp. Educ.* **2011**, *33*, 208–224. [CrossRef]

Proceeding Paper

Alternatives for Locating People Using Cameras and Embedded AI Accelerators: A Practical Approach [†]

Ángel Carro-Lagoa *, Valentín Barral, Miguel González-López, Carlos J. Escudero and Luis Castedo

CITIC Research Center & Department of Computer Engineering, University of A Coruña, 15071 A Coruña, Spain; valentin.barral@udc.es (V.B.); miguel.gonzalez@udc.es (M.G.-L.); escudero@udc.es (C.J.E.); luis.castedo@udc.es (L.C.)
* Correspondence: angel.carro@udc.es
† Presented at the 4th XoveTIC Conference, A Coruña, Spain, 7–8 October 2021.

Abstract: Indoor positioning systems usually rely on RF-based devices that should be carried by the targets, which is non-viable in certain use cases. Recent advances in AI have increased the reliability of person detection in images, thus, enabling the use of surveillance cameras to perform person localization and tracking. This paper evaluates the performance of indoor person location using cameras and edge devices with AI accelerators. We describe the video processing performed in each edge device, including the selected AI models and the post-processing of their outputs to obtain the positions of the detected persons and allow their tracking. The person location is based on pose estimation models as they provide better results than do object detection networks in occlusion situations. Experimental results are obtained with public datasets to show the feasibility of the solution.

Keywords: indoor localization; computer vision; neural networks; embedded devices

1. Introduction

During recent years, the interest in indoor human location has increased due to the large number of applications in various fields, such as security surveillance, activity monitoring, behavioral analysis, and healthcare [1].

Traditionally, when it is necessary to locate people indoors, radio-based technologies are used, which can be affected by the characteristics of the environment and also force target users to carry specific devices. An alternative to these technologies is video-based localization using security cameras, which are increasingly common in buildings and public places. Due to advances in computer vision and Deep Learning (DL), the detection of people on video is more reliable.

The localization and tracking of people is usually performed in two steps: people are first detected in each individual frame to obtain their position in the image. Then, these detections are associated across frames to obtain the path followed by each person.

Typically, these tasks are performed by processing the video from each camera in a centralized way. However, it is possible to perform this processing in a distributed manner due to the advances in edge-computing. Cameras can use AI accelerator chips that allow for fast and low-power neural network inference. Several chips are available on the market, such as Google Coral, Intel Movidius, or Nvidia Jetson.

In this work, we focus on the task of detecting people in security camera images by performing the processing on an embedded device with a Google Coral's Edge TPU. The tracking methods that can be applied to the obtained results are not addressed.

2. Person Location Method

Pedestrian location is performed by processing the input images with a person detector that will locate the persons present in the image. Then, the output of the detector is

processed to determine the real-world position of each person. To perform this last step, the camera calibration information and the vertical vanishing point are also used.

2.1. Person Detection

The most common alternatives for person detection using convolutional neural networks (CNNs) are object detectors, which provide bounding boxes of the persons, and pose estimation, which provides the position of the different key body joints of each person. Cosma et al. [2] compared these two methods, obtaining better results with pose detection networks, which are more resistant to occlusions. Moreover, the correct processing of the detected pose allows for estimation of the position of the person's feet more accurately even when they do not appear in the image.

The PoseNet neural network [3] is used in this work. This model uses a bottom-up approach where all the keypoints of every person are first predicted using a CNN, providing a heatmap for every body part. Then, these keypoints are grouped into individuals using a custom greedy algorithm. This last step can fail if the image has several persons close to each other, mixing the keypoints of two or more persons.

There are several pretrained PoseNet networks available with different CNN backbones and input resolutions. We selected the ResNet50 backbone with a 416×288 resolution as it provides a good balance between inference speed and reliability.

2.2. Post-Processing of Person Keypoints and Projection to 2D Map

The keypoints of each person are used to predict the position of the feet, even if they are not detected or they are occluded. Each keypoint obtained has a score, allowing discarding the keypoints with low reliability. With these reliable keypoints, our post-processing algorithm predicts the feet and head position of each person taking into account the proportions of the human being. These positions are estimated using the least squares method. The vertical vanishing point of the image is also taken into account to correct the inclination of people in the image, depending on the camera perspective.

Cosma et al. [2] used a similar method with the following differences: they only performed these calculations when the feet positions were not detected, and they attempted to determine the inclination of people without taking into account the vanishing point.

Once the feet position in the image is known, the information from the camera is used to determine the map position of each person. The correspondence between each pixel on the image and the 2D floor map coordinates can be calculated with a homography transformation. The homography matrix can be obtained from the position of, at least, four pixels and the map coordinates of each of them. This matrix can also be calculated from the camera projection matrix.

In certain situations, when a person is very close to the camera and only the head is detected, the estimation of the feet position is very poor. This problem can be corrected by assuming that the person has an average height and using the known position of the camera, thus, providing a better estimation of the person's position.

3. Experimental Results

The CamLoc [2] and ICG Lab6 [4] datasets were processed with our person positioning system. Unlike other datasets that only provide the bounding boxes of each person, these datasets annotate the groundtruth position of each person in the map and provide the camera calibration information. This enables us to directly obtain the mean error of the estimated positions.

The CamLoc dataset contains only one person in several scenarios with varying levels of occlusion. Table 1 shows the obtained results with the CamLoc dataset. The mean error of the positions and the percentage of missing predictions are compared, showing that our system obtained better results with all the cameras.

Table 1. The results with the CamLoc dataset compared with the original results.

Camera	Mean Error (cm)		Missing Predictions (%)	
	CamLoc	This Work	CamLoc	This Work
S1_Wide_cam1	36.26	27.49	9.18%	3.46%
S1_Wide_cam4	53.58	45.39	4.47%	0%
S2_Narrow_cam2	45.27	30.96	-	5.72%

The ICG Lab6 dataset [4] consists of one room that is simultaneously recorded by four cameras. There are six scenarios where several persons perform different activities in the room. Table 2 shows the obtained results jointly with the results in [4]. In addition to the mean error, the detected true positives (TP), false positives (FP), and false negatives (FN), i.e., the missing detections) are shown.

Table 2. The mean error column only considers the error of the TP detections.

Scenario	Algorithm	Mean Error (m)	TP	FP	FN
CHAP	ICG Lab6	0.102	1555	2	6
CHAP	This work	0.105	1513	33	25
LEAF1	ICG Lab6	0.107	464	2	2
LEAF1	This work	0.092	422	8	39
LEAF2	ICG Lab6	0.097	930	41	41
LEAF2	This work	0.102	517	15	453
MUCH	ICG Lab6	0.111	783	9	9
MUCH	This work	0.098	780	28	10
POSE	ICG Lab6	0.123	485	14	14
POSE	This work	0.150	428	31	57

The ICG Lab6 method uses a specific tracking algorithm for this kind of scenario with several cameras covering a common area and obtains good results. Our results were obtained by performing a merge of the near positions detected in each camera, and then using a simple tracking algorithm to filter out some FP and FN, only considering the positions of the detections and not the appearance of each person. Moreover, the results are also affected by the difficulty of the pose estimator to distinguish between people when they are very close to each other.

4. Conclusions

We described the developed person location method based on computer vision techniques and provided our experimental results. The obtained results showed the high accuracy that this kind of positioning system can provide. However, in complex scenarios, an adequate tracking algorithm that takes into account the appearance of each person is needed to obtain reliable results.

Funding: This work has been funded by the Navantia-UDC Joint Research Unit under Grant IN853B-2018/02, the Xunta de Galicia (by grant ED431C 2020/15, and grant ED431G 2019/01 to support the Centro de Investigación de Galicia "CITIC"), the Agencia Estatal de Investigación of Spain (by grants RED2018-102668-T and PID2019-104958RB-C42) and ERDF funds of the EU (FEDER Galicia 2014–2020 & AEI/FEDER Programs, UE).

Conflicts of Interest: The authors declare no conflict of interest.

References

1. Morar, A.; Moldoveanu, A.; Mocanu, I.; Moldoveanu, F.; Radoi, I.E.; Asavei, V.; Gradinaru, A.; Butean, A. A Comprehensive Survey of Indoor Localization Methods Based on Computer Vision. *Sensors* **2020**, *20*, 2641. [CrossRef] [PubMed]
2. Cosma, A.; Radoi, I.E.; Radu, V. CamLoc: Pedestrian Location Estimation through Body Pose Estimation on Smart Cameras. In Proceedings of the 2019 International Conference on Indoor Positioning and Indoor Navigation (IPIN), Pisa, Italy, 30 September–3 October 2019; pp. 1–8. [CrossRef]
3. Papandreou, G.; Zhu, T.; Chen, L.C.; Gidaris, S.; Tompson, J.; Murphy, K. PersonLab: Person Pose Estimation and Instance Segmentation with a Bottom-Up, Part-Based, Geometric Embedding Model. In Proceedings of the European Conference on Computer Vision (ECCV), Munich, Germany, 8–14 September 2018.
4. Possegger, H.; Sternig, S.; Mauthner, T.; Roth, P.M.; Bischof, H. Robust Real-Time Tracking of Multiple Objects by Volumetric Mass Densities. In Proceedings of the IEEE Conference on Computer Vision and Pattern Recognition (CVPR), Portland, OR, USA, 23–28 June 2013.

Proceeding Paper

Mixed Reality in an Operating Room Using Hololens 2—The Use of the Remote Assistance from Manufacturers Techinicians during the Surgeries [†]

Rita Veloso [1,‡], Renato Magalhães [1,‡], António Marques [1,‡], Paulo Veloso Gomes [1,*,‡] and Javier Pereira [2,‡]

1. LabRP-CIR, Psychosocial Rehabilitation Laboratory, Center for Rehabilitation Research, School of Health, Polytechnic Institute of Porto, 4200-374 Porto, Portugal; rita.veloso@chporto.min-saude.pt (R.V.); renato.magalhaes@ipoporto.min-saude.pt (R.M.); ajmarques@ess.ipp.pt (A.M.)
2. CITIC, Research Center of Information and Communication Technologies, Talionis Research Group, Universidade da Coruña, 15071 A Coruña, Spain; javier.pereira@udc.es
* Correspondence: pvg@ess.ipp.pt
† Presented at the 4th XoveTIC Conference, A Coruña, Spain, 7–8 October 2021.
‡ These authors contributed equally to this work.

Abstract: The aim of this work is that the participants, using HoloLens 2 and Dynamics 365 Remote Assistance, can receive all the training and information necessary for the correct application of prosthesis and medical devices remotely, from a support center of the manufacturers, avoiding the displacement and presence of these technicians during surgeries. After implementing this method, an analysis will be made on its impact, avoiding displacement and the presence of technicians during surgery, in terms of increasing satisfaction and improving the experience of the participants, reduction of various risks (including the risk of infection) and on reduction of some economic and environmental costs.

Keywords: immersive environments; mixed reality; medical remote assistance; extended reality; augmented reality

1. Introduction

Mixed reality (MR) was first mentioned in 1994 by Paul Milgram, and is a blend of physical and digital worlds, unlocking the links between human, computer, and environment interaction, based on advancements in computer vision, graphical processing power, display technology, and input systems [1]. By using holographic devices, such as Microsoft HoloLens 2, the participants could take advantage of the ability to place digital content in the real world as if it were there. This technology allows participants to see through display and see the physical environment while wearing the headset and allows a full six-degrees-of-freedom movement, both rotation and translation. The participants can hold "hands-free" and "heads-up" teams video calls with experts anywhere in the world, with all of benefits in this kind of experience [1,2].

Recent research has shown that with the use of advanced technological solutions such as MR, the spaces of the operating rooms tend to decrease and the number of professionals present during a surgery too [3], improving the efficiency in the use of resources in a hospital, whether they are human, of space, or technicians and materials. MR is a concept which provide an "ideal virtual space with [sufficient] reality essential for communication" [4]. The combination of computer processing, human input, and environmental input sets the stage for creating true MR experiences. Movement through the physical world translates to movement in the digital world and improves the experience and better outcomes of the participants and tasks [5], once it did not blind doctors' original view of the real world, showing a new vision with mutual correction function, which improved the safety of surgery [6].

Currently, surgeons and nurses focus their attention on operating room, both on the patient's body and on surgical monitors, to get all the information needed [7]. To help them in their procedures, MR starting been in operating rooms all over the world [8]. This kind of technology is also a powerful for better training and improving education on surgical tactics and methods [9]. During the last few decades, changes in surgical materials are constantly being developed and incremental to improve better outcomes [10], most of them needs accomplishment by the manufacturer's technicians during the surgeries. Their presence in the operating room increases the risk of infection [11,12], the delays in surgeries, and the logistic costs of the prosthesis, particularly, in orthopedic field.

Every year in Portugal, orthopedic surgeons perform around 5000 arthroplasties (surgical replacements of necrotic or fractured with a prosthesis), mostly hip and knees arthroplasties [13]. Through displaying specific images in the HoloLens 2 and using in the Dynamics 365 Remote Assistance application, all the assistance could be virtual with a better accuracy of the patient instrumentation, scaling up the expert support all over the world with less costs. There are numerous complex surgeries that require the physical presence of technicians from the prosthesis manufacturers during the surgery to help the participants with their correct application. These technicians, despite being trained for the surgical environment, increase the number of professionals within the operating room, with all the associated risks, namely, the risk of infection.

The objectives of this study are: Test the effectiveness use of MR technology, in the surgical environment as a pilot example for future projects, as a tool for aiding participants during arthroscopies (position and collocation of the prosthesis) without the presence of the manufacturer's technicians, firstly from the identification of the main requirements for this process: analyzing its impact of avoiding displacement and the presence of technicians during surgery, reducing the risk of infection, increasing satisfaction and improving the experience of the participants, the eventual reduction of surgery time, increasing flexibility in scheduling surgeries, increasing the profitability of the technicians' time to perform assistance to a greater number of surgeries and finally, with no physical visits to hospitals, reducing the CO_2 emissions.

2. Methods

Preliminary systematic review, document analysis, analysis of similar previous cases in the industry, in particular the automotive industry using HoloLens 2 and Dynamics 365 Remote Assistance [14], identification of requirements to implement with professionals involved in surgeries with prosthesis, and initial exploratory interviews with orthopaedic surgeons.

3. Results

The development of a system that allows the use of HoloLens 2 as a tool for aiding participants during arthroscopies, and analyze its impact on several factors such as reducing the risk of infection; increasing satisfaction and improve the experience of the participants, using the video recording feature for future training; improve patient experience, sharing some previous videos of the procedure collected from the HoloLens 2; reducing surgery time increasing flexibility in scheduling surgeries; increasing the profitability of the technicians' time to perform assistance to a greater number of surgeries; reducing the CO_2 emissions; reducing of the global costs of the prosthesis.

4. Conclusions

Using HoloLens 2 to support the surgical team in the operating rooms during the arthroplasty's surgeries, participants will be able to share, in real-time, their vision of the patient's specific location where the prosthesis will be applied. While communicating with the manufacturer's specialist technician via Dynamics 365 Remote Assistance, to monitor the correct sequence of application of the parts, maintaining constant visual and voice interaction with technicians, they can be watched continuing its activity in a concentrated and focused way with the patient and the rest of the team. The collected data have shown that the use of HoloLens 2, while an immersive technology of mixed reality, could be useful to eliminate the presence of the manufacturer's technicians during these surgeries, improving participants and patient experience, reducing the risk of infection and the duration of the surgeries while reducing the price of the prosthesis in a future negotiation with the manufacturers.

Author Contributions: Conceptualization, R.V., R.M.; methodology, R.V., R.M., A.M.; validation, R.V., R.M., P.V.G.; investigation R.V., R.M.; writing—original draft preparation, R.V., R.M.; writing—review and editing, R.V., R.M., P.V.G.; visualization, R.V., R.M.; supervision, A.M., J.P.; project administration, R.V., R.M. All authors have read and agreed to the published version of the manuscript.

Funding: This research received no external funding.

Institutional Review Board Statement: Not applicable.

Informed Consent Statement: Not applicable.

Acknowledgments: This research was carried out and used the equipment of the Psychosocial Rehabilitation Laboratory (LabRp) of the Research Center in Rehabilitation of the School of Allied Health Technologies, Polytechnic Institute of Porto.

Conflicts of Interest: The authors declare no conflict of interest.

References

1. Microsoft. "What is Mixed Reality?". 2021. Available online: https://docs.microsoft.com/en-us/windows/mixed-reality/discover/mixed-reality (accessed on 3 August 2021).
2. Gallagher, J.A.L. Mixed-Reality Headsets in Hospitals Help Protect Doctors and Reduce Need for PPE. 2020. Available online: https://www.imperial.ac.uk/news/197617/mixed-reality-headsets-hospitals-help-protect-doctors/ (accessed on 3 August 2021).
3. Joseph, A.; Allison, D. Designing A Safer OR. 2018. Available online: https://healthcaredesignmagazine.com/trends/research-theory/designing-a-safer-or/ (accessed on 3 August 2021).
4. Milgram, P.; Kishino, F. Taxonomy of mixed reality visual displays. *IEICE Trans. Inf. Syst.* **1994**, *77*, 1321–1329.
5. Carlos, F.; Sergio, I.-S.; Carlos, O. The impact of virtual, augmented and mixed reality technologies on the customer experience. *J. Bus. Res.* **2019**, *100*, 547–560.
6. Hu, H.Z.; Feng, X.B.; Shao, Z.W.; Xie, M.; Xu, S.; Wu, X.H.; Ye, Z.W. Application and Prospect of Mixed Reality Technology in Medical Field. *Curr. Med. Sci.* **2019**, *39*, 1–6. [CrossRef] [PubMed]
7. Galati, R.; Simone, M.; Barile, G.; Luca, R.D.; Cartanese, C.; Grassi, G. Experimental Setup Employed in the Operating Room Based on Virtual and Mixed Reality: Analysis of Pros and Cons in Open Abdomen Surgery. *J. Healthc. Eng.* **2020**, *2020*, 8851964. [CrossRef] [PubMed]
8. Ferrari, V.; Klinker, G.; Cutolo, F. Augmented reality in healthcare. *J. Healthc. Eng.* **2019**. [CrossRef] [PubMed]
9. Zhu, E.; Hadadgar, A.; Masiello, I.; Zary, N. Augmented reality in healthcare education: An integrative review. *PeerJ* **2014**, *2*, e469. [CrossRef] [PubMed]
10. Keeney, J.A. Innovations in total knee arthroplasty: Improved technical precision, but unclear clinical benefits. *Orthopedics* **2016**, *39*, 217–220. [CrossRef] [PubMed]
11. Rebelo, S., Segurança do Doente no Bloco Operatório. Dissertação (Mestre em Enfermagem Médico-Cirúrgica), Escola Superior de Enfermagem de Coimbra, Coimbra, Portugal, 2013.
12. Cristina, M.L.; Sartini, M.; Schinca, E.; Ottria, G.; Spagnolo, A.M. Operating room environment and surgical site infections in arthroplasty procedures. *J. Prev. Med. Hyg.* **2016**, *57*, E142. [CrossRef] [PubMed]
13. Portuguese Arthroplasty Register (RPA). Available online: http://www.rpa.spot.pt/Quick-Links/Home.aspx?lang=en-GB (accessed on 3 August 2021).
14. Mercedes-Benz Has Begun Using HoloLens 2 To Provide Maintenance Support. 2021. Available online: https://www.vrfocus.com/2020/09/mercedes-benz-has-begun-using-hololens-2-to-provide-maintenance-support/ (accessed on 3 August 2021).

Proceeding Paper

Application for Decision-Making on Mild Cognitive Impairments [†]

Erick Gonzalez-Martin [1], Alberto Alvarellos [1,2], Virginia Mato-Abad [1], Juan Manuel Pias-Peleteiro [3,4], Isabel Jimenez-Martin [3,4] and Francisco Cedron [1,2,*]

[1] Software Engineering Laboratory, Computer Science Faculty, University of A Coruña, 15071 A Coruña, Spain; erick.gonzalez@udc.es (E.G.-M.); alberto.alvarellos@udc.es (A.A.); virginia.mato@udc.es (V.M.-A.)
[2] Research Center on Information and Communication Technologies, University of A Coruña, 15071 A Coruña, Spain
[3] Department of Neurology, University Clinical Hospital of Santiago de Compostela, 15706 Santiago de Compostela, Spain; juan.manuel.pias.peleteiro@sergas.es (J.M.P.-P.); isabel.jimenez.martin@sergas.es (I.J.-M.)
[4] Clinical Health Research Institute of Santiago de Compostela (IDIS), Universidade de Santiago de Compostela, 15706 Santiago de Compostela, Spain
* Correspondence: francisco.cedron@udc.es
[†] Presented at the 4th XoveTIC Conference, A Coruña, Spain, 7–8 October 2021.

Abstract: Life expectancy in Western countries is increasing. The fact that humans are living longer lives presents new challenges to people's quality of life. Some of the problems that most affect older people are the problems associated with cognitive impairment. The development of a tool that helps psychologists to carry out different types of tests is the main objective of this work. To this end, an interdisciplinary group of psychologists and engineers have joined forces to create a tool that generates a series of standardised metrics to guide clinicians and help them make decisions about a patient's cognitive impairment.

Keywords: depression; cognitive impairment; neuropsychological test

1. Introduction

Despite the problems that continually arise in our society (social, political, economic, health, etc.), it has been proven that, in Western countries, the ageing of the population is a growing trend, i.e., the life expectancy of the elderly is increasing [1]. The fact that humans are living longer and longer lives has brought a series of challenges to the quality of life. One of the problems that most affect the elderly are the problems associated with cognitive impairments [2]. Among the cognitive problems, the best known is Alzheimer's disease, which causes very serious problems such as personality changes, deterioration in the ability to move or walk, difficulty communicating, memory loss, attention and orientation problems, among many others [3]. Alzheimer's disease usually occurs in people over the age of 65, although there are documented cases of people who may have developed it from the age of 40 onwards [4]. The big problem with Alzheimer's, and many other types of cognitive impairment, is that they are currently incurable, the only possibility being early detection and then carrying out activities and/or taking medication that can slow down the disease [5].

2. Objective

The main objective of this work is the creation of a tool that helps psychologists to carry out different types of tests to help diagnose their patients. To do this, the tool has to generate a series of standardised metrics to guide clinicians in making the final decision about the patient's cognitive impairment.

3. State-of-the-Art

Without a doubt, the health field is evolving towards an environment where technology is more omnipresent and where there are more and more applications to help doctors make decisions. The world of neuropsychology is no exception and those that seek to improve cognitive functioning through a set of activities related to memory, reasoning, calculation and communication stand out. Some existing applications are detailed below:

- Imentia [6]: It is a tool that detects possible cognitive impairment through the ENM.dem test. It then generates cognitive stimulation sessions [7]. This tool is designed for people who have already been diagnosed with Alzheimer's disease. The tool costs EUR 288 per year.
- Cantab [8]: It has a battery of neuropsychological tests to detect neurological diseases, disorders, pharmacological manipulations and neurocognitive syndromes. The tool is not intended to study cognitive impairment. It costs EUR 30,000.
- Stimulus [9]: This is an application that allows cognitive stimulation and rehabilitation. The cost of the tool is EUR 1296 per year.
- Accexible [10]: It is a cognitive impairment detection platform in which the patient's acoustic data is extracted. Their price is not public.

The main difference between the application developed and those available on the market is that it does not focus on the use of one or several specific tests. The tool that has been created allows the clinician to perform the necessary tests and then have a report on which to make a final decision.

4. Methodology

This paper presents a system for decision making in cases of mild cognitive impairment. The application allows to have several patients and to perform certain operations on them, such as viewing previous reports or performing new tests for a report (Figure 1). Figure 2 shows the different tests that were applied to the patient, where the clinician enters the PD value, which indicates the real value of the test, while the PZ value is the standardised value obtained and calculated by the application from the PD value entered by the clinician. It is important to mention that the clinician chooses at any time the tests he wants for the report and that at any time he can finalise the report by indicating the clinical suspicion of the patient (Figure 3).

Figure 1. List of the patients registered in the application and quick actions that can be performed on them.

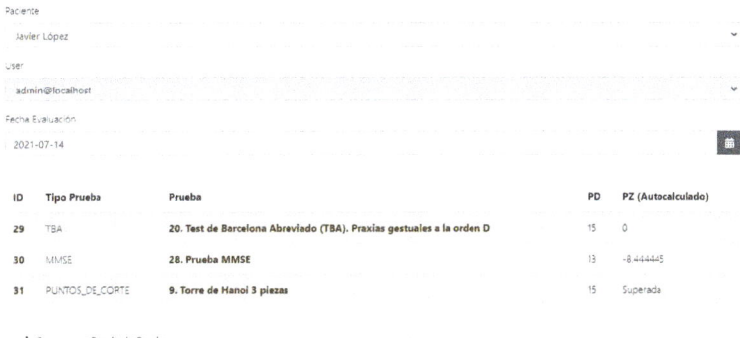

Figure 2. A view of the tests that have been performed at one point in time on the patient. The PD value is entered by the clinician and is the direct score of a test. The PZ value is automatically calculated by the system using normalised values.

Figure 3. Patient report screen where the clinician can view the tests that were performed on a patient. The clinician to indicate the type of clinical suspicion based on the tests performed.

Author Contributions: Conceptualization, J.M.P.-P. and I.J.-M.; methodology, A.A., V.M.-A. and F.C.; software, E.G.-M. and F.C.; validation, E.G.-M., J.M.P.-P. and I.J.-M.; writing—original draft preparation, F.C.; writing—review and editing, F.C.; visualization, E.G.-M.; supervision, F.C. All authors have read and agreed to the published version of the manuscript.

Funding: This research received no external funding.

Institutional Review Board Statement: Not applicable.

Informed Consent Statement: Not applicable.

Data Availability Statement: Not applicable.

Conflicts of Interest: The authors declare no conflict of interest.

References

1. World Health Organization (WHO). *The World Health Report 2000. Health Systems: Improving Performance*; WHO Office of Publications: Geneva, Switzerland, 2000.
2. Christidi, F.; Migliaccio, R.; Santamaria-Garcia, H.; Santangelo, G.; Trojsi, F. Social Cognition Dysfunctions in Neurodegenerative Diseases: Neuroanatomical Correlates and Clinical Implications. *Behav. Neurol.* **2018**, *2018*, 1849794. [CrossRef] [PubMed]
3. Sun, B.; Li, W.; Zhu, C.; Jin, W.; Zeng, F.; Liu, Y.; Bu, X.; Zhu, J.; Yao, X.; Wang, Y. Clinical Research on Alzheimer's Disease: Progress and Perspectives. *Neurosci. Bull.* **2018**, *34*, 1111–1118. [CrossRef] [PubMed]
4. Hvidsten, L.; Engedal, K.; Selbæk, G.; Wyller, T.; Bruvik, F.; Kersten, H. Quality of Life in People with Young-Onset Alzheimer's Dementia and Frontotemporal Dementia. *Dement. Geriatr. Cogn. Disord.* **2018**, *45*, 91–104. [CrossRef] [PubMed]
5. McDade, E.; Bateman, R. Stop Alzheimer's before it starts. *Nature* **2017**, *547*, 153–155. [CrossRef] [PubMed]
6. Imentia: La App de Estimulación Cognitiva. Available online: https://www.imentia.com (accessed on 5 August 2021).
7. Deví-Bastida, J.; Domínguez-Luque, P.; Jofre-Font, S. Evaluación neuropsicológica de la demencia avanzada: ¿son de utilidad los instrumentos psicométricos de valoración cognitiva? Una revisión sistemática. *Rev. Neurol.* **2021**, *72*, 239–249. [PubMed]

8. CANTAB Cognitive Research Software | Cambridge Cognition. Available online: https://www.cambridgecognition.com/cantab (accessed on 5 August 2021).
9. Profesional (Stimulus ® PRO). Available online: https://stimuluspro.com/profesional-stimulus-pro (accessed on 5 August 2021).
10. acceXible. Available online: https://accexible.com (accessed on 5 August 2021).

Proceeding Paper

An Analysis of the Current Implementations Based on the WebAuthn and FIDO Authentication Standards [†]

Martiño Rivera-Dourado [1,2,*], Marcos Gestal [1,2,3], Alejandro Pazos [1,2,3] and José M. Vázquez-Naya [1,2]

[1] Grupo RNASA-IMEDIR, Departamento de Ciencias de la Computación y Tecnologías de la Información, Facultade de Informática, Universidade da Coruña, Elviña Campus, 15071 A Coruña, Spain; marcos.gestal@udc.es (M.G.); alejandro.pazos@udc.es (A.P.); jose@udc.es (J.M.V.-N.)
[2] Centro de Investigación CITIC, Universidade da Coruña, Elviña Campus, 15071 A Coruña, Spain
[3] IKERDATA S.L., ZITEK, University of Basque Country UPVEHU, Rectorate Building, 48940 Leioa, Spain
* Correspondence: martino.rivera.dourado@udc.es
[†] Presented at the 4th XoveTIC Conference, A Coruña, Spain, 7–8 October 2021.

Abstract: During the last few years, some of the most relevant IT companies have started to develop new authentication solutions which are not vulnerable to attacks like phishing. WebAuthn and FIDO authentication standards were designed to replace or complement the *de facto* and ubiquitous authentication method: username and password. This paper performs an analysis of the current implementations of these standards while testing and comparing these solutions in a high-level analysis, drawing the context of the adoption of these new standards and their integration with the existing systems, from web applications and services to different use cases on desktop and server operating systems.

Keywords: WebAuthn; authentication; FIDO

1. Introduction

Username and password is the *de facto* authentication method used in almost every web application, but it is threatened by several attacks. The most relevant one is phishing. During the last few years, some of the most relevant IT companies have started to develop new solutions which are not vulnerable to these attacks. In this context is where they form the FIDO Alliance to start developing a protocol to use hardware devices and public-key cryptography to perform authentication.

WebAuthn [1] is a new W3C authentication API for browsers to make use of hardware or software FIDO security keys [2] for replacing or complementing the username and password authentication method. Therefore, this new method can be applied in two different use cases: (1) using the security key as a second factor authentication method, usually after a password; (2) using the security key as a first factor authentication method, identifying and authenticating the user, without the need of a username or password. Moreover, web applications are not the unique systems where FIDO security keys can be of use. Operating Systems, like Windows and Linux, have solutions that make use of this new authentication method.

2. Materials and Methods

The analysis carried out in this paper has involved two main scenarios that implied two different approaches: web applications and Operating Systems. For both of them, the Solo Hacker from Solokeys, the Yubikey 5 NFC from Yubico and the Titan Security Keys from Google were used as a FIDO hardware authenticators and a PC as a host for the tests. Regarding web applications, the testers have used the Chromium browser (v.91.0) as a client and developer tool for debugging the operations, using the DebAuthn web application [3]. On the other hand, Windows 10 and Ubuntu 20.04 LTS Operating Systems were tested inside Virtual Machines using Virtualbox, interfacing with the FIDO hardware key through USB.

3. Web Applications

As the aforementioned two use cases are different and involve specific configuration of the registration and authentication operations, the current implementations among the different existing and compatible web services is also diverse. In this paper, we analyzed and identified the different use cases two of the most relevant online platforms present in the FIDO Alliance: Google and Microsoft free accounts.

Google free accounts offer the usage of security keys as a second-factor authentication method, which they name as 2-Step Verification. As shown during the tests, the implementation from Google avoids the usage of resident credentials (a.k.a. discoverable credentials) [1], which limits their solution to use WebAuthn authenticators only as a second-factor authentication method, maintaining the password always as a first-factor. During registration, user verification trough a PIN was not required nor a user handle identifier was installed in the device. Although Google offers an Advanced Protection Program [4] which enforces the usage of a second-factor authentication mechanism with security keys, the first-factor authentication method is still based on a password. However, this implementation requires using two WebAuthn authenticators with non-resident credentials: one device for daily usage and the other as a backup in case of device loss. For this purpose, Google has developed their own Titan Security Keys, although the current version only supports non-resident credentials.

On the contrary, Microsoft free accounts implement WebAuthn only as a first-factor authentication option in their Advanced security options, excluding it from the list of second-factor authentication methods. However, Microsoft also implements other first-factor authentication methods, like push notifications to a smartphone application, SMS codes, Windows Hello or even sending a code via email.

When registering or authenticating with a WebAuthn authenticator as a first-factor, Microsoft requires the usage of resident credentials and user verification via PIN. During the registration operation, the credential with the user handle identifier is installed in the device and, during the authentication operation, this identifier is returned together within the authenticator response. It is worth mentioning that, when registering the Solokey device in the Microsoft account, the server aborts the operation. Microsoft cancels the registration when a specific FIDO authenticator is not in their list of allowed manufacturers, filtering them during the attestation verification process. For this reason, the Yubikey authenticator was used instead.

4. Operating Systems

The FIDO CTAP standard can be used to communicate with FIDO authenticators natively and defines their behaviour and available operations, so it can be used in other online and offline systems. In this context, Yubico has developed a PAM (Pluggable Authentication Module) [5] for using FIDO authenticators as a token to authenticate users on Linux-based Operating Systems. It includes a binary to obtain key handles and public keys from the authenticator, allowing to create an entry in the configuration file that maps an user with a credential.

Regarding the Windows Operating System, Microsoft has developed their own Window's native WebAuthn API, for which Yubico has recently added support in their libfido2 library [6]. The problem of this approach is that developers are not able to interact with FIDO devices natively, so FIDO CTAP2 extensions which are not included in the Windows API will not be used. In this context, we have tested different configurations of WebAuthn requests on the browser, concluding all of them in Windows launching their native platform for the interaction with the FIDO devices. This approach diverges from the solution in Linux systems, where browsers and PAM modules are in charge of performing the FIDO CTAP communication.

Although Windows has included an utility for managing security keys in their sign-in options, it does not yet support native sign-in with FIDO security keys for local accounts. However, Microsoft offers a business solution for FIDO2 authentication with security keys through their Azure Active Directory Multi-Factor feature, using Kerberos tickets to authorize users with on-premise Active Directory controllers [7]. For this reason, Yubico has developed their Yubico Login [8] solution that allows Windows sign-in with Yubikeys, although they not use FIDO CTAP2 features, so they are not compatible other security keys. This implementation uses Yubico HMAC challenge-response programmable slots available in Yubikey 4 and 5.

5. Conclusions

WebAuthn has been implemented as an authentication option in some of the most relevant web services, like Google and Microsoft free accounts. While Google has developed their own security keys to be used as a second-factor, Microsoft has chosen WebAuthn as a first-factor authentication method with resident credentials in devices of their allowed list of manufacturers. This makes the implementation from Google more conservative, as it uses WebAuthn as a second-factor, making their solution more compatible with browsers, platforms and FIDO devices. In contrast, Microsoft allows users to avoid passwords with WebAuthn, as they have been doing with other first-factor sign-in options like push notifications.

Operating Systems have started to support WebAuthn and FIDO standards for other authentication mechanisms, further than web applications. For this reason, Yubico developed local OS authentication solutions both for Linux and Windows. However, while the Linux PAM module can be used with any authenticator compatible with WebAuthn, the solution for Windows is only available for Yubikeys. Finally, Microsoft native implementations make difficult to some developers to completely use FIDO functionalities, and make their Azure AD software the only option for using any FIDO device as a sign-in option in their Operating System.

Author Contributions: Conceptualization, M.R.-D.; Methodology, M.R.-D., M.G. and J.M.V.-N.; Testing, M.R.-D.; Investigation, M.R.-D., M.G., A.P. and J.M.V.-N.; Resources, M.G., A.P. and J.M.V.-N.; Writing—original draft preparation, M.R.-D.; Writing—review and editing, M.R.-D., M.G., A.P. and J.M.V.-N.; Supervision, M.G., A.P. and J.M.V.-N. All authors have read and agreed to the published version of the manuscript.

Funding: CITIC, as Research Center accredited by Galician University System, is funded by "Consellería de Cultura, Educación e Universidade from Xunta de Galicia", supported in an 80% through ERDF, ERDF Operational Programme Galicia 2014–2020, and the remaining 20% by "Secretaría Xeral de Universidades" (Grant ED431G 2019/01). This project was also supported by the "Consellería de Cultura, Educación e Ordenación Universitaria" via the Consolidation and Structuring of Competitive Research Units—Competitive Reference Groups (ED431C 2018/49).

Conflicts of Interest: The authors declare no conflict of interest.

References

1. Web Authentication: An API for Accessing Public Key Credentials Level 2. Available online: https://www.w3.org/TR/webauthn-2/ (accessed on 18 May 2021).
2. Client to Authenticator Protocol (CTAP). Available online: https://fidoalliance.org/specs/fido-v2.0-ps-20190130/fido-client-to-authenticator-protocol-v2.0-ps-20190130.html (accessed on 18 May 2021).
3. Debauthn: WebAuthn Authenticator Debugging Tool. Available online: https://debauthn.tic.udc.es/ (accessed on 19 July 2021).
4. Advanced Protection Program. Available online: https://landing.google.com/advancedprotection/ (accessed on 19 July 2021).
5. Pluggable Authentication Module (PAM) for U2F. Available online: https://github.com/Yubico/pam-u2f (accessed on 29 June 2020).
6. Pull Request #336 · Yubico/libfido2. Available online: https://github.com/Yubico/libfido2/pull/336 (accessed on 19 July 2021).
7. Azure Active Directory Passwordless Sign-In | Microsoft Docs. Available online: https://docs.microsoft.com/en-us/azure/active-directory/authentication/concept-authentication-passwordless (accessed on 19 July 2021).
8. Computer Login Security with YubiKey | Yubicoand . Available online: https://www.yubico.com/products/computer-login-tools/ (accessed on 19 July 2021).

Proceeding Paper

A Deep Learning-Based Strategy to Predict Self-Interference in SFN DTT [†]

Dariel Pereira-Ruisánchez *, Darian Pérez-Adán and Luis Castedo

Department of Computer Engineering & CITIC Research Center, University of A Coruña, Campus de Elviña S/N, 15071 A Coruña, Spain; d.adan@udc.es (D.P.-A.); luis.castedo@udc.es (L.C.)
* Correspondence: d.ruisanchez@udc.es
† Presented at the 4th XoveTIC Conference, A Coruña, Spain, 7–8 October 2021.

Abstract: A deep learning-based strategy for the analysis of the self-interference in single frequency networks (SFNs) for digital terrestrial television (DTT) broadcasting is considered. Several laboratory measurements were performed to create a dataset that relates the self-interference parameters and some quality metrics of the resulting received signal. The laboratory setup emulates an SFN scenario with two DTT transmitters. The strongest received signal and the relative values of attenuation and delay between the signals stand for the input parameters. The modulation error ratio (MER) of the strongest received signal, the MER of the resulting signal, and the SFN gain (SFNG) are the output parameters. This dataset is used to train four different multi-layer perceptron (MLP) models to predict accurate maps of interference and signal quality metrics. The considered models are suitable as complements for any multiple frequency network (MFN) coverage software with the capability to return the signal strength and the position data. This way, the SFN self-interference behavior can be predicted by considering only a proper description of the MFN coverage.

Keywords: SFN; deep learning; broadcasting; self-interference

1. Introduction

The remarkable growth of mobile services and wireless communication technologies has led to a revision of the way the available spectrum bands are allocated. In digital terrestrial television (DTT) broadcasting, the spectral efficiency achieved with multiple frequency networks (MFNs) is significantly improved when moving to single frequency networks (SFNs). Furthermore, the deployment of SFNs leads to a more homogeneous distribution of the electric-field strength in the coverage area and to savings in transmission power [1].

In previous works, self-interference in SFNs is only considered when the interfering signals arrive with a delay longer than the guard interval. However, this only represents a critical scenario where the interference is mostly destructive. Signals arriving within the guard interval also produce self-interference, and it can be either constructive or destructive. The effect of this kind of interference is called SFN gain (SFNG) and it must be properly controlled to obtain a good performance in SFN systems [2–4].

Several network planning strategies based on deep learning (DL) algorithms are being considered as a reasonable alternative for the configuration of broadcasting systems. These strategies allow reducing the computational complexity of theoretical models and the planning cost of the field-testing-based approaches [5–7]. The predictive capability of DL algorithms and the lack of works about using them for SFN interference analyses have motivated this research. The major contributions of this work can be summarized as follows:

- The development of a laboratory test-based dataset that relates the parameters of the received signals to several metrics of interference and signal quality.
- The implementation of deep learning-based models to predict the interference and the resulting signal quality metrics.

2. Dataset and Proposed Deep Learning-Based Models

The proposed laboratory setup emulates an SFN scenario with two interfering transmitters. The interfering signals were generated by using a Broadcast Test Center (BTC) from Rohde and Schwarz and the signal quality metrics were measured by using the S7000 TV Analyzer professional receiver. The electric-field strength of the main signal ($E_{\text{MainSignal}}$), and the values of *Attenuation* and *Delay* of the secondary signal, were configured to emulate self-interference scenarios. These parameters are the input features in the proposed dataset. The modulation error ratio (MER) was the metric employed to quantify the signal quality. The measured values of modulation error ratio (MER) of both the main signal (MER_{MFN}) and the resulting received signal (MER_{SFN}) are output features. The SFN gain (G_{SFN}) is the third output feature, which is calculated as the difference between the MER_{SFN} and the MER_{MFN} parameters.

The resulting dataset was employed to train four multi-layer perceptron (MLP) models by using a supervised-learning strategy (Table 1). The first models are regression models; thus, they were trained to predict the exact values of their respective output features. The last one is a binary classification model and it was trained to predict whether the value of G_{SFN} is positive or negative. Positive G_{SFN} values stand for the cases where the received signal improves when moving to SFN while the negative values correspond to a signal degradation.

Table 1. Proposed deep learning-based models.

MLP Models	Output Feature	Type
MLP_MfnMER	MER_{MFN}	Regression
MLP_SfnMER	MER_{SFN}	Regression
MLP_SfnG	G_{SFN}	Regression
MLP_SfnGclass	$Gclass_{\text{SFN}}$	Classification

3. Results

Table 2 summarizes the accuracy values obtained by employing the proposed regression models. The coefficient of determination (R^2), the mean absolute error (MAE), the mean square error (MSE) and the root mean square error ($RMSE$) are the metrics used to measure the performance. A lower accuracy is obtained with the MLP_SfnG model since the correspondence between G_{SFN} and the input features cannot be easily determined.

Table 2. Performance metrics of the regression models.

MLP Models	R^2	MAE	MSE	RMSE
MLP_MfnMER	0.998	0.159	0.036	0.191
MLP_SfnMER	0.997	0.134	0.041	0.203
MLP_SfnG	0.909	0.151	0.049	0.221

In Figure 1, the predicted values are plotted versus the measured values. As expected, a higher dispersion can be observed in the G_{SFN} predictions because the performance of this model is lower than the others. Some dispersion can also be observed in the edge values of the parameters due to the instrument measuring ranges.

Figure 2 shows the confusion matrix for the MLP_SfnGclass classification model. From the 317 samples considered for the validation process, the 91.5% were well predicted

(184 true negatives and 106 true positives). The remaining 8.5% of the predictions were either false positives or false negatives.

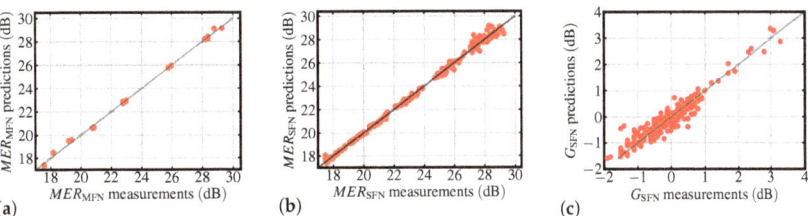

Figure 1. Predicted values versus measured values of (**a**) MER_{MFN}, (**b**) MER_{SFN} and (**c**) G_{SFN}.

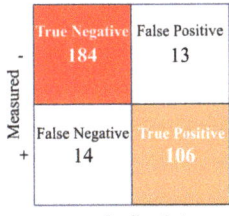

Figure 2. Confusion matrix of the MLP_SfnGclass model.

4. Conclusions

This paper proposes a deep learning-based strategy to analyze the self-interference in SFNs for DTT broadcasting. Unlike most planning-oriented researches, interference in SFNs is analyzed over the entire overlapping area and not only in critical cases where delays are especially long. A dataset obtained from laboratory measurements is employed to train four MLP models for predicting signal quality parameters in an SFN DTT deployment. The prediction results exhibit the high degree of relation between the received signal's parameters and the resulting signal quality. The proposed dataset and the MLP models are suitable for any SFN interference analysis since this approach is not limited to specific terrain or transmission variables.

Author Contributions: Conceptualization, formal analysis, investigation, visualization and writing original draft, D.P.-R. and D.P.-A.; writing—review and editing original draft, D.P.-R., D.P.-A. and L.C.; project administration and funding acquisition, L.C.

Funding: This work has been funded by the Xunta de Galicia (by grant ED431C 2020/15, and grant ED431G2019/01 to support the CITIC, Centre for Information and Communications Technology Research, from the University System of Galicia), the Agencia Estatal de Investigación of Spain (by grants RED2018-102668-T and PID2019-104958RB-C42) and ERDF funds of the EU (FEDER Galicia 2014–2020 & AEI/FEDER Programs, UE), and the predoctoral grant BES-2017-081955.

Institutional Review Board Statement: Not applicable.

Informed Consent Statement: Not applicable.

Data Availability Statement: The dataset used to train the deep learning-based models is publicly available at https://github.com/DarielPereira/SFN_Dataset.git (accessed on 30 September 2021).

Conflicts of Interest: The authors declare no conflict of interest.

References

1. Mattson, A. Single frequency networks in DTV. *IEEE Trans. Broadcast.* **2005**, *51*, 413–422. [CrossRef]
2. Plets, D. On the Methodology for Calculating SFN Gain in Digital Broadcast Systems. *IEEE Trans. Broadcast.* **2010**, *56*, 331–339. [CrossRef]
3. Plets, D.; Joseph, W.; Angueira, P.; Arenas, J.A.; Verloock, L.; Martens, L. SFN gain in broadcast networks. In Proceedings of the IEEE International Symposium on Broadband Multimedia Systems and Broadcasting (BMSB), Nuremberg, Germany, 8–10 June 2011.
4. Ruisánchez, D.P. Estudio de la interferencia mutua en SFN para DTMB. *RIELAC* **2020**, *41*, 73–88.
5. Moreta, C.E.G. Prediction of Digital Terrestrial Television Coverage Using Machine Learning Regression. *IEEE Trans. Broadcast.* **2019**, *65*, 702–712. [CrossRef]
6. Liu, D. Optimizing Wireless Systems Using Unsupervised and Reinforced-Unsupervised Deep Learning. *IEEE Netw.* **2020**, *34*, 270–277. [CrossRef]
7. Kibria, M.G. Big Data Analytics, Machine Learning, and Artificial Intelligence in Next-Generation Wireless Networks. *IEEE Access* **2018**, *6*, 32328–32338. [CrossRef]

Proceeding Paper
Low Cost Automated Security Audit System †

Pedro Fernández-Arruti *, Julio J. Estévez-Pereira *, Francisco J. Nóvoa, Jose C. Dafonte and Diego Fernández

Research Center of Information and Communication Technologies (CITIC), Campus de Elviña, s/n, 15071 A Coruña, Spain; francisco.javier.novoa@udc.es (F.J.N.); carlos.dafonte@udc.es (J.C.D.); diego.fernandez@udc.es (D.F.)

* Correspondence: pedro.fernandez-arruti@udc.es (P.F.-A.), julio.jairo.estevez.pereira@udc.es (J.J.E.-P.)
† Presented at the 4th XoveTIC Conference, A Coruña, Spain, 7–8 October 2021.

Abstract: In recent years, a quick transition towards digitization has been observed in most organizations. Along with it, certain inherent problems have appeared, such as the increase in cyber threats. Large organizations are able to adapt easily, but this does not happen with small and medium-sized companies. Currently, there are very few solutions aimed at fulfilling the needs of these small enterprises, so we have worked on a tool for them. Our tool is capable of displaying key, easy-to-interpret information related to each organization's network assets. To achieve this, we used passive and active analysis techniques and successfully evaluated the viability of using machine learning techniques to get more meaningful information. All of the information obtained is displayed in a simple web application, which is designed to be used by managers in organizations without them needing to handle complex concepts and vocabulary.

Keywords: network audit; passive analysis; active analysis; machine learning

1. Introduction

Organizations of all sizes are now significantly reliant upon information technology and networks for the operation of their business activities. Therefore, they have the added requirement of ensuring that their systems and data are appropriately protected against security breaches. However, there is evidence to suggest that security practices are not strongly upheld within small and medium-sized enterprise (SME) environments [1].

There are different approaches in the literature that attempt to address this problem. However, many of them require those responsible for organizations to handle complex concepts and vocabulary and provide results that managers of this type of organization do not know how to interpret.

Our project involves building a modular tool that implements the creation of an inventory of the organization's assets (final and intermediate devices, active services, and identification of application-layer protocols) and an information visualization through a dashboard (providing key information to the organization's managers, indicating the technical risk of the organization). In addition, we evaluate the viability of machine learning techniques for offering advanced knowledge of the state of the network from the data collected by using unsupervised exploration techniques. There are non-functional characteristics that are key to the success of our tool: a low-cost, scalable, modular, and easy-to-use solution.

2. State of the Art

Nowadays, there are many solutions for carrying out network audits. Many of them produce satisfactory results, allowing their customers to improve the security of their networks. However, only a reduced number of them are both low-priced and easy to use. It is for this reason that small and medium-sized businesses cannot afford a secure network infrastructure.

An example of a currently available wired network audit tool is the Raspberry Pwn [2]. This tool is an open-source software created by the company Pwnie Express, which is aimed at detecting vulnerabilities in a network using a Raspberry. The disadvantage of this tool is its maintenance, since it has not been revised since 2014. On the other hand, there is a project called Wireless Attack Toolkit (WAT) [3] that allows one to convert a Raspberry Pi into a security auditing system for different types of networks. Its main disadvantage is the same as in the previous case, as the last revision of its code was in 2016.

3. Materials and Methods

3.1. Architectural Design

This project is about designing and building a scalable, low-cost, and easy-to-use system that performs audits on corporate networks with minimal intervention by the end user. For this, two types of analysis are performed: a passive analysis, which consists in a device that passively listens to the network traffic and makes an inventory of the active devices on the network, as well as the protocols that make some kind of broadcast communication on it; and an active analysis, which detects each asset's operating system, hostname, IP, and the status of its ports and services.

Moreover, we not only show the retrieved data, but also process them in order to generate a dataset on which unsupervised machine learning techniques can be applied. Concretely, we use data involving services and protocols to train a self-organizing map (SOM) [4] that clusterizes our samples, providing an easy-to-understand and very visual way to distinguish the devices in our network, which are atypical when it comes to the services running or protocols used.

To build a system that implements the desired functionalities and meets the non-functional requirements of low cost, scalability, and ease of use, we propose the design that can be seen in Figure 1.

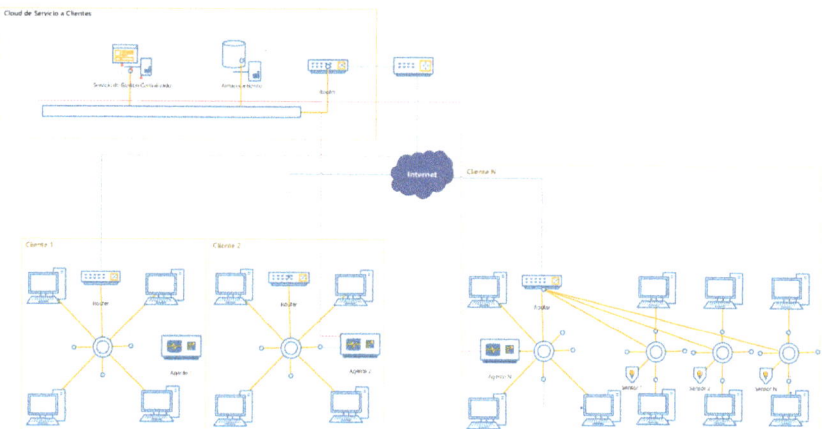

Figure 1. System architecture.

The system relies on three different types of elements. First of all, we have a hardware agent connected to the client network. If the network has multiple subnets, sensors will be placed to collect information from each segment. These sensors will send the added information to the agent of its organization. Finally, a server is used to store the data related to the operation of the network.

3.2. Software and Hardware

To achieve the objectives discussed above, we employ hardware devices based on a low-cost board where we run our application code. This code is written in Python 3 and uses well-known network tool libraries, such as Scapy and Nmap. In addition, the Django framework is utilized to create the web interface. Finally, for performing the machine learning tasks, we relied mainly on Numpy, Pandas, and MiniSom.

4. Results

As a result of the implementation of the tool, a network scanning software was obtained and is executed periodically every hour. The information collected is reflected in a web interface.

The data obtained through passive analysis are the following: IPv4 addresses, IPv6 addresses, device network adapter manufacturer data (OUI), device name, the last time it was detected, domain names (through LLMNR and MDNS), operating system (through the TTL value of the packets), and the broadcast protocols used by each host.

On the other hand, the data obtained for each of the hosts detected by the active analysis are the following: IPv4 addresses, IPv6 addresses, computer name, possible operating systems that run on it, and open ports and services that run on said ports.

Finally, concerning the use of SOMs to clusterize the detected devices according to both their services and protocols, we found that the results are promising. To reach this conclusion, we relied on two metrics: average quantization error and topographic error measurement. In this project, we reached the values 0.30 and 0.15, respectively, for these metrics.

Although being anomalous is not the same as posing a threat, it is interesting for security purposes to discover and analyze devices that are different from others according to the topological distance between the clusters defined.

5. Discussion

After developing the first version of our tool, we came to the conclusion that it is possible to build a low-cost product that performs security audits in networks of small organizations. Our solution provides to SMEs a much-needed cybersecurity solution that is exclusively oriented to them and, therefore, affordable.

When contemplating future work, we plan to use agents as devices that not only perform network audits, but also carry out continuous monitoring. This is intended to perform network anomaly detection on a day-to-day basis by creating normal network profiles against which to compare network traffic at all times. We think that this is a very promising line of work, as good anomaly prevention could translate into effective attack prevention.

Author Contributions: Conceptualization J.C.D. and F.J.N.; methodology, J.C.D. and F.J.N.; software, P.F.-A. and J.J.E.-P.; validation, J.C.D, D.F., and F.J.N.; formal analysis, P.F.-A.; research, P.F.-A. and J.J.E.-P.; resources, P.F.-A. and J.J.E.-P.; data curation, P.F.-A. and J.J.E.-P.; writing—original draft preparation, P.F.-A. and J.J.E.-P.; writing—review and editing, P.F.-A., J.J.E.-P, J.C.D., D.F., and F.J.N.; visualization, P.F.-A. and J.J.E.-P.; supervision, J.C.D, D.F., and F.J.N. All authors have read and agreed to the published version of the manuscript.

Funding: CITIC, as a Research Center accredited by the Galician University System, is funded by "Consellería de Cultura, Educación e Universidade from Xunta de Galicia", supported in an 80% through ERDF, ERDF Operational Programme Galicia 2014–2020, and the remaining 20% by "Secretaría Xeral de Universidades (Grant ED431G 2019/01). This work was also funded by the research consolidation grant ED431B 2021/36, Art.83 collaboration F19/17, the Ministry of Economy and Competitiveness of Spain, and the FEDER funds of the European Union (Project PID2019-111388GB-I00).

Conflicts of Interest: The authors declare no conflict of interest.

References

1. Kurpjuhn, T. The SME security challenge. *Comput. Fraud. Secur.* **2015**, *3*, 1–3. [CrossRef]
2. Raspberry Pwn. Available online: https://github.com/pwnieexpress/raspberry_pwn (accessed on 29 July 2021).

3. Wireless Attack Toolkit (WAT). Available online: https://sourceforge.net/projects/piwat/ (accessed on 29 July 2021).
4. Del Coso, C.; Fustes, D.; Dafonte, C.; Nóvoa, F. J.; Rodríguez-Pedreira, J. M.; Arcay, B. Mixing numerical and categorical data in a Self-Organizing Map by means of frequency neurons. *Appl. Soft Comput.* **2015**, *36*, 246–254. [CrossRef]

Proceeding Paper

Design of Machine Learning Models for the Prediction of Transcription Factor Binding Regions in Bacterial DNA [†]

Sara Alvarez-Gonzalez [1,2] and Ivan Erill [3,*]

1. Departamento de Ciencias de la Computación y Tecnologías de la Información, Universidade da Coruña, 15071 A Coruña, Spain; sara.alvarezg@udc.es
2. CITIC-Centro de Investigación en Tecnologías de la información y las Comunicaciones, Universidade da Coruña, 15071 A Coruña, Spain
3. Department of Biological Sciences, University of Maryland Baltimore County, Baltimore, MD 21250, USA
* Correspondence: erill@umbc.edu
† Presented at the 4th XoveTIC Conference, A Coruña, Spain, 7–8 October 2021.

Abstract: Transcription Factors (TFs) are proteins that regulate the expression of genes by binding to their promoter regions. There is great interest in understanding in which regions TFs will bind to the DNA sequence of an organism and the possible genetic implications that this entails. Occasionally, the sequence patterns (motifs) that a TF binds are not well defined. In this work, machine learning (ML) models were applied to TF binding data from ChIP-seq experiments. The objective was to detect patterns in TF binding regions that involved structural (DNAShapeR) and compositional (kmers) characteristics of the DNA sequence. After the application of random forest and Glmnet ML techniques with both internal and external validation, it was observed that two types of generated descriptors (HelT and tetramers) were significantly better than the others in terms of prediction, achieving values of more than 90%.

Keywords: transcription factor; machine learning; protein binding

1. Introduction

The prediction of specific transcription factor (TF) binding regions in the DNA of bacterial organisms is a challenging task, especially when the TF binding motifs are not well defined or there are certain structural parameters of the DNA structure at play that classical models do not take into account. Advances in machine learning (ML) techniques have made it possible to create models capable of incorporating DNA structural parameters in the prediction of TF binding sites in genomic sequences.

In this work, using ML techniques, we were able to predict with high accuracy whether a nucleotide sequence would be a region where the TF would bind or not. Our work has been previously published as a Master's Thesis at the Universitat Oberta de Catalunya (UOC) [1]. The DNA sequences used as positive data were extracted from the article by Adhikari et al. [2], obtained using the ChIP-seq technique with the GcrA TF in the bacterial organism *Brevundimonas subvibrioides*.

2. Materials and Methods

2.1. Creation of Negative Sequence Set

From the 879 peaks (nucleotide sequences where the target TF had bound), two types of nucleotide sequences were created from these in order to generate the database of negative sequences.

On the one hand, biologically plausible replicates, here termed Replicates, were created. For these, the *peaks* were located in the reference genome, and their subsequences were classified according to whether they were located relative to a gene: intergenic, intragenic, upstream, or downstream. From this, 879 sequences homologous to the positive

dataset were generated matching the composition of each one but using regions of the organism's genome where the TF had not been bound.

On the other hand, a negative dataset was generated with a pseudo-replicate process, termed Boots replicates. In this case, the generation of negative data was carried out by extracting trimers that existed in the original peak until the target length was completed.

2.2. Descriptor Extraction

The FASTA file of each of the datasets (879 peaks + 879 replicates for each of the cases) was introduced to the R DNAshapeR library, and vectors of values were obtained for each of the 4 selected elements: HelT, MGW, ProT, and Roll. From the data vectors obtained for each sequence, histograms generated for each sequence were used as descriptors. In this case, 25 descriptors were chosen by DNAshape and dataset algorithms.

Descriptors were also calculated by counting the appearance of k-mers in each of the sequences. Monomers, dimers, and tetramers (4, 16, and 256 combinations, respectively) were studied.

2.3. Machine Learning Models

Random forest [3] and generalized linear model (Glmnet) [4] were used in this work. A nested cross-validation was carried out, using a validation for the search of the best hyperparameters through a holdout and a second validation with a 10-fold CV to validate the model, taking the average of 5 iterations of this technique. Thus, the performance values reflected in Figure 1 represent the average of the 50 models generated for each descriptor and each ML model.

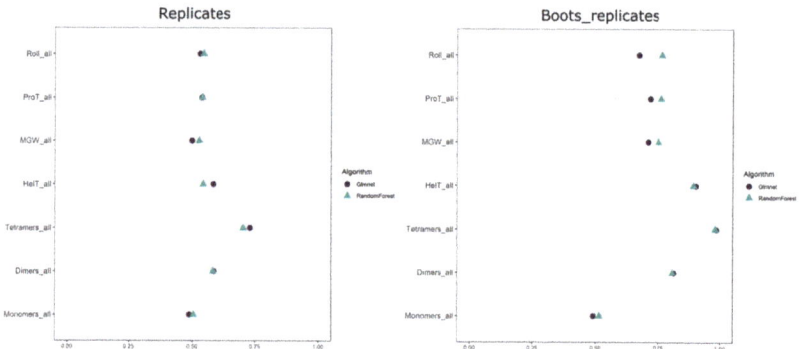

Figure 1. Dot plot showing the mean of each of the models. The mean corresponds to the 50 replicates obtained using the CV in replicates. The image on the left corresponds to the models in the dataset of Replicates, while the image on the right matches the models in the dataset of Boots_replicates.

3. Results

The total number of datasets to carry out the ML models was seven sets for each of the datasets (Replicates and Boots_replicates), resulting in a total of fourteen sets of descriptors to be trained with the two algorithms. The models obtained by the algorithms were evaluated using the *area under the receiver operating characteristics curve* (AUCROC). The main results are described in the subsection presented below.

HelT and Tetramers as Key Descriptors

Figure 1 illustrates the performances of the AUCROC for both datasets and all descriptors. On the left side, we can observe the results obtained for the Replicates, while the right side shows those corresponding to Boots_replicates. The first four sets represented belong to the structural descriptors extracted by the DNAshape library, while the last three correspond to k-mers counts.

As can be observed, both the HelT and tetramers descriptors produce the ML models with the highest performance, reaching up to 0.75 in the Replicates and almost 0.9–1 in the Boots_replicates.

4. Discussion

The use of these descriptors is due to the fact that we seek to represent the sequences not only in terms of base reading but also in terms of their structural features. These have been described as two different modes for protein–DNA recognition that are key and necessary to predict the behavior of TFs in DNA [5].

Of the seven descriptors studied, it was observed that different ML models with a high level of prediction could be developed to determine the TF binding regions across the genome. In particular, both HelT and tetramer counts proved to be particularly predictive.

Similarly, it has been found that the most significant tetramers for ML algorithms largely correspond to the motif that was found in the reference paper for the data used [2] with the MEME program, as presented in Figure 2.

Figure 2. Motif found in reference article [2] for GcrA TF in Brevundimonas subvibrioides.

Funding: This work has received financial support from the Xunta de Galicia and the European Union (European Social Fund (ESF)).

Data Availability Statement: The database used for the development of this study it is available at the Gene Expression Omnibus (GEO) under accession number GSE138845.

Acknowledgments: This project was also supported by the General Directorate of Culture, Education and University Management of Xunta de Galicia (Ref. ED431G/01, ED431D 2017/16).

References

1. Alvarez-Gonzalez, S. *Desarrollo de un sistema de Machine Learning para obtener modelos de unión a Factores de Transcripción en datos ChIP-seq*; Universitat Oberta de Catalunya (UOC): Barcelona, Spain, 2021. Available online: http://hdl.handle.net/10609/133102 (accessed on 23 September 2021).
2. Adhikari, S.; Erill, I.; Curtis, P.D. Transcriptional rewiring of the GcrA/CcrM bacterial epigenetic regulatory system in closely related bacteria. *PLoS Genet.* **2021**, *17*, e1009433. [CrossRef] [PubMed]
3. Friedman, J.; Hastie, T.; Tibshirani, R. Regularization paths for generalized linear models via coordinate descent. *J. Stat. Softw.* **2010**, *33*, 1. [CrossRef] [PubMed]
4. Breiman, L. Random forests. *Mach. Learn.* **2001**, *45*, 5–32. [CrossRef]
5. Abe, N.; Dror, I.; Yang, L.; Slattery, M.; Zhou, T.; Bussemaker, H.J.; Rohs, R.; Mann, R.S. Deconvolving the recognition of DNA shape from sequence. *Cell* **2015**, *161*, 307–318. [CrossRef] [PubMed]

Proceeding Paper

Robust Methods for Soft Clustering of Multidimensional Time Series [†]

Ángel López-Oriona [1,*], Pierpaolo D'Urso [2], José A. Vilar [1,3] and Borja Lafuente-Rego [1]

1. Research Group MODES, Research Center for Information and Communication Technologies (CITIC), University of A Coruña, 15071 A Coruña, Spain; jose.vilarf@udc.es (J.A.V.); borja.lafuente@udc.es (B.L.-R.)
2. Department of Economics, Sapienza University of Rome, Piazzale Aldo Moro 5, 00185 Rome, Italy; pierpaolo.durso@uniroma1.it
3. Technological Institute for Industrial Mathematics (ITMATI), 15782 Santiago de Compostela, Spain
* Correspondence: oriona38@hotmail.com
† Presented at the 4th XoveTIC Conference, A Coruña, Spain, 7–8 October 2021.

Abstract: Three robust algorithms for clustering multidimensional time series from the perspective of underlying processes are proposed. The methods are robust extensions of a fuzzy C-means model based on estimates of the quantile cross-spectral density. Robustness to the presence of anomalous elements is achieved by using the so-called metric, noise and trimmed approaches. Analyses from a wide simulation study indicate that the algorithms are substantially effective in coping with the presence of outlying series, clearly outperforming alternative procedures. The usefulness of the suggested methods is also highlighted by means of a specific application.

Keywords: multidimensional time series; fuzzy C-means; unsupervised learning

1. Introduction

Clustering of time series is a pivotal problem in statistics with several applications [1,2]. Generally, the goal is to divide collection of unlabelled time series into uniform groups so that intra-cluster similarity is maximized wheres the inter-cluster similarity is minimized. Most of the current techniques deal with univariate time series (UTS), while clustering of multidimensional time series (MTS) has received limited attention. This paper proposes three robust clustering methods for MTS. All of them are aimed at neutralizing the effect of outlying series while detecting the underlying grouping structure.

2. Robust Clustering Methods for Multivariate Time Series

Let $\{X_t, t \in \mathbb{Z}\} = \{(X_{t,1}, \ldots, X_{t,d}), t \in \mathbb{Z}\}$ be a d-variate real-valued strictly stationary stochastic process. Let F_j the marginal distribution function of $X_{t,j}$, $j = 1, \ldots, d$, and let $q_j(\tau) = F_j^{-1}(\tau)$, $\tau \in [0,1]$, the corresponding quantile function. Fixed $l \in \mathbb{Z}$ and an arbitrary couple of quantile levels $(\tau, \tau') \in [0,1]^2$, consider the cross-covariance of the indicator functions $I\{X_{t,j_1} \leq q_{j_1}(\tau)\}$ and $I\{X_{t+l,j_2} \leq q_{j_2}(\tau')\}$

$$\gamma_{j_1,j_2}(l, \tau, \tau') = \text{Cov}\Big(I\{X_{t,j_1} \leq q_{j_1}(\tau)\}, I\{X_{t+l,j_2} \leq q_{j_2}(\tau')\}\Big), \qquad (1)$$

for $1 \leq j_1, j_2 \leq d$. Taking $j_1 = j_2 = j$, the function $\gamma_{j,j}(l, \tau, \tau')$, with $(\tau, \tau') \in [0,1]^2$, so-called quantile autocovariance function (QAF) of lag l, generalizes the traditional autocovariance function.

For the multivariate process $\{X_t, t \in \mathbb{Z}\}$, we can consider the $d \times d$ matrix $\Gamma(l, \tau, \tau') = \big(\gamma_{j_1,j_2}(l, \tau, \tau')\big)_{1 \leq j_1, j_2 \leq d}$, which simultaneously gives information about both the cross-dependence (when $j_1 \neq j_2$) and the serial dependence (since there is a lag l).

Under appropriate summability conditions (mixing conditions), we can define the the Fourier transform of the cross-covariances. In this regards, the *quantile cross-spectral density* is given by

$$\mathfrak{f}_{j_1,j_2}(\omega,\tau,\tau') = (1/2\pi)\sum_{l=-\infty}^{\infty}\gamma_{j_1,j_2}(l,\tau,\tau')e^{-il\omega}, \quad (2)$$

for $1 \leq j_1, j_2 \leq d$, $\omega \in \mathbb{R}$ and $\tau, \tau' \in [0,1]$. Note that $\mathfrak{f}_{j_1,j_2}(\omega,\tau,\tau')$ is complex-valued.

The quantile cross-spectral density contains information about the general dependence patterns of a given stochastic process. For a specific realization of the process, this quantity can be consistently estimated by means of the so-called smoothed CCR-periodogram, $\hat{G}_{T,R}^{j_1,j_2}(\omega,\tau,\tau')$, proposed by [3].

Based on previous remarks, a simple dissimilarity measure between two realizations of the d-variate process (MTS) can be defined as follows. Given the i-th MTS, $X_t^{(i)}$, consider the set $G^{(i)} = \{\hat{G}_{T,R}^{j_1,j_2}(\omega,\tau,\tau'), j_1, j_2 = 1,\ldots,d, \omega \in \Omega, \tau, \tau' \in \mathcal{T}\}$, where Ω is the set of Fourier frequencies and $\mathcal{T} = \{0.1, 0.5, 0.9\}$. Let $\Psi^{(i)}$ be the vector formed by concatenating the elements of the set $G^{(i)}$. The dissimilarity measure between the series $X_t^{(1)}$ and $X_t^{(2)}$ is defined as the Euclidean distance between the complex vectors $\Psi^{(1)}$ and $\Psi^{(2)}$. We call this dissimilarity d_{QCD}.

The dissimilarity d_{QCD} is used to develop three robust fuzzy clustering methods. All of them assume that we want to group n MTS into C clusters, and are based on the traditional fuzzy C-means clustering algorithm. They look for the set of centroids $\overline{\Psi} = \{\overline{\Psi}^{(1)},\ldots,\overline{\Psi}^{(C)}\}$, and the $n \times C$ matrix of fuzzy coefficients, $U = (u_{ic})$, $i = 1,\ldots,n$, $c = 1,\ldots,C$, which define the solution of a given minimization problem. The quantity u_{ic} represents the membership degree of the i-th MTS in the c-th cluster. The minimization problem for the first method is the following:

$$\min_{\overline{\Psi},U} \sum_{i=1}^{n}\sum_{c=1}^{C} u_{ic}^m \left[1 - \exp\left\{-\beta\left\|\Psi^{(i)} - \overline{\Psi}^{(c)}\right\|_2^2\right\}\right] \text{ w.r.t } \sum_{c=1}^{C} u_{ic} = 1 \text{ and } u_{ic} \geq 0,$$

where β is an hyperparameter that needs to be set in advance and m is a parameter which determines the fuzziness of the partition, frequently called the fuziness parameter.

The exponential distance is used in the previous model because it is capable of neutralizing the effect of outlying series by spreading out their membership degrees between the different clusters [4].

The second robust procedure follows the noise cluster approach, and takes into account the following minimization problem:

$$\min_{\overline{\Psi},U} \sum_{i=1}^{n}\sum_{c=1}^{C-1} u_{ic}^m \left\|\Psi^{(i)} - \overline{\Psi}^{(c)}\right\|_2^2 + \sum_{i=1}^{n}\delta^2\left(1 - \sum_{c=1}^{C-1} u_{ic}\right)^m \text{ w.r.t } \sum_{c=1}^{C} u_{ic} = 1 \text{ and } u_{ic} \geq 0,$$

where $\delta > 0$ is the a parameter known as the noise distance, which has to be specified in advance.

The previous model includes C groups, but only $(C-1)$ are "real" clusters. The noise cluster is artificially created for outlier identification purposes. The aim is to locate the outliers and place them in the noise cluster, which is represented by a fictitious prototype that has a constant distance from every MTS (the noise distance, δ).

The third technique can be expressed by means of the minimization problem:

$$\min_{Y,U} \sum_{i=1}^{H(\alpha)}\sum_{c=1}^{C} u_{ic}^m \left\|\Psi^{(i)} - \overline{\Psi}^{(c)}\right\|^2 \text{ w.r.t } \sum_{c=1}^{C} u_{ic} = 1 \text{ and } u_{ic} \geq 0.$$

where Y ranges on all the subsets of $\Psi = \{\Psi^{(1)}, \ldots, \Psi^{(n)}\}$ of size $H(\alpha) = \lfloor n(1-\alpha) \rfloor$. The model attains its robustness by removing a certain proportion of the series and requires the specification of the fraction α of the data to be trimmed.

The three previously presented robust models have been analysed by means of a broad simulation study containing a wide variety of generating processes. Two alternative dissimilarities were taken into account for comparison purposes [5,6]. In all cases, the three proposed algorithms outperformed the competitors.

3. Application to real data

The three techniques proposed in Section 2 were applied to perform clustering in a real MTS database. Specifically, we considered daily stock returns and trading volume of the top 20 companies of the S&P 500 index, thus obtaining 20 bivariate MTS. Table 1 shows the membership degrees of the series concerning the trimmed approach.

Table 1. Membership degrees for the top 20 companies in the S&P 500 index by considering the trimmed approach and a 6-cluster partition.

Company	C_1	C_2	C_3	C_4	C_5	C_6
AAPL	0.083	0.146	0.299	**0.365**	0.066	0.041
MSFT	0.107	0.049	0.213	**0.356**	0.099	0.176
AMZN	**0.865**	0.017	0.051	0.032	0.010	0.025
GOOGL	**0.682**	0.032	0.092	0.128	0.025	0.040
GOOG	**0.902**	0.010	0.031	0.028	0.008	0.022
FB	0.002	**0.983**	0.006	0.004	0.003	0.002
TSLA	0.023	0.012	0.056	**0.885**	0.013	0.010
BRK.B	-	-	-	-	-	-
V	0.004	0.014	0.015	0.017	**0.941**	0.009
JNJ	0.004	0.015	0.019	0.013	**0.937**	0.013
WMT	-	-	-	-	-	-
JPM	0.002	0.001	0.003	0.003	0.002	**0.989**
MA	0.005	0.006	**0.968**	0.010	0.005	0.006
PG	0.015	0.012	0.028	0.016	0.019	**0.909**
UNH	0.006	**0.924**	0.026	0.013	0.022	0.008
DIS	0.020	0.038	**0.772**	0.099	0.042	0.030
NVDA	0.025	0.020	0.085	**0.804**	0.043	0.024
HD	-	-	-	-	-	-
PYPL	0.155	**0.301**	0.297	0.115	0.057	0.075
BAC	0.076	0.086	0.225	0.067	0.060	**0.485**

The symbols in bold correspond to the companies which were trimmed away, Berkshire Hathaway (BRK.B), Walmart (WMT) and Home Depot (HD). Similar clustering solutions were obtained with the remaining two methods.

4. Conclusions

This work proposes three robust methods to perform fuzzy clustering of MTS. They are based on the so-called exponential, noise and trimmed ideas. Each approach attains robustness to outlying series in a different way. The three procedures have been presented and assessed through a wide simulation study, substantially outperforming alternative approaches. A real data application has been also carried out in order to show the usefulness of the presented techniques.

Acknowledgments: This research has been supported by MINECO (MTM2017-82724-R and PID2020-113578RB-100), the Xunta de Galicia (ED431C-2020-14), and "CITIC" (ED431G 2019/01).

References

1. Liao, T.W. Clustering of time series data—A survey. *Pattern Recognit.* **2005**, *38*, 1857–1874. [CrossRef]
2. Aghabozorgi, S.; Shirkhorshidi, A.S.; Wah, T.Y. Time-series clustering—A decade review. *Inf. Syst.* **2015**, *53*, 16–38. [CrossRef]

3. Baruník, J.; Kley, T. Quantile coherency: A general measure for dependence between cyclical economic variables. *Econom. J.* **2019**, *22*, 131–152. [CrossRef]
4. Wu, K.L.; Yang, M.S. Alternative c-means clustering algorithms. *Pattern Recognit.* **2002**, *35*, 2267–2278. [CrossRef]
5. D'Urso, P.; Maharaj, E.A. Autocorrelation-based fuzzy clustering of time series. *Fuzzy Sets Syst.* **2009**, *160*, 3565–3589. [CrossRef]
6. D'Urso, P.; Maharaj, E.A. Wavelets-based clustering of multivariate time series. *Fuzzy Sets Syst.* **2012**, *193*, 33–61. [CrossRef]

MDPI
St. Alban-Anlage 66
4052 Basel
Switzerland
Tel. +41 61 683 77 34
Fax +41 61 302 89 18
www.mdpi.com

Engineering Proceedings Editorial Office
E-mail: engproc@mdpi.com
www.mdpi.com/journal/engproc

www.ingramcontent.com/pod-product-compliance
Lightning Source LLC
LaVergne TN
LVHW070451100526
838202LV00014B/1704